Family Law and Practice

AUSTRALIA
The Law Book Company Ltd.
Sydney : Melbourne : Brisbane : Perth

CANADA
The Carswell Company Ltd.
Toronto : Calgary : Vancouver : Ottawa

INDIA
N. M. Tripathi Private Ltd.
Bombay
and
Eastern Law House Private Ltd.
Calcutta

M.P.P. House
Bangalore

ISRAEL
Steimatzky's Agency Ltd.
Jerusalem : Tel Aviv : Haifa

PAKISTAN
Pakistan Law House
Karachi

Family Law and Practice

Second Edition

PETER D. REEKIE,
Solicitor, Senior Lecturer, The College of Law

and

RICHARD TUDDENHAM, M.A., LL.B.,
Barrister, Member of the Board of Management,
The College of Law

LONDON
SWEET & MAXWELL
1990

Published in 1990 by
Sweet and Maxwell Limited of
South Quay Plaza, 183 Marsh Wall, London E14 9FT
Computerset by P.B. Computer Typesetting, N. Yorks
Printed in Great Britain by
Butler & Tanner Limited,
Somerset

British Library Cataloguing in Publication Data

Reekie, Peter D.
   Family law and practice.—2nd. ed.
   1. England. Families. Law
   I. Title   II. Tuddenham, Richard
   344.20615

   ISBN 0–421–42490–7

To Anita and Jane, our wives,
with our love and thanks, and to whom
we remain married despite having written
this second edition

Preface

Our main aim in writing this book was to provide a clear and comprehensive text for use by students on the Law Society's Final Examination course. However, the areas covered by the syllabus are the same mainstream ones as those with which the matrimonial practitioner is concerned in his or her everyday work, and we believe the first edition of this book therefore also proved useful to articled clerks and newly qualified practitioners. We hope it may also have been of use to those studying for other professional examinations.

Since the first edition was published there have been a number of fairly radical changes to the subject. Accordingly the chapters on Tax and Welfare Law have been completely re-written and the chapters on Legal Aid and the Unmarried Family have been substantially revised. However, the largest single development, which has necessitated revision throughout the book, was the passing of the Children Act 1989. This Act has been described by the Lord Chancellor as "the most comprehensive and far reaching reform of child law which has come before Parliament in living memory." The Act has presented us with a number of problems, not the least of which is that it is not yet in force, nor is it expected to be until October 1991. Further, it entails a number of procedural changes which will be introduced by delegated legislation which is not yet in existence. In order to present both the existing law relating to children and the law as it will be once the Act is passed, we have divided the section on children into four chapters. There are two dealing with the current law (relevant until the Children Act is in force) and two dealing with the new law.

Family law is, of course, in a constant state of flux and it is already possible to discern further changes on the horizon. The Law Commission is currently considering changes to the basis for divorce and the Lord Chancellor has established an interdepartmental working party to oversee a "rolling programme for review of family law and procedure." On a much smaller scale it is worth noting that when the Courts and Legal Services Act comes into force, registrars, who play such an important role in family proceedings, will be renamed "district judges." Although, as with the Children Act, we have anticipated some of these changes, in general, we have tried to state the law as at July 1, 1990.

Finally, we would like to acknowledge the assistance and advice we have received from those of our colleagues who have helped us in a variety of ways in the preparation of this edition. In particular we would like to thank Allun Thomas and Jane Chapman of the College of Law at Guildford and Imogen Burton of The College of Law at Chancery Lane for reading and commenting on various sections of the book. We are also grateful to the editorial staff of Sweet and Maxwell Ltd. for their help and advice in seeing this second edition through to publication. For any errors that remain we blame each other.

July 1990
Peter Reekie
Richard Tuddenham

Contents

CONTENTS

Abbreviations of Statutes

C.A. 1975	Children Act 1975 (c. 72)
C.A. 1989	Children Act 1989 (c. 41)
C.A.C.A. 1985	Child Abduction and Custody Act 1985 (c. 60)
C.C.A. 1980	Child Care Act 1980 (c. 5)
C.G.T.A. 1979	Capital Gains Tax Act 1979 (c. 14)
C.Y.P.A. 1933	Children and Young Persons Act 1933 (c. 12)
C.Y.P.A. 1969	Children and Young Persons Act 1969 (c. 54)
D.M.P.A. 1973	Domicile and Matrimonial Proceedings Act 1973 (c. 45)
D.P.M.C.A. 1978	Domestic Proceedings and Magistrates Courts Act 1978 (c. 22)
D.V.M.P.A. 1976	Domestic Violence and Matrimonial Proceedings Act 1976 (c. 50)
F.L.R.A. 1969	Family Law Reform Act 1969 (c. 46)
F.L.R.A. 1987	Family Law Reform Act 1987 (c. 42)
G.A. 1973	Guardianship Act 1973 (c. 29)
G.M.A. 1971	Guardianship of Minors Act 1971 (c. 3)
H.A. 1985	Housing Act 1985 (c. 68)
I.C.T.A. 1988	Income and Corporation Taxes Act 1988 (c. 1)
I.H.T.A. 1984	Inheritance Tax Act 1984 (c. 51)
L.P.A. 1925	Law of Property Act 1925 (15 & 16 Geo. 5, c. 20)
M.C.A. 1973	Matrimonial Causes Act 1973 (c. 18)
M.F.P.A. 1984	Matrimonial and Family Proceedings Act 1984 (c. 42)
M.H.A. 1983	Matrimonial Homes Act 1983 (c. 19)
M.W.P.A. 1882	Married Women's Property Act 1882 (45 & 46 Vict. c. 75)
S.S.A. 1986	Social Security Act 1986 (c. 50)

Abbreviations

A.B.W.O.R.	Assistance by Way of Representation
C.C.B.	Community Charge Benefit
C.G.T.	Capital Gains Tax
D.S.S.	Department of Social Security
E.S.C.D.6	Extra-Statutory Concession D6
F.C.	Family Credit
H.B.	Housing Benefit
H.P.	Hire Purchase
I.R.	Inland Revenue
I.S.	Income Support
I.H.T.	Inheritance Tax
J.P.	Justice of the Peace
M.C.R. 1977	Matrimonial Causes Rules 1977
M.I.R.A.S.	Mortgage Interest Relief at Source
M.P.S.	Maintenance Pending Suit
N.F.C.A.	National Foster Care Association
N.H.S.	National Health Service
V.A.T.	Value Added Tax

Table of Cases

xiii

Table of Statutes

Table of Statutory Instruments

1. Introduction

1. The Scope of Family Law 1–01

Matrimonial clients generally come to see a solicitor with an immediate problem which usually falls into one of four categories. These are divorce, finance, children and domestic violence. For this reason this book is divided into four sections based on the same categories. It should be appreciated at the outset, however, that family law and practice should not be seen as a series of self-contained topics. In many cases the topics are interdependent, so that, for example, a client, whose first concern is to obtain an injunction to exclude a violent husband, may subsequently want a divorce, maintenance and a custody order. A related difficulty is that applications for these forms of relief are not usually made one after another, but may often be proceeding simultaneously, though at different rates of progress. For the purposes of exposition it is necessary to divide the topics into separate categories, but reminders have been included where appropriate about the way one topic relates to another.

Another difficulty that must be faced by the lawyer who 1–02 wants to be successful in the practice of family law, is that it requires an accurate and up-to-date knowledge of at least some aspects of many other branches of the law, such as those relating to taxation, welfare benefits, real property, inheritance and conveyancing.

However, a wide familiarity with the relevant branches of law 1–03 is not enough. The family lawyer needs more than just the skills of a lawyer. He or she will often have to combine those skills with those of an advocate, negotiator and even a counsellor. No book can teach these skills; most can be acquired only by practice and experience.

2. Preliminary Matters 1–04

Before embarking on a detailed consideration of the four main categories of matrimonial problem with which this book is concerned, we must consider three matters which do not fit conveniently into any one of those categories, but which may, nevertheless, be relevant to all of them. These are the topics of the family courts system, conciliation and legal aid, advice and assistance. This last topic is so important to the family law practitioner that it deserves a chapter to itself, and is, therefore, dealt with in Chapter 2.

1–05 THE FAMILY COURTS

Family disputes, depending on their nature, may be dealt with in the magistrates' courts, the county court, or the Family Division of the High Court. In some cases all three levels of court have jurisdiction to hear applications under a particular statute, whereas in other cases jurisdiction is confined to one or two of them. This does make the system unnecessarily complicated, and is one of the reasons for the frequently heard calls for a new Family Court. Although such a court will no doubt be established eventually, there seems no immediate prospect of its arrival.

1–06 At present, the majority of family law work is handled by the county court. So, for example, all matrimonial causes (*e.g.* divorce petitions) must be started in a divorce county court,[1] that is a county court which has been designated as a divorce county court by the Lord Chancellor.[2] However, under section 39 of the M.F.P.A. 1984, the county court has a discretion to transfer family proceedings to the High Court, and, indeed, under section 38 the High Court has a corresponding discretion to transfer certain family proceedings to the county court. These discretions are subject to directions issued by the President of the Family Division (*i.e.* the senior judge who presides over that division). The current direction[3] requires that cases should be dealt with in the High Court, where the "complexity, difficulty or gravity" of the issues demand it, although there are certain matters that must be transferred to the High Court for trial. These will be indicated when they arise in the text.

1–07 Much of the matrimonial work that is done in the county court is handled by registrars.[4] In particular, they deal with

1 M.F.P.A. 1984, s.33(3).
2 *Ibid.* s.33(1).
3 *Practice Direction* [1988] 1 W.L.R. 558.
4 When the Courts and Legal Services Act 1990 comes into force, registrars will become known as "district judges."

most aspects of divorce proceedings and hear most of the applications for financial and property orders. County court registrars must be solicitors of at least seven years' standing.

The system in London is slightly different, in that, although there are several divorce county courts there, the Principal Registry of the Family Division of the High Court (also known as the Divorce Registry) is treated as a divorce county court as well.[5] Registrars in the Principal Registry are generally barristers or solicitors of at least 10 years' standing, and barristers are often appointed to these posts.

CONCILIATION

(i) Definition   1–08
The first question to consider is what is meant by the term "conciliation." A widely accepted definition is that given in the Report of the Finer Committee on One-Parent Families,[6] which referred to it as the process of

> "assisting the parties to deal with the consequences of the established breakdown of their marriage by reaching agreements or giving consents or reducing the area of conflict upon custody, support, access to and education of the children, financial provision, the disposition of the matrimonial home, lawyer's fees and every other matter arising from the breakdown which calls for a decision on future arrangements."

More briefly, it may be described as the process of helping the parties to come to terms with the consequences of marriage breakdown, and to resolve their differences by agreement, rather than through contested court proceedings.

It can be seen from this that it is quite distinct from reconciliation, which aims to reunite the parties and to avoid an irretrievable breakdown of the relationship. It also differs from counselling, which by analysing the parties' relationship, usually seeks to preserve it.

(ii) The lawyer's role   1–09
The good family practitioner will certainly encourage his or her client to adopt a conciliatory rather than a litigious approach in resolving disputes. In particular he or she will emphasise the detrimental effect which a litigious approach may have on the relationships between parents and their

5 M.F.P.A. 1984, s.42(4).
6 Cmnd. 5629 (1974).

children. This need for a conciliatory approach, which emphasises that a family dispute is not a contest in which there is a winner and a loser, but rather a search for fair solutions, is one of the items of the Code of Practice published by the Solicitors' Family Law Association, which it recommends any solicitor practising family law to adopt.

However, it must be emphasised that the solicitor advising one of the parties cannot act as a conciliator. A conciliator must be able to see a problem from both sides, and the solicitor's involvement with his own client will often make this objective assessment impossible. For example, a problem may arise over access because a young child becomes extremely distressed whenever her father calls to take her out. He may blame the child's mother for promoting this reaction. The mother may blame the father for somehow causing the child's behaviour. Each solicitor may well advance his or her own client's view. An independent conciliator will be better placed to make an objective assessment, and may suggest, for example, that the reason for the child's behaviour is that she has come to associate the occasions when both parents are together with arguments and distress.

The lawyer's role, therefore, cannot go beyond promoting a conciliatory approach to the problem, but he or she may be able to give practical help by referring the parties to a conciliation service.

1–10 (iii) Conciliation services

There are two types of conciliation service—in-court, and out-of-court. Both services have the same general aims, although their methods of achieving it differ. Although conciliation can be used to resolve many types of dispute, the majority of cases involve custody and access matters.

1–11 *In-court conciliation*

Conciliation services within the court system are part of the court welfare service provided by court welfare officers. The first service started in Bristol County Court in 1976, and was initially confined to defended divorces, but was later exended to undefended divorces in which there was a custody or access dispute. Such services now exist in a number of other county courts in different parts of the country. One of the best known schemes is that which operates in the Principal Registry in London. Here conciliation appointments are made in cases involving disputed custody or access. The first appointment takes place before a registrar sitting with a court welfare officer. The parties, who must both be present with

4

their legal advisers, will be encouraged to settle their dispute by negotiation and, if necessary, the appointment can be adjourned, while the parties retire to a private room with the welfare officer in an attempt to resolve the matter.

Out-of-court conciliation   **1–12**

Out-of-court services are independent of the courts. Again, the first such scheme began in Bristol, in 1977, but since then many similar independent schemes have been started. Conciliators working in these services will be people with some form of social work training, though many of them may also have received specialised conciliation training as well.

The main differences that distinguish these services from in-court services are that they are available before the institution of proceedings, and that their procedures are more informal and more flexible than those which can be adopted by the courts. In particular, the absence of legal advisers and the registrar can help create a more relaxed atmosphere. On the other hand, it is important that independent services should maintain certain common standards. Consequently, in 1983, the National Family Conciliation Council was founded as a means of establishing certain uniform standards and to provide a central body through which independent services can liaise.

(iv) The future of conciliation   **1–13**

There seems little doubt that the two forms of conciliation service have been successful, at least in terms of avoiding embittering disputes. Thus, for example, in some areas where conciliation services operate, disputed access cases that proceed to a full trial are a rarity.

At present, however, these services are by no means comprehensive and their ad hoc nature means that in some parts of the country both in-court and out-of-court services operate, whereas in other areas there are none. Many family law practitioners had hoped that such anomalies would be removed by the establishment of a publicly-funded national conciliation service, but such a step seems unlikely in view of the report of a conciliation project unit from the University of Newcastle. This report, commissioned by the Lord Chancellor and published in 1989, estimates that conciliation increases the cost of settling disputes by between £150 and £250. The report suggests that there is insufficient evidence that these costs are substantially off-set by the conciliation process itself (for example, in reduced litigation costs), and concludes that a national conciliation service would cost between £2 million and £3.5 million a year to run, depending on whether it was an in-court or an out-of-court service.

It seems that the current thinking in the Lord Chancellor's Department is that, while there is much to be said for a process which helps the parties to a divorce to resolve their differences with a minimum of bitterness, the introduction of a national conciliation service is not the only way of achieving this. It may be done instead as part of the overall reform of the law of divorce and the procedural changes this will entail. More is said about this in Chapter 3.

In the meantime, some encouragement has been offered to existing conciliation services, by a Practice Direction, issued in 1986,[7] which instructs judges and registrars to consider referring disputes over children to any local conciliation service that may exist, before ordering a welfare report to be prepared.

1–14 A further notable development was the establishment in 1988 of the Family Mediators' Association, which introduced the American concept of divorce mediation into this country. Mediation, for which the parties pay a fee, extends to all the issues arising from the breakdown of the marriage. A couple meet together with a family mediator and a solicitor mediator, neither of whom gives specific advice to either party, but will instead help them achieve a resolution of their differences. This project appears to be working very successfully, but is, of course, available only to those who can pay for it.

7 [1986] 2 F.L.R. 171.

2. Legal Aid and Legal Advice and Assistance

Throughout this book, whenever procedure is being considered, references are made to the legal advice and assistance and the civil legal aid schemes. However, it is convenient to set out the main principles and procedures in one chapter early on. This will give an idea from the outset of how the schemes work, but will also provide an account which the reader may want to consult at later stages when studying a particular procedural topic.

1. The Nature of the Schemes

When a marriage breaks down one or both parties usually seek legal advice on how best to regulate their affairs. In many cases one, and sometimes both, of the parties may seek assistance from the state for payment of their solicitor's fees. Legal aid and legal advice and assistance play such a large part in most matrimonial practices that every family practitioner must be fully conversant with these schemes.

What many clients fail to realise is that, unlike most other forms of state assistance provided by the welfare state (*e.g.* the National Health Service) legal aid is not "free," but is more in the nature of a loan. In return for a contribution assessed on the client's means the state agrees to pay the solicitor's fees, both profit costs and expenses (expenses are referred to as disbursements). In some cases the applicant's means are such that no contribution is payable. Even when the applicant is required to make a contribution, the contribution will be refunded to the extent that any of the solicitor's fees are recovered from the other party, by means of a subsequent order for payment of costs.

It is not uncommon, however, for there to be a deficit between the solicitor's fees and the contribution plus costs recovered (if any). In these circumstances the state is entitled to a share in any property recovered or preserved for the assisted party in the court action. The share may be secured by a charge over the property in question. This legal aid charge (or "statutory charge" as it is often called) is considered in detail at 2–18 to 2–34, below. In most cases, therefore, legally aided litigants are in no worse or better position than privately paying clients as they will be ultimately liable for their solicitor's fees. However, if there is no property recovered or preserved and no contribution payable (because, *e.g.* the client is in receipt of income support) then the litigant may truly be in receipt of free legal aid.

2–02 **2. Administration**

The schemes are administered by the Legal Aid Board on behalf of the state. The Board is composed of between 11 and 17 members comprising both lawyers and non-lawyers. The Legal Aid Act 1988, which created the Board, contains very wide powers to enable the Board to change the whole structure of legal aid and legal advice and assistance, although as yet the system remains broadly the same as the old system which was administered before April 1989 by the Law Society.

England and Wales are divided into 13 legal aid areas. The areas are divided into five groups. For administrative reasons there are area managers and group managers in charge of the two tiers. These managers, together with their staff, deal with the administration of the system. Rather confusingly, for the purpose of the various statutory provisions, all the managers are designated "area directors" and that is how they will be referred to throughout the book. The area director has the power to grant or refuse legal aid, subject to an appeal to a local area committee. These committees are staffed by practising solicitors and barristers who sit on the committees part time. Any solicitor with a practising certificate may undertake legal aid work, but not all wish to do so. However, a solicitor is under a duty to advise a client of the availability of legal aid, even if he does not do such work himself. Failure to so advise a client may be professional misconduct.

There are three main types of financial assistance which are of concern to the family practitioner; these are legal advice and assistance, legal aid and assistance by way of representation.

3. Legal Advice and Assistance (the Green Form Scheme)

2–03 THE SCOPE OF THE SCHEME

The Green Form scheme was introduced to enable a client to obtain financial assistance for legal advice before the receipt of legal aid, which can take several weeks and sometimes months to obtain. It covers advice and assistance (*e.g.* correspondence) on behalf of a client on any question of English law or procedure up to a maximum amount.[1] It does not, however, cover any step in court proceedings and therefore legal aid must, generally, be obtained for this.

There are some exceptions to this rule, one of which is very important in matrimonial work. Legal aid used to be available for undefended divorce proceedings but was withdrawn in 1977.[2] For this reason the Green Form scheme was extended to provide financial assistance to a petitioner applying for an undefended divorce to cover limited steps in court proceedings (*e.g.* the preparation of court documents). The maximum financial limit on advice and assistance is increased in these circumstances.[3]

PROCEDURE   2–04

The client will attend at his or her solicitor's office, and one of the first topics which is normally discussed is the possibility of obtaining financial assistance to cover the work to be undertaken by the solicitor.

The solicitor will have a supply of Green Forms and will complete one of these for the client.[4] Brief details of the applicant's income and capital are required. The solicitor will then assess the client's financial eligibility by means of the "key card." This is a form which allows the solicitor to calculate the client's disposable capital and income and to make appropriate deductions for dependants, and from this the solicitor can work out whether the client is financially eligible, and, if so, whether any contribution will have to be paid towards the cost of assistance.

The client will then be told whether he is eligible for legal advice and assistance under the Green Form and, if so, the amount of his maximum contribution. The client may then choose not to proceed further, or, if ineligible for Green Form advice, may pay privately, or may avail himself of some other

---

[1] See 2–05, below.
[2] Legal Aid (Matrimonial Proceedings) Regs. 1977, now replaced by the Civil Legal Aid (Matrimonial Proceedings) Regulations 1989.
[3] For more details about this, see para. 4–14, below.
[4] Generally the application for advice and assistance must be made personally by the client to his solicitor. In certain circumstances (*e.g.* ill health) it is possible for someone else to apply on the client's behalf (Legal Advice and Assistance Regulations 1989, reg. 10).

scheme that the particular solicitors' firm provides (*e.g.* the fixed fee interview scheme).[5]

If he decides to proceed under the Green Form, then, after reading the form and in particular the warning relating to the impact of the statutory charge,[6] he must sign the form and pay his contribution (if any) to the solicitor.

2–05 FINANCIAL LIMITS ON WORK

These limits are drawn by reference to the time that a solicitor may spend on a case. Thus, in general matters the limit is two hours' work and where the solicitor is advising a petitioner in a divorce or judicial separation it is three hours' work. The hourly rate varies depending on the legal aid area relevant to the particular firm. For most areas it is currently £39.25. This means that in general cases the maximum is £78.50 and for cases where the solicitor is advising a petitioner it is £117.75.[7] In the London area the amounts allowed are higher. These limits include disbursements (*e.g.* the cost of obtaining a marriage certificate) but are exclusive of V.A.T. If the solicitor feels that these limits should be extended in a particular case he may apply to the area director for permission.

The authorisation for an extension must be obtained *before* the additional expenditure is incurred. An example of where this might be done is when the client believes his spouse is committing adultery and the solicitor wishes to instruct an enquiry agent to obtain evidence, as no other methods of proof are available.

2–06 ONLY ONE GREEN FORM PER MATTER

If the client has received advice and assistance on his matrimonial affairs under a Green Form in the past, either from the same solicitor or another solicitor, then the maximum limit still applies. Even if the client returns for further advice many months later authorisation to extend the limit must be obtained if the initial limit is to be exceeded by this further advice.

Sometimes a client has previously received advice from one solicitor under a Green Form and then consults a second solicitor on the same matter. In these circumstances the

---

[5] Under this scheme for a small payment (*e.g.* £5 + V.A.T.) the solicitor will give advice following a half-hour interview with the client.
[6] See 2–18, below.
[7] Legal Advice and Assistance Regulations 1989, reg. 4(1).

second solicitor must seek authorisation from the area director in order to continue advising the client under the original Green Form.[8] Of course, if the previous advice concerned a separate matter (*e.g.* a consumer problem) and the current advice relates to a matrimonial matter, then a separate Green Form may be completed.

In matrimonial work matters connected with, or arising out of, divorce or judicial separation proceedings cannot be treated as separate matters. Thus the divorce, and any proceedings for custody, an injunction and financial relief must all be dealt with on one Green Form. As legal aid is available for matters other than the undefended divorce, it is usual practice to apply for legal aid to cover the ancillary work as soon as possible.

PAYMENT OF SOLICITORS' FEES   2–07

Once the matter has been completed the solicitor will submit a bill to the area committee. This bill is completed on the back of the Green Form itself, and includes a summary of the number of letters written, telephone calls made, time spent with the client and other work undertaken. If relevant, any authority to exceed the Green Form limit should be included.

Occasionally it may be necessary for the solicitor to deduct the Green Form costs from money received on behalf of the client. This is dealt with further at 2–34, below. The bill is then subject to approval by the area committee and if found reasonable will be paid.

4. Legal Aid[9]   2–08

CIRCUMSTANCES WHERE LEGAL AID IS AVAILABLE FOR DIVORCE

As has been mentioned (at 2–03, above), legal aid generally is no longer available to finance an undefended divorce suit. Where a solicitor is consulted in such a matter his fees are covered by the Green Form scheme, but he does not "act" for the client in the suit. The client is treated as a litigant in person whom the solicitor is merely "advising and assisting."

---

[8] Legal Advice and Assistance Regulations 1989, reg. 16.
[9] Legal aid is split into civil and criminal legal aid (hence sometimes a legal aid certificate is referred to as civil aid certificate). Clearly, for our purposes criminal legal aid is irrelevant and the expressions legal aid and legal aid certificate will be used but will refer only to civil legal aid.

There are some exceptions to this. Paragraph 5A of Part II of Schedule 2 to the Legal Aid Act 1988 provides that legal aid shall be available:

   (i) where a cause has become defended, or to defend a divorce; or

  (ii) where the petition is directed to be heard in open court; or

 (iii) where, by reason of physical or mental incapacity, it is impracticable for the applicant to proceed without representation.

2–09 OTHER WORK FOR WHICH LEGAL AID IS AVAILABLE

Legal aid is, however, still available for representation on ancillary matters. The above provision goes on to state that it is available for making or opposing an application:

   (i) for an injunction;

  (ii) for ancillary relief;

 (iii) for an order relating to custody, access, education, care or supervision of a child (but only if there is reason to believe that the application will be opposed);

 (iv) for an order under M.C.A. 1973, s.41 (but only if there is reason to believe that the application will be opposed);

  (v) relating to any other matter which raises a substantial question for determination by the court.

2–10 MAKING THE APPLICATION

The legal aid application is made by completing the appropriate form and sending this to the area director at the legal aid office of the area in which the solicitor's office is situated or in which the client lives.

The solicitor should complete the form and not ask the client to do so. The cost of the work involved can be covered by the Green Form. The solicitor should then explain the mechanics and consequences of being legally aided, and, in particular, should advise the client of the impact of the legal aid charge. The legal aid application form includes a "tear off" section which contains various explanatory notes for the client including one relating to the charge. This has the advantage of providing solicitors and legal aid offices with confirmation that applicants have been informed.[10]

The appropriate forms are:

CLA1.— General form of application. (This is used rarely in family law matters but where this form is to be used it will be mentioned in context in the relevant section of the book).

CLA2.— Application for Legal Aid in Matrimonial Proceedings. (This is used for almost every application in matrimonial cases.)

CLA3.— Application for an Emergency Certificate (which accompanies, in appropriate cases, one of the other forms).

SJ1.— Application for Legal Aid for Authorised Summary Proceedings (This form is rarely used, because of the availability of A.B.W.O.R.— see 2–35 below).

CLA4.— Statement of information concerning the client's means. This will accompany the appropriate application form. It is sent on by the area director to the D.S.S. for means assessment (see below).

ASSESSING ELIGIBILITY   2–11

A financial assessment must be made to determine the client's eligibility for legal aid. This is undertaken by the legal aid assessment offices of the Department of Social Security. The merits of the application are considered by the local legal aid office. This process can take from six weeks to two months (or more). It is necessary to show that the applicant has reasonable grounds for taking, defending or being a party to the proceedings.[11] This means that the applicant must have some sort of reasonable case which he should be allowed to

---

[10] See the *Legal Aid Handbook* 1990, p. 51. This book is indispensable for any solicitor with a legal aid practice.
[11] Legal Aid Act 1988, s.15(2).

take to court. There are two occasions on which legal aid may be refused which deserve special mention here:

(i) Where only a trivial advantage would be gained by the applicant from the proceedings to which the application relates.[12] This is often given as justification for refusing legal aid to defend a divorce. This is covered below at 4–87.

(ii) Where it is more appropriate to grant assistance by way of representation,[13] (as to which, see below). This may be because proceedings are cheaper in the magistrates' court than in the county court.

If the application is granted, and no contribution is payable (because, for example, the client is on income support) two copies of the legal aid certificate are sent to the solicitor and one copy to the applicant. If a contribution is payable, the applicant will be sent an offer of legal aid which should be accepted within 28 days. If it is accepted the certificate will then be issued as before. The contribution will be payable in one sum if it is payable from capital, or in monthly instalments if it is payable from income.[14]

2–12 EMERGENCY LEGAL AID

It is possible in cases of urgency to apply for emergency legal aid. In this way legal aid can be granted without full investigation of either the applicant's means, or the merits of the application.

The emergency legal aid application (form CLA3) must be completed and sent with the appropriate application form (usually form CLA2) for full legal aid to the local office as explained above. An emergency application should be processed by the legal aid office on the day of receipt. In cases of extreme urgency, for example an application for an *ex parte* injunction) an application may be made over the telephone, although it is still essential to complete and send the appropriate application forms to the local office. If an emergency certificate is issued it will only last for a limited period of time (usually six weeks). It is important to ensure

---

[12] The Civil Legal Aid (General) Regulations 1989, reg. 29.
[13] Legal Aid Act 1988, s.15(3).
[14] Two contribution figures may be used in appropriate cases; the actual contribution will be based on the likely cost of the solicitor's fees. However, if the costs are greater than expected a further contribution will be necessary, and therefore the certificate will specify a maximum contribution figure as well.

that the full legal aid certificate is received within this time limit. If there is some delay in this then an application should be made for the time limit to be extended.

Emergency legal aid is granted only for a limited purpose, pending full investigation of the claim, and it may be revoked should it transpire that the applicant is ineligible. If this happens the client will be liable to repay all the costs paid out to his solicitor by the Legal Aid Board. The solicitor should make this clear to his client when the application is made.

NOTIFICATION   2–13

It is necessary to inform the court and the other side that the client is legally aided. This obligation arises either on the issue of the certificate or the commencement of court proceedings. The court is notified by the assisted person's solicitor filing the top copy of the certificate. The opponent is notified by the service on him of a separate typed form, called a "notice of issue of certificate." To show the court that this step has been taken, a copy of the notice of issue is filed at court.

SOLICITOR AND CLIENT RELATIONSHIP   2–14

This is not affected by the issue of a legal aid certificate. A legally aided client may select his own solicitor and counsel and the privileged relationship which exists between the lawyer and the client is not generally affected. However, there are provisions in the Civil Legal Aid (General) Regulations 1989 which do impinge on a client's privilege in certain respects.

(i) The assisted person's solicitor is under a duty to report a client's abuse of legal aid to the area director. For example, if a client unreasonably wishes to continue with an unwinnable case, or where a client has lied about his means.[15]

(ii) The solicitor must report on the progress and disposal of the proceedings on being requested to do so by the director. He should also report whenever reasonable offers are made or money is paid into court, which the client has refused. If another party in the case is granted legal aid he is required to inform the director.[16]

[15] The Civil Legal Aid (General) Regulations 1989, reg. 67.
[16] *Ibid.* reg. 70.

(iii) A solicitor is not precluded by the existence of any right of privilege from disclosing any information to the area committee which may enable it to perform its functions.[17]

Example

A solicitor, S., has been informed that his client has recently inherited a large sum of money.

The privilege of confidentiality which is owed to a client does not prevent S. from informing the area committee of the change in the client's means, if the client refuses to report this change himself.

2–15 SCOPE OF LEGAL AID CERTIFICATE

There is a temptation to believe that, once a client is legally aided, all work done for the client will be paid by the legal aid fund. There are, however, various limitations to this.

(i) Wording of the certificate
The certificate will set out what work it covers. For example, certificates for financial relief applications usually cover all such applications, but are limited to the securing of one substantive order only. Therefore, should proceedings be necessary to enforce an order (*e.g.* for periodical payments) an application to amend the certificate to include this would be necessary.

(ii) General limitations imposed by regulations[18]
Prior approval should be obtained before certain work is undertaken, for example, where an expert's report or opinion is needed. Even where authority is obtained the solicitor should always obtain his client's consent before incurring any unusual expense, since the client may eventually be paying for it out of his contribution or by virtue of the statutory charge.

2–16 PAYMENT OF SOLICITOR

Once a client has been issued with a legal aid certificate the solicitor may not take any payment from the client in respect of work done in those proceedings.[19]

---

[17] *Ibid.* reg. 73.
[18] *Ibid.* regs. 59–61.
[19] Legal Aid Act 1988, s.15(b) and the Civil Legal Aid (General) Regulations 1988, reg. 64; see *Littaur* v. *Steggles Palmer* [1986] 1 W.L.R. 287 for further details.

The solicitor's fees will in due course be paid by the Legal Aid Board from the legal aid fund. The solicitor's costs will have to be approved before they are paid by the Legal Aid Board. This approval may take the form of an assessment by the area director if, for example, the case is settled before court proceedings are commenced, or where the cost of court proceedings is low.[20] In most cases, however, the costs will be "taxed" by the court following an order for legal aid taxation. If the costs are beyond what is fair and reasonable then they will be disallowed.

ORDERS FOR COSTS   2–17

Essentially costs are always in the discretion of the court, but the general principle of civil litigation is that costs are usually awarded to the successful party. Where one or both of the parties are legally aided this general principle is subject to amendment by statute.

If the legally aided party is successful then the general principle does apply and an order for costs will be made in his favour. Clearly the actual costs recovered will be paid into the legal aid fund.

If, however, the assisted party loses the case, then the Legal Aid Act 1988, section 17(1) provides that a legally aided party should only be liable for costs to the extent that it is reasonable for him to be required to pay them. This is having regard to all the circumstances, including the financial resources of the parties and their conduct in connection with the dispute. Financial resources do not include such things as a person's home and contents. The size of a person's contribution to his own legal aid is a good indication of the extent of his resources and it is unlikely that an order would be made against a legally aided party with a low or nil contribution.[21] In practice orders for costs are rarely made against legally aided parties.

Finally, there is limited (and rarely exercised) power for the courts to award costs out of the legal aid fund to a successful party who is not in receipt of legal aid. Section 18 of the Legal Aid Act 1988 provides that payment can be ordered from the fund if:

---

[20] The Civil Legal Aid (General) Regulations 1988, reg. 105.
[21] Resources can include a lump sum awarded to a party in the proceedings, *McDonnell* v. *McDonnell* [1977] 1 W.L.R. 34.

(i) an order for costs was not made against a legally aided party because of the provisions of section 17; and

(ii) the original proceedings (as opposed to any appeal) were instituted by the legally aided party and the claimant would suffer severe financial hardship if the order were not made; and

(iii) it is just and equitable for an order to be made.

Similar provisions apply to persons in receipt of A.B.W.O.R.[22]

5. The Statutory Charge

2–18   THE LEGAL AID FUND

The operation of the Legal Aid Fund can be represented by the following diagram:

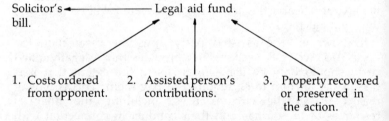

Solicitor's bill. ◄─────────── Legal aid fund.

1. Costs ordered from opponent.
2. Assisted person's contributions.
3. Property recovered or preserved in the action.

2–19   As was explained above, legal aid is essentially a loan by the legal aid fund of the amount required to pay the assisted party's costs. However, this "loan" is only repayable from certain sources. The first source is any costs ordered to be paid by the other side. If this amount is insufficient to cover the costs, any contribution made by the assisted person will be used. If there is then a surplus, the balance will be returned to the assisted person. If, however, there is still a deficit, and if the client has been successful in the proceedings, any property recovered or preserved for the assisted party may be used to repay the fund.

2–20   In order to facilitate collection of the money, the regulations provide that any money payable to an assisted person under

---

[22] Legal Aid Act 1988, ss.12 and 13.

an agreement or order made in connection with the matter covered by the legal aid certificate must be paid to the assisted person's solicitor. He must, in turn, pay this to the Legal Aid Board for the benefit of the legal aid fund. This includes money received in respect of costs, or money paid in settlement of a claim. The regulations also provide that the solicitor should inform the Board of any property recovered or preserved for the assisted person.[23]

Example

S., a solicitor, acts for Wendy in her matrimonial problems. S. advises her and assists her in obtaining a decree of divorce under the Green Form. She is then granted a legal aid certificate to obtain a custody order (as this is contested) and financial ancillary relief.

At the end of the case S.'s bill is £1,000. Orders for costs are made against Wendy's husband in the custody application, but not in respect of the ancillary relief application. Wendy's husband pays those costs to S. in the sum of £400. S. pays these to the Legal Aid Board, reducing the fund's deficit to £600.

Wendy has paid her maximum contribution to the fund which was assessed at £100. This now leaves a deficit of £500.

In the ancillary relief application Wendy obtained an order that her husband pay her a lump sum of £5,000. Her husband pays this to S. who sends the whole sum to the Legal Aid Board.[24] After deduction of the £500 deficit, the Board will pay £4,500 to Wendy.

THE OPERATION OF THE STATUTORY CHARGE 2–21

Section 16(6) of the Legal Aid Act 1988 gives the Legal Aid Board a first charge for the benefit of the legal aid fund on any property "recovered or preserved" for the assisted party in "the proceedings." The meaning of these terms must now be considered in more detail.

(i) Recovered or preserved 2–22

If the assisted party successfully pursues a claim for property it will be "recovered" by him, or if he successfully defends a claim against his property it will be "preserved" by him.

---

[23] The Civil Legal Aid (General) Regulations, regs. 87 and 90.

[24] There is power given to the area committee (by reg. 90(2)) to direct that only part of the money received by the solicitor should be paid to the Board and the balance to the assisted party, if the legal aid fund would be sufficiently protected by payment of a lesser sum.

Example

Henry and Wanda own a house in joint names. Wanda seeks an order that the property be transferred to her; Henry defends this claim and seeks an order transferring the house to him. Wanda succeeds in her claim. She will have "recovered" Henry's half share and "preserved" her own. The charge will attach to the whole property.

2–23   The House of Lords in *Hanlon* v. *The Law Society*[25] has made it clear that, before property can be said to have been recovered or preserved, there must have been a real (as opposed to theoretical) contest over entitlement to it. The phrase adopted by the court to signify this was that the property must have been "in issue". Theoretically all the matrimonial property may be divided by the court following divorce, but it is clear that it is only where entitlement to this property is "in issue" that the charge will operate. Whether property is in issue may be ascertained from a variety of sources, for example, the court documents (pleadings), the evidence, the judgment or order of the court and even the correspondence[26] between the two sides.

Example

Susan and John own a house in joint names. On divorce, Susan seeks an order from the court transferring the house into her sole name. John objects to this but does not seek to make a claim against Susan's half share. Susan is successful. The statutory charge will only attach to the half share which Susan has "recovered" from John, because her half was never "in issue".

2–24   The charge will also attach if there is an issue as to possession of property, even if title to the property is undisputed. In *Curling* v. *The Law Society*[27] the parties agreed that they owned the matrimonial home in equal shares, but the wife wanted an immediate sale and division of the proceeds, whereas the husband sought an order allowing him to remain in the house. Eventually the proceedings were compromised by payment of a sum of money to the wife. The Court of Appeal held that the charge attached to this sum of money. The wife had, in effect, succeeded in her claim and had recovered

---

[25] [1981] A.C. 124.

[26] The mere fact that a formal claim has been made in the petition will not necessarily be sufficient to put property in issue; see *Curling* v. *The Law Society* [1985] 1 W.L.R. 470; and *Jones* v. *The Law Society* [1983] 4 F.L.R. 733.

[27] [1985] 1 W.L.R. 470. See also the Law Society's Gazette of 1.5.85 for an article giving guidance about the further effects of this decision.

property, even if this was only by accelerating her right to the possession of property which both sides agreed was hers.

Section 16(7) of the Legal Aid Act 1988 ensures that, if the **2–25** proceedings are settled or avoided, any property to which the assisted party has a right under any compromise shall be subject to the charge. Section 16(7) is very wide in its operation, so that even if no proceedings are commenced at all but, after the grant of legal aid, a settlement is reached to avoid court proceedings, the charge will attach to the property which is the subject of the settlement. It will attach even if the property recovered was not itself in issue.

Example

Hugh, a legally aided husband makes a claim on the matrimonial home and his wife, Wilma, agrees to transfer instead "Greenacre," another property owned by her to Hugh. "Greenacre," will be subject to the charge.[28]

(ii) The proceedings **2–26**
The proceedings include the whole cause, action or matter so that if, for example, in divorce proceedings, there is a contested issue as to custody and an injunction application, the costs of these proceedings will be included within the charge. If there is then an ancillary relief application any property recovered or preserved will be subject to a charge in respect of the costs of the application for ancillary relief, the injunction costs and the cost of the contested custody application. To these will also be added the original divorce costs under the Green Form.[29]

EXEMPTIONS[30] **2–27**

In matrimonial cases the following property is exempt from the charge:

(i)   periodical payments;

(ii)   the first £2,500 of any money, or the value of any property, recovered or preserved in, *inter alia*, proceedings under the following:

---

[28] *Van Hoorn* v. *The Law Society* [1985] Q.B. 106.
[29] The Green Form costs are added to the legal aid costs and both form part of the charge (Legal Aid Act 1988, s.16(9)).
[30] The Civil Legal Aid (General) Regulations 1989, reg. 94.

(i)   the Matrimonial Causes Act 1973 for a lump sum or property adjustment order;

(ii) the Domestic Proceedings and Magistrates' Courts Act 1978 for a lump sum;

(iii) the Married Women's Property Act 1882, s.17;

(iv) the Guardianship of Minors Act 1971.

Whilst this would cover most applications involving married couples, it is important to note that it does not include many orders made in proceedings relating to unmarried partners. This is dealt with further at 15–42, below.

Example

Harold and Jane divorce and Jane commences proceedings for a lump sum order, a transfer of property order and periodical payments.

The court awards her £2,000 cash, orders the transfer of the matrimonial home, which is owned solely by Harold, into her name and also orders periodical payments for herself and the children.

Jane has a nil contribution towards her legal aid and no order for costs is made. The periodical payments are exempt. Jane is entitled to set off the £2,500 exemption against first the cash[31] and then the balance of £500 against the value of the matrimonial home. If the net value (after deducting the outstanding mortgage) of the matrimonial home is £8,500, £8,000 of this will be subject to a charge in favour of the Legal Aid Board for the amount of her solicitor's bill.

2–28   ENFORCEMENT OF THE CHARGE

The Legal Aid Board can enforce their charge in any way which would be available to an individual who had been given a charge. Where it relates to land the charge will immediately be protected by a suitable registration. In the case of cash, enforcement should present few problems as there is a duty on a solicitor to forward any cash received to the Board. This has been dealt with at 2–20 above. However, in appropriate cases the Board can postpone enforcement.

(i) *Land*[32]

If the property in question is land, then the area director can agree to postpone enforcement if the property is to be used as a home by the assisted person or his dependants *and this*

---

[31] This is understood to be the practice of the Legal Aid Board.
[32] The Civil Legal Aid (General) Regulations 1989, reg. 97.

purpose is recited in the order or agreement. This means that the Board will not generally take steps to force the sale of the property but will wait for their money until the property is sold voluntarily by the assisted person. The property must provide adequate security for the charge and the assisted person must agree to pay interest, currently at the rate of 12 per cent. per annum. This is simple, rather than compound, interest and, rather than being paid by instalments, it can be added to the outstanding capital sum if the assisted person wishes.

The charge may be transferred to another property, thus enabling the assisted person to move house. The substituted property must provide adequate security and interest will continue to accrue. The Board have issued guidelines as to when they will agree to a substitution.[33] In essence the house must be required as a home for the assisted party and at least one child under the age of 18; or it must be necessary for the assisted person to move for reasons of health, disability or employment.

A second substitution will only be authorised in exceptional circumstances.

(ii) *Cash*[34]

If the assisted person has recovered or preserved cash (*e.g.* a lump sum has been awarded in his favour) then enforcement can only be postponed if this is to be used to buy a home. Again the purpose must be *recited in the court order or agreement*. The property must be purchased within one year and will be subject to a charge. Interest will again accrue at the rate of 12 per cent. per annum. A new property can be substituted, and the charge transferred, on similar terms to those outlined above.

REDUCING THE IMPACT OF THE CHARGE

(i) Tell the client   2–29

Clearly the client must be informed of the impact of the charge as soon as legal aid is applied for and reminded of it throughout the case. Advice then given about the charge should be confirmed in writing to the client. This may not only make matters clearer to the client, it also gives the solicitor a safeguard should the client later deny that the advice was given. The client will also receive information

---

[33] *Legal Aid Handbook* 1990, p. 547.
[34] The Civil Legal Aid (General) Regulations 1989, reg. 96.

about the charge by means of a "tear off" section attached to the legal aid application form. During the course of ancillary proceedings it is important to remember that the real value of any order may be affected by the charge, and this may act as an incentive to the client to keep the costs as low as possible.

2–30 **(ii) Obtain an order for costs whenever possible**
This is the obvious method of reducing the charge, although it is not always possible. Costs are not, for example, normally awarded against a legally aided party. The practice of the court relating to orders for costs is discussed in more detail at 2–17 above.

2–31 **(iii) Make use of the exemptions**
It will be apparent from what was said about exemptions in 2–27 above, that it may be sensible to seek orders to which the charge cannot apply. Thus, other things being equal, periodical payments orders are to be preferred to lump sum orders. In some cases the court itself may take the impact of the charge into account in deciding on the most appropriate order.[35] The charge must, however, be kept in perspective. The costs in many cases will amount only to a few hundred pounds and the operation of the charge should not then lead the client to accept an order which does not properly cater for his or her needs.

2–32 **(iv) Avoid putting property in issue**
If the parties have agreed about the distribution of property before legal aid is applied for, the charge cannot attach to that property. So, for example, if the parties have agreed what is to happen to the matrimonial home, but are disputing custody of the children, the charge cannot attach to the home, even if legal aid is granted for the custody dispute.

Even if there is a dispute about property, it may be possible to reduce the impact of the charge by showing that only part of the property was in issue.

Example

The matrimonial home is in the joint names of Margaret and Denis. On divorce Denis accepts that Margaret should have a half share of the property, but Margaret wants it all. If she succeeds, with the

---

[35] See, *e.g. Simmons* v. *Simmons* [1984] Fam. 17; but note *Collins* v. *Collins* [1987] 1 F.L.R. 187, in which the Court of Appeal held that a judge had been wrong to include an amount for costs in a lump sum order. This decision was apparently overlooked by Anthony Lincoln J. in *B.* v. *B. (Real Property)* [1988] 2 F.L.R. 490 when, in assessing the amount of a lump sum order he expressly increased it to allow for the legal aid charge.

*help of legal aid, the charge should attach only to half the value of
the property, because the other half was never in issue.*

In such cases, however, it is important to make it clear
when applying for legal aid exactly what is in issue between
the parties and what has already been agreed.

(v) Artificial devices? 2–33
The court has said that legal advisers have a responsibility to
the legal aid fund and should not try to manipulate the
destination of money or property so as to avoid the charge.[36]
The charge will not attach if an order is made in favour of
someone who is not an assisted person. This is because
section 16(6) of the Legal Aid Act 1988 refers only to property
recovered or preserved for the assisted person, so that
provision for children is not caught. However, in *Draskovic* v.
Draskovic,[37] Balcombe J. refused to make a consent order
transferring property to the children, rather than the assisted
wife, on the basis that it was not in the public interest for the
statutory charge to be defeated in this way.

THE OPERATION OF THE CHARGE IN GREEN FORM 2–34
CASES

As has been mentioned, the costs under the Green Form are
added to the legal aid costs and are included in the charge. If,
however, no legal aid is applied for, because, for example, the
case is settled at an early date, a charge still operates, but in
favour of the solicitor, not the Legal Aid Board.[38]

Example

*S., a solicitor, advises Bill under the Green Form. Bill wants to
divorce his wife, Sally, and is seeking to claim half of the money in
his joint building society account from Sally. The money represents
their sole capital asset.*

*S. advises and assists Bill to obtain the divorce, and at an early
stage of negotiations S. receives a cheque from Sally's solicitor for
£3,000 representing half the money in the joint account.*

*S.'s bill under the Green Form totals £109.50. Bill has no
contribution under the Green Form and no order for the costs of the
divorce is made against Sally.*

---

[36] *Manley* v. *The Law Society and Another* [1981] 1 W.L.R. 335.
[37] (1981) 11 Fam.Law. 87.
[38] Legal Aid Act 1988, s.11(2). By virtue of Legal Advice and Assistance
Regulations 1989, reg. 23, a solicitor with the authority of the area
committee need not enforce the charge if, *e.g.* it would cause hardship to
the client or could only be enforced with unreasonable difficulty.

Of the £3,000 paid to S., £2,500 is exempt from the charge, but £109.50 must be deducted from the balance before it is paid to the client.

2–35 6. Assistance by Way of Representation

This form of financial assistance has almost entirely replaced legal aid in domestic proceedings before magistrates.[39] In principle the scheme allows a client who is in receipt of Green Form advice and assistance to extend the scope of the Green Form to cover representation at a hearing in the magistrates' court.

It is generally quicker to obtain A.B.W.O.R. than legal aid as the means test is carried out by the solicitor in completing the Green Form, rather than by the D.S.S.[40]

The calculation required is very similar. However, A.B.W.O.R. has a higher capital limit than for advice and assistance, so occasionally a client who is ineligible for Green Form advice may still qualify for A.B.W.O.R.

Once approval for A.B.W.O.R. has been granted, the solicitor may take the necessary steps in the court proceedings and represent the client at the hearing. There ceases to be any fixed financial limit, but of course his bill must be approved prior to payment by the Legal Aid Board.

Apart from this, there are slight procedural differences between A.B.W.O.R. and legal aid.

Following the completion of a Green Form the solicitor will complete an application form for A.B.W.O.R. (A.B.W.O.R. 1.) and send this to the area director. Apart from increased capital limits for A.B.W.O.R., financial eligibility and the contribution are identical to that under the Green Form so there will be no need for a separate means assessment. The application will be considered on its merits and if granted a form called "Approval of Assistance by way of Representation" will be sent to the assisted person and his solicitor. The solicitor will then have to inform the court and the other side that A.B.W.O.R. has been granted. There is no prescribed form for this.

---

[39] It covers, *e.g.* proceedings for financial provision in the magistrates' court on marriage breakdown, proceedings in the magistrates' court under G.M.A. 1971, proceedings for a family protection order under s.16 of the D.P.M.C.A. 1978 and for proceedings under the C.C.A. 1980.

[40] As the financial limits for eligibility for Legal Aid are slightly more generous than for A.B.W.O.R., if a client is ineligible for A.B.W.O.R. it may still be possible to apply for legal aid for proceedings before the magistrates' court, see 2–10, above.

It is also possible to apply for A.B.W.O.R. on the telephone in cases of emergency (*e.g.* where protection from violence is sought). There is no equivalent to the emergency application form for legal aid, as by the nature of A.B.W.O.R. there will not be an investigation of the applicant's means by the D.S.S.

7. Representation within the Precincts of the Court   2–36

Regulations 7 and 8 of the Legal Advice and Assistance (Scope) Regulations 1989 allow extension of the Green Form to cover representation before the court. Under these regulations a solicitor, who perhaps has not been able to apply for emergency legal aid, can ask a magistrates' or county court to authorise representation on the Green Form. Alternatively the court can request any solicitor within the precincts of the court to represent a party under these regulations.

Unlike A.B.W.O.R., approval under this provision does not alter the normal financial limits on the work that may be done under the Green Form. Consequently it was not much used at all except occasionally in cases of domestic violence where an application has had to be made with great urgency. Owing to a change in the regulations relating to emergency certificates, it is likely to be even less used in the future. Nowadays it is possible for work to be paid for under the legal aid scheme even though it was done prior to the issue of an emergency certificate. The conditions relating to this provision are very restrictive however. The legal aid area office must have been closed so that no application for an emergency certificate could have been made, and the application for such a certificate must be made at the first available opportunity.[41] This is discussed in more detail at 20–35, below.

[41] Civil Legal Aid (General) Regulations 1989, reg. 103(6).

PART I

DIVORCE AND OTHER DECREES

3. Divorce—The Law

1. Background

The first steps towards the present law of divorce were taken in 1857 with the passing of the first Matrimonial Causes Act. Before that Act a divorce, in the sense in which we understand the term, could be obtained only by a complicated and expensive procedure that included the passing of a private Act of Parliament. The 1857 Act established a Court for Divorce and Matrimonial Causes with power to grant decrees of dissolution of marriage, though only on the ground of the other spouse's adultery. The grounds for divorce were broadened by the Matrimonial Causes Act 1937 to include cruelty, desertion and incurable insanity and these, with adultery, remained the only grounds until the Divorce Reform Act 1969 came into force on January 1, 1971.

The changes that this Act introduced were the result of widespread dissatisfaction with the law's reliance on the matrimonial offence as the normal ground for divorce. The need, in most cases, to brand one spouse as the "guilty" party was felt by many to be unrealistic and unfair. In 1966 the report of a committee set up by the Archbishop of Canterbury recommended that the grounds for divorce should be replaced by an investigation into whether the marriage had in fact broken down.[1] This report was referred to the Law Commission, which in turn reported in favour of making the irretrievable breakdown of the marriage the sole ground for divorce, although it was felt impracticable and undesirable for there to be a detailed investigation into each marriage that had allegedly broken down.[2] Ultimately it was agreed that the breakdown should be established by proof of one of five facts, three of which bore a strong resemblance to the former grounds for divorce. These were embodied in the Divorce

[1] *Putting Asunder* (S.P.C.K., 1966).
[2] *Reform of the Grounds of Divorce: The Field of Choice*: (Cmnd. 3123 (1966)).

Reform Act 1969; this was subsequently consolidated into the M.C.A. 1973, which contains the present law. Not surprisingly, however, dissatisfaction has continued with the law's failure to move very far from the concept of the matrimonial offence. As a result, the Law Commission is once again considering possible reform of the ground for divorce.

3–03 In a discussion paper entitled *Facing the Future* (Law Com. No. 170) published in 1988, the Commission concludes that the irretrievable breakdown of the marriage should remain as the sole ground on which a divorce decree should be granted. It suggests, however, that this should no longer be judged according to the present guidelines with their emphasis on fault. It proposes instead that a divorce should be obtainable only after a fixed period of separation, (*e.g.* one year) or more radically, only after a period of transition, during which time the parties are encouraged to settle the arrangements for their future before the divorce is finalised.

No firm legislative proposals to this effect have been forthcoming as yet. The Lord Chancellor has, however, indicated that he intends to promote a rolling programme of reform in family law matters over the next few years and that reform of divorce law is high on this agenda.

3–04 2. Terminology

Before embarking on an explanation of divorce law, the following points about terminology must be made. The party seeking a decree of divorce is known as "the petitioner" and the party against whom the decree is sought is known as "the respondent." A person with whom the respondent is alleged to have committed adultery is known as "the co-respondent." A decree of divorce is granted in two stages. The initial decree is called "the decree nisi"; this does not dissolve the marriage. Dissolution occurs, usually at least six weeks later, when the decree is made "absolute."

3–05 3. The One-Year Bar

The Law Commission,[3] Parliament, and no doubt many other people, think that it would be wrong to allow a married couple to divorce within the very early stages of a marriage. Couples might not consider the prospect of marriage seriously

---

[3] *Time Restrictions on Presentation of Divorce and Nullity Petitions* Law Com. No. 116 (1982).

enough if they knew they could petition for divorce the day after the ceremony. Furthermore, newly-weds who encountered early marital problems might be tempted to resort to a quick divorce, without making any serious attempt to resolve these problems.

Accordingly, section 3(1) of the M.C.A. 1973 provides that no **3–06** petition for divorce shall be presented to the court before the expiration of the period of one year from the date of the marriage. This bar was inserted by the M.F.P.A. 1984. It cannot be waived under any circumstances. However, although no divorce petition can be filed within the first year of marriage, section 3(2) makes it clear that this does not preclude a petition subsequently being based on events which occurred during that time. So, for example, adultery committed within the first year of a marriage might be relied on in a petition filed after that year has expired.

Of course, the fact that divorce is impossible within the first **3–07** year of marriage does not preclude those parties who do encounter early marital problems from seeking other remedies. For example, injunctions may be sought by those faced with domestic violence; applications for maintenance and custody may be made independently of a divorce petition and in some cases a decree of judicial separation (to which there is no time bar) may be appropriate. These remedies are dealt with in detail elsewhere in the book.

4. The Ground for Divorce   3–08

By section 1(1) of the M.C.A. 1973, a petition for divorce may be presented to the court by either party to a marriage on the ground that the marriage has broken down irretrievably. Although this is the sole ground for divorce, section 1(2) goes on to say that the court shall not hold the marriage to have broken down irretrievably unless the petitioner satisfies the court of one or more of five facts, which are then set out. They may be summarised as adultery, unreasonable behaviour, two years' desertion, two years' separation with the respondent's consent to divorce and five years' separation, regardless of the respondent's consent:

These facts, therefore, assume a crucial role in obtaining a **3–09** divorce and, although they are not formally grounds for divorce, it is understandable that they should often be thought of as if they were. This tendency is reinforced by the provision in section 1(4) that, once the court is satisfied that one of the facts has been made out, it must normally grant a decree of divorce unless it is satisfied that the marriage has not broken down irretrievably. In practice, therefore, proof of one of the facts leads to a decree being granted. Conversely, the court may be satisfied that the marriage has irretrievably broken down, but will refuse a decree if none of the five facts has been proved.[4]

3–10   5. The Five Facts in Detail

A large body of case law has developed around the five facts. Some of this goes back beyond the reforms introduced by the Divorce Reform Act 1969, because the first three facts closely resemble the former grounds for divorce. However the procedural reforms of the 1970s, which are dealt with in Chapter 4 below, have reduced the importance of substantive law in this field. The great majority of divorce petitions are undefended and are dealt with by county court registrars without any hearing taking place. Section 1(3) of the M.C.A. 1973 provides that "on a petition for divorce it shall be the duty of the court to inquire, so far as it reasonably can, into the facts alleged by the petitioner and into any facts alleged by the respondent." Therefore a registrar may take the view that an alleged fact has not been made out, even though it is undisputed by the other party. In practice, however, this seldom happens.

3–11   ADULTERY AND INTOLERABILITY

The first fact, set out in section 1(2)(*a*) of the M.C.A. 1973, is that "the respondent has committed adultery and the petitioner finds it intolerable to live with the respondent."

Adultery continues to be a common basis for divorce, partly no doubt because it allows a divorce to be obtained more quickly than do most of the other facts. In 1988, the year for which the latest statistics are available, nearly 30 per cent. of the 154,788 divorce decrees granted were based on adultery.[5]

---

[4] As in *Richards* v. *Richards* [1972] 1 W.L.R. 1073, and *Buffery* v. *Buffery* [1988] 2 F.L.R. 365.
[5] Judicial Statistics 1988 (Cm. 745 (1989)), Table 5.3.

Section 1(2)(*a*) requires proof of two elements; adultery and intolerability. These must be considered in turn.

(i) Adultery

Definition   3–12

There has never been a statutory definition of adultery, but it would be generally accepted that it consists of voluntary sexual intercourse between two members of the opposite sex, one or both of whom are married, though not to each other.[6] Penetration of the woman by the man is sufficient to amount to intercourse for the purpose of this definition.[7] As the intercourse must be voluntary, it follows that the victim of rape does not commit adultery,[8] nor does a woman who lacks the "capacity to consent" through, for example, involuntary drunkenness or the effect of drugs. In all these cases, however, the man commits adultery on which his wife could base a divorce petition.

Proof of adultery   3–13

In the past, when adultery was regarded as being akin to a criminal offence, the courts required it to proved beyond reasonable doubt. This attitude was gradually relaxed, however, and nowadays adultery may be proved on the civil standard of proof on a balance of probabilities.[9]

However, an allegation of adultery is still regarded as a very serious matter, so the courts have continued to insist that there are degrees of probability and that, where adultery is alleged, proof on a simple balance of probabilities is not enough.[10] In other words it is not enough for the court to feel that it is just more probable than not that adultery occurred. It is unclear from this exactly how far the balance must tip in favour of the party making the allegation.

Fortunately, however, this is not often a problem, because in   3–14
many cases the respondent admits the adultery. To facilitate this, the form of acknowledgment of service, which the

---

[6] For a variation on the same theme, see *Rayden on Divorce* (15th ed., 1988) p. 228, accepted in, *e.g. Dennis* v. *Dennis* [1955] P. 153.

[7] *Dennis* v. *Dennis* (above).

[8] Though the burden of proving that intercourse was not consensual apparently rests on the respondent: *Redpath* v. *Redpath* [1950] 1 All E.R. 600.

[9] The presumption that a child born in wedlock is legitimate may be rebutted by proof on a balance of probabilities (F.L.R.A. 1969, s.26). As this is one method of proving adultery it follows that the same standard of proof applies to all other methods.

[10] *Serio* v. *Serio* [1983] 4 F.L.R. 756.

respondent and co-respondent each receive with the petition alleging adultery, asks whether they admit it. They are not obliged to answer, but are warned that an admission given in this form will be treated by the court as one on which the petitioner is entitled to rely.[11] If a party does admit the adultery on the acknowledgment of service form, he must sign the form personally, regardless of whether a solicitor is acting for him. The petitioner will later identify the signature (at least in the case of the respondent) in the affidavit filed in support of the petition. (This is considered in more detail at 4–61 below.)

3–15   Besides this, it is common practice, before the petition is filed, to ask the respondent to provide a confession statement in which the respondent formally admits the adultery, giving brief details of dates and places and, perhaps, naming the co-respondent. It may seem superfluous to obtain such a statement if the respondent is later going to admit adultery in the acknowledgment of service, but it may be worthwhile for three reasons. First, it will show at the outset that the respondent is prepared to allow a divorce petition based on adultery to go through undefended; secondly, it will provide particulars of adultery which can be used in drafting the petition, and thirdly it can be relied on as evidence of the adultery should the respondent fail to sign or return the acknowledgment of service.

3–16   If the respondent refuses to admit adultery, it may be difficult to prove. Direct evidence of adultery from someone who was present is rarely available, and some kind of circumstantial evidence will normally be needed. This make take a variety of forms. In the past evidence of what was quaintly known as "inclination plus opportunity" was sometimes relied on. This would often take the form of showing that the parties had spent the night together in the same room.[12] Evidence that the respondent had given birth to an illegitimate child, or had contracted venereal disease which could not have come from the petitioner, would be other ways of proving adultery.

3–17   It can also be proved by reference to previous court proceedings, as where, for example, a husband has been convicted of rape,[13] or where he has been found to be the

---

[11] Matrimonial Causes (Amendment) Rules 1980, r. 4.
[12] Though this does not create an irrebuttable presumption that adultery occurred. *England* v. *England* [1953] P. 16.
[13] Civil Evidence Act 1968, s.11(1).

father of an illegitimate child in previous civil proceedings.[14] Usually the threat of resorting to one of these methods of proof is enough to persuade the respondent to admit adultery.

(ii) Intolerability

3–18

Besides proving adultery, the petitioner must find it intolerable to live with the respondent. No doubt in many cases it will be the fact of adultery which the petitioner finds intolerable, but it need not be so. Section 1(2)(a) does not say that the intolerability must be in consequence of the adultery, and in *Cleary* v. *Cleary*[15] the Court of Appeal held that section 1(2)(a) was not to be construed as if it did say this. So Mr. Cleary, who had forgiven his wife for her adultery, was still entitled to a decree even though he had given evidence to the effect that it was his wife's behaviour after her adultery rather than the adultery itself which he found intolerable. This decision was followed, somewhat reluctantly, by a differently constituted Court of Appeal in *Carr* v. *Carr*,[16] but the court in that case suggested that it might be desirable for the point to be decided by the House of Lords, after full consideration of the arguments in favour of requiring a causal connection between the adultery and the intolerability. However, this has never happened.[17]

It is clear from the wording of section 1(2)(a) that the test of **3–19** intolerability is purely subjective; provided the petitioner finds it intolerable to live with the respondent, it is irrelevant that any reasonable person would find it perfectly supportable. On the other hand, the court has to believe the petitioner's assertion if it is to grant a decree. As Lord Denning M.R., for example, said in *Cleary* v. *Cleary*, the court should not necessarily accept a petitioner's bare assertion that married life is intolerable.[18] In practice, however, this is what usually happens. In an undefended case, where there is no oral hearing, the petitioner is asked to complete a standard form affidavit, which, in adultery cases, poses the question "Do you find it intolerable to live with the respondent?"[19] A

---

[14] *Ibid.* s.12(1) (as amended by the F.L.R.A. 1987).
[15] [1974] 1 W.L.R. 73.
[16] [1974] 1 W.L.R. 1534.
[17] For a summary of the arguments for and against requiring a causal connection, see Cretney and Masson, *Principles of Family Law* (5th ed., 1990), pp. 105–106.
[18] At [1974] 1 W.L.R. 76.
[19] M.C.R. 1977, Form 7(a).

simple "Yes" is all that is normally required to satisfy the court on the point.

3–20 **(iii) Cohabitation after discovery of adultery**
By virtue of section 2(1) of the M.C.A. 1973, one party is not entitled to rely on adultery committed by the other if the parties cohabit for more than six months after the adultery has been discovered.

3–21 Several points should be noted about this potential bar to a divorce based on adultery:

(i) Time does not start to run until the adultery has been discovered. It is immaterial how long ago the adultery was committed.

(ii) The six months' cohabitation may be made up of any number of shorter periods of living together following the discovery, as might occur where the parties make several attempts at reconciliation.

(iii) The fact that the parties cohabit for more than six months, following the petitioner's discovery of the respondent's adultery with a particular individual, does not preclude the petitioner from relying on subsequent acts of adultery by the respondent with that same individual.

Example

On January 1, Wendy discovers that her husband Henry has committed adultery with Carol. She forgives him and they live together until October 1, when Wendy discovers that Henry and Carol committed adultery again in February. Wendy can base a petition on the adultery in February.[20]

The six months' bar operates until decree absolute (when the marriage is finally dissolved). So a petitioner who obtains a decree nisi based on adultery, and then cohabits with the respondent for more than six months, will be refused a decree absolute and the decree nisi will be rescinded.[21]

3–22 The main purpose behind section 2(1) is to allow the parties a reasonable period of time in which to achieve a reconciliation.

[20] *Carr* v. *Carr* (above) shows that it is important to identify the actual adultery being relied upon in construing s.2(1). Here the fact that a wife lived with her husband for 18 months after discovering his adultery was held to be no bar to her relying on his adultery with the same woman after the parties had separated.
[21] *Biggs* v. *Biggs* [1977] Fam. 1.

In order to ensure that a petitioner who takes advantage of this provision is not later prejudiced as a result, section 2(2) provides that the court must disregard cohabitation for less than six months after the discovery of adultery, in deciding whether the petitioner finds it intolerable to live with the respondent.

BEHAVIOUR

The second fact, set out in section 1(2)(*b*), is that "the respondent has behaved in such a way that the petitioner cannot reasonably be expected to live with the respondent." Behaviour has consistently proved the most popular of all the facts. This is probably because, like adultery, it can be used without waiting for any period of separation to elapse first. In 1988, over 43 per cent. of all divorce decrees were based on this fact.[22]

3–23

(i) The test of behaviour

3–24

When the respondent's behaviour was first introduced as a basis for divorce there was a tendency to treat it as requiring evidence of the "grave and weighty" misconduct which had been needed to establish the old grounds of cruelty and constructive desertion (behaviour which drove the petitioner to leave the respondent) which this fact, in effect, replaced.[23] However, in *Livingstone-Stallard* v. *Livingstone-Stallard*[24] Dunn J. rejected the idea of applying tests derived from the old law to the modern statute. He took the view that the language of section 1(2)(*b*) was clear enough as it stood, and that the court should think of itself as a properly-directed jury faced with the question: "Would any right-thinking person come to the conclusion that this husband has behaved in such a way that this wife cannot reasonably be expected to live with him, taking into account the whole of the circumstances and the character and personalities of the parties?". Applying this test to the facts of this case the judge found that a wife was entitled to a decree on the basis of her husband's behaviour, even though many of the incidents alleged against him were trivial in themselves. Taken together they had resulted in the wife being subjected to a constant atmosphere of criticism, disapproval and boorish behaviour which she could not reasonably be expected to tolerate.

---

[22] Judicial Statistics 1988 (Cm. 745 (1989)), Table 5.3.
[23] See, *e.g. Pheasant* v. *Pheasant* [1972] Fam. 202.
[24] [1974] Fam. 47.

3-25 This approach to section 1(2)(*b*) was subsequently approved of by the Court of Appeal in *O'Neill* v. *O'Neill*,[25] where, however, the allegations against the husband were somewhat stronger. They included the fact that the husband, on his retirement as an airline pilot, had embarked on a project to renovate the matrimonial home. This had entailed removing some 30 tons of rubble from underneath the floorboards and depositing it in the garden, mixing cement in the living-room and removing the lavatory door for eight months, all of which caused the wife inconvenience and embarrassment. Nevertheless the trial judge had considered the wife's complaints to be trivial, and had dismissed her petition, quoting the marriage vow in which the parties promise to take each other "for better or worse". The Court of Appeal, allowing the wife's appeal, held that it was the Act, and not the Book of Common Prayer, which provided the relevant test. Applying the simple wording of section 1(2)(*b*) to the facts of this case, it was clear that the wife could not reasonably be expected to live with the husband.

3-26 It will be seen that the test propounded by Dunn J., and approved by the Court of Appeal, requires the court to consider the character and personality of the parties themselves. In other words the test is not purely objective, and involves making allowances for the individual foibles of the parties to the case. This had been recognised earlier by Bagnall J. in *Ash* v. *Ash*,[26] a case in which a wife petitioner was granted a decree on the basis of her husband's behaviour after he had lost a well-paid job, and the parties' living standard had drastically declined. Although some wives might have borne this set-back cheerfully, the judge said that he must take into account the fact that this wife "was prepared to take advantage of the good and to enjoy prosperity but has not been able to tolerate the disadvantages of the bad and of adversity".

Bagnall J. also suggested that this need to consider each party's temperament meant that spouses could not complain of each other's behaviour if both were bad in similar respects. So, for example, "a violent petitioner can reasonably be expected to live with a violent respondent, a petitioner who is addicted to drink can reasonably be expected to live with a respondent similarly addicted" and so on. This, with respect, is taking the subjective approach too far. Where the parties

---

[25] [1975] 1 W.L.R. 1118. The decision was followed in *Buffery* v. *Buffery* [1988] 2 F.L.R. 365.
[26] [1972] Fam. 135.

are, for example, continually making drunken assaults on each other, it would seem extraordinary if a petition brought by either on the basis of the other's behaviour were dismissed because they could reasonably be expected to live with each other on such terms.[27] This would be to place too much emphasis on the subjective element in section 1(2)(*b*), and too little on the ground for divorce itself, the irretrievable breakdown of the marriage.

(ii) Examples of behaviour   3–27
The ingenuity of both spouses and lawyers will no doubt ensure that there can never be an exhaustive list of the kinds of behaviour which will justify the granting of a divorce decree. The following, therefore, are no more than examples of the allegations which are commonly made in behaviour petitions and which, either alone or more often in combination, will generally satisfy the registrar that a decree should be granted:

(a) physical violence;

(b) "verbal violence": this can take many forms, *e.g.* threats, abuse, nagging and constant criticism;

(c) persistent drunkenness;

(d) sexual behaviour; this can range from demanding intercourse too often, to not wanting it at all; it also includes requiring a partner to engage in perverted sexual practices;

(e) regular association with another person, falling short of adultery, sometimes referred to as an "improper association." Homosexual or lesbian relationships can be included in this category;

(f) lack of affection and attention, as where one spouse never talks to the other or never plays a part in looking after the children or the home.[28]

---

[27] Though see *Shears* v. *Shears* (1972) 117 S.J. 33, in which Hollings J. dismissed a wife's petition containing complaints of the husband's violence and drunkenness, saying that the parties came from a "rumbustious community" and that drinking was a way of life in their "strata of society."

[28] But see *Pheasant* v. *Pheasant* (above), in which a husband's complaint that his wife had failed to give him the "spontaneous demonstrative affection which his nature demanded and for which he craved" was held not to justify a decree. And in *Richards* v. *Richards* [1984] A.C. 174, where a wife's allegations against her husband included his failure to bring her flowers on the birth of their child, the judge at first instance described the allegations as "rubbishy."

3–28   **(iii) The mentally-ill respondent**

A special difficulty arises when the respondent's behaviour is seen to be the result of mental illness. The fact that the respondent is not behaving as he does out of any malice towards the petitioner may sometimes be seen as a mitigating factor and may lead the court to refuse a decree, which in different circumstances it might have granted.[29]

Nevertheless, the fact that the respondent is mentally ill is not necessarily a sufficient answer to a behaviour petition. The court will have particular regard to the effect which the behaviour has had on the petitioner, and, as in any other case, should grant a decree if it concludes that this petitioner cannot reasonably be expected to live with this respondent.[30] A decree may even be granted in a case in which the illness has reduced the respondent to the state of a "human vegetable," requiring indefinite institutional care. Passive inactivity can still be classified as "behaviour" within section 1(2)(*b*).[31]

3–29   **(iv) Cohabitation after the final incident**

Section 2(3) of the M.C.A. 1973 provides that the court must disregard cohabitation of up to six months following the final incident of behaviour relied on by the petitioner in deciding whether the petitioner can reasonably be expected to live with the respondent. As with section 2(2) relating to adultery, this provision is designed to allow attempts at reconciliation, without ultimate prejudice to the petitioner should the attempts fail.

3–30   The following points concerning section 2(3) should be noted.

    (i)   To help the court decide whether cohabitation is continuing or not, the standard form affidavit, which must be filed in support of an undefended behaviour petition, requires details of the living arrangements where the parties have lived at the same address for more than six months after the final incident relied on, or after the filing of the petition, if the behaviour is continuing.

    (ii) Section 2(3) does not constitute a bar to a decree being granted where cohabitation has exceeded six months. The court retains a discretion to grant a decree in such

---

[29] As in *Richards* v. *Richards* [1972] 1 W.L.R. 1073.

[30] See, *e.g. Katz* v. *Katz* [1972] 1 W.L.R. 955 where the husband's behaviour drove the wife to attempt suicide.

[31] *Thurlow* v. *Thurlow* [1976] Fam. 32.

cases, and may do so if there is a good reason for the continued cohabitation.[32]

(iii) Where the parties are still cohabiting it should often be possible to avoid difficulties by ensuring that the petition alleges an incident of behaviour occurring within the six months prior to the petition being filed.

(iv) Many registrars are suspicious of all cases where the parties are still living together at the time a behaviour petition is filed. It is, therefore, wise to be able to explain the fact that the parties are still living together, whatever the period of cohabitation since the final incident relied on.

DESERTION

3–31

The third fact, set out in section 1(2)(c), is that "the respondent has deserted the petitioner for a continuous period of at least two years immediately preceding the presentation of the petition." This is the least used of the facts; in 1988, under 2 per cent. of all divorce decrees were based on it.[33] No doubt this is largely because, once the parties have lived apart for the necessary two-year period, they often prefer to divorce by consent under the next fact. Furthermore, desertion is legally the most complex of the five facts, and few solicitors would advise their clients to run the risk of becoming entangled in the problems of proving desertion when a simpler alternative is often available.

It might be thought that a further reason why desertion is so little used is that a petitioner cannot reasonably be expected to live with a respondent who is in desertion. Consequently, where one party deserts the other, it would seem quicker to petition on the basis of section 1(2)(b) and avoid a two-year wait. The courts, however, have refused to allow this, since otherwise section 1(2)(c) would never be used at all, which cannot have been Parliament's intention. In *Stringfellow* v. *Stringfellow*,[34] where a wife tried to divorce her husband under section 1(2)(b) after he had been gone for less than three months, the Court of Appeal held that desertion, and steps leading up to desertion, could not be pleaded as

3–32

---

[32] *e.g. Bradley* v. *Bradley* [1973] 1 W.L.R. 1291, where the wife had nowhere else to live.

[33] Judicial Statistics 1988 (Cm. 745 (1989)), Table 5.3.

[34] [1976] 1 W.L.R. 645.

behaviour. The court did not explain how it is possible to distinguish between behaviour of the kind encompassed by section 1(2)(*b*) and behaviour which merely constitutes "steps leading up to desertion." However, in cases where behaviour is relied on after the respondent has left the home, it is clearly important to ensure that ample particulars of behaviour unrelated to the desertion are included in the petition.

3–33 **(i) The elements of desertion**
Desertion is not defined by statute and the courts have also refrained from laying down a comprehensive definition. However, it has long been accepted that four matters must be proved in order to establish desertion.

3–34 *Factual separation*

Normally this is the most straightfoward element to prove. Complications have arisen in cases in which the parties have remained living under the same roof, but have had so little contact with each other that it becomes possible for them to maintain that they are living apart. Perhaps the best test of this is that put forward by Denning L.J. in *Hopes* v. *Hopes*.[35] He suggested that a decision should be based on the question of whether the parties were in effect occupying separate flats: "They may meet on the stairs or in the passageway, but so they might if they each had separate flats in one building." If contact between the parties is as minimal as this, they will be treated as living apart.

3–35 *The intention to desert*

This consists of an intention to bring cohabitation permanently to an end. This intention must subsist throughout the period of desertion. Should it lapse, as where, for example, a spouse in desertion offers to come home, then the desertion lapses too.[36]

3–36 *Absence of consent*

Consensual separation cannot amount to desertion. However, the mere fact that the deserted spouse is glad that the other has gone does not make the separation a consensual one. Something more positive is required, as where, for example,

---

[35] [1949] P. 227.
[36] An exception to this is contained in s.2(4) of the M.C.A. 1973. Where a deserter becomes incapable of maintaining an intention to desert, the court may, by virtue of s.2(4), treat the desertion as continuing despite the supervening mental incapacity.

the parties enter into a separation agreement, or where one party actively prevents the other from returning by changing the locks on the doors of the matrimonial home.[37]

It might be thought that the fact that a deserted spouse had obtained an injunction or order excluding the other spouse from the home would similarly prevent desertion running. This is not necessarily so, however. Section 4(4) of the M.C.A. 1973[38] gives the court a discretion to treat any period when such injunction or order is in force as a period of desertion. In practice, however, a spouse who had succeeded in obtaining an exclusion order, and who wanted a divorce, would probably rely on the behaviour which had justified the granting of the order to get a decree under section 1(2)(b).

Absence of just cause   3–37

One spouse is not in desertion if he has just cause for living apart from the other. This normally takes the form of a complaint about the other spouse's behaviour, which either drove the alleged deserter out of the home, or prevented him from returning after he had left. If the alleged deserter can show just cause for living apart it usually follows that he is entitled to a divorce decree of his own, on the basis of either the other spouse's adultery or behaviour.

(ii) Cohabitation during desertion   3–38

Despite the fact that section 1(2)(c) of the M.C.A. 1973 requires the two-year period of desertion to have been continuous, section 2(5) provides that no account shall be taken of up to six months' cohabitation after the period of desertion has started to run. This, like the other provisions of section 2 already referred to, is designed to allow attempts at reconciliation without precluding the possibility of divorce if these attempts are unsuccessful.

Any period of cohabitation cannot be included in the two-year period of desertion. Although the two years of living apart do not have to be literally continuous, there must nevertheless be a total of two years before a petition can be filed.

Example   3–39

Harry deserts Wilma on January 1, 1989. On January 1, 1990 they resume living together until July 1, 1990 when Harry leaves again, and they never resume cohabitation. Wilma cannot petition until

---

[37] As in *Barnett* v. *Barnett* [1955] P. 21.
[38] Inserted by the D.P.M.C.A. 1978, s.62.

after July 1, 1991 when a full two years of desertion will have elapsed.

3–40 TWO YEARS' SEPARATION AND RESPONDENT'S CONSENT

The fourth fact, set out in section 1(2)(*d*), is "that the parties to the marriage have lived apart for a continuous period of at least two years immediately preceding the presentation of the petition and the respondent consents to a decree being granted." This is the first of the five facts seen so far which does not involve any allegation of misconduct against the respondent. When it was introduced in 1971 it allowed divorce by consent for the first time and not surprisingly it is often used. In 1988, nearly 19 per cent. of all divorce decrees were based on this fact.[39] Even so it is not nearly as much relied upon as adultery and behaviour.

The two elements of separation and consent must now be considered in more detail.

(i) Two years' separation

3–41 *Factual separation*

As with desertion, there is generally no problem in showing that the parties are indeed living apart, although problems have occasionally arisen where the parties have remained living under the same roof. In this case, however, the M.C.A. 1973 provides some guidance. According to section 2(6) which applies to this fact but not to desertion, "a husband and wife shall be treated as living apart unless they are living with each other in the same household." At first sight this appears to be the same as the "separate flats test" suggested in *Hopes* v. *Hopes*[40] for the purpose of desertion. This test similarly emphasises that it is living in a household, rather than a house, which is important in determining whether the parties are living together or not. However, section 2(6) has been given a broader interpretation than this by the Court of Appeal in the exceptional case of *Fuller* v. *Fuller*.[41] Here a wife had left her husband to go and live with her lover. The husband became seriously ill, and, on his discharge from hospital, went to live with his wife and her lover in the lover's house. The wife there looked after her husband by cooking and washing for him, for which the husband paid,

---

[39] Judicial Statistics 1988 (Cm. 745 (1989)), Table 5.3.
[40] See 3–34, above.
[41] [1973] 1 W.L.R. 730.

and the husband, although occupying the spare bedroom, shared the rest of the house with the wife and her lover. When, four years later, the wife subsequently petitioned for divorce, relying on the fact of separation, the Court of Appeal held that she should succeed. The court held that section 2(6) was to be read as meaning that the parties were to be treated as living apart "unless they are living with each other *as husband and wife* in the same household." Here the parties, though living in the same houshold, were not living as husband and wife, but rather as lodger and landlady.

The two-year period

3–42

The actual day of separation must not be counted in calculating the period of separation. So, where an impatient wife petitioned under section 1(2)(*d*) on the second anniversary of the separation, it was held that she was a day too early.[42]

Although, as with desertion, the period of separation is supposed to be continuous, section 2(5) of the M.C.A. 1973,[43] which requires a period or periods of cohabitation not exceeding six months in all to be disregarded, applies to this fact as well.

The mental element

3–43

In *Santos* v. *Santos*[44] the Court of Appeal held that the mere fact that the parties have lived in separate places for two years is not enough to constitute the two years' separation required by section 1(2)(*d*). At least one of the parties must have recognised that the marriage was at an end throughout the two-year period, although it is not necessary for this recognition to have been communicated to the other party. The court felt that, in the absence of such a requirement, absurd cases could arise where the parties had lived apart through force of circumstance. For example, a husband, who had worked abroad for two years, but had remained on excellent terms with his wife at home, could divorce her after they had had a row while he was home on leave. This possibility is removed by requiring that one party must have regarded the marriage as over throughout the two-year period of separation.

---

[42] *Warr* v. *Warr* [1975] Fam. 25. No doubt the same rule applies to the previous fact (desertion) and the next fact (five years' separation), and to all other provisions in the M.C.A. 1973 which require the computation of time (*e.g.* the one-year bar to divorce).

[43] See 3–38, above.

[44] [1972] Fam. 247.

It is doubtful, however, whether Parliament intended section 1(2)(*d*) to include any mental element. After all, absurdities of the kind outlined above could be avoided by the court finding that the marriage had not broken down irretrievably, if that was indeed the case. Furthermore, the insistence on an early recognition that the marriage is finished militates against attempts at reconciliation, which the Act elsewhere seeks to promote, although few potential petitioners would, of course, know about the need for a mental element until they consulted a solicitor.

3–44 Somewhat surprisingly, perhaps, the need to prove a mental element appeared to cause few difficulties in practice, and nowadays, as a result of the procedural changes introduced since *Santos* v. *Santos* was decided, it is normally sufficient for the petitioner[45] to respond correctly to the following request, which appears in the standard form affidavit required in support of a petition based on section 1(2)(*d*): "State the date when and the circumstances in which you came to the conclusion that the marriage was in fact at an end."[46]

Nevertheless, it will be apparent that the reply must be carefully worded if the court is to be satisfied that the necessary mental element is present.

(ii) The respondent's consent

3–45 *Proof of consent*

The way in which the respondent's consent to a decree being granted should be given is governed by rule 16 of the M.C.R. 1977. This provides that the respondent must give the registrar a notice indicating his consent, signed by the respondent personally. Rule 16 also provides that it is sufficient for this purpose for the respondent to indicate his consent in the acknowledgment of service form, which he returns to the court after being served with the divorce petition. If a solicitor acts for the respondent the solicitor will sign this form, but in order to comply with rule 16 it is essential that the respondent should sign as well, if he is consenting to the decree being granted. Rule 16 does not insist that the respondent's consent must be indicated to the

---

[45] It was not suggested in *Santos* v. *Santos* that it must be the petitioner who formed the recognition that the marriage was over rather than the respondent. Nevertheless both Sir George Baker P. in *Beales* v. *Beales* [1972] Fam. 210, and the Matrimonial Rules Committee, who approved the affidavit in support of a s.1(2)(*d*) petition, have assumed that it must be the petitioner who forms the recognition.

[46] M.C.R. 1977, Form 7(*d*).

court on the acknowledgment of service form, and no doubt it could be given in other ways, for example, by letter. In practice, however, it is normally convenient to prove consent by the respondent's signature on the acknowledgment of service. The petitioner will later identify this signature as the respondent's in the affidavit which is filed in support of the petition. (This is considered in more detail at 4–61 below.)

The nature of consent   **3–46**

It is well established that, whatever the form in which the respondent gives his consent, it must be expressed in a positive manner. It is not enough for the respondent merely to use words such as "I have no objection to a divorce." Thus in *Matcham* v. *Matcham*[47] Dunn J. dismissed a wife's petition based on section 1(2)(*d*) because her husband, who had since disappeared, had indicated his consent only in those words and this "passive negative attitude," said the judge, was not enough.

The consequences of consent   **3–47**

It is essential that the respondent should be capable of understanding the nature and consequences of giving his consent to a decree, and, where this is in doubt, the burden of proving it lies on the petitioner.[48] All respondents who are served with a petition based on section 1(2)(*d*) have the consequences of giving their consent drawn to their attention in the Notice of Proceedings form, which accompanies the petition. Besides being warned of the obvious consequence that consent will normally lead to a divorce decree being granted, they are also warned that pension rights, rights of occupation in the matrimonial home and rights of inheritance may all be affected by divorce. (The consequences of divorce are considered in more detail at 3–77 to 3–85 below.)

Conditional consent   **3–48**

As the respondent's consent is crucial to a divorce under section 1(2)(*d*), the respondent may be able to use it as a powerful bargaining counter in negotiations with the petitioner. A respondent may, for example, make his consent conditional on the petitioner agreeing to a favourable financial settlement. He can also make his consent conditional upon not being ordered to pay the costs of the suit.[49]

---

[47] (1976) 120 S.J. 570. See also *McGill* v. *Robson* [1972] 1 W.L.R. 237.
[48] *Mason* v. *Mason* [1972] Fam. 302.
[49] *Beales* v. *Beales* [1972] Fam. 210.

3–49 *Withdrawal of consent*

Even if the respondent does consent to the divorce, he may withdraw his consent at any time until a decree nisi has been granted, whereupon the proceedings will be stayed.[50] Indeed, even where a decree nisi has been granted, it may be possible to have it rescinded by virtue of section 10(1) of the M.C.A. 1973. This provides that the court may rescind a decree nisi based on section 1(2)(*d*) "if it is satisfied that the petitioner misled the respondent (whether intentionally or unintentionally) about any matter which the respondent took into account in deciding to give his consent."

3–50 The following points should be noted concerning section 10(1):

(i) The respondent must have been misled by the petitioner. It is not enough that the respondent was, for example, misled by his own solicitor, or simply misunderstood some matter on which he based his consent.

(ii) Although, no doubt, section 10(1) would normally be invoked when a respondent was misled as to some financial or property matter, there is in theory no restriction on the kind of matter that could be relevant. So, for example, a wife could seek to have a decree rescinded if her husband had obtained her consent by pretending that he did not intend to marry his secretary after the divorce. However the court has a discretion as to whether to rescind the decree and would be unlikely to do so in cases such as this.

(iii) Section 10(1) refers only to rescission of a decree nisi, not a decree absolute. Since the normal minimum interval between the two is only six weeks, it can be seen that there is little scope for respondents to make use of section 10(1).

3–51 FIVE YEARS' SEPARATION

The fifth and last fact, set out in section 1(2)(*e*) is "that the parties to the marriage have lived apart for a continuous period of at least five years immediately preceding the presentation of the petition." The consent of the respondent

---

[50] M.C.R. 1977, r. 16(2).

is not required, so this fact can be used by a petitioner who cannot prove any matrimonial offence against the respondent where the respondent is opposed to a divorce. Fears that it would become a "Casanova's charter" have, however, proved unfounded. Approximately 6 per cent. of all decrees were based on this fact in 1988 and, as with all the other facts, more of these were granted to wives than to husbands.[51]

Apart from the longer period of separation required and the fact that the respondent's consent is not needed, this fact has several features in common with the previous one. All the points made at 3–41 to 3–44 above, concerning separation, apply equally here. Thus section 2(6) defining "living apart," applies; the actual day of separation must not be included in calculating the five-year period, and the mental element laid down in *Santos* v. *Santos* must be proved.

6. The Grave Hardship Defence   3–52

One difference between the two facts, however, lies in section 5 of the M.C.A. 1973. This provides a special defence to a petition based on section 1(2)(*e*), where that fact is the only one proved by the petitioner. By virtue of section 5(1) a respondent to a petition based on this fact may oppose it "on the ground that the dissolution of the marriage will result in grave financial or other hardship to him and that it would in all the circumstances be wrong to dissolve the marriage." The defence was included to meet the objections of those who feared that section 1(2)(*e*) would be used to divorce "innocent" respondents, who opposed a decree because they feared being left destitute. In fact, however, it is little used in practice.

The nature of the defence can best be examined by dealing in turn with its two essential elements; that is to say, first, hardship and, secondly, the fact that it would be wrong to dissolve the marriage.

HARDSHIP

(i) The nature of financial hardship   3–53
The hardship alleged must result from the dissolution and not simply the breakdown of the marriage. So, in *Talbot* v. *Talbot*[52]

---

[51] Judicial Statistics 1988 (Cm. 745 (1989)), Table 5.3. (In *Reiterbund* v. *Reiterbund* [1975] Fam. 99, Finer J. pointed out that the fear that this fact would become a "Casanova's charter" could "with roughly equal ineptitude have been expressed by a reference to Messalina.")

[52] (1971) 115 S.J. 870.

a wife's attempt to rely on section 5 failed, because the undoubted financial hardship she was suffering was largely the result of the husband's failure to comply with maintenance orders made against him. The court held that divorce would not, in itself, cause any greater hardship so the husband's petition should not be dismissed.

Partly as a result of this decision, subsequent cases have often been concerned with the loss of prospective pension rights, because the potential loss of, for example, a widow's pension is a direct result of divorce, rather than the breakdown of the marriage. In order to counter the argument that the prospective loss of a widow's pension cannot be hardship, because such loss would never materialise if the respondent predeceased the petitioner, section 5(3) provides that "hardship shall include the loss of the chance of acquiring any benefit which the respondent might acquire if the marriage were not dissolved." Obviously this provision could apply also to loss of rights of inheritance on the husband's intestacy.

3–54 In assessing alleged financial hardship, the court may be prepared to take into account the fact that the respondent is eligible for welfare benefits. In *Reiterbund* v. *Reiterbund*[53] a wife, who was living on supplementary benefit (now called income support), sought to have her husband's petition dismissed under section 5, because she stood to lose the widow's state pension if divorced. She failed because it was shown that her total income would remain the same whether she was divorced or not. If the decree was granted, she would go on receiving supplementary benefit. If the decree was refused, and her husband predeceased her, she would indeed receive the widow's pension, but her supplementary benefit would then be reduced by the amount of the pension, leaving her income unchanged.

3–55 This does not mean that it is always open to a petitioner to point to the availability of welfare benefits as a means of mitigating hardship which the respondent would otherwise suffer. In *Reiterbund* v. *Reiterbund* both parties were badly off, and to ignore the availability of welfare benefits in such cases would effectively prevent a petitioner from ever getting a decree based on section 1(2)(e), if the respondent chose to invoke section 5. However, in cases where a petitioner has the means to make proper provision for the respondent, the court would not expect the respondent to rely on welfare

[53] [1975] Fam. 99.

benefits to avoid suffering grave financial hardship. Therefore, in some cases where the court has concluded that such hardship will result from divorce (as where, for example, the parties are middle-aged and the wife has a prospective entitlement to a substantial widow's pension) the court may require the husband to make alternative provision to compensate the wife for her potential loss.[54] If he cannot do so his petition may, in the last resort, be dismissed.[55]

(ii) Non-financial hardship

3–56

The wording of section 5(1) makes it clear that a respondent may cite other grave hardship as a reason for dismissing the petition. The Act gives no clue as to what form such hardship might take, but almost all the cases that have arisen on the point have concerned foreign wives who alleged that, if divorced, they would become social outcasts because of their communities' abhorrence of divorce. Although the Court of Appeal has accepted that this is capable of constituting hardship within section 5(1),[56] the defence has never yet succeeded because the courts have never been persuaded that the consequences of divorce will be as disastrous as the parties concerned have maintained.[57]

WRONG TO DISSOLVE MARRIAGE

3–57

Even if a respondent can establish grave hardship, for which the petitioner cannot compensate, it does not automatically follow that the petition will be dismissed. The respondent must also show that it would in all the circumstances be wrong to dissolve the marriage. Section 5(1) indicates that among the circumstances which the court must consider are "the conduct of the parties to the marriage and the interests of those parties and of any children or other parties concerned." Thus, while proof of grave hardship would normally lead to the conclusion that it would be wrong to dissolve the marriage, cases can arise in which the court feels

---

[54] As in, e.g. Parker v. Parker [1972] Fam. 116 where the husband was able to take out an insurance policy to compensate the wife for the contingent loss of a police widow's pension and where the obligation to pay the premiums could be secured by second mortgage on his house. This approach was approved by the Court of Appeal in Le Marchant v. Le Marchant [1977] 1 W.L.R. 559.

[55] As in, e.g. Julian v. Julian (1972) 116 S.J. 763, where the husband's offer of alternative insurance provision was insufficient to compensate the wife.

[56] In Banik v. Banik [1973] 1 W.L.R. 874.

[57] See, e.g. Banik v. Banik (No. 2) (1973) 117 S.J. 582 and Rukat v. Rukat [1975] Fam. 63.

that the marriage should be dissolved despite the hardship which will result. For example, in *Brickell* v. *Brickell*[58] the Court of Appeal held that a husband was entitled to a decree based on section 1(2)(*e*), even though the wife would suffer grave financial hardship, because the wife had behaved so disgracefully during the marriage that the court thought it would be wrong *not* to dissolve it.

3–58 SECTION 5 AS A BARGAINING TACTIC

In practice the threat of using this defence may be enough to extract a satisfactory financial offer in settlement from the petitioner. The complications of a defended divorce are such that they are to be avoided if at all possible: see 4–85 to 4–92, below.

3–59 7. The Respondent's Financial Position in Separation Cases

Where the court has granted a decree nisi on the basis of two or five years' separation under section 1(2)(*d*) or (*e*), and on no other basis, the respondent can apply to the court under section 10(2) of the M.C.A. 1973 for consideration of his or her financial position as it will be after the divorce. Unlike section 5, discussed above, this provision is not a defence to the petition, but, once it has been invoked, the court cannot make the decree absolute unless it is satisfied either:

(a) that the petitioner should not be required to make any financial provision for the respondent, or

(b) that the financial provision made by the petitioner for the respondent is reasonable and fair or the best that can be made in the circumstances.[59]

This provision is seldom relied on, but it may occasionally prove useful to a respondent who feels that the petitioner will agree to a better financial settlement if he knows that the marriage will not be dissolved until satisfactory terms have been concluded. The petitioner will not normally be able to

[58] [1974] Fam. 31.
[59] M.C.A. 1973, s.10(3).

satisfy the court merely by promising to make provision for the respondent, and the court will require provision actually to be made before the decree absolute is granted.[60]

However, under s.10(4) of the M.C.A. 1973 the court has a **3-60** discretion to make the decree absolute, without satisfactory provision having been made, if:

(a) it appears that there are circumstances making it desirable that the decree should be made absolute without delay, and

(b) the court has obtained a satisfactory undertaking from the petitioner that he will make such financial provision for the respondent as the court may approve.

Even here the petitioner must present the court with an outline of his proposals rather than simply promise to make proposals in the future.[61]

It is important to understand, however, that the court has no **3-61** power to make financial or property adjustment orders under section 10. The section is unconnected with the general powers to make orders for ancillary relief contained in sections 23 and 24 of the Act, which are discussed in Chapter 6, below. This is unsatisfactory in that, if the court decides that financial or property orders are required, it cannot make them unless the respondent has also made the appropriate application for such orders.[62] On the other hand, the fact that section 10 allows the court to withhold the decree absolute enables it to insist on the petitioner making provision for the respondent in ways which it has no power to order under sections 23 and 24. So, for example, one use of an application under section 10(2) is to compel a husband to make adequate insurance provision for a wife who stands to lose a widow's pension as a result of the divorce. This may be of some help to a respondent who defends a section 1(2)(e) petition under section 5, but fails because the court decides that it would not be wrong to dissolve the marriage.[63]

---

[60] *Wilson* v. *Wilson* [1973] 1 W.L.R. 555.

[61] *Grigson* v. *Grigson* [1974] 1 W.L.R. 228.

[62] The Matrimonial Causes Procedure Committee (the Booth Committee) recommended in its report, published in July 1985, that s.10 should be amended to include applications for ancillary relief.

[63] See *Brickell* v. *Brickell* [1974] Fam. 31 where the Court of Appeal, in rejecting the wife's defence under s.5, emphasised that this did not prejudice any application she might make under s.10(2).

3–62 ## 8. The Welfare of the Children of the Family— Existing Law

The existing law requires the court to consider the welfare of the children of the parties whenever there is a divorce. The manner in which this consideration takes place has been the subject of some criticism and so the Children Act 1989 sets out a new way in which the children's welfare is to be considered by the court within divorce proceedings. This section considers the existing law. When the Children Act 1989 comes into force the new law will apply. This is set out at paragraphs 3–74 to 3–76 below.

3–63 ### THE IMPORTANCE OF A DECLARATION

Under the existing law section 41 of the M.C.A. 1973 provides that the court must in all cases consider the arrangements made for the welfare of any relevant children of the family. "Welfare" is defined for this purpose as including custody, education and financial provision for the child.[64] No decree of divorce can be made absolute until the court has made a declaration in the terms laid down in section 41. If, by some oversight, a decree were made absolute without such a declaration it would be void.[65] Bearing in mind that this would, in turn, render void any subsequent marriage of either of the parties, it can be seen that the section 41 declaration is of crucial importance.

3–64 ### THE TERMS OF THE DECLARATION

Section 41(1) requires the court to declare by order that it is satisfied:

(a) that for the purposes of this section there are no children of the family to whom this section applies; or

(b) that the only children who are or may be children of the family to whom this section applies are the children named in the order and that:

(i) arrangements for the welfare of every child so named have been made and are satisfactory or are the best that can be devised in the circumstances; or

---

[64] M.C.A. 1973, s.41(6).
[65] M.C.A. 1973, s.41(3).

(ii) it is impracticable for the party or parties appearing before the court to make any such arrangements[66]; or

(c) that there are circumstances making it desirable that the decree should be made absolute ... without delay, notwithstanding that there are or may be children of the family to whom this section applies and that the court is unable to make a declaration in accordance with paragraph (b) above.

If the court does make a declaration in terms of section 41(1)(c) it must obtain a satisfactory undertaking from either or both of the parties to bring the question of arrangements before the court within a specified time.[67] Such declarations are sometimes made where the long-term arrangements for the children are uncertain, because no final orders for financial provision, property adjustment or custody have been made. The Court of Appeal has emphasised that uncertainty about future financial or custody arrangements does not normally justify a refusal of a section 41 declaration unless any delay occasioned is likely to be short.[68] If a refusal would cause a delay of several months, the judge should base his declaration on the existing arrangements, unless the delay would be of positive advantage to the children. **3–65**

In any case where the court is not satisfied with the arrangements proposed, either party can require it to make an order declaring its non-satisfaction.[69] This then constitutes an order against which either party can appeal, although, in practice, it would often be preferable to change the arrangements in a way likely to meet with the judge's approval, and then seek a fresh appointment before the judge. **3–66**

THE CHILDREN TO WHOM SECTION 41 APPLIES   3–67

Section 41(5) provides that the section applies to the following children of the family:

---

[66] This declaration might be made where, for example, the parents were for some reason unable to cope with the children, so that the children had been placed in the care of a local authority.
[67] M.C.A. 1973, s.41(2).
[68] *Yeend* v. *Yeend* (1984) 14 Fam. Law 314; *A.* v. *A.* [1979] 1 W.L.R. 533.
[69] M.C.A. 1973, s.41(4).

(a) any minor child of the family who at the date of the order under subsection (1) above is:

  (i) under the age of 16, or

  (ii) receiving instruction at an educational establishment or undergoing training for a trade, profession or vocation, whether or not he is also in gainful employment; and

(b) any other child of the family to whom the court ... directs that this section shall apply; and the court may give such a direction if it is of opinion that there are special circumstances which make it desirable in the interest of the child that this section should apply to him.

3–68 Thus, all children of the family under 16 must be considered, but children between the ages of 16 and 18 need be considered only if they are receiving some kind of education or training. Other children of the family need not be considered at all in the absence of a special direction, which might be given where, for example, an adult child of the family was suffering from some physical or mental disability, which justified the court in paying special attention to the arrangements for his welfare.

DEFINITION OF "CHILD OF THE FAMILY"

3–69 The term "child of the family," which occurs in many sections of the Act, is defined in section 52(1) as meaning:

(a) a child of both parties to a marriage; and

(b) any other child, not being a child who has been boarded out with those parties[70] by a local authority or voluntary organisation, who has been treated by both of those parties as a child of their family.

3–70 Whether a child is indeed a child of both parties may sometimes be a matter of dispute, though the dispute usually arises in the context of an application for maintenance, rather than in the divorce proceedings. The court has power to direct the use of blood tests on blood taken from the child,

---

[70] When the Children Act 1989 comes into force the words "who has been boarded out with those parties" will be replaced by the words "is placed with those parties as foster parents." (Sched. 12, para. 33).

the mother and the alleged father of the child. This should resolve a paternity dispute.[71]

Whether a party has treated a child as a child of the family is **3–71** a question of fact, the answer to which depends on that party's behaviour towards the child. For example, it will be relevant to ask whether the party has assumed any responsibility for maintaining the child and whether he refers to the child as his son or daughter. It has, however, been held that it is irrelevant that a party was deceived as to the paternity of the child,[72] though the child must have been born before it can be treated as a child of the family at all.[73] In general, the courts do not require much evidence to be persuaded that the child was treated as a child of the family.

The wording of section 41(1), quoted above, makes it clear **3–72** that, if the court is in any doubt as to whether a particular child is a child of the family, that child should nevertheless be included in the declaration.

THE EFFECT OF AN INACCURATE DECLARATION **3–73**

Although a failure to make a declaration renders void any subsequent decree absolute, the same is not true if a declaration is made but is later found to have been inaccurate.[74] So, for example, where a mother concealed from the court the fact that a child of the family had been born between decree nisi and decree absolute, so that that child was not referred to in the section 41 declaration, the court, in upholding the validity of the subsequent decree absolute, held that the inaccurate declaration did not even render the decree voidable.[75]

9. The Welfare of the Children of the Family under the Children Act 1989

Under the terms of the Children Act 1989 the provisions of **3–74** section 41 will be revised.[76] It has been widely felt that the original objectives behind section 41, (*i.e.*: to ensure that divorcing parents make the best possible arrangements for their children and that special cases requiring protective

---

[71] See F.L.R.A. 1969 Part III (considered in more detail at 15–07 *et seq.* below).
[72] *W.* v. *W.* [1972] Fam. 152.
[73] *A.* v. *A.* [1974] Fam. 6.
[74] M.C.A. 1973, s.41(3).
[75] *Healey* v. *Healey* [1984] Fam. 111.
[76] See Children Act 1989, Schedule 12, para. 31.

measures are identified) are not always being attained. Consequently the new section 41 imposes a more limited duty on the court.

In future the court in divorce proceedings will have to consider:

(a) whether there are any children of the family to whom section 41 applies; and

(b) if there are, whether the court should exercise any of its powers under the Children Act 1989 in respect of them in view of the actual or proposed arrangements for the children's upbringing and welfare.[77]

3–75 Both the above paragraphs require further explanation. In general, section 41 will apply only to children under the age of 16 at the date when the court considers the case, unless the court otherwise directs.[78] The court might make such a direction where, for example, the child in question suffers from some disability, or where the court thinks that the child, though over 16, is vulnerable in some other way.

Assuming there are children to whom the new section 41 applies, the court will then consider whether there is any need for it to make an order regulating, for example, with whom the child is to live, and what contact the other parent should have with the child. (The orders that the court can make under the Children Act 1989 are considered in detail in Chapter 17 below.)

In many cases the court will not find it necessary to make any such order because the parents will themselves have made or proposed satisfactory arrangements of their own.

3–76 The general effect of the amendment will therefore be to remove the need for a declaration of satisfaction as an essential prerequisite of a valid divorce decree. However, the new section 41 does contemplate the possibility of a delay being imposed on the granting of a decree under certain conditions. This possibility will arise in cases where the court does consider that it may need to make an order under the Children Act 1989 in respect of a child, but cannot do so without giving the case further consideration. In such cases the court has power to delay the grant of the decree absolute if it considers that there are exceptional circumstances which make it desirable to do so in the interests of the child.[79]

[77] s.41(1) as substituted.
[78] s.41(3) as substituted.
[79] s.41(2) as substituted.

10. Consequences of Divorce 3–77

The most obvious effect of the granting of a decree absolute is that the parties' marriage is dissolved, and they thereupon become free to marry again. However, the fact that they cease to be husband and wife has other consequences which should be borne in mind both by the parties and by their legal advisers.

RIGHTS OF OCCUPATION IN THE MATRIMONIAL HOME 3–78

Under the M.H.A. 1983, where one spouse is the sole legal owner of the matrimonial home, the other spouse has statutory rights of occupation in the home. These rights can be registered, and will then bind a subsequent purchaser or mortgagee of the home. However, on divorce the statutory rights of occupation are brought to an end, unless a direction to the contrary has previously been obtained from the court. Where continued protection is needed it will therefore be necessary to obtain such a direction, or consider alternative means of protection instead. (This problem is considered in detail in Chapter 9, below.)

WILLS AND RIGHTS OF INHERITANCE 3–79

A testator's will is not wholly revoked by his divorce (as it is by his marriage). However, by virtue of section 18A of the Wills Act 1837,[80] any gift to the former spouse lapses on divorce, and any appointment of the former spouse as an executor or trustee will be ineffective, unless, in both cases, a contrary intention is indicated in the will itself. It would, of course, be unusual for a testator to specify that gifts to his spouse under his will should remain effective even if the marriage should end before his death.

In the case of intestacy, a former spouse will not be able to 3–80 take advantage of the provisions governing intestate succession under the Administration of Estates Act 1925. The rules specifying the property to be taken by a spouse on intestacy do not extend to a former spouse.

A former spouse is entitled to apply under the Inheritance 3–81 (Provision for Family and Dependants) Act 1975 for reasonable financial provision out of the estate of a deceased former spouse. In general, however, such applications are unlikely to

---

[80] Inserted by Administration of Justice Act 1982, s.18(2).

succeed, since, where there has been a divorce, the divorce court will usually have tried to deal comprehensively with the parties' property and assets at that time. Furthermore, the court has power, on the divorce, to direct that future applications shall not be made under the 1975 Act. This can be done whether the parties agree to it or not.[81]

3–82 It will often be appropriate on divorce for the parties' solicitors to advise their clients to have new wills prepared. The parties may not only want to consider making fresh provision for the devolution of their property; it may also be necessary to consider, for example, whether new provision should be made for the care of their children should the custodial parent die before they grow up.

3–83 LIFE INSURANCE POLICIES

It is also wise to review any existing life insurance policies on or before divorce. Where, for example, a policy exists on the husband's life for the benefit of the wife, the husband will probably let the premiums lapse on divorce. However, if the husband is likely to be paying maintenance for some years to come, the wife might want to have some protection against his premature death. In this case the wife might take over the premiums, provided she is the named beneficiary under the policy. This would be pointless if the policy simply provides that the proceeds should go to the policy-holder's "wife," because this would only benefit whoever the husband was married to at the time of his death. In this case the wife might consider taking out a new policy on her husband's life, although this would require the husband's co-operation in providing the insurance company with evidence as to his state of health.

3–84 PENSION RIGHTS

One of the consequences of divorce is that a wife loses the chance of becoming a widow. She thus loses her prospective entitlement to a widow's pension under her husband's pension scheme. This may be a serious problem for a divorced woman who has young children to care for, and so may not be able to pursue pensionable employment of her own. It is even more serious for an older woman who may

---

[81] See Inheritance (Provision for Family and Dependants) Act 1975, s.15 (as amended by M.F.P.A. 1984, s.8).

have sacrificed her own career prospects to bring up a family, and is now too old, either to find pensionable employment, or to build up a worthwhile pension entitlement of her own.

Although the court may be able to make orders for ancillary **3–85** relief which may, at least partially, compensate for this loss (*e.g.* by the award of a lump sum), there is, as yet, no purpose-built solution to the problem. It may be that in the future the courts will be given power to make an order on divorce for the preservation of a wife's contingent pension expectation.[82]

---

[82] See *e.g. Occupational Pension Rights on Divorce* (1985), a consultation paper issued by the Lord Chancellor's Department.

4. Divorce Procedure

4–01 This chapter deals with the procedure for obtaining a decree of divorce. Whilst the procedure for obtaining a decree of judicial separation is very similar, it is not exactly the same; for example, there is only one decree of judicial separation whereas there are two of divorce (see further at 3–04, above). The procedure for obtaining a decree of nullity and a decree of presumption of death is completely different and will be outlined in Chapter 5, below.

Before considering step by step the procedure that should be followed in order to obtain a decree of divorce, the jurisdiction of the court to entertain the application must be examined.

4–02 ## 1. Jurisdiction

The court in England and Wales has jurisdiction to grant a decree of divorce, nullity or judicial separation if, at the date of the petition, either of the parties was:

(a) domiciled in England and Wales; or

(b) habitually resident in England and Wales throughout the period of one year ending with that date.[1]

4–03 DOMICILE

Domicile is a concept which indicates a single legal system according to which certain questions affecting an individual's personal status must be decided. It is completely independent from any other concept which may be used to link a person with a country or state. Thus citizenship or nationality have

---

[1] Domicile and Matrimonial Proceedings Act 1973, s.5.

no direct bearing on a person's domicile. It will be noted that an individual can only be domiciled in a territory which has a separate legal system. So, for example, it is possible for someone to be domiciled in England and Wales, *or* Scotland, but not in the United Kingdom.

There are three types of domicile; domicile of origin, dependence and choice. It is important to appreciate that a person may have one or more of these types of domicile, but only one can be operative at any one time.

(i) Domicile of origin

4–04

This is the domicile of a child's parents at the date of the child's birth. Should the parents have separate domiciles, a legitimate child has the domicile of his father, an illegitimate child that of his mother.[2] It is irrelevant where the child was born. A person's domicile of origin is never lost, and, although it may be held in abeyance during the period of a domicile of choice, it will revive should that domicile of choice be abandoned without a new domicile of choice having been acquired. For an example of the operation of these principles see 4–09 below.

(ii) Domicile of dependence

4–05

Until a child attains the age of 16 his domicile will change with that of his parents. Therefore, if his parents acquire a domicile of choice in another territory, the child's domicile of origin will be held in abeyance and he will acquire a domicile of dependence which is the same as that of his parents. Should the parents have different domiciles, a legitimate child will follow the domicile of his father, an illegitimate child that of his mother. If the parents separate and a legitimate child lives with his mother, his domicile will follow hers, unless and until he acquires a home with his father.[3]

(iii) Domicile of choice

Acquisition

4–06

Anyone not of unsound mind and over the age of 16[4] may acquire a domicile of choice. To do so a person must satisfy two criteria:

---

[2] If the parents of a "legitimate child" are living apart at the time of birth then the child will probably have the domicile of his mother. Domicile and Matrimonial Proceedings Act 1973 (D.M.P.A. 1973), s.3.

[3] D.M.P.A. 1973, s.4.

[4] Or the date of marriage, if they marry at an age earlier than 16, which is only possible in a foreign territory. (D.M.P.A. 1973, s.3).

(a) he must reside in a territory; and

(b) have formed the intention to reside there permanently.

It has been said that a person must intend to live in the territory "until the end of his days unless and until something happens to make him change his mind."[5]

4–07 Many factors are relevant in determining this intention. Declarations of intention are admissible, though clearly they may carry little weight. Length of residence, the purchase of a house or naturalisation may also be relevant, but no one factor will be decisive.

Example

Audrey, whose domicile of origin is English, moved from England to New York State, U.S.A. 30 years ago. She has owned an apartment there for many years. She worked for the United Nations for most of that time until she retired recently.

She has been awarded the status of "resident alien" by the U.S.A. However, she has visited England on a regular basis, she has a British passport and has always declared that England is her home and that she will return here in her old age.

According to English law Audrey will not have acquired a domicile of choice in New York State.

4–08 *Abandonment*

A domicile of choice will be abandoned if the individual both:

(a) ceases to reside in a territory; and

(b) has no intention of returning there as a permanent home.

Unless the individual immediately acquires a new domicile of choice his domicile of origin will then revive.

4–09 The following example illustrates the operation of the various types of domicile.

Example

Eve's parents were both domiciled in France at her birth. She therefore has a French domicile of origin. When she was six years old her parents acquired a domicile of choice in England and Wales. She then had a domicile of dependence in this country, her domicile of origin being held in abeyance. When she was 18 she met Jimmy, a

---

[5] *Per* Buckley L.J. in *I.R.C.* v. *Bullock* [1976] 1 W.L.R. 1178 at p. 1185.

Scot, *and married him. They then set up home in Scotland where Eve and Jimmy intended to remain for life. Eve had acquired a domicile of choice in Scotland.*

Some years later she and Jimmy separated. She met an American serviceman, Hank, and they now propose to marry and move to the U.S.A. Last month she returned to live temporarily with her parents in England, intending never to return to Scotland.

She has abandoned her Scottish domicile of choice. However, she has not acquired a domicile of choice in England, as she does not intend to reside here permanently. In these circumstances her domicile of origin will be her only domicile. As she is domiciled in France it will not be possible for an English court to entertain her application for a divorce.

HABITUAL RESIDENCE   4–10

This has been defined as "voluntary residence with a degree of settled purpose."[6] Therefore, if someone arrives in this country for a holiday, they will not be habitually resident here, whereas, if they had intended to stay for some years and work in this country, they would be. In the example in 4–09, if Eve changes her mind and does not go to the United States immediately to marry Hank, but remains with her parents for one year, she will be able to apply for a divorce (assuming she is able to prove the ground for divorce).

It must be remembered that to found the jurisdiction of the court, either party must be habitually resident in England and Wales for the *period of one year* prior to the date of the petition.

RECOGNITION OF A FOREIGN DECREE   4–11

Before an English court can grant a divorce, it must, of course, be satisfied that there is a marriage in existence capable of being dissolved. Consequently, if the parties have been granted a decree dissolving the marriage in another jurisdiction, the court will not grant a decree here if it is prepared to recognise the foreign decree.

The detailed law on this topic is not within the scope of this book. It is contained in Part II of the Family Law Act 1986.[7]

In general, foreign divorces or annulments obtained in judicial   4–12
or other proceedings will be recognised in the United

---

[6] *Per* Lord Scarman in *R.* v. *Barnet London Borough Council, ex p. Nilish Shah* [1983] 2 W.L.R. 16, accepted by Bush J. in *Kapur* v. *Kapur* (1985) 15 Fam. Law 22.
[7] See, in particular, s.46.

Kingdom if the divorce or annulment is effective under the law of the country in which it was obtained, and if, at the time proceedings were started, one of the parties was habitually resident, or domiciled, in that country or was a national of that country.

If the foreign divorce or annulment was not obtained by judicial or other proceedings, it may still be recognised if both parties were domiciled in that country at the time it was obtained, or one of them was, and the other was domiciled in a country which also recognises the divorce or annulment.

These rules of recognition are deliberately broad so as to avoid as far as possible the difficulties that arise when people are treated as married in one jurisdiction and not in another.

In the past cases were sometimes bitterly contested because, if the court was prepared to recognise a foreign decree, it was not able to grant ancillary relief.[8] However, the courts now have the power to grant financial relief after a foreign decree. There will, therefore, be fewer disputes in future as to whether a foreign divorce should be recognised. The topic of financial relief after a foreign decree is dealt with at 6–31 to 6–33.

4–13 2. Divorce Procedure

Owing to the changes in divorce procedure in recent years, the vast majority of divorces are not contested and are obtained through the post. This had led to a devaluation of the significance of the law relating to divorce, so that the procedure is now often more important to the family practitioner than the law. The Children Act 1989 will have an impact on divorce procedure. In so far as it is possible to ascertain what these changes will be, they are covered at 4–93. The Children Act is unlikely to come into force until October 1991 at the earliest, and the following procedure will be correct until that time.

4–14 LEGAL ADVICE AND ASSISTANCE

This topic has been dealt with at 2–03 to 2–07. As legal aid is not generally available for undefended divorce proceedings

---

[8] See, *e.g. Quazi* v. *Quazi* [1980] A.C. 744.

the Green Form scheme has been extended to cover such work. The limit is increased to three hours and the amount of work that may be done for a petitioner without prior approval is extended to the preparation of court documents. The *Legal Aid Handbook* contains a list of matters which would be covered.[9]

(1)   Preliminary advice on:

    (i)   the ground for, and effect of, a decree,

    (ii) future arrangements for the children,

    (iii) financial matters,

    (iv) housing and the matrimonial home.

(2)   Drafting and typing the petition and statement of arrangements.

(3)   Advising on filing and subsequent procedure including service.

(4)   Advising on, and typing the application for, directions for trial and the affidavit in support.

(5)   Advising on the children appointment (but not attending court).

(6)   Advising on obtaining the decree absolute.

Despite the way the above is set out in the *Legal Aid Handbook*, in practice, many solicitors will actually do the work for the client rather than merely "advising on" the appropriate step. For example, the form of application for the decree absolute will be completed by the solicitor, sent to court, and, on receipt of the decree from the court, it will be sent to the client.

THE PETITION   4–15

The M.C.R. 1977, r. 8(1) provides that every cause shall be begun by a petition. The rules also provide[10] for the information which must be contained in the petition, although

---

[9] *Legal Aid Handbook* (1990), pp. 63–64.
[10] Rule 9 and Appendix 2.

it is possible for an application to be made for leave to omit some of the prescribed details.

4–16 THE CONTENTS OF THE PETITION

Although the layout of this document is a formality, it is important to ensure that it complies with the requirements of the rules. Failure to do so may mean that the document is not accepted by the court, or that an application for leave to amend is required at a later time. More drastically, if the correct claims for ancillary relief are not included, the petitioner may later be barred from claiming ancillary relief. Printed forms are available from legal stationers which are designed to meet the provisions of each of the facts for divorce.[11] Nonetheless it is important to appreciate the details which must be included on the forms. In an attempt to make the provisions of the rules more palatable, there follows a draft petition which has annotated references to the relevant provisions of the M.C.R. 1977.

4–17 EXAMPLE PETITION

IN THE
CHRISFORD COUNTY COURT[12]

No. 90D 1258

1. On the 14th day of August 1969 the petitioner SUSAN SMITH was lawfully married to MARK SMITH (hereinafter called "the respondent") at St. Martha's Church, in the Parish of Ambleforth in the County of Blandshire.[13]

2. The petitioner and respondent last lived together at Glebe Cottage, Ambleforth in the County of Blandshire.[14]

---

[11] Some county courts are prepared to provide blank forms free of charge for use by solicitors.

[12] This is the court reference number which is inserted by the court office when the petition is received by them.

[13] Every petition shall state the names of the parties to the marriage and the date and place of marriage. It is important to copy the details of the place of marriage exactly from the marriage certificate. If this is not done many courts will reject the petition.

[14] The last address at which the parties to the marriage have lived together as husband and wife must be stated.

3.　The petitioner is domiciled in England and Wales[15] and is by occupation an estate agent and resides at Glebe Cottage Ambleforth aforesaid and the respondent is unemployed and resides at 12 London Road Ambleforth in the County of Blandshire.[16]

4.　There are no children of the family now living except WAYNE JUSTIN SMITH who was born on the 19 March 1974 and who is receiving full time education at Chrisford Comprehensive School.[17]

5.　No other child, now living, has been born to the petitioner during the marriage *except* POLLY ANN JONES who was born on the 1 January 1990.[18]

6.　There are or have been no other proceedings in any court in England and Wales or elsewhere with reference to the marriage (or to any child of the family) or between the petitioner and respondent with reference to any property of either or both of them *except* that on the 3 February 1989 at the Ambleforth Magistrates' Court the respondent was adjudged to have failed to provide reasonable maintenance for the child of the family WAYNE JUSTIN SMITH and custody of the said child

---

[15] Where it is alleged that the court has jurisdiction based on domicile (see 4-03 to 4-09, above) details of the petitioner's domicile must be given. If this is not England and Wales then details are also required of the respondent's domicile. If jurisdiction is based on the habitual residence of either party then details must be given including addresses and periods of residence at each address.

[16] The occupation and addresses of both parties must be given. Should the petitioner wish to conceal her address (*e.g.* to prevent molestation by the respondent) an application may be made *ex parte* to the registrar to omit this. It is important in such cases to remember not to include the address in other documents with which the respondent will be served.

[17] The petition must state whether there are any living children of the family and if so:

    (a)　their full names and dates of birth or (if it is the case) that they are over 18; and

    (b)　in the case of each minor child over the age of 16, whether he is receiving instruction at an educational establishment or undergoing training for a trade, profession or vocation.

[18] It should be stated whether any other child now living has been born to the wife during the marriage. If the petitioner is the husband then this statement should be made "to the knowledge of the petitioner." If there are any children, details of their full names and dates of birth should be given. For the definition of child of the family see 3-69, above. If there is any dispute as to whether a child is a child of the family then this must be stated.

was awarded to the petitioner with reasonable access to the respondent and the respondent was ordered to make periodical payments to him in the sum of £17.00 per week.[19]

7. There are no proceedings continuing in any country outside England and Wales which are in respect of the marriage or are capable of affecting its validity or subsistence.[20]

8.[21] The said marriage has broken down irretrievably.[22]

9. The respondent has committed adultery and the petitioner finds it intolerable to live with the respondent.[23]

10. *PARTICULARS*
On or about the 10th day of April 1989 at 12, London Road, Ambleforth, Blandshire the respondent committed adultery with Elizabeth Robinson (the co-respondent). Since then at that address the respondent has cohabited and frequently committed adultery with the co-respondent.[24]

PRAYER[25]
The petitioner therefore prays:

---

[19] This must be stated and if there have been any such proceedings then the following details must be given:

    (a)   the nature of the proceedings;

    (b)   the date and effect of any decree or order; and

    (c)   in the case of proceedings with reference to the marriage, whether there has been any resumption of cohabitation since the making of the decree or order.

[20] Again this fact must be stated and if there are any such proceedings then details must be given. Where such proceedings have already started, the English court has a discretion (or in some cases a duty) to stay the proceedings in this country. See the D.M.P.A. 1973, Sched. 1.

[21] In the case of petitions based on fact E only, a statement should be included as to whether any agreement has been made or is proposed to be made for the support of the respondent or petitioner or any child of the family, and if so details of the arrangement should be given.

[22] This must be stated in petitions for divorce.

[23] The fact alleged should be stated following the wording of the M.C.A. 1973, s.1(2).

[24] Brief particulars of the fact alleged should be given but not the evidence by which those particulars are to be proved.

[25] The petition must finish with a prayer setting out the particulars of relief claimed including any claims for custody, costs and ancillary relief which it is intended to claim.

(1) That the said marriage be dissolved.
(2) That the petitioner may be granted the custody of WAYNE JUSTIN SMITH.
(3) That the respondent may be ordered to pay the costs of this suit, should it become defended.[26]
(4) That the petitioner may be granted the following ancillary relief:

    (a) an order for maintenance pending suit
    a periodical payments order
    a secured provision order
    a lump sum order

    (b) a periodical payments order ⎱
    a secured provision order ⎰ for the children of the family
    a lump sum order

    (c) a property adjustment order[27]

Signed *Susan Smith*[28]

The names and addresses of the persons to be served with this petition are:

respondent: Mark Smith of 12, London Road, Ambleforth, Blandshire.

co-respondent: Elizabeth Robinson of 12, London Road, Ambleforth, Blandshire.[29]

The petitioner's address for service is: c/o Richards, Rowe & Co., 1, High Street, Ambleforth, Blandshire.[30]

[26] As to the alternative claims for costs see 4–23, below.
[27] All forms of ancillary relief which are to be sought should be claimed. If in doubt it is best to include the application for relief as otherwise an application will have to be made for leave to apply for the relief if it is wanted later. See 10–08, below.
[28] M.C.R. 1977, r. 11. The petition must be signed by the petitioner if acting in person (*e.g.* where receiving Green Form advice and assistance); or by the solicitor acting for the petitioner if the petition was prepared by him (or in the name of his firm); or by counsel if the petition was prepared by him.
[29] The names and addresses of persons to be served should be given and it should be indicated if any of them are suffering from a disability.
[30] The petitioner's address for service is either:

    (a) her solicitor's if a solicitor is acting for her; or
    (b) the address of any place in England and Wales at, or to which, documents for the petitioner may be delivered or sent, if she is acting in person.
    (c) as here, if she is in receipt of Green Form advice and assistance, the solicitor's name or firm and address may be given in this fashion if the solicitor agrees.

Dated this 1st day of September 1990.

Address all communications for the court to: The Registrar, County Court, Chrisford.

The court office at High Street, Chrisford, Blandshire is open from 10 a.m. to 4 p.m.

4–18   DRAFTING OF PARTICULARS

The main variation of format in the petition arises from the fact relied upon to obtain a decree. In each case the fact should be recited as contained in section 1(2) of the M.C.A. 1973. The particulars of the relevant fact must, however, be drafted with care and the following points should be borne in mind:

4–19   (i) Fact A

As can be seen from the example above only the barest details of the adultery are required. It is usual to state merely where, when and with whom[31] the adultery was committed.

4–20   (ii) Fact B

The particulars of this fact are the most difficult of all to draft. The incidents of unreasonable behaviour should be set out one by one in separate paragraphs in chronological order, starting, in each case, with the date on which the incident occurred. They should be drafted in the third person.

Example

On August 6, 1990 the respondent returned home in the early hours of the morning. When the petitioner asked him where he had been the respondent refused to tell her. When she repeated the inquiry he struck the petitioner with his fists about the body and face causing severe bruising to her chest and a cut lip.

It is necessary to plead sufficient incidents to illustrate the general picture of the breakdown of the marriage. In most cases six to eight incidents should be sufficient, including, in

---

[31] For further points concerning the identity of the co-respondent, see 4–33.

particular, the first, worst and last incidents. Obviously, if the petition is based on fewer, but more serious, incidents then the particulars will be limited to these. In particular, where the behaviour alleged includes incidents of violence, three or four paragraphs should be adequate.[32]

(iii) Fact C   4–21

An example should suffice to explain how the particulars should be set out. It is important to plead the apparent intention on the part of the respondent to bring the cohabitation to an end. It should also be pleaded that the desertion has continued without consent or just cause.

Example

On June 1, 1987 the respondent left the matrimonial home at 3, Hurricane Close, Chrisford, Blandshire with the intention of bringing cohabitation permanently to an end. She has ever since that date remained living apart from the petitioner without just cause and without the petitioner's consent.

(iv) Facts D and E   4–22

It is sufficient to plead the date of separation and details of any periods during which the parties lived together and that, with the exception of those periods, the parties have lived apart.

COSTS   4–23

The likelihood of obtaining an order for costs is considered below at 4–70 to 4–71. If they are unlikely to be awarded in accordance with those principles then careful consideration should be given before making a claim. For example, as will be seen, in fact D cases it is usual to agree orders for costs prior to any consent being given.

If costs are wanted they should be applied for in the prayer, otherwise leave will be required to insert a claim at a later date. However, problems arise with Green Form clients. Technically they are litigants in person, and, although entitled to their costs and expenses under the Litigants in Person (Fees and Expenses) Act 1975 these will usually be small. In particular a Green Form client will be exempted from payment of the filing fee (see below at 4–28). To avoid any risk of

---

[32] *Brice* v. *Brice* (1974) 4 Fam. Law. 88.

unnecessarily alarming the respondent in such cases and, perhaps, inducing him to defend a petition, many practitioners do not claim costs in Green Form cases.

This does have the drawback that, if the petition is defended and the petitioner obtains legal aid to be represented by his solicitors, they will have to apply for leave to amend the petition to insert a prayer for costs. To avoid this it is usual in Green Form cases to insert a prayer asking for costs only if the petition is defended.

4–24 THE SUPPORTING DOCUMENTS

Together with the petition must be filed:

(i) A statement of arrangements
This is a statement as to the arrangements that are to be made for the care of any children of the family referred to in the petition and to whom M.C.A. 1973, s.41 applies. The details of this section were discussed in the previous chapter at 3–63 to 3–73. This statement must contain the information required by Form 4.[33] In the vast majority of cases a printed blank form (available from law stationers) will be used. The marginal notes on this form give full instructions on how to complete this relatively straightforward document. Essentially details relating to the accommodation, education, maintenance and access arrangements for the child are required. The form also requires particulars of any health problems suffered by any of the children,[34] and details of any child who is in the care, or under the supervision, of a local authority.

It is important to bear in mind when completing this form that it is the proposed future arrangements that the court particularly wishes to know about, not merely the current arrangements.

4–25 It is possible that the petitioner has little or no information concerning the arrangements because, for example, the children live with the respondent and he has not seen them for some years. In these circumstances the petitioner must still file a statement of arrangements giving such information as he has. The respondent will then be invited by the court to file a separate statement of arrangements. If the court is doubtful about the adequacy of the information it might order a

---

[33] This is the number of the prescribed form contained in Appendix 2 to the M.C.R. 1973.

[34] If a child suffers from a serious illness or disability then a medical report should be filed with the statement of arrangements. M.C.R. 1977, r. 8(2).

welfare report at the children appointment. (See 4–75 to 4–78, below.) It is worth noting that this form should always be signed by the petitioner personally whether or not he is represented by a solicitor.

(ii) Marriage certificate 4–26
This should be filed at court. It should either be the original copy that was given to the parties on marriage or a certified copy. This is available, on payment of a fee, from the General Registry of Births, Deaths and Marriages in London or from the register office for the district in which the parties were married. A photocopy of a certificate will not be accepted.

The cost of obtaining a marriage certificate can be met under the Green Form scheme, but the solicitor will probably want to apply for an extension to the initial financial limit to cover this extra cost.

In some cases it may not be possible to file the certificate at the same time as the other papers. This might occur, for example, where an urgent application is being made in the divorce proceedings to exclude a violent husband from the home, and the certificate is not readily available. In such cases an *ex parte* application for directions should be made to the registrar,[35] who will generally accept an undertaking to file the certificate at a later date.

If the marriage certificate is in a foreign language it must be accompanied by an authenticated translation.

(iii) A certificate as to reconciliation[36] 4–27
If a solicitor is acting for the petitioner, he is required to file this form stating whether or not he has discussed with the petitioner the possibility of a reconciliation. The solicitor is also required to state *whether or not* he has given the petitioner details of persons qualified to help in such matters. It is important to note that this form should not be filed where the client is in receipt of Green Form advice and assistance. This is because in such cases the solicitor is not *acting* for the client, who is technically a litigant in person. Further it should be noted that the rules require merely the completion of the form, not the formal reference to a conciliation or reconciliation service. The completion of the form entirely in the negative is perfectly acceptable and by no means unusual.

This does not mean that it should be treated as a mere form-filling exercise, and it is clear that in appropriate cases

[35] M.C.R. 1977, r. 12(2).
[36] Again a printed form is available and will normally be used for this. See M.C.A. 1973, s.6(1) and M.C.R. 1977, r. 12(3).

expert help will enable the parties to resolve, with the minimum of emotional damage, many of the issues as to finance, custody and the divorce, even if divorce itself cannot be avoided. Expert help and counselling is available from a number of organisations including "Relate" (formerly the Marriage Guidance Council) and certain religious organisations. This topic is discussed generally at 1–08 to 1–14, above.

4–28 **(iv) Fee or certificate of exemption from fee**
A fee of £40 is payable on filing a divorce petition. However, if the petitioner is in receipt of Green Form advice and assistance, an application for exemption should be filed requesting exemption from paying the fee. This exemption is also available if the petitioner is in receipt of income support or family credit, although, of course, in these circumstances he will probably be in receipt of advice and assistance as well.

4–29 **(v) Previous orders**
Copies of any previous court orders relating to the parties or the children of the family and referred to in the petition should also be filed.

4–30 **(vi) Copies for service**
Sufficient copies of the petition must also be filed for service on all the parties to the divorce (*i.e.* the respondent and co-respondent). A copy of the statement of arrangements must also be filed for service on the respondent.

4–31 The documents may be filed in any divorce county court or the divorce registry in London. (Most, but by no means all, county courts have divorce jurisdiction). Obviously, in most cases the divorce county court nearest the petitioner or his solicitors will be selected.

4–32 PARTIES

Clearly the parties will consist of the two parties to the marriage, being the petitioner and the respondent. Any third party at this stage is called a co-respondent.

4–33 **(i) Naming the co-respondent**
Sometimes the petitioner does not wish to name the person with whom the other spouse is alleged to have committed adultery. Nonetheless, the name must be given, unless:

    (a) the alleged adulterer's name and identity are unknown to the petitioner and the petition contains a statement to that effect; or

(b)   the petition alleges that the respondent has been guilty of rape. The victim will not be made a co-respondent unless otherwise directed[37]; or

(c)   the court otherwise directs.

(ii) Improper association   4–34

Sometimes, although the petition is based on fact B, it contains allegations of an improper association which does not amount to adultery. For example, allegations of homosexual behaviour, or of heterosexual behaviour of an intimate nature which falls short of adultery.

In this case the court will direct whether or not that person should be made a co-respondent. It is advisable in such cases for the petitioner to make an early application for such a direction to avoid undue delay. Notice of the application should be given to the named person.[38]

SERVICE OF THE DOCUMENTS

(i) Postal service

How effected   4–35

The service of a petition will usually be undertaken by the court. The usual procedure is that the county court registrar will serve the following documents by post on the respondent and any co-respondent:

(a)   petition;

(b)   notice of proceedings.[39] This is a notice to the other parties explaining how to complete the acknowledgment of service;

(c)   acknowledgment of service.[40] This form contains certain questions, the answers to some of which govern how the divorce will proceed. The important questions will be discussed in context below. This form should be signed, in order to acknowledge service, either by the party's solicitor or, if he is not represented, then by the party in person. In certain circumstances the form must, in any event, be signed by the party in person; for example, to admit adultery (see below, 4–61);

---

[37] M.C.R. 1977, r. 13.
[38] M.C.R. 1977, r. 13(3).
[39] Appendix 1 of the M.C.R. 1977, Form 5.
[40] *Ibid.* Form 6.

(d) where the party being served is the respondent, a copy of the statement of arrangements.

4–36 *The return of the acknowledgment of service*

On receipt of the documents from the court the respondent and co-respondent (if any) are required to return the acknowledgment of service within eight days.

There is no presumption as to due service of the petition by post. Service is usually proved by the return by the party of the acknowledgment of service duly signed. In due course the petitioner will be asked to identify the signature on the acknowledgment of service returned by the respondent. This proves service of the documents.

In the case of the acknowledgment of service returned by the co-respondent, service is presumed to have been effected merely by the return of that document signed by the co-respondent.

In either case if the party is represented by solicitors who sign and return the acknowledgment of service then again service is presumed to have been effected without further evidence.

As soon as the court receives the acknowledgment of service it will send a copy to the solicitors for the petitioner. In many county courts, if the court has not received the acknowledgment after a certain time the registrar will notify the petitioner.[41]

4–37 *Procedure following non-return of the acknowledgment*

If the acknowledgment of service is not returned to the court, it will, in most cases, be necessary to attempt to serve the documents personally. In some cases, however, it may be possible to seek an order for deemed service, rather than attempt personal service.

4–38 *Order for deemed service*[42]

This is not a method of service but a means whereby the registrar can order that either postal or personal service has been effective. However, it is extremely unlikely that this would be necessary in the case of personal service. (This is considered further at 4–44).

If there is some evidence that the party has received the documents then an *ex parte* application can be made to the

---

[41] The period of time varies from court to court although it is often one month. In some courts no notification at all is sent.
[42] M.C.R. 1977, r. 14(6).

registrar, supported by an affidavit giving the necessary evidence, for an order deeming service. Applications for this order which are supported only by the evidence of the petitioner are treated with caution and some registrars will require independent evidence of receipt.

Example   **4–39**

You act for June, the petitioner in divorce proceedings, against Simon. Postal service of the petition and supporting documents has been attempted but no acknowledgment has been received by the court. June's mother spoke to Simon on the telephone a few days ago when he mentioned that he would not co-operate in any way with the divorce proceedings. He also said that he had thrown away the divorce papers which he had received through the post.

You would probably advise June to make an application for deemed service, filing an affidavit from her mother in support.

(ii) Personal service   **4–40**
In some circumstances personal service (essentially, handing the document to the party) may be initially effected without any attempt to serve by post. This might be because, for example, the respondent has no postal address; or because an application is also being made for an injunction where personal service of that application is required in any event.

How effected   **4–41**

Personal service will be effected either by the county court bailiff, if the registrar so directs, on the petitioner's request, or by the petitioner's solicitors (usually by a process server instructed by them).[43] If the petitioner has a solicitor acting for him (rather than simply giving advice and assistance under the Green Form) the reason for requesting bailiff service, rather than attempting service through the petitioner, must be given.[44] In no circumstances may personal service be effected by the petitioner himself.

The return of the acknowledgment   **4–42**

Usually, however, personal service will only be attempted if postal service has failed. The party who is served personally may then return the acknowledgment of service to the court office. In this case service is proved exactly as at 4–36 above.

However, to guard against the possibility that the acknowledgment may not be returned it is necessary to obtain

---

[43] M.C.R. 1977, r. 14(2)(b).
[44] *Practice Direction* [1977] 1 All E.R. 845.

other means of evidence that the party served received the documents.

4–43 *Failure to return the acknowledgment*

Where the county court bailiff effected service, he will file a certificate stating that the petition was served. The bailiff will usually attempt to obtain the respondent's signature in receipt of the document, or ask the party to identify himself by some other means. It is usual for the petitioner to supply the bailiff with a recent photograph of the respondent to aid identification. Should the bailiff be successful in obtaining the signature of the respondent, this signature may be identified by the petitioner in his affidavit in support of the petition (see 4–58 to 4–62, below). Otherwise the petitioner will have to confirm in his affidavit in support that the photograph attached to the bailiff's certificate is that of the respondent.

Should the petitioner employ a process server to attempt personal service, the procedure is similar to that involving the bailiff, except that an affidavit of service from the process server will be required rather than a certificate of service.

4–44 *Failure to effect personal service*[45]

If personal service is impossible because the party cannot be located, then an application must be made for an order relating to service.

4–45 **(iii) Orders of the court relating to service**

It should be stressed that applications for an order relating to service are not granted lightly and the registrar will require comprehensive evidence as to the failure of attempts to locate the party to be served.

4–46 *Substituted service*[46]

If every effort to trace the party has failed then the petitioner might consider applying for an order for substituted service. Enquiries relating to the whereabouts of the other party should be thorough, as a failure to make all reasonable enquiries might be treated by the court subsequently as a defect in service rendering a decree voidable.[47] The assistance of various government agencies (*e.g.* the D.S.S.) may be sought in trying to locate the party.[48] The court would be

---

[45] M.C.R. 1977, r. 14(3).
[46] M.C.R. 1977, r. 14(9).
[47] *Purse* v. *Purse* [1981] Fam. 143.
[48] See *Practice Direction* (Disclosure of Addresses: 1989) [1989] 1 W.L.R. 219.

extremely reluctant to grant this order unless every possibility of serving the respondent personally had been exhausted.

This order would only be appropriate if there were some evidence that the method of substituted service proposed would be likely to bring the proceedings to the attention of the party. The usual method of substituted service is by an advertisement in a newspaper that the party is known to read regularly. The registrar must be satisfied that there is a "reasonable possibility"[49] of the advertisement coming to the attention of the party. If the registrar is not so satisfied, then the only alternative is to apply for an order dispensing with service (as to which see below).

There are other methods of substituted service which might **4–47** be ordered in appropriate cases. For example, service on a relative whom the party is believed to visit regularly.

Application for this order is made *ex parte* to the registrar, supported by an affidavit giving evidence of the need for this form of service.

Order dispensing with service[50] **4–48**

The registrar may grant this order if it is impracticable to serve a party or if it is otherwise expedient to dispense with service. Application for such an order is made in the same way as above. This application should only be made very much as a last resort and, again, it will only be granted if evidence is given that all reasonable attempts to locate the other party have been made.

(iv) Service on a party under a disability[51] **4–49**
Special rules govern the service of the documents on a person under a disability.

Minors **4–50**

In this case the proceedings must be served on the child's father or guardian or person with whom he resides or in whose care he is. The court may make orders relating to service.

Mental patients **4–51**

Service should be effected on the person authorised under the Mental Health Act 1983, or, if no one is so authorised, the

---

[49] M.C.R. 1977, r. 14(9).
[50] M.C.R. 1977, r. 14(11).
[51] M.C.R. 1977, rr. 112 and 113.

Official Solicitor if he consents to act, or the person with whom the patient resides or in whose care he is.

4–52   DIRECTIONS FOR TRIAL

In the normal case, once a completed acknowledgment of service has been returned to the court by the respondent, the court sends a photocopy of this document to the petitioner's address for service. What happens next depends on whether the respondent (or any co-respondent) has expressed an intention to defend the divorce. The acknowledgment of service contains a question asking the recipient to indicate whether or not he intends to defend the divorce. If he answers "yes," this is treated as "notice of intention to defend." Such a notice may also be given in some other manner (*e.g.* by letter or formal notice).

Giving notice of intention to defend suspends the proceedings for a period of time to enable the respondent to file an answer to the divorce petition. If an answer is filed the divorce becomes a defended cause, and may not proceed to a contested trial for many months.

4–53   If no notice of intention to defend is given, or no answer is filed, then the matter will proceed as an undefended divorce. (Fewer than one per cent. of cases are dealt with as defended divorces[52]). Directions for trial will be given, and the matter will normally be dealt with through the post as a "special procedure" divorce. Nowadays this is a misleading term, since it is the procedure followed in the great majority of cases.

Undefended divorce procedure will be considered first, then defended divorces will be dealt with in outline.

4–54   **(i) Time limits**
The registrar can only give directions for trial once the time limits set out below have expired. There is, therefore, no point in making an application for such directions until these time limits have expired.

4–55   (i) Where an acknowledgment of service has been filed which does not give notice of intention to defend, at least eight days must have expired from service of the petition.

---

[52] Judicial Statistics 1988 (Cm. 745 (1989)), Tables 5.5 and 5.6.

(ii) Where notice of intention to defend has been given in **4–56** the acknowledgment of service, the time for filing an answer, being 29 days from service of the petition, must have expired.

(iii) If no acknowledgment of service has been returned, **4–57** the registrar must be satisfied that the petition and supporting documents were nevertheless served. He must still be satisfied that the above time limits for filing a notice of intention to defend and answer (if relevant) have expired. Where personal service was effected, the date of service will be the date stated by the server. Evidence as to this will be given in the affidavit of service or the certificate of service, referred to at 4–43, above.

Alternatively, the court may have made an order relating to service. In the case of an order deeming service, the above time limits will apply from the date when service was deemed to have been effected. If an order for substituted service has been made, the order will specify the periods for giving notice of intention to defend and filing an answer. In the case of an order dispensing with service, application for directions for trial may be made forthwith.

(ii) The affidavit in support of the petition **4–58**
The petitioner must at this stage swear an affidavit in support of the petition. This is filed with the application for directions for trial. The M.C.R. 1977 prescribe a form to be used containing the information which must be given. There are five versions of the affidavit, one for each of the five facts.[53] The court normally sends a blank copy of the appropriate affidavit to the petitioner together with the photocopy of the acknowledgment of service, although blank copies of the form may also be obtained from law stationers. The first part of the form contains a series of questions relating to the petition and the divorce which must be answered by the petitioner.

In all cases, the petitioner is asked whether the contents of **4–59** the petition are true, and whether he wishes to alter or add to any statement in the petition. If the petitioner wishes to make a material change to something already in the petition it may be necessary at this point to seek leave of the registrar to amend the petition, which will then have to be re-served on the other parties. If the petitioner wishes to add matters that have occurred *since* the filing of the petition, such as fresh

---

[53] M.C.R. 1977, r. 33(3), Appendix 2 Form 7(A)—(E).

allegations of behaviour, leave to file a supplemental petition will be required. The supplemental petition will then have to be served on the other parties.

The other questions in the affidavit vary according to the fact relied on. The main variations may be summarised as follows:

4–60 Fact A (adultery): petitioners are required to state:

(i)   reasons for saying the respondent committed adultery;

(ii) when the adultery was first discovered;

(iii) whether it is intolerable to live with the respondent.

Fact B (behaviour): petitioners are required to state:

(i)   whether the behaviour has affected their health;

(ii) whether they are still living at the same address as the respondent, and, if so, the precise living arrangements adopted.

Fact C (desertion): petitioners are asked to state:

(i)   the date on which the parties separated and whether they agreed to separate;

(ii) the facts supporting the allegation of desertion and the reason for saying it continued up to the presentation of the petition;

(iii) whether the respondent ever offered to resume cohabitation.

Fact D and E (two and five years' separation): petitioners are asked to state:

(i)   the date of separation;

(ii) the reason for the separation;

(iii) the date when and the circumstances in which they concluded the marriage was at an end.

In fact C, D and E cases, petitioners also have to state where they and the respondent have lived since the separation and whether they ever resumed cohabitation and, if so, for how long.

4–61 It will be gathered from what has already been said about divorce law (Chapter 3, above) that some of these questions pose a trap for the unwary. However, where a solicitor is advising the petitioner, he should already have satisfied himself that the relevant fact can be proved and can ensure that each question is answered accurately.

In all cases the petitioner must identify the signature of the respondent, if he has signed the acknowledgment of service, in order to prove service. (see 4–36, above). This document should be exhibited (attached) to the affidavit in support.

Even if the respondent is represented by solicitors, he (as well as his solicitors) must sign the acknowledgment of service in two cases. If the fact on which the divorce is proceeding is fact A or D the respondent must sign, admitting adultery or consenting to the divorce, as appropriate. This also applies to the co-respondent in adultery cases. In these two cases the petitioner must identify the respondent's signature on the acknowledgment, and the acknowledgment must be exhibited to the affidavit, for the purpose of proving the fact relied on.

It may be that there is other evidence supporting the fact **4–62** alleged; *e.g.* a letter or formal confession statement admitting adultery; an affidavit sworn by a neighbour supporting allegations of unreasonable behaviour; or a medical report. In these circumstances the relevant document should also be exhibited to the affidavit.

It may also be necessary to confirm the accuracy of a photograph relied on by the person who effected personal service, or to identify the signature on any receipt given by the respondent for the documents.

Any affidavit of service sworn by a process server should be filed with the affidavit.

(iii) The application for directions **4–63**
This is made by completing a simple form of application for directions which contains a large section in blank for completion by the registrar giving his directions. Again the court normally supplies the form with the photocopy of the acknowledgment of service. The solicitor (or the petitioner in Green Form cases) completes and signs the form requesting directions and returns it to the county court together with the petitioner's affidavit in support. The registrar then gives directions by placing the cause on the Special Procedure List.

REGISTRAR'S CERTIFICATES

(i) Registrar's certificate as to decree nisi **4–64**
The registrar then considers the petition, affidavit in support and any corroborative evidence and, using the form of Request for Directions, certifies either:

4–65   (i) That he is satisfied that the petitioner is entitled to a decree; or

4–66   (ii) That he is not so satisfied. In this case he may withdraw the matter from the Special Procedure List or give the petitioner an opportunity to file further evidence. It is for the particular registrar to decide in any given case whether or not the petitioner has sufficiently proved the fact alleged. Clearly, this is an area where local practice varies. Certain matters do, generally, cause difficulty. For example:

—allegations of adultery with unknown co-respondents.

—allegations of adultery where the co-respondent does not admit the adultery but the respondent does.

—behaviour petitions where the allegations are weak or slight, or the effect on the petitioner's mental well-being is pleaded as a main factor in the petition.

—separation petitions where the parties continue to live under the same roof.

4–67   The registrar may choose to give the petitioner an opportunity to file further evidence first, and may only remove the case from the Special Procedure List and set it down for hearing before the judge, if he remains dissatisfied with this further evidence.

4–68   *Example*

Hugh alleges in his petition that Wendy has committed adultery with Julian. Wendy and Julian admitted this to him orally in the presence of Shirley, a mutual friend, but only Wendy signed a confession statement. She also answered the acknowledgment of service admitting the adultery. Julian, however, has been obstructive during the divorce, and the papers had to be served on him personally. He has not returned the acknowledgment of service to the court.

On reading the affidavit in support of the petition the registrar might be prepared to grant a decree based on Wendy's adultery with a man against whom the allegation cannot be proved. Alternatively, the registrar might be prepared to accept the statement in Hugh's affidavit that Julian admitted the adultery orally, and might make a finding of adultery against him. The registrar might, however, feel that corroboration by means of an affidavit from Shirley would be preferable, and adjourn the application for this further evidence to be submitted. If this is not forthcoming, the registrar might then set the case down before the judge so that he can hear oral evidence from Hugh. However, the registrar might feel that the case is so doubtful that it should be removed from the Special Procedure list at once and heard by the judge in any event.

Where the registrar is satisfied that the petitioner is entitled to   **4–69**
a decree nisi, he will fix a date for the pronouncement of the decree by the judge in open court. He uses the form of Request for Directions for this purpose.

(ii) Registrar's certificate as to costs   **4–70**
As noted at 4–23, above, costs are not generally claimed in Green Form cases. Where, however, the petition does contain a prayer for costs, the registrar must consider the claim. The normal principle which applies in civil litigation that the winning party should be awarded costs, does not always apply to undefended divorce. Essentially costs are always in the discretion of the court. Nonetheless certain principles have evolved.

(i) Costs will usually be ordered from a co-respondent as well as the respondent. (See further as to grounds for objecting to payment of costs, 4–71, below).

(ii) In fact B and fact C cases costs will usually be awarded against the respondent.

(iii) In the case of fact D petitions it is usual for the parties to come to an agreement as to payment of the costs (*e.g.* the respondent will pay half the costs). In some cases the respondent will only consent to the decree subject to no order being made as to costs.

(iv) Fact E petitions should not contain a prayer for costs.[54] No doubt if they did, no order for costs would be made.

The acknowledgment of service contains a question asking the   **4–71**
respondent or co-respondent if they object to any claim for costs made in the petition. Any objections are considered by the registrar, and, if he feels that the objection deserves further consideration, he will adjourn the question of costs.

---

[54] *Chapman* v. *Chapman* [1972] 1 W.L.R. 1544.

This will then be considered by the judge at the time he pronounces the decree nisi. The objecting party will be notified of this and will be given the opportunity of attending.[55]

Objections are most likely to arise in adultery cases. A party against whom costs are claimed, who can show that the order would be unjust because the adultery took place after the breakdown of the marriage, might succeed in defending the claim. In the case of a claim against a co-respondent, it is a defence to establish that the co-respondent did not know, and could not be expected to have known, that the respondent was married. If no objection is made to a claim for costs, the registrar has power to certify that the petitioner is entitled to costs, and does so on the form of Request for Directions.

4–72   (iii) Registrar gives date for children appointment
Apart from fixing a date for the pronouncement of the decree nisi (as to which see 4–64, above), the registrar may also fix a date for the children appointment. In cases involving children of the family to whom the M.C.A. 1973, s.41 applies, this should be done unless:

    (i)   there is a pending application by the respondent for custody or access; or

    (ii) the registrar thinks it inappropriate.[56]

Despite the fact that there is a pending application for custody, the petitioner is at liberty to make an express application for a hearing date for the section 41 declaration, This may be given, in certain circumstances, despite an apparent custody dispute.[57]

4–73   (iv) Other directions by the registrar
There are other directions that the registrar might make in some cases. If the registrar feels that the petitioner should have obtained a medical report or a welfare report on a child who is in care, he may make suitable directions for the report to be obtained.

In a case where the parties have been able to reach agreement concerning ancillary finance then, provided the

---

[55] M.C.R. 1977, r. 49.
[56] M.C.R. 1977, r. 48(4). The registrar might take this view if, *e.g.* the respondent had filed his own statement about the arrangements for the children which was seriously at odds with that filed by the petitioner.
[57] See 3–65, above.

appropriate procedure for obtaining a consent order has been followed, (see 11–06, below) the registrar may certify that the parties are entitled to an order for ancillary relief in the agreed terms. The judge will then so order when pronouncing the decree nisi.

PRONOUNCEMENT OF THE DECREE NISI 4–74

The registrar, having fixed the date for the judge to pronounce a decree in open court, will notify all the parties. At the appointed time a list of the cases is read, and the judge sitting in a court room empty of litigants will pronounce the decree nisi in each case. There is no need for any party to attend. It is for this reason that the special procedure is often referred to as a "postal divorce." Should there be an objection to the payment of costs this will normally be dealt with by the judge at this stage.

THE CHILDREN APPOINTMENT 4–75

Many courts list the children appointments for the same day as, but at a later time than, the pronouncement of the decree nisi. At the same time as the registrar notifies the parties of the date for the pronouncement of the decree, he will notify them of the time and place for the children appointment which will take place in chambers before the judge. It is important to note that the registrar cannot deal with the children appointment. As will be seen later, with some very minor exceptions, applications relating to the welfare, custody and access of children can only be dealt with by a judge. It is necessary for the petitioner to attend this appointment and the respondent may do so if he wishes.

(i) Procedure 4–76
There is no formal procedure at such appointments. The petitioner and the judge will discuss the arrangements proposed for the children, the judge having as a guide the statement of arrangements filed by the petitioner. The appointment will take place in the judge's chambers. The petitioner is unlikely to be represented. Certainly under the Green Form scheme no payment will normally be made for attendance at a children appointment.[58]

---

[58] See 2–03, above, but note in a contested case Legal Aid may be available, see 2–09, above.

4–77   **(ii) Declaration under section 41 of the Matrimonial Causes Act 1973**
The judge may then make one of the declarations discussed at 3–64, above. The law relating to the M.C.A. 1973, s.41 is considered fully at 3–62 to 3–73, above.

4–78   **(iii) Custody and access orders**
The judge will normally make custody orders and orders for reasonable access, if satisfied that there is no dispute relating to this between the parties. If there is a current dispute he will usually adjourn these matters to a date to be fixed. He may also take the opportunity to make an order for welfare reports. The procedure which is followed when there is a contested custody dispute, both as to custody and the M.C.A. 1973, s.41 declarations, is dealt with at 16–25, below.

The custody order will also contain provisions restricting the right to the custodial parent to remove the child from the jurisdiction and to change its name. These provisions are considered further at 16–26 and 16–27, below.

4–79   THE DECREE NISI

The decree nisi and copies of the orders that may have been made on the children appointment will be sent to the parties by the court.

THE DECREE ABSOLUTE

4–80   **(i) Time limit**
After six clear weeks (in practice six weeks and one day from decree nisi) the petitioner may apply for the decree to be made absolute. This is done by completing a form and sending it to the county court,[59] with the appropriate fee. There is no need to give notice to the respondent. The registrar will grant the decree absolute if he is satisfied:

(i)   that no proceedings have been commenced in relation to an appeal or a rehearing or to rescind the decree nisi; and

(ii)   that no intervention by the Queen's Proctor or any other person is pending; and

(iii)   that a declatation under section 41 of the M.C.A. 1973 has been made in relation to the children of the family; and

[59] M.C.R. 1977, r. 65(1). Appendix 1 to M.C.R. 1977, Form 8.

(iv) that the provisions of section 10(2) to (4) (which relate to consideration of the respondent's financial position after the divorce) do not apply or have been complied with.

It is a matter of good practice not to apply for the decree absolute automatically, but only after having taken specific instructions from the petitioner. It is possible for the petitioner to change his mind, even at this late stage, and a reconciliation might have been effected. It would then be unfortunate if his solicitor were to have applied for the decree absolute at the first opportunity. Of course, where the petitioner is being advised under the Green Form scheme and so is a litigant in person, the petitioner must sign the application for the decree. **4–81**

(ii) The respondent's application   **4–82**
The petitioner might delay making the application for the decree absolute. In some cases this might be because the petitioner knows that the respondent is very anxious to remarry and wants to use the right to apply for the decree absolute as a bargaining counter in negotiations about finance and property. The petitioner might also want the continued protection of the M.H.A. 1983[60]; which normally ends on decree absolute. Stalling tactics are of limited value, however, because three months from the date when the petitioner could first have applied for it, the respondent may apply for the decree to be made absolute. The rules require the respondent to give notice of this application to the petitioner.[61]

(iii) Expediting the decree   **4–83**
An application may be made by the petitioner, but not the respondent, for the decree absolute to be expedited. This might be done, for example, where the petitioner is anxious to remarry to ensure that an expected child is born after the marriage of its parents. Application should be made on notice supported by an affidavit from the petitioner. Such applications are not granted readily by the courts.

(iv) Delay   **4–84**
Should the application for the decree absolute be delayed for more than 12 months the court will require a written explanation for the delay. The registrar may require an affidavit to be filed and may either grant or refuse the application or refer it to the judge. On some occasions the

---

[60] See 9–15, below.
[61] M.C.R. 1977, r. 66(2).

reason for the delay is an oversight on the part of the petitioner or his advisers. In these circumstances the application will normally be granted. If, however, the delay is due to an attempted reconciliation, the parties will be subject to the provisions of the M.C.A. 1973, s.2(1). In fact A cases if they live together for a period of more than six months after knowledge of the last act of adultery the decree nisi will be rescinded.[62]

4–85 3. Defended Causes

This topic is to a large extent outside the scope of this book. Fewer than one per cent. of all divorces are heard as defended causes. Many divorces are defended for a short period of time and become compromised, usually over matters of ancillary relief, and are then dealt with as undefended cases. Certain points, however, should be made.

4–86 NOTICE OF INTENTION TO DEFEND

This has already been considered at 4–56, above. As was explained, the main purpose of giving notice is to prevent directions for trial being given for a period of 29 days from service of the petition to allow the respondent time to file his answer. Although, for this reason, it is prudent to give notice of intention to defend if there is any possibility of the respondent wanting to file an answer, it should be noted that a respondent is entitled to file an answer even if no notice of intention to defend has been given.[63] Conversely, a respondent who does give notice is under no obligation to file an answer if he subsequently changes his mind.

4–87 LEGAL AID

Legal aid is available to defend a divorce petition. Once a petition becomes defended it is open to the petitioner to apply for legal aid as well. However, whether a party is the petitioner or respondent to the divorce will be irrelevant when questions of ancillary relief, custody or access fall to be decided. Nonetheless, the question of either party's conduct may be relevant in such ancillary matters and an uncontested allegation in a petition may, therefore, in certain cases, lead to a party being prejudiced in the subsequent issue. For

[62] See 3–20, above.
[63] M.C.R. 1977, r. 18(2).

example, in a small percentage of cases a party's conduct may be relevant in an application for ancillary relief.[64] If a serious allegation of conduct appears in the petition, the respondent may wish to defend the petition to ensure that he is not •subsequently bound by a finding that he committed the conduct alleged, which would be the result of allowing the petition to proceed undefended.

The Legal Aid Board consider that it is the duty of the Area director to ensure that legally-aided cases are not defended without good reason. In cases of the type mentioned above it is sometimes possible that a compromise can be reached whereby the particular allegation to which objection is made can be deleted from the petition. If this is not possible then legal aid may be granted to defend. In cases where there will be no detriment to the proper interests of the parties it is extremely unlikely that legal aid will be granted.[65] If, therefore, the respondent wishes to contest an allegation of conduct only because he considers it exaggerated or untrue, he may be refused legal aid to do so.

However, the Court of Appeal have expressed the opinion that if, for example, the respondent wishes to contest certain allegations of misconduct, he should be allowed to do so, even if this would have no bearing on the subsequent ancillary proceedings.[66]

THE ANSWER   4–88

(a) This must be filed within 21 days from the expiration of the time limit for giving notice of intention to defend the petition.[67] It must be remembered that, if no notice of intention to defend has been given, it is possible for the registrar to give directions for trial eight days after service of the petition. The answer must, however, be filed before directions for trial are given.

(b) This period is often too short. In many cases legal aid may   4–89
have been applied for and this is unlikely to be determined for some time. In such cases an application might be made, on notice, for the period to be extended. Hopefully this can be agreed with the other side as, of course, in these circumstances legal aid will not yet have been granted to the respondent.

---

[64] See 6–60, below.
[65] *Legal Aid Handbook*, pp. 65–66.
[66] See *McCarney* v. *McCarney* [1986] 1 F.L.R. 312.
[67] M.C.R. 1977, r. 18(1).

4–90   (c) If the period has expired, and the respondent wishes to defend, it will be necessary to apply for leave to file an answer out of time. If directions for trial have been given, as will normally be the case, the registrar will probably already have certified that the petitioner is entitled to a decree. It has been held that this is tantamount to a decree nisi and therefore an application for leave to defend should, in these circumstances, be dealt with on a similar basis to an application for a rehearing of a decree nisi.[68]

This means that the application will be refused unless there are substantial grounds for believing that the decree was obtained contrary to the interests of justice. This might be so where, for example, the failure to file an answer was due to ignorance or lack of advice and the respondent's case, if put before the court, might lead to a different result.[69]

4–91   SUBSEQUENT PROCEDURE

Prior to 1986 all defended divorces were transferred to the High Court. Now, however, these cases will nearly always remain in the county court unless the registrar decides that, owing to the "complexity, difficulty or gravity" of the case, it is more appropriate for it to be transferred to the High Court for hearing.[70]

In a defended case further pleadings may be filed (*e.g.* a reply to the answer may be filed). An application for directions for trial will then be made. The case will usually be listed for a pre-trial review at which the case will be considered by the registrar with the parties and an attempt made to settle the matter. If this is unsuccessful the case will be listed for hearing before the judge. There is usually a waiting period of a few months before the trial date.

4–92   COSTS

Following the pronouncement of the decree nisi the judge will make an award of costs.

The general principle is that the unsuccessful party will be ordered to pay the costs of the successful party. However, as in other fields of civil litigation, it is unlikely that costs will be

---

[68] *Day* v. *Day* [1979] 2 W.L.R. 681.

[69] See *Mitchell* v. *Mitchell* [1984] Fam. 1; *Moosa* v. *Moosa* [1983] 4 F.L.R. 131; *Ali Ebrahim* v. *Ali Ebrahim* [1983] 1 W.L.R. 1336.

[70] The discretion is contained in the M.F.P.A. 1984, s.39 and is subject to *Practice Direction (Family division: Business: Distribution)* [1988] 1 W.L.R. 558.

awarded against a legally aided party. The position is further complicated because the other principles set out in the context of undefended divorces also apply (see 4–70, above).

4. Procedure under the Children Act 1989   4–93

The Act amends M.C.A. 1973, s.41[71] so that it will no longer be necessary for the court always to make a declaration of satisfaction regarding the arrangements for the children (see 4–77). This is because the Law Commission felt that this procedure sometimes leads to unnecessary orders being made for custody and access.[72] The whole emphasis of the Act is to avoid making orders regarding children wherever possible. Indeed section 1(5) provides that the court "shall not make the order or any of the orders (under the Act) unless it considers that doing so would be better for the child than making no order at all."[73]

The parties will still have to provide the court with details of the proposed arrangements for the children, but this is for the purpose of enabling the court to consider whether to exercise its powers under the Act. Its powers include ordering a welfare report, making a residence order or contact order, or, in appropriate cases, delaying the decree absolute until it has had time to consider the case. These orders are considered in more detail in Chapter 17.

Once the Act is in force regulations will provide precisely how divorce procedure will change. A statement of arrangements, possibly in a new format, will still be filed, but it will only be in rare cases that any orders in relation to children will be necessary.

---

[71] See 3–74.
[72] Report No. 172, paras. 3.5 *et seq.*
[73] See 17–05 and 17–06.

5. Nullity, Judicial Separation and Presumption of Death

5–01 This chapter deals with the three other decrees which are occasionally considered as an alternative to divorce—nullity, judicial separation and presumption of death and dissolution of the marriage. By comparison with divorce, however, few such decrees are granted each year.[1]

1. Nullity

5–02 VOID AND VOIDABLE MARRIAGES

The term "nullity" is used to refer to the decree which is granted in respect of both void and voidable marriages. A void marriage is one which suffers from such a fundamental defect that it is treated as having never taken place. Indeed, if the parties were sufficiently confident of the existence of the defect, they could treat the marriage as a nullity without obtaining a decree. A voidable marriage, on the other hand, is regarded as a valid and subsisting marriage until a nullity decree has been obtained in respect of it. Although the marriage suffers from some defect, the law leaves it to one of the parties to decide whether it should be annulled.

Section 11 of the M.C.A. 1973 sets out the grounds on which a marriage is void, and section 12 sets out the grounds on which a marriage is voidable. Both sections relate to marriages celebrated after July 31, 1971.[2]

---

[1] In 1988, 1,917 petitions for judicial separation and 389 for nullity were granted (Table 5.4, Judicial Statistics 1988: Cm. 745 (1989)).

[2] The Nullity of Marriage Act 1971, which was consolidated into the M.C.A. 1973, came into force on August 1, 1971. Marriages celebrated before then are still subject to the pre-1971 law, which in many respects is the same as that under the Act.

THE GROUNDS ON WHICH A MARRIAGE IS VOID

Section 11 of the M.C.A. 1973 provides that a marriage shall be void on the following grounds only: **5–03**

(i) That it is not a valid marriage under the provisions of the Marriage Acts 1949 to 1986 **5–04**
This covers three types of case:

   (i)   the parties are too closely related to each other (*i.e.* within the "prohibited degrees"). The relationship may be by blood (*e.g.* brother and sister) or by marriage (*e.g.* a man may not marry his mother-in-law while either his former wife or his father-in-law are still alive)[3]; or,

   (ii) either party is under 16[4]; or,

  (iii) the parties have married in disregard of certain formalities.

         The formalities concerned are of the most fundamental kind (*e.g.* a marriage celebrated according to the rites of the Church of England must be solemnised by a person in Holy Orders) and even then the marriage is void only if the parties disregarded them "knowingly and wilfully."[5]

(ii) That at the time of the marriage either party was already lawfully married **5–05**

(iii) That the parties are not respectively male and female **5–06**
It was held in *Corbett* v. *Corbett*[6] that the law is, for this purpose, concerned only with biological sex, and, for legal purposes a person's sex is fixed at birth. It cannot subsequently be changed, either by natural development or by medical or surgical means. This case was, however, decided under common law and would not necessarily bind a court that was called on to interpret the provisions in section 11.

(iv) In the case of a polygamous marriage entered into outside England and Wales, that either party was at the time of the marriage domiciled in England and Wales **5–07**

---

[3] s.1 and Sched. 1 of the Marriage Act 1949 (as amended).
[4] *Ibid.* s.2.
[5] *Ibid.* s.25.
[6] [1971] P. 83.

The effect of this provision is that a person domiciled in England and Wales lacks the capacity to enter into a valid polygamous marriage. This is so whether the marriage is actually or only potentially polygamous.

5–08   THE GROUNDS ON WHICH A MARRIAGE IS VOIDABLE

Section 12 of the M.C.A. 1973 provides that a marriage shall be voidable on the following grounds only:

5–09   (i) That the marriage has not been consummated owing to the incapacity of either party to consummate it
Consummation has been held to require "ordinary and complete" sexual intercourse,[7] but it is irrelevant that either party is infertile so that intercourse could not have resulted in conception. The incapacity must be permanent and incurable.[8] It is not clear, from the wording of section 12(a), whether the incapacity must have existed at the date of the marriage, but the fact that this is a ground of nullity rather than divorce suggests that this should also be a requirement, as indeed it was before the Act was passed.

5–10   (ii) That the marriage has not been consummated owing to the wilful refusal of the respondent to consummate it
This is (with the possible exception of section 12(a), above) the only ground of nullity which arises after the date of the marriage. Wilful refusal has been defined as "a settled and definite decision come to without just excuse" not to consummate the marriage.[9] Mere indecision on the part of the respondent cannot, therefore, entitle the petitioner to a decree.

5–11   (iii) That either party to the marriage did not validly consent to it, whether in consequence of duress, mistake, unsoundness of mind or otherwise

Duress

It has been said that, to prove duress, it must be shown that the will of one of the parties was overborne "by a genuine and reasonably held fear caused by a threat of immediate

---

[7] *D—e* v. *A—g* (1845) 1 Rob.Ecc. 279; applied, *e.g.* in *W.* v. *W.* [1967] 1 W.L.R. 1554.
[8] See *e.g. S.Y.* v. *S.Y.* [1963] P. 37. The unreasonable refusal of a person suffering the incapacity to undergo an operation to rectify it, entitles the court to regard the incapacity as incurable.
[9] *Horton* v. *Horton* [1947] 2 All E.R. 871.

danger, for which the party is not himself responsible, to life, limb or liberty."[10] Although this suggests an objective test, the courts have in some cases been prepared to consider only the effect of pressure on the individual petitioner, and have not always defined the nature of the duress so narrowly. It may be enough to ask simply whether the duress has destroyed the reality of the consent. Thus, for example, family pressure put on a Hindu girl to submit to an arranged marriage has been treated as vitiating her consent.[11] As this indicates, the duress need not emanate from the other party to the marriage; indeed it can be imposed by external events, as when a party contracts a marriage to escape from the oppression of a totalitarian regime.[12]

Mistake

A mistake can vitiate consent only if it relates to the identity of the other party or to the nature of the ceremony.[13] Such cases obviously very rarely arise.

Unsoundness of mind

A party's unsoundness of mind will vitiate consent only if it prevents him from understanding the nature of the contract he is making.[14] This entails an appreciation of the duties and responsibilities of marriage, but it is difficult to prove that a party lacked this low degree of understanding.[15] In cases of mental disorder, it will be easier to rely on the next ground.

(iv) That at the time of the marriage either party, though capable of giving a valid consent, was suffering (whether continuously or intermittently) from mental disorder within the meaning of the Mental Health Act 1983 of such a kind or to such an extent as to be unfitted for marriage 5–12

A decree may be granted on this ground where one of the parties suffers from a mental disorder which, while not preventing that party from understanding the duties and responsibilities of marriage, makes it impossible for him to carry them out.

---

[10] *Per* Sir J. Simon P. in *Szechter* v. *Szechter* [1971] P. 286.

[11] *Hirani* v. *Hirani* [1982] 4 F.L.R. 232.

[12] As in *Szechter* v. *Szechter*, above.

[13] See, *e.g. Mehta* v. *Mehta* [1945] 2 All E.R. 690: decree granted because petitioner believed marriage ceremony was one of conversion to the Hindu faith.

[14] *Durham* v. *Durham* (1885) L.R. 10 P.D. 80.

[15] *Re Park* [1954] P. 112: testator who lacked mental capacity to make a will, held to have had capacity to consent to marriage on the same day.

5–13 **(v) That at the time of the marriage the respondent was suffering from venereal disease in a communicable form**

5–14 **(vi) That at the time of the marriage the respondent was pregnant by some person other than the petitioner**

5–15 BARS TO A DECREE

There can be no bars to the obtaining of a decree in respect of a void marriage since, as already indicated, such a marriage is a nullity regardless of whether a decree is granted in respect of it. However, section 13 of the M.C.A. 1973 sets out three bars to a decree being granted in respect of a voidable marriage.

5–16 **(i) General bar: section 13(1)**
The court must not grant a decree if the respondent satisfies the court:

(a) that the petitioner, with knowledge that it was open to him to have the marriage avoided, so conducted himself in relation to the respondent as to lead the respondent reasonably to believe that he would not seek to do so; *and*

(b) that it would be unjust to the respondent to grant the decree.

Example

When the parties discover that the wife is physically incapable of consummating the marriage, the husband, knowing that he could obtain a nullity decree, nevertheless agrees to the adoption of a child. If the husband subsequently petitioned for a decree on the basis of the wife's incapacity, the wife could, no doubt, establish the first part of the bar, but might, nevertheless, find it very difficult to establish the second part.[16] Even if the husband were now to be denied a decree, he could still, eventually, petition for a divorce. Furthermore, the wife can make the same applications for financial provision, property adjustment and custody orders in the nullity proceedings as she could on divorce.

5–17 **(ii) Three-year time-bar: section 13(2)**
The court must not grant a decree in respect of a marriage which is voidable for any reason, other than non-consummation, unless either the petition is presented within three years

---

[16] See *D.* v. *D.* [1979] 10 Fam. 53.

of the date of the marriage, or leave is granted to petition outside this time. A judge may grant such leave under section 13(4) if the petitioner suffered from a mental disorder within the meaning of the Mental Health Act 1983 at some time during the three-year period, and the judge considers it would be just to grant leave. The application for leave may itself be made more than three years after the date of the marriage (section 13(5)).

Non-consummation is excluded from this time-bar because it sometimes takes a period of years to establish incapacity or wilful refusal to consummate a marriage.

(iii) Bar based on petitioner's knowledge: section 13(3)   **5–18**
The court must not grant a decree on the basis that the respondent suffered from venereal disease or was pregnant by another at the date of the marriage, unless the petitioner was ignorant of these facts at the time.

THE EFFECT OF A DECREE

(i) Children   **5–19**
As a void marriage is a complete nullity and a decree simply gives formal recognition to this fact, it follows that any children the parties may have had are prima facie illegitimate. They will, however, be treated as legitimate if the conditions prescribed by section 1 of the Legitimacy Act 1976 (as amended by the F.L.R.A. 1987) apply. These conditions are:

(i)   that at the time of insemination resulting in the birth, or where there was no such insemination, the child's conception (or at the time of the celebration of the marriage if this was later) both or either of the parties reasonably believed that the marriage was valid; and

(ii)   that the father was domiciled in England and Wales at the date of the child's birth, or died domiciled here if he died before the birth.

It will be seen from the above wording that the statute does not expressly deal with the situation in which a child is born to a couple who are not married to each other at the time, but who do subsequently contract a void marriage. It refers only to the possibility of insemination or conception, but not birth, preceding the ceremony. As a result, it has been held that the section does not apply to a child whose parents entered into a void marriage after the child's birth.[17] Such a child remains

---

[17] See *In re Spence, decd.* [1990] 2 W.L.R. 1430.

(for want of a better word) "illegitimate." In future, however, this should be of no importance since the Family Law Reform Act 1987 and the Children Act 1989 have removed the legal disadvantages which previously attached to those whose parents were unmarried.

Where the marriage is only voidable, it is provided by the M.C.A. 1973, s.16 that the decree shall operate to annul the marriage only as respects any time after the decree has been made absolute, and the marriage shall be treated as if it had existed up to that time. Consequently any children born during the marriage are legitimate.

5–20 **(ii) Wills**

Although a will is normally revoked by a testator's marriage,[18] a void marriage cannot have this effect. A voidable marriage, however, does revoke a previous will whether it is subsequently annulled or not.[19]

When a decree of nullity is granted, whether in respect of a void or a voidable marriage, it has the same effect on an existing will as a decree of divorce; the will takes effect as if the appointment of the former spouse as an executor or trustee were omitted and any gift to the former spouse lapses, except, in either case, in so far as a contrary intention appears in the will.[20]

5–21 **(iii) Ancillary relief**

The parties to a nullity suit can apply for ancillary relief in respect of finance, property and children in the same way as parties to a divorce.

5–22 OBTAINING A DECREE

The only way of obtaining a nullity decree is by a hearing in open court before a judge. The special procedure does not apply. Legal Aid is available for the hearing in the ordinary way. As with divorce, the decree is granted in two stages, and a declaration of satisfaction in respect of any relevant children must be made under section 41 of the M.C.A. 1973 before the decree can be made absolute.

---

[18] By virtue of s.18 of the Wills Act 1837 (substituted by s.18 of the Administration of Justice Act 1982).

[19] See *Re Roberts* [1978] 1 W.L.R. 653.

[20] See s.18A of the Wills Act 1837 (inserted by s.18 of the Administration of Justice Act 1982).

DIVORCE OR NULLITY? 5–23

In some cases a petitioner has a choice between petitioning for divorce or nullity. For example, a spouse's refusal to consummate the marriage could be treated as unreasonable behaviour under section 1(2)(*b*) of the M.C.A. 1973. Where a choice does exist, the client is usually better advised to petition for divorce. This usually means that the matter will not be heard in open court, unless it is defended, and thus the petitioner will be spared both the ordeal of giving oral evidence and the publicity that may surround such a case.

2. Judicial Separation

THE GROUNDS FOR A DECREE 5–24

By virtue of section 17(1) of the M.C.A. 1973, the grounds on which a decree of judicial separation may be sought are the facts set out in section 1(2) of the Act. These provide evidence of the irretrievable breakdown of the marriage for the purpose of a divorce, but, in the case of judicial separation, the court is not concerned with whether the marriage has broken down irretrievably or not.[21] (The five facts are considered in detail at 3–10 to 3–51 above). Section 2 of the M.C.A. 1973, with its provisions concerning the effect of cohabitation on the section 1(2) facts, applies to judicial separation as it does to divorce.

THE REASONS FOR USING JUDICIAL SEPARATION 5–25

Since the grounds for judicial separation are the same as the facts on which a divorce petition is based, the question naturally arises as to why judicial separation should be chosen in preference to divorce. The reasons for choosing judicial separation can be summarised as follows:

(i) There is no one-year time-bar to the presentation of a 5–26 petition, as there is with divorce. A petition for judicial separation may be presented at any time after the marriage, provided one of the grounds is satisfied.

(ii) Some clients have a fundamental objection to divorce, 5–27 usually for religious reasons. For such clients judicial separation may be an acceptable alternative.

---

[21] M.C.A. 1973, s.17(2).

5–28   (iii) The ancillary relief that can be obtained in conjunction with a petition for judicial separation is the same as that which can be obtained on divorce. In particular, the courts' powers to order property adjustment and the sale of property under sections 24 and 24A of the M.C.A. 1973 are available. There are no such powers under the non-ancillary financial jurisdictions contained in section 27 of the M.C.A. 1973 and in the D.P.M.C.A. 1978 (for which, see Chapter 14, below).

It is also possible to obtain non-molestation and exclusion injunctions as part of the proceedings for judicial separation. The availability of a wide range of ancillary relief may be particularly attractive to the client who needs such relief, but is, as yet, undecided about ending the marriage with a petition for divorce.

Nevertheless, in many cases where a divorce is not immediately possible, but financial relief or custody orders are wanted by the client, the solicitor will often prefer to apply for orders in the magistrates' courts. (See Chapter 14).

5–29   THE EFFECT OF THE DECREE

A decree of judicial separation does not, of course, dissolve the marriage; it simply relieves the parties from the duty of living together.[22] In practical terms this only means that neither party can be in desertion once the decree has been granted. A decree of judicial separation also affects the devolution of property on intestacy; property belonging to a spouse who dies intestate while a decree of judicial separation is in force and the separation is continuing, devolves as if the other spouse were already dead.[23] On the other hand, a decree of judicial separation, unlike divorce and nullity decrees, has no effect on the wills the spouses may have made. If, therefore, one party does not want the other to benefit under their will, it may be necessary to make a new one.

5–30   OBTAINING THE DECREE

The procedure for obtaining a decree of judicial separation is broadly the same as that for obtaining a decree of divorce. Thus, as long as the petition is undefended, the special

---

[22] *Ibid.* s.18(1).
[23] *Ibid.* s.18(2). Note that the survivor spouse would still be able to apply for provision out of the deceased spouse's estate under the Inheritance (Provision for Family and Dependants) Act 1975.

procedure usually applies and legal aid is not normally available. Instead the client may be advised under the Green Form scheme, with the same initial limit of three hours' work available to the solicitor who drafts the petition.

The provisions of section 6 of the M.C.A. 1973, which are **5–31** designed to promote a reconciliation, apply to judicial separation as well as divorce.[24] Thus, where a solicitor is acting for a petitioner (rather than just advising under the Green Form scheme) he must file a certificate in Form 3 stating whether he has discussed reconciliation with the client (see 4–27, above). Also, the court has power to adjourn the proceedings if there appears to be a reasonable possibility of reconciliation.

Unlike divorce and nullity decrees, a decree of judicial **5–32** separation is not granted in two stages; the court simply grants the decree once a ground has been proved. However, as section 41 of the M.C.A. 1973 applies (*i.e.* the court must make a declaration regarding the welfare of any relevant children of the family) the children appointment will be held before the decree is granted, rather than after the decree nisi as in divorce cases.

No doubt because judicial separation does not terminate the **5–33** marriage, some of the safeguards available to respondents to divorce petitions are not available in cases of judicial separation. Thus, a respondent to a petition based on five years' separation cannot defend it on the grounds of grave financial hardship, under section 5 of the M.C.A. 1973. Respondents to petitions based on two years' separation plus consent cannot use section 10(1) to have a decree rescinded because they were misled into giving their consent, nor can respondents to petitions based on two or five years' separation seek to delay the decree by applying under section 10 for consideration of their financial position.

DISCHARGE OF THE DECREE **5–34**

The M.C.A. 1973 contains no provision for the discharge of a decree of judicial separation. No doubt the court could rescind the decree under its inherent jurisdiction if it were shown that there had been some fundamental irregularity in its being granted (*e.g.* the ground on which it was based was shown to be non-existent). It has also been held that the court can

[24] M.C.A. 1973, s.17(3).

discharge the decree on the application of either party if cohabitation is resumed.[25] It has never been decided whether a resumption of cohabitation automatically discharges the decree.

5–35 DIVORCE AFTER JUDICIAL SEPARATION

Section 4(1) of the M.C.A. 1973 expressly provides that the grant of a decree of judicial separation is no bar to a subsequent divorce decree being granted on the same facts. Indeed section 4(2) goes on to provide that, in such cases, the court may treat the decree of judicial separation as sufficient proof of the fact on which it was based (*e.g.* adultery, behaviour etc.). The petitioner is still required to give evidence, but in an undefended case, this can usually take the form of a Form 7 affidavit sworn in support of the petition.

Special provision is made by section 4(3) for the case where the decree of judicial separation was based on desertion. The decree itself prevents further desertion running, but, if the decree was based on two years' desertion and has remained continuously in force, the desertion on which it was based is deemed to have immediately preceded the presentation of the divorce petition, in order to satisfy the requirements of section 1(2)(c) of the M.C.A. 1973.

Example

Wilma obtains a decree of judicial separation against Hubert on the basis of his having deserted her for two years. The decree remains in force for a year, after which Wilma decides to petition for divorce. Although Hubert's desertion came to an end on the granting of the decree, Wilma is still entitled to seek a divorce on the basis that his desertion immediately preceded the presentation of her divorce petition.

3. Presumption of Death and Dissolution of Marriage

5–36 THE GROUND FOR THE DECREE

By virtue of section 19 of the M.C.A. 1973, a party to a marriage who can show that reasonable grounds exist for supposing the other party to be dead can present a petition for a decree of presumption of death and dissolution of the

---

[25] *Oram v. Oram* (1923) 129 L.T. 159.

marriage. Section 19(3) provides that, if the other party has been continually absent for seven years and the petitioner has no reason to believe the other party to have been alive during that time, it may be presumed that the other party is dead. However, a petitioner would never normally wish to rely on this presumption as he could instead obtain an ordinary decree of divorce based on five years' separation under section 1(2)(*e*) of the M.C.A. 1973. Nevertheless, section 19 could prove useful to a petitioner who had other reasonable grounds for supposing his spouse to be dead after a shorter period of absence, and was anxious to have the marriage dissolved in order to be free to remarry.

OBTAINING THE DECREE   5–37

The petition would be heard by a judge in open court and the decree would be granted in two stages as with an ordinary decree of divorce.

PART II

FINANCIAL PROVISION

6. The Law Relating To Financial Provision And Property Adjustment

This chapter deals primarily with the powers of the divorce **6–01** court to make orders under the M.C.A. 1973 for financial provision and property adjustment, following a petition for divorce, nullity or judicial separation. Very occasionally a husband or wife who are in dispute about the ownership of property may have to resort to the alternative jurisdiction of the M.W.P.A. 1882, under which the court can make a declaration as to the ownership of the matrimonial property. This jurisdiction is considered briefly at the end of this chapter. Cases also sometimes arise in which a spouse wants maintenance or a lump sum without instituting matrimonial proceedings. The jurisdictions under which such orders may be obtained are considered in Chapter 14, below.

Increasingly nowadays problems arise when parties who have never been married seek advice about financial provision and property adjustment on the breakdown of their relationship. In Chapter 15, below, we consider the more limited powers of the courts to make orders where the parties have never been married.

1. Financial Provision and Property Adjustment **6–02** Under the Matrimonial Causes Act 1973

Disputes about money and property are much more common than disputes about the divorce itself. Even if the parties ultimately agree to the making of a consent order, this is often only after protracted negotiations between their respective solicitors, and sometimes only after the case has been argued before the registrar or judge.

This section deals first with the orders for ancillary relief which are available under the M.C.A. 1973; then the statutory criteria according to which those orders should be made are considered; finally it looks at the way the court uses its powers in practice. In all the examples used in this section it is assumed that any maintenance is to be paid by the husband, although orders can be made against either party.

6–03 THE ORDERS

Sections 22 to 24A of the M.C.A. 1973 set out the orders which can be granted in connection with proceedings for divorce, nullity or judicial separation. The orders can be categorised as orders for maintenance pending suit, financial provision, property adjustment and the sale of property.

6–04 **(i) Maintenance pending suit**

Section 22 of the M.C.A. 1973 gives the court power to make orders for maintenance pending suit (M.P.S.) on a petition for divorce, nullity, or judicial separation. M.P.S. consists of periodical payments in favour of *either* party to the marriage. So, for example, the wife may be the respondent in the divorce proceedings, but is still entitled to apply for M.P.S. Children cannot be awarded M.P.S. because, unlike parties, they can receive periodical payments under section 23 of the M.C.A. 1973 before any decree is granted. As the name suggests, M.P.S. is maintenance that is awarded pending the outcome of the proceedings. It cannot begin earlier than the date of the presentation of the petition (though it can, if ordered later, be back-dated to the date of the petition), and it cannot continue beyond the date of the determination of the suit. The suit will usually be determined when the decree is made absolute (in the case of divorce or nullity) or when the decree is granted (in the case of judicial separation). Alternatively, it would be determined if the petition were dismissed. Within these limits the court may order M.P.S. for such term as it thinks reasonable.

6–05 Although applications for M.P.S. are made as a matter of routine in the prayer of many divorce petitions, these applications are often not proceeded with. This is because income support provides many wives with a better alternative, at least until a full order for periodical payments can be made under section 23 of the M.C.A. 1973 (see 6–08, below). The relative advantages of income support may be summarised thus:

Speed

A wife who has, for example, been deserted by her husband will receive any benefit to which she is entitled within a few days of her application to the D.S.S. If she applies for M.P.S., she will no doubt need legal aid. Emergency legal aid is not normally granted for applications for M.P.S., so she may well have to wait for two months, or more, before a legal aid certificate is issued. There may then be a further delay waiting for a hearing date for her application in the county court.

Amount

Even if M.P.S. is awarded, it is unlikely to be as much as a wife might expect to receive by way of periodical payments under section 23 of the M.C.A. 1973. It may well not be enough even to take the wife off income support, so she will be no better off for having obtained the order.

Security

A wife in receipt of income support knows that, as long as her circumstances remain the same, she will be able to collect her benefit each week. Even if she obtains an order for M.P.S., she may find that her husband defaults and she will then have to try to enforce the order in further court proceedings. This, in itself, is a difficult process, particularly as M.P.S. will not normally be registered in the magistrates' court for enforcement (see 13–10 to 13–11).

This is not to say that there is never any point in pursuing a claim for M.P.S. Clearly, if a wife can reasonably expect to obtain an order for substantial M.P.S., she may be well advised to proceed. Even if the wife is eligible for income support and any order for M.P.S. would probably be insufficient to take her off benefit, she may find she will be encouraged by the D.S.S. to obtain an order against her husband (see 8–48, below). In some cases too, the husband may positively wish to be able to pay maintenance under a court order, because he will then be able to claim tax relief up to a certain level on the payments. (See 7–08, below). In *Peacock* v. *Peacock*,[1] Booth J. held that this tax advantage was enough in itself to justify making an order for M.P.S., even though the wife would be no better off, as the amount ordered was insufficient to take her off what is now income support.   **6–06**

(ii) Financial provision orders   **6–07**
Section 23 of the M.C.A. 1973 gives the court power to make financial provision orders in favour of either party to the marriage and any children of the family. Financial provision consists of periodical payments (which may be secured) and lump sums.

Periodical payments   **6–08**

Periodical payments orders normally take the form of weekly or monthly amounts of money which one party is ordered to

[1] [1984] 1 W.L.R. 532.

pay the other and any children of the family. Orders in favour of children can provide that the money shall be paid either to a party for the benefit of the child or direct to the child. For tax reasons it is generally better for the order to make the money payable to a party for the benefit of the child. This may entitle the payer to tax relief on the payments. (For more detail see 7–09 below.)

6–09 *Secured periodical payments*

The court also has power, under section 23(1) to order that the obligation to make periodical payments to parties and children shall be secured. This means that the court can require some capital asset belonging to the payer spouse to be charged as security for the payments. If the payer then defaults, any income from the asset (for example, dividends from shares) can be used to satisfy the order, or the asset can be sold and the proceeds used for this purpose. Obviously it is possible to make this type of order only if the payer has sufficient capital assets to provide worthwhile security, and the court will not normally require the payer's sole capital asset (usually his home) to be charged as security.[2] Consequently orders for secured periodical payments are rare.

6–10 *Lump sum orders*

Under section 23(1)(*c*) of the M.C.A. 1973 the court can order either party to pay the other a lump sum. Under section 23(1)(*f*) the court can order either party to pay a lump sum to, or for the benefit of, a child of the family, though these orders for children are not often made.

Although section 23(1)(*c*) says that a party to the marriage may receive "such lump sum or sums" as may be specified, it has been held in *Coleman* v. *Coleman*[3] that only one lump sum order can ever be made under this provision. In that case a wife, who had already been awarded a lump sum on the divorce, made a subsequent application for another, but Sir George Baker P. held that the court had no jurisdiction to grant it. The judge held that a lump sum for a party is intended as a "once and for all" provision. The plural reference in section 23(1)(*c*) was explained as allowing the court to make provision for more than one lump sum payment within the one order. So, for example, a wife in urgent need of capital might receive an immediate payment

---

[2] Though this may be done if the payer is unlikely to make ordinary periodical payments: *Aggett* v. *Aggett* [1962] 1 W.L.R. 183.
[3] [1973] Fam. 10.

on the making of the order, but that order could also provide that she should later receive a further sum out of the proceeds of the former matrimonial home when that had been sold.

This restriction does not apply to orders for children. Section 23(4) provides that the power to make financial provision orders for children "shall be exercisable from time to time," which would allow more than one lump sum order to be made in favour of a child.

Lump sum orders may be made for a variety of purposes. **6–11** They are often ordered to be paid out of the proceeds of sale of the former matrimonial home and in such cases represent a division of capital between the parties. Such lump sums will often be used towards the purchase of a new home. In other cases, however, a lump sum payment may be regarded as maintenance; for example, where the court decides to effect a "clean break" between the parties and wishes to capitalise the periodical payments that might otherwise have been awarded. Furthermore, section 23(3) expressly provides that lump sums may be awarded to a party to cover maintenance expenses incurred before the application for a lump sum was made. This would be useful in cases where income support, or an order for maintenance pending suit, had proved inadequate to cover expenses incurred before the divorce. Section 23(3) also allows a lump sum order to be paid by instalments, and the obligation to make such payments may be secured in the same way as the obligation to make periodical payments.

Where a lump sum is ordered to be paid by instalments, or **6–12** where the court orders payment of a lump sum to be deferred, (because, for example, the payer needs time to raise the money) the court has power under section 23(6) to order that interest shall be paid on the instalments or the deferred sum. Interest may be payable under section 23(6) from the date of the order until the date when payment is due. It should be noted that this provision is not designed to deal with the case of the payer who fails to pay by the due date. This does not matter when the lump sum order was made in the High Court, as the lump sum automatically carries interest as a judgment debt under the Judgments Act 1838. However, where, as in the majority of cases, the order was made in the county court, no interest is payable in the case of default since there is at present no provision for interest to be paid on county court judgments or orders.[4]

---

[4] For a full consideration of the problems involved, see [1989] Fam. Law 379.

6–13 **(iii) Property adjustment orders**
Section 24 of the M.C.A. 1973 gives the court power to make property adjustment orders in favour of either party to the marriage and any children of the family. Property adjustment consists of transfers and settlements of property and orders varying ante-nuptial and post-nuptial settlements.

6–14 *Transfers of property*

Under section 24(1)(*a*) of the M.C.A. 1973 the court can order one party to the marriage to transfer property to the other, or to a child of the family, or to someone else for the benefit of such a child. The transferor must be entitled to the property either in possession or reversion. The majority of orders made under this section relate to the former matrimonial home, but any other property could be made the subject of a transfer order; for example, the contents of the home, cars and shares. It has also been established that the court can order the transfer of certain tenancies under section 24. The extent to which this is possible is considered in more detail at 6–120 to 6–125, below.

6–15 *Settlements of property*

Under section 24(1)(*b*) of the M.C.A. 1973 the court can order one party to settle any property to which he is entitled for the benefit of the other party, or any children of the family. This power could be used to create a settlement of all kinds of property for the continuing benefit of the wife and children, but it is most commonly used in relation to the former matrimonial home. Thus the home, formerly in the name of one of the parties, may be settled on both parties on trust for sale, with sale postponed until the occurrence of certain specified events, such as the youngest child of the family reaching 18, or the death of the spouse in occupation. (These orders are discussed in detail at 6–99 to 6–112, below.)

6–16 *Variation of ante- and post-nuptial settlements*

Under section 24(1)(*c*) and (*d*) of the M.C.A. 1973 the court can vary ante- and post-nuptial settlements for the benefit of the parties or any children of the family, and can also extinguish or reduce the interest of one party under such a settlement, even if this does not benefit the other.

In the past these powers were more important than they are today and the terms "ante- and post-nuptial settlements" were widely defined. Now, however most of the property adjustment orders the courts make can be seen as being either transfers or settlements of property under section 24(1)(*a*) and (*b*). Strictly speaking, however, where the matrimonial home is already held on trust for sale in the joint names of the parties, and the court makes an order varying the terms of the trust to postpone sale for a period of time (see 6–104 to 6–109, below), the court is using its jurisdiction to vary a post-nuptial settlement.

(iv) Duration of the Orders

Parties to the marriage:

The starting point: Applications for financial provision and **6–17** property adjustment orders can be made on, or at any time after, the presentation of the petition, but no application will be heard until a decree has been granted. In the case of divorce and nullity petitions it is sufficient that a decree nisi should have been granted; even so, any order cannot take effect until decree absolute.[5] Orders for periodical payments can, however, be backdated to the date on which the petition was filed.[6] This may be useful to the payee as a means of compensating for a deficiency of income support or maintenance pending suit before the divorce. Periodical payments should, however, never be backdated as a matter of routine. Careful consideration needs to be given to the means of the payer before this is done, because that party will often lack the capital resources to pay the lump sum that backdating entails.

Termination: All orders for periodical payments must cease **6–18** on the remarriage of the payee.[7] Orders for unsecured payments cease on the death of either party[8] but orders for secured payments need cease only on the death of the payee[9]; the existence of assets charged as security for the payments allows those payments to continue even though the payer is dead. Thus, although secured payments are sought primarily as a means of protection against a payer liable to default, they may also be worth seeking in cases where the payer is likely to die before the payee.

Limited periodical payments: The court itself can limit the **6–19** duration of orders for secured and unsecured periodical payments. Section 25A(2) of the M.C.A. 1973 provides that,

---

[5] ss.23(5) and 24(3) of the M.C.A 1973.
[6] s.28(1) of the M.C.A. 1973.
[7] *Ibid.* Note, however, that settled cohabitation is not to be equated with remarriage for this purpose: *Atkinson* v. *Atkinson* [1988] Fam. 93.
[8] *Ibid.*
[9] *Ibid.*

when a court makes an order for periodical payments in favour of a party, it shall consider *"whether it would be appropriate to require those payments to be made or secured only for such term as would in the opinion of the court be sufficient to enable the party in whose favour the order is made to adjust without undue hardship to the termination of his or her financial dependence on the other party."* Such a limitation might be appropriate where, for example, children of the family would soon be old enough for the mother to go out to work again, or where a wife needed maintenance only while training for a qualification which would enable her to get a better job.

6–20   Limited term maintenance orders are most likely to be made by consent. If the payer suspects that the payee's circumstances will improve in future to such an extent that maintenance will be unnecessary, it will always be open to him to seek a variation of the order under section 31 of the M.C.A. 1973 when that situation arises. (The use of limited term maintenance orders is considered in more detail at 6–24 below.)

6–21   Even when the court does make a limited term maintenance order the payee will generally be entitled to apply for an extension of the term under section 31 of the M.C.A. 1973, provided the application is made before the term expires. (An application made after this would be too late since no order capable of variation would then exist).[10] However, section 28(1A) of the M.C.A. 1973 does give the court power to direct that the payee shall not be entitled to apply for an extension of the term specified in the order. Again, such directions will in practice be rare, since there will normally be no point in precluding the possibility of variation regardless of any change of circumstance in future. For an example of this see *Waterman* v. *Waterman*.[11] In this case the marriage had been of very short duration, having lasted only 17 months, although the couple did have a child of five, custody of whom was granted to the wife. The judge awarded a lump sum and periodical payments to the wife, but limited the wife's periodical payments to a term of five years, as he held that she had a real earning capacity and had indeed been training to improve her secretarial skills. He therefore ordered that the wife should not be entitled to apply for an extension of the limited term. The Court of Appeal held that this latter restriction was wrong. The court felt that it would be unjust

---

[10] See *Minton* v. *Minton* [1979] A.C. 593. See also *T.* v. *T.* [1988] 1 F.L.R. 481.
[11] [1989] 1 F.L.R. 380.

to impose a limited term on the maintenance ordered in view of the fact that the child was still very young and that there remained some uncertainty as to the wife's future earning prospects.

The "remarriage trap": Orders for lump sums and for **6–22** property adjustment, being "once and for all" orders, are obviously not subject to the same limitations as orders for periodical payments. However, section 28(3) of the M.C.A. 1973 prevents a party who has remarried from applying for a financial provision order in his or her own favour (as opposed to one in favour of a child), and for any kind of property adjustment order. It has been held that section 28(3) only prevents an application from being *made* after remarriage, not from being heard. Provided, therefore, an application has been made before remarriage, the court retains jurisdiction to deal with it on its merits after remarriage.[12] This has no relevance to orders for periodical payments, which would cease on remarriage anyhow. It may be important, however, where a lump sum or property adjustment order is wanted. A party who remarried, without having applied for either of these provisions, would be prevented from making such applications in future. This is not normally a danger when acting for a petitioner, because the applications will normally be made in the petition itself. However, when acting for a respondent who, like most respondents, is not defending the petition by filing an answer, it is important to file an application for capital provision before decree absolute, especially if there is any prospect of the client remarrying in the near future. (See Chapter 10 for details of the procedure for applying for ancillary relief.)

Children of the family

The starting point: As with parties to the marriage, **6–23** applications for financial provision and property adjustment orders in favour of children of the family can be made on, or at any time after, the presentation of the petition. However, unlike applications for parties, applications for financial provision (but not property adjustment) for children can be heard, and orders made, before any decree is granted. Indeed, such orders can be made for children even if the proceedings for a decree are dismissed, provided this is done forthwith or within a reasonable period after the dismissal.[13]

---

[12] *Jackson* v. *Jackson* [1973] Fam. 99.
[13] M.C.A. 1973, s.23(2).

As with parties, any order for periodical payments can be backdated to the date of the application for the order.[14]

6–24   *Age limits*: Section 29(2) of the M.C.A. 1973 imposes certain age limits on periodical payments for children. In the first instance these should not extend beyond a child's seventeenth birthday, unless the court thinks it right to specify a later date. A court may do this if it is obvious at the time the order is made that the child will require maintenance beyond 17, because, for example, he is going to stay on at school. But in any event, the original order cannot normally be expressed to extend beyond the child's eighteenth birthday. Furthermore, by virtue of section 29(1), a financial provision order and a transfer of property order cannot normally be made in the case of a child who is already 18 or older. There are, however, exceptions to these general rules. Section 29(3) provides that periodical payments orders can be made to extend beyond a child's eighteenth birthday, and financial provision and transfer of property orders can be made, in respect of those who are already 18 or more, if they are, or will be, receiving education or vocational training, irrespective of whether they are also in gainful employment. Such orders can also be extended beyond 18 under section 29(3) if there are "special circumstances" justifying this. This, for example, allows the court to extend periodical payments to children of the family who are suffering from physical or mental disabilities. If any of the exceptions set out in section 29(3) apply, there is no further age limit at which periodical payments must cease, or beyond which financial provision orders or transfer of property orders cannot be made. There is no age limit at all on the making of the other property adjustment orders (*e.g.* settlements of property) in favour of children of the family.

6–25   *Applications by older children*: Occasionally an older child of the family, whose parents are divorced, may want financial provision, but finds that neither parent is willing to provide it. This happened in *Downing* v. *Downing*,[15] where a 20 year old daughter, whose parents had been divorced 10 years ago, had gone to University, but neither parent was prepared to make the proper parental contribution to supplement her grant. Payne J. held that the daughter could be given leave to intervene in the parents' divorce suit to apply for financial provision on her own behalf.[16]

---

[14] *Ibid*. s.29(2).
[15] [1976] Fam. 288.
[16] Such leave may now be given under M.C.A. 1977, r. 69.

Termination: As with payments for a party to the marriage, **6–26**
ordinary periodical payments for a child will cease if the payer
dies, but secured payments can continue after the payer's
death. Payments for children do not, of course, cease on the
remarriage of either party, although the remarriage of a
custodial parent might give the other party grounds for
applying for a variation of the payments for the child. It
might, for example, be argued that the effect of remarriage
had been to release more of the custodial parents' resources
for the support of the child, so justifying a reduction in the
amount of maintenance paid for the child.

(v) Orders for the sale of property

6–27

Under section 24A of the M.C.A. 1973 (inserted in 1981), the
court has power to order a sale of any property in which
either party to the marriage has a beneficial interest, either in
possession or reversion. This power is sometimes described as
being "parasitic," because it can be exercised only if the court
also makes an order for:

   (i)   secured periodical payments; or

   (ii) a lump sum; or

   (iii) a property adjustment order.

The order for sale can be made at the same time as one of
these orders, or at any time afterwards. It cannot take effect
until decree absolute.[17]

The order for sale may contain consequential or supplementary provisions, such as a provision requiring a payment to be
made out of the proceeds of sale, and a provision specifying
the person or persons to whom the property is to be offered
for sale.[18]

Other examples, though not expressly mentioned in section
24A, would be provision for the valuation of the property
before sale, and a direction as to which party's solicitor
should have the conduct of the sale. However, the court have
taken a restrictive view of their powers to make consequential
orders. It has been held, for example, that the court cannot
order that debts owed to a third party with no beneficial
interest in the property should be paid out of the proceeds of
sale of the property.[19] It has also been held that section 24A
does not allow the court to make a possession order against
one of the parties where that party is a joint tenant of the

---

[17] M.C.A. 1973, s.24A(3).
[18] *Ibid.* s.24A(2).
[19] See *Burton* v. *Burton* [1986] 2 F.L.R. 419.

property in question.[20] This can cause problems where a joint tenant remains living in the property and will not co-operate with the sale. It would seem, therefore, that, if there is any prospect of the other party not being prepared to co-operate with the sale, it would be unwise to seek an order under section 24A at all. In such cases it would be better instead to order a transfer of the property outright from one party to the other, with the transferor receiving a lump sum in return. Alternatively, if the parties were still married, it might be possible to apply under the Matrimonial Homes Act 1983 to have the other party excluded pending a sale.

6–28   The main object behind the introduction of section 24A was to give the court a power, previously lacking under the M.C.A. 1973 itself, to order the sale of the former matrimonial home so as to allow a division of the proceeds between the parties. So, for example, the court can order the husband to sell the house of which he is the sole owner, and share the proceeds with the wife by way of a lump sum payment. However, section 24A also provides a useful means of enforcing lump sum orders. If, for example, a husband fails to pay a lump sum by the date specified, the wife can apply for an order that the husband sell specified assets, such as shares, and pay the lump sum out of the proceeds. Indeed, the original lump sum order may provide for its own enforcement by including a provision for the sale of property if the money is not paid by a certain date.

6–29   The court has power under section 24A(4), to direct that the sale shall not take place until a specified event has occurred or a specified period has expired. So, for example, the court could back a lump sum order in favour of a wife, with an order that the husband should sell the former matrimonial home in which he is still living, but could postpone the date of the sale to give the husband an opportunity to raise the money without having to sell the house.

6–30   Section 24A is not confined to property which is owned only by the parties. The power to order a sale can be exercised in respect of property in which other people also have a beneficial interest; for example, a parent of one of the parties who also lives in the matrimonial home. However, section 24A(6) provides that any other person with a beneficial interest must be given an opportunity to make representations with respect to the order, and those representations must be

[20] See *Crosthwaite* v. *Crosthwaite* [1989] 2 F.L.R. 86.

considered among the other circumstances to which the court is required to have regard under section 25. (See 6–34 to 6–66, below.)

(vi) Orders after a foreign decree   **6–31**
Although, of course, the vast majority of orders for ancillary relief are made in respect of divorce decrees obtained in this country, the court[21] does have certain powers to make orders following the granting of a decree abroad. The conditions under which this may be done are laid down in Part III of the M.F.P.A. 1984.

The essential conditions are: **6–32**

(1) The parties' marriage must have been dissolved or annulled, or they must have been legally separated, by means of judicial or other proceedings abroad, and the decree or separation must be recognised as valid by the English court.[22] (The rules governing the recognition of foreign decrees are summarised at 4–12 above.)

(2) The English court must have jurisdiction based on

   (a) the domicile of either party in England and Wales; or

   (b) the habitual residence of either party for one year in England and Wales; or

   (c) the fact that either party has a beneficial interest in a dwelling-house in England and Wales which has at some time been a matrimonial home of the parties.[23]

Provided these conditions are satisfied, an application can be   **6–33**
made (though only with the leave of the court) for orders for financial provision, property adjustment and an order for the sale of the property.[24]

THE STATUTORY CRITERIA   **6–34**

Section 25 of the M.C.A. 1973 (as amended by the M.F.P.A. 1984, and section 25A of the M.C.A. 1973, inserted by

---

[21] These powers are normally exercised only by the High Court; see *Practice Direction* [1988] 1 W.L.R. 560.
[22] M.F.P.A. 1984, s.12.
[23] *Ibid.* s.15.
[24] *Ibid.* s.17.

M.F.P.A. 1984) sets out the matters to which the court is to have regard in exercising its powers to order financial provision and property adjustment. Strictly speaking these sections do not apply to applications for maintenance pending suit under section 22, although a number of the factors set out in section 25 would in practice be taken into account on such applications.[25] Since, however, decisions on maintenance pending suit are often made on the basis of limited information about the parties' resources, it would be impracticable to require all the section 25 and section 25A factors to be taken into account in such cases.

6–35 **(i) General criteria**

Section 25(1) requires the court to consider "all the circumstances of the case" in exercising its powers under sections 23, 24 and 24A. This is so broad as to be meaningless, but as a "catch-all" phrase it is sometimes useful when the court wants to take into account a particular matter which is not expressly referred to elsewhere. More specifically, section 25(1) also requires the court to give "first consideration" to "the welfare while a minor of any child of the family who has not attained the age of 18." This provision (inserted by M.F.P.A. 1984) marks an increasing emphasis on the need to make proper provision for the children of the family. It suggests that the children should receive a higher proportion of the income available on divorce than was previously the case, and can even be read as requiring the court to calculate maintenance for the children before maintenance for a spouse.

6–36 Two further points should be emphasised concerning the reference to the children's welfare in section 25(1). First, the reference is to "children of the family," so such children are presumably to take priority over other children who may be involved in the case—for example, the children of another woman with whom the husband is now living.

Secondly, section 25(1) does not provide that the children's welfare is a *paramount* consideration as is the case in custody disputes. This means that when making orders for a party to the marriage the court must ultimately be concerned to do justice between the parties, even if this is not necessarily the best solution from the children's point of view. In particular, there are other factors in section 25 and section 25A (discussed below) which are designed to encourage *the parties*

---

[25] See *Peacock* v. *Peacock* [1984] 1 W.L.R. 532.

to become financially independent of each other as soon as is reasonably possible after divorce.[26]

(ii) Criteria relevant to parties   **6–37**
Section 25(2) sets out a list of matters which the court must consider when making orders under sections 23, 24 and 24A in favour of a party to the marriage. It is not intended to be an exhaustive list, but it covers most of the matters that are likely to be relevant. Each paragraph of section 25(2) is listed and discussed below.

The income, earning capacity, property and other financial resources   **6–38**
of the parties (section 25(2)(a))

Income: The parties' income is obviously a relevant factor in every case. Everybody has income of some kind, though, in practice one of the most common problems lies in finding out exactly how much. (More will be said about this in Chapter 10.) Income is always relevant in assessing the amount of maintenance that one party should pay and the other should receive, but it may also be relevant in making capital and property orders. There is, for example, no point in ordering the husband to transfer the matrimonial home to the wife if she will be unable to pay for its upkeep.

Earning capacity: Earning capacity is much less likely to be   **6–39**
relevant. The question of whether this should be taken into account arises most commonly in the case of the wife who is not working, or not working full-time. The attitude of registrars to this varies widely, but in general a woman with young children to look after would not be expected to go out to work. In any case, earning capacity is by definition, a hypothetical matter, and is only likely to affect the amount of an order in those rare cases where the court considers that a party is blatantly avoiding work.

When earning capacity is taken into account, it is more likely   **6–40**
to affect the term for which periodical payments are ordered than the amount. This is reinforced by the fact that section 25(2) requires the court to consider any increase in earning capacity which it would be reasonable to expect a party to acquire in future. This may prompt the court to consider whether, for example, a wife should be awarded periodical payments for a limited term only, after which she could be expected to have obtained a qualification and become

---

[26] Though sometimes a "clean break" between parents will be in the best interests of the children by putting an end to protracted and bitter disputes about maintenance; see *S. v. S.* [1986] 1 F.L.R. 492.

financially independent. If the parties agree to such a provision this may prove satisfactory, but, in the absence of agreement, there is rarely any point in limiting the term of periodical payments in the expectation of an increase in earnings. This is usually best left to be dealt with by an application to vary the order when circumstances change. (Limited term maintenance orders are considered in more detail at 6–24, below.)

6–41 As with income, earning capacity may be relevant in assessing capital property orders as well as maintenance. In *Mitchell* v. *Mitchell*[27] for example, the Court of Appeal took account of the fact that the wife would be able to earn more when the children had grown up, in deciding to increase the husband's eventual share of the sale proceeds of the matrimonial home. Although this would give the wife less capital with which to buy a new home, her increased earning capacity would allow her to take out a mortgage with which to finance the purchase.

6–42 *Property*: The reference to "property" in section 25(2)(a) has been broadly construed by the courts, so that any property which either party owns may be taken into account. It is irrelevant that the property was not acquired as a "family asset" during the marriage. Thus, for example, in *Daubney* v. *Daubney*,[28] the Court of Appeal held that it was correct to take into account property which the wife had bought with a sum of damages awarded her as a result of a car accident. This indicates that the court will look at the reality of the parties' financial situation; if an asset is available to a party it should be considered, regardless of how that party came by it.

6–43 *Other resources*: The term "other financial resources" in section 25(2)(a) is designed to catch any other assets which might have escaped the preceding words, and gives the court a wide discretion to take into account a number of resources not mentioned earlier. For example:

6–44 *Benefits in kind*: It is common enough for a party to enjoy certain "perks" that go with his job, and the court will take these into account in comparing the parties' financial position. Company cars are an obvious example of this kind of benefit, as are free or subsidised meals, private health insurance, and cheap loans. However, almost any benefit might be considered, provided some monetary value can be attributed to

[27] [1984] 4 F.L.R. 387.
[28] [1976] Fam. 267.

it. In one case the court took into account the fact that the husband, a part-time butcher, received payment by way of £5 worth of meat each week.[29]

Income of other members of the household: A common source of **6–45** dispute is the extent to which the income of a husband's second wife should be considered in assessing what he should pay his first wife. The same problem may arise where the husband is cohabiting with another woman who has earnings of her own. The Court of Appeal has said in *Slater* v. *Slater*[30] that this income should not simply be added to the husband's, and the total treated as a joint fund out of which ·periodical payments can be made. On the other hand, the court also said that the other woman's income may be considered to the extent that it releases more of the husband's income to provide periodical payments for his first wife. This may seem at first sight to be a distinction without a difference, but this is not really so. If, for example, the husband had married a rich second wife and her income were simply added to his in calculating the maintenance payable to the first wife, the result might be that the husband would be ordered to pay all his income in maintenance. In practice the court would never do this. It would though be prepared to consider the second wife's income to the extent that she could provide for her own needs and thus release some of the husband's income for the payment of maintenance. However, any income of the second wife which exceeded the amount she could be expected to contribute to her own living expenses would be disregarded. A similar approach may be adopted to the income of other members of the household, such as older children who are in employment but are still living at home.[31]

Welfare benefits: Many parties, usually wives, have to claim **6–46** welfare benefits on the initial breakdown of their marriage, and the question then arises as to whether the court should take into account the availability of, for example, income support, in deciding how much the husband should be ordered to pay. In general, the courts will not allow the husband to case the burden of maintaining his wife and children on to the State, and, indeed, the D.S.S. can take steps to obtain contributions to the family's maintenance from a so-called "liable relative" (see 8–44 to 8–48, below).

[29] *Rodewald* v. *Rodewald* [1977] Fam. 192.
[30] [1982] 3 F.L.R. 364.
[31] See *Rodewald* v. *Rodewald* (above).

However, cases often arise in which it would clearly be impracticable to order a husband to pay his wife and children enough maintenance to take them off benefit completely. In such cases, the court must have regard to the fact that the wife can claim income support or other welfare benefits. This may be so, not just where the husband is poor,[32] but also, sometimes, where the husband has entered into new and reasonable commitments (for example, by remarriage) which leave him without enough money to support his former wife fully.[33]

One benefit which can always be taken into account is child benefit and, where available, the additional one-parent benefit.[34] These are not means-tested benefits and are payable to all those who have children to care for. (See 8–04 to 8–11, below for the details of these benefits.)

6–47 In deciding whether to take account of the availability of welfare benefits to the wife, the courts are also guided by the principle that the husband should not be depressed below what they call "subsistence level."[35] Indeed if he was, it is unlikely that he would obey the order anyhow, and problems of enforcement would inevitably arise. "Subsistence level" is often taken to be the amount which a person in the husband's position would receive by way of income support and housing benefits if he were eligible for them, but this cannot be treated as a universal definition. In some cases the courts have been prepared to leave the husband with more than this,[36] while, on the other hand, it was held in one case[37] that a man who was actually in receipt of what is now income support should still be required (for reasons of "public policy") to pay maintenance to his children.

6–48 Money available to a party under the terms of a discretionary trust can be taken into account as a resource in appropriate cases. This was recognised in *Browne* v. *Browne*,[38] in which the Court of Appeal accepted that it would be wrong to put pressure on discretionary trustees to make payments which they otherwise would not have made. However, the reality of the situation in this case was that the wife had access to the

---

[32] See, *e.g. Barnes* v. *Barnes* [1972] 2 All E.R. 872.
[33] See, *e.g. Stockford* v. *Stockford* [1982] 3 F.L.R. 58.
[34] See *Slater* v. *Slater* [1982] 3 F.L.R. 364.
[35] *Shallow* v. *Shallow* [1979] Fam. 1.
[36] *e.g. Stockford* v. *Stockford* (above).
[37] *Freeman* v. *Swatridge* [1984] F.L.R. 762.
[38] [1989] 1 F.L.R. 291.

trust funds whenever she liked and indeed had effective control over them. The court therefore upheld the judge's decision that the wife should be ordered to pay a lump sum of £175,000 to the husband. Much depends, however, on the purpose underlying the trust. In *J. v. J. (C intervening)*[39] the Court of Appeal, while accepting that two children's interests under their mother's will trust were relevant resources within section 25, held that, as the fund had not been established to provide for the children's maintenance, it would be wrong to treat the whole of the income from the fund as being available to the children. Their father could not, therefore, be allowed to treat the fund as a windfall absolving him from paying increased periodical payments for their benefit.

Future prospects: Section 25(2)(*a*) requires the court to **6-49** consider not only the resources which the parties currently have, but also those which they are "likely to have in the foreseeable future." In general, however, the courts will not take prospective assets into account unless the prospect of their receipt is certain, and their size can be accurately predicted at the time of the hearing. So, for example, in *Calder v. Calder*,[40] the husband's entitlement under a family settlement, when the present tenant for life died, was considered a relevant factor in deciding the size of a lump sum payment to the wife. Usually prospects of an inheritance will be too uncertain to merit consideration, however,[41] and the courts will not require a third party to disclose his testamentary intentions in advance.[42] The best tactic to adopt where it is thought that the other party will be much better off in the future, is to make an application for a lump sum or property transfer, but to ask for the hearing of the application to be adjourned generally, until the assets have been received. This was allowed in *Hardy v. Hardy*,[43] where a husband stood to gain a large inheritance when his father died. It has also been used by wives whose husbands were likely to be paid a lump sum on retirement.[44] However, the court will grant an adjournment only if the assets will be received in the reasonably foreseeable future[45] and it may be that, with the

---

[39] [1989] Fam.Law. 270.
[40] (1976) 6 Fam.Law. 242, C.A.
[41] See *Michael v. Michael* (1986) 130 S.J. 713.
[42] *Morgan v. Morgan* [1977] Fam. 122.
[43] [1981] 2 F.L.R. 321.
[44] *e.g. Priest v. Priest* [1980] 1 F.L.R. 189.
[45] See, *e.g. Roberts v. Roberts* [1986] 2 All E.R. 483, in which the judge said that the longest period for granting such an application would be between four and five years.

increased emphasis on encouraging early financial independence for each party, adjournments of this kind will become harder to obtain.

6–50 One contingency with which the courts will not concern themselves is the prospective remarriage of either party.[46] It would obviously be offensive and unjust if, for example, the court were to attempt to assess a wife's general prospects of remarriage in deciding what orders to make in her favour. In any case, as we have already seen, any periodical payments awarded to a party cease on remarriage, so the question could be relevant only to capital provision. Here two qualifications need to be made. First, although the court cannot be asked to assess prospects of remarriage, it may be prudent for the parties themselves to consider the matter in deciding what offers to make and to accept. A husband, for instance, would sometimes be well advised to bear in mind the fact that any maintenance paid to the wife will cease on remarriage, whereas lump sum payments and property transfers are normally irrevocable.[47] Secondly, a distinction can be drawn between prospects of remarriage in the hypothetical sense and those situations where there is a settled intention to remarry. Such an intention must be disclosed to the other party and to the court,[48] and might well affect the order which the court would then make.

6–51 *The financial needs, obligations and responsibilities which each of the parties has or is likely to have in the foreseeable future (section 25(2)(b))*

This paragraph, like the previous one, refers to matters which must be relevant in every case. In particular, the need for a home is often one of the most decisive factors in allocating the available resources between the parties. This is especially true were there young children still to be brought up, so that priority must be given to providing a home for the custodial parent.

6–52 Similarly all parties have obligations and responsibilities. Obviously commitments such as mortgage or rent payments, food, fuel and telephone bills, and loan instalments, have to be taken into account, although it is common to hear arguments about whether the size of such commitments is reasonable. Usually arguments about the size of essential

---

[46] See, *e.g. Wachtel* v. *Wachtel* [1973] Fam. 72 at p. 96.
[47] See 12–20, below.
[48] *Livesey* v. *Jenkins* [1985] A.C. 424.

outgoings are pointless, however, unless one party is obviously wasting money. Indeed, even when an item cannot properly be described as essential (*e.g.* television and video rental) it will normally be taken into account if a party has already committed himself to paying for it.

One of the responsibilities which causes the bitterest **6–53** arguments is that of a husband for another woman, and, perhaps, for that woman's children too. However, it is well established that a man's responsibilities to a second wife, or to a woman with whom he is now living, must be given as much weight as his other responsibilities, and it is not open to the first wife to demand that she be given priority over the second.[49] Where there is too little money to go round both households, the court may have to take into account the fact that income support is often available to the first wife, but not to the husband's new family.

The standard of living enjoyed by the family before the breakdown of **6–54**
the marriage (section 25(2)(c))

In the majority of cases it is impossible to preserve the parties' former standard of living, because, although the parties' resources will remain roughly the same, those resources will now be needed to support two households. The court will, however, try to ensure that no great disparity of standards arises between the two households. Both parties may be worse off, but, in theory, each should be worse off to a similar extent.

The age of the parties and the duration of the marriage (section **6–55**
25(2)(d))

The age of the parties may seem relevant to many of the decisions that have to be made. For example, the amount and duration of any periodical payments, or the question of whether the matrimonial home should be preserved for the occupation of one of the parties. However, in most cases, the court is really more influenced by the needs rather than the age of the parties. For example, a young working wife does not need to be compensated for loss of prospective life insurance benefits; she may not need substantial or any periodical payments, and she may not need the former matrimonial home to live in, because she can afford to take out a mortgage of her own. On the other hand, a middle-aged wife who has not worked for many years may need all of these things.

[49] See *Barnes* v. *Barnes* [1972] 1 W.L.R. 1381.

6–56 Similarly, the duration of the marriage, although an apparently important factor, is usually not one to which the court needs to give much specific attention. If the marriage has lasted many years there will probably be more assets available for distribution than in the case of a short marriage, and very often the parties will have made both financial and non-financial contributions to the marriage which the court will feel should be reflected in the orders it makes.

6–57 In fact, despite the wording of section 25(2)(*d*), it is the duration of cohabitation within marriage which is relevant, rather than the duration of the marriage itself. The courts attach little weight to the fact that a marriage lasted several years if the parties lived apart for most of that time.[50] On the other hand, cohabitation outside marriage will not be considered under this heading. This was established by the Court of Appeal in *Foley* v. *Foley*[51] in upholding a judge's refusal to take into account under this paragraph the fact that a marriage, which had lasted five years, had been preceded by a period of seven years' cohabitation. However, as the Court of Appeal also pointed out, pre-marital cohabitation may sometimes be considered relevant as one of the "circumstances of the case" referred to in section 25(1). This has been done where, for example, the parties were unable to marry for many years, but together built up a business during a long relationship which ended soon after they were married.[52]

6–58 *Any physical or mental disability of either of the parties to the marriage (section 25(2)(e))*

This is obviously a factor which will be relevant only in a minority of cases. Again, disabilities are likely to increase the financial needs of the sufferer, and so would also be considered under section 25(2)(*b*), above.

6–59 *The contributions which each of the parties has made or is likely in the foreseeable future to make to the welfare of the family, including any contribution by looking after the home or caring for the family (section 25(2)(f))*

The value of this paragraph lies in the fact that it allows the court to take into account non-financial contributions by a party, in considering how to exercise its powers to make financial provision and property adjustment orders. In the

---

[50] As happened in, *e.g. Taylor* v. *Taylor* (1974) 119 S.J. 30.
[51] [1981] Fam. 160.
[52] *Kokosinski* v. *Kokosinski* [1980] Fam. 72.

days when the courts' powers were limited to declaring the existing property rights of the parties in matrimonial property, only contributions to which some monetary value could be attributed were taken into account. Nowadays, however, the courts have jurisdiction to adjust existing property rights and, in doing this, can, by virtue of this paragraph, take into account the fact that, for example, a wife devoted herself to bringing up the children instead of following a career outside the home.

The conduct of each of the parties, if that conduct is such that it   **6–60**
would in the opinion of the court be inequitable to disregard it
(section 25(2)(g))

The question of whether a party's conduct, or, more accurately, misconduct, should have any bearing on the orders the court makes, is one which has been vigorously debated. In fact the courts very rarely do take conduct into account, and, even when they do, could usually have reached the same conclusion by reliance on other factors in section 25(2). Where conduct has been treated as relevant, it has usually been because one party's conduct could be clearly seen to be a great deal worse than the other's, or because the conduct has had a direct effect on the financial resources of the parties.

Thus, to take an example of the first type of case, in *West* v. *West*[53] the court took into account a wife's refusal to live with her husband, apparently for no good reason, in fixing her periodical payments at a lower level than she might otherwise have received.

Examples of cases in which a spouse's conduct has affected the parties' financial position, and therefore been relevant, are *Martin* v. *Martin*,[54] in which the husband dissipated some £33,000 worth of capital in unsuccessful business ventures during the marriage, and *Jones* v. *Jones*,[55] where a husband permanently impaired his wife's earning capacity as a nurse by injuring her hand in a knife attack. This latter case is also notable for the fact that the attack occurred after the dissolution of the marriage, but was still held to be a relevant factor.

All of these cases were decided before the M.F.P.A. 1984   **6–61**
inserted section 25(2)(g) in the M.C.A. 1973, and at a time when the test normally applied was whether the conduct was

[53] [1978] Fam. 1.
[54] [1976] Fam. 335.
[55] [1976] Fam. 8.

so "obvious and gross" as to demand consideration.[56] However the introduction of the present test was probably not intended to bring about any change in the courts' attitude to allegations of misconduct in ancillary proceedings.

6–62 Any doubt on this point could have been dispelled conclusively by the Court of Appeal in *Kyte* v. *Kyte*,[57] but in fact the opportunity was lost. Indeed, if anything, the court created doubts about the matter, because Purchas L.J., referring to the present wording, said: "It may be that the words ... give a broader discretion than that available under the pre-existing law." It is unlikely, however, that this heralds any significant alteration to the court's attitude to allegations of misconduct. What Purchas L.J. said was clearly *obiter*, because he took the view that in this case the wife's behaviour should be taken into account on any test. During the marriage Mr. Kyte had displayed suicidal tendencies, and Mrs. Kyte, who had started having an affair with another man, did nothing to dissuade him. Indeed on one occasion when her husband telephoned her from work to say that he wanted to commit suicide, she duly arrived at his office bearing alcohol and tablets. When her husband then changed his mind, Mrs. Kyte told him: "I knew you had no guts." The Court of Appeal accepted that a proper approach to such cases is to ask: "Would a right-thinking man or woman say that the conduct was such as to extinguish or reduce the applicant's entitlement?" On the facts of this case, the court held that the judge's award of a lump sum to the wife of £14,000 should be reduced to £5,000.

6–63 One unusual example of a case in which conduct was treated as relevant is *B.* v. *B.*[58] The conduct which was considered relevant in this case was the wife's persistent failure to make full and frank disclosure of her means in the ancillary proceedings. The judge accepted that this was conduct which it would be inequitable to disregard in assessing the amount of the lump sum award. Unfortunately, however, it is impossible to tell what discount the judge made for the wife's conduct in this case, as the judge made no reference to a specific figure and the wife was awarded a lump sum of £35,000. Nevertheless, the case provides additional ammunition for practitioners wanting to extract accurate information about means from recalcitrant spouses.

[56] A test adopted by the Court of Appeal in *Wachtel* v. *Wachtel* [1973] Fam. 72.
[57] [1988] Fam. 145.
[58] [1988] 2 F.L.R. 490.

It should be noted that section 25(1)(*g*) does not in terms refer **6–64** to "misconduct" at all, so that the paragraph may sometimes be invoked as a convenient "catch-all" provision under which almost any kind of behaviour could be taken into account. Thus, for example, in *Atkinson* v. *Atkinson*,[59] which was a variation application, the Court of Appeal held that although a wife's settled cohabitation with another man was not to be equated with remarriage (which would automatically have brought her periodical payments to an end) it was conduct which should be considered under section 25(*g*).

In some cases, the court has been influenced by the fact that **6–65** no allegations of misconduct were made against the other spouse. This does create a danger of conduct being seen as relevant in cases where no counter-allegations are made, and, if this attitude gained currency, such allegations would increase and result in more contested ancillary proceedings and, perhaps, more defended divorce proceedings. At present, however, there are no signs of such a trend developing. One powerful reason for this is that ancillary proceedings involving "substantial contested allegations of conduct" may be transferred from the county court to the High Court, thus greatly increasing both the length and cost of the proceedings.[60]

In the case of divorce or nullity proceedings, the value to each of the **6–66** *parties of any benefit (for example, a pension) which, by reason of the dissolution or annulment, that party will lose the chance of acquiring (section 25(2)(h))*

This factor does not apply to proceedings for judicial separation, as such proceedings do not terminate the marriage.

Section 25(2)(*g*), by referring to pension rights, provides a good example of the kind of loss which the courts should consider under this heading. Thus, for example, a respondent to a petition based on five years' separation who has unsuccessfully defended the petition on the basis of grave financial hardship under section 5 of the M.C.A. 1973, can still ask the court for compensation for the loss of prospective pension rights, as, of course, can any party who can show that the loss of such rights will prejudice their financial position after divorce. Under this heading the court could also consider the loss of rights of inheritance which may result

[59] [1988] Fam. 93.
[60] See M.F.P.A. 1984, s.39 and *Practice Direction* [1988] 1 W.L.R. 560.

from the divorce, as well as the loss of the chance of sharing in assets which the other party is expected to acquire in future. However, as we have already seen in 6–49 (above), the courts will often refuse to speculate about contingencies like this.

6–67 **(iii) Criteria relevant to children**
We have already seen that section 25(1) of the M.C.A. 1973 requires the courts to give first consideration to the welfare of any children of the family in the general exercise of its powers under sections 23, 24 and 24A. However, section 25(3) also sets out more specific criteria to be considered when making financial provision and property adjustment orders, and orders for sale in favour of children, and section 25(4) adds some special criteria for those cases where such orders are sought against a party to the marriage who is not a parent of the child concerned. These criteria are summarised below, but do not call for further comment.

6–68 Section 25(3) requires the court to have regard to:

(a) the financial needs of the child;

(b) the income, earning capacity (if any), property and other financial resources of the child;

(c) any physical or mental disability of the child;

(d) the manner in which he was being and in which the parties expected him to be educated or trained;

(e) the considerations mentioned in relation to the parties to the marriage in section 25(2)(a), (b), (c) and (e), which are set out above (*i.e.* the parties' resources, needs, standard of living and any disability from which they suffer).

6–69 Section 25(4) requires the court to consider in addition:

(a) whether the party who is not a parent assumed any responsibility for the child's maintenance, and if so to what extent, on what basis and for how long;

(b) whether that party knew the child was not his or her own;

(c) the liability of any other person to maintain the child.

6–70 **(iv) The clean break**
One of the aims of the M.F.P.A. 1984 was to promote the idea of achieving as early an end as possible to one party's dependence on the other after a marriage has been dissolved

or annulled. The desirability of achieving what has come to be known as a "clean break" between the parties was emphasised by the House of Lords in *Minton* v. *Minton*[61] several years before the Act was passed, and the position has now been reached where it can be said that a clean break is to be favoured "wherever possible".[62]

The essence of a clean break is that, once the terms of the order have been fully complied with, there should be no provision capable of subsequent variation under section 31 of the M.C.A. 1973 (for which see Chapter 12, below). This means that: **6–71**

(i)   the only orders that are made must be of a capital nature, (*i.e.* lump sum and property adjustment orders);

(ii) any applications for periodical payments made by the parties for their own benefit must be dismissed outright, or any orders that are made must be expressed to last only for a precisely defined period of time, with no possibility of this period being extended;

(iii) any outstanding applications should be formally dismissed. If the break is to be truly "clean," both parties should apply for all forms of relief and, in so far as they are not granted, the applications should be dismissed.

Additionally:

(iv) advantage should be taken of section 15 of the Inheritance (Provision for Family and Dependants) Act 1975. This allows the court to prohibit future applications for provision out of the estate of a deceased former spouse.

The statutory provisions designed to promote a clean break are contained in section 25A of the M.C.A. 1973 (inserted by the M.F.P.A. 1984) and are summarised below. It must be emphasised, however, that these provisions have no bearing on orders made in favour of children. The fact that children are involved does not preclude a clean break between the parties, at least as regards finance and property,[63] but as orders for financial provision in favour of children can be   **6–72**

---

[61] [1979] A.C. 593.
[62] See *Harman* v. *Glencross* [1986] Fam. 81, *per* Balcombe L.J.
[63] See, *e.g. Suter* v. *Suter* [1987] 3 W.L.R. 9.

made "from time to time"[64] there can never be a final dismissal of their claims for such provision.

6–73 Section 25A(1) of the M.C.A. 1973 imposes on the court in divorce and nullity cases a general duty to consider whether to exercise its powers under sections 23, 24 and 24A so as to end the parties' financial obligations to each other, as soon after the decree as is just and reasonable.

Of course, there will be many cases where a clean break would not be just and reasonable, but the court (and practitioners) should always consider the matter to avoid missing the case where it is an appropriate solution.

6–74 Similarly, section 25A(2), already considered in 6–19 (above), requires the court to consider limiting the term of any periodical payments order to a party, although, again, this will often not be an appropriate order to make. In *Barrett* v. *Barrett*[65] the Court of Appeal emphasised that this provision does not create any presumption in favour of limited term maintenance which the wife has to rebut. In this case the court held that a judge had been wrong to limit periodical payments for a wife in her forties to a four-year term, in the absence of clear evidence that she could adjust without hardship to the termination of the payments.

6–75 Section 25A(3) confers on the court in divorce and nullity cases a power to dismiss outright a party's application for periodical payments, if the court considers that no continuing obligation should be imposed on one party to make payments to the other.

When it dismisses the application, the court may direct that the applicant shall not be entitled to make any further applications for periodical payments. Although the point has not yet been settled, it may be that, if the application were dismissed without this further direction, it would remain open to the applicant to seek an order in the future. What is clear from section 25A(3), however, is that there is no need for the applicant to have consented to the dismissal of the claim, although the courts are often reluctant to impose a clean break in the absence of consent.

6–76 This reluctance can be seen in a number of cases decided since the 1984 Act was passed. For example, in *Whiting* v. *Whiting*[66] the parties had been divorced in 1975 and the

---

[64] M.C.A. 1973, s.23(4).
[65] [1988] 2 F.L.R. 516.
[66] [1988] 1 W.L.R. 565.

husband had paid the wife maintenance while she qualified as a teacher. By 1979 the wife had become financially independent and the order was reduced to a nominal 5p. a year. Subsequently the husband was made redundant, and his income now amounted to about £4,500 a year. The wife, on the other hand, earned £10,500 as a teacher. Accordingly, the husband now sought the complete discharge of the order. The Court of Appeal, however, upheld (by a 2–1 majority) the judge's refusal to do this. The decision of the majority was based on their reluctance to interfere with the way in which the judge exercised her discretion. The judge had considered that the wife was entitled to a nominal order as a "last backstop" against a future change in her fortunes. Balcombe L.J. dissented strongly, however. He took the view that to adopt the judge's approach would be to negate entirely the clean break principle. Nevertheless, in *Hepburn* v. *Hepburn*[67] the Court of Appeal again declined to interfere with a judge's refusal to impose a clean break in circumstances in which one might have expected it. This case, like the previous one, was an application to vary periodical payments in favour of a wife. The parties had been divorced in 1980 and soon afterwards another man had moved in to live with the wife, and indeed they remained living together as husband and wife. The wife now sought an increase in her periodical payments, while the husband sought their discharge on the ground (*inter alia*) of the wife's long-term cohabitation. The judge, however, refused to discharge the order completely and made a nominal order in favour of the wife. It was this decision with which the Court of Appeal refused to interfere.

There have, however, been cases in which the court has been **6–77** prepared to impose a clean break against the wishes of the applicant. One example is provided by the case of *Seaton* v. *Seaton*.[68] Here the Court of Appeal upheld a judge's dismissal, without consent, of a husband's application for periodical payments. After a marriage of 14 years the husband, aged 42, had no capital or earning capacity, having suffered a disabling stroke. He lived with his elderly parents and received a disability pension. The wife, on the other hand, was aged 36, worked as a teacher and lived with the co-respondent. The Court of Appeal accepted that the wife should not be ordered to pay the husband anything, as his needs were already reasonably satisfied. This was clearly an unusual case,

---

[67] [1989] 1 F.L.R. 373.
[68] (1986) 16 Fam. Law 267.

however, and it is interesting to speculate whether the result would have been the same had the parties' positions been reversed.

6–78 Another case in which a clean break may be an appropriate solution is that in which the husband is on a low income and the wife is already in receipt of state benefits, so that anything the husband pays the wife below her benefit entitlement will make no difference to her income. It is a well-established principle that the courts will not allow a husband to pass his maintenance responsibilities on to the state. In *Ashley* v. *Blackman*,[69] however, the judge accepted that in low-income cases it may well not be appropriate to insist on the husband continuing to make maintenance payments, and a clean break may be imposed.

THE COURTS' USE OF THEIR POWERS

6–79 **(i) Introduction**
Although the section 25 guidelines do include most of the matters which the courts would want to consider in most cases, they do not provide any ready guide to the actual calculation and assessment of maintenance and property orders. The courts are really more concerned with figures than events when, for example, they have to decide how much maintenance a wife and children should receive each week. Not surprisingly, then, the courts have devised for themselves ways of calculating maintenance and capital orders which, while taking account of the section 25 factors, do provide a standardised method of deciding the appropriate order in many of the routine cases which are being heard every day.

6–80 In this section these methods are outlined, first in relation to maintenance, and then in relation to capital and property orders. It must be appreciated at the outset, however, that, in practice, maintenance and capital cannot normally be considered in isolation from each other. Very often the court has got to arrange a "package deal" which is fair to both sides. So, for example, if a clean break order is being made, in which the wife is to receive no maintenance, it might well be appropriate to give her a larger lump sum, or a more generous property adjustment order than could be expected by a wife who was to continue receiving periodical payments. Also, in cases where the court has to decide what is to

[69] [1988] Fam. 85.

happen to the matrimonial home, it will sometimes be sensible to make this decision first, and then calculate the appropriate maintenance orders in the light of it. For example, the court may be able to calculate what a wife needs by way of periodical payments only after it has decided whether she is to remain living in the former matrimonial home.

(ii) Assessing maintenance

The one-third starting point for parties   **6–81**

Initially the courts, guided by Lord Denning's judgment in *Wachtel* v. *Wachtel*,[70] adopted the "one-third rule" as a guide to assessing maintenance for a party. The object of this is to give the wife periodical payments which will bring her income up to one-third of the parties' joint incomes.

Example

	£
Henry's gross income:	24,000 p.a.
Wendy's gross income:	6,000 p.a.
Total	30,000 p.a.

$\frac{£30,000}{3}$ = £10,000; so Wendy needs £10,000−£6,000=£4,000 p.a. by way of periodical payments to give her one-third of the parties' joint incomes.

Although subsequent attempts were made to make the test **6–82** more sophisticated, by, for example, allowing deductions for National Insurance contributions and the cost of travel to work, the "one-third rule" remained a fairly blunt instrument for assessing maintenance, and it gradually became discredited, largely because (contrary to what was ever intended) it was often used mechanically, without enough consideration for whether the results it produced were really appropriate for the circumstances of the particular case. Despite this, it remains a possible starting point in calculating periodical payments in cases where no other figure is available. However, as a result of the changes in the income tax treatment of maintenance payments introduced in 1988, which leave maintenance untaxed in the hands of the recipient and give only very limited tax relief to the payer, a one-third calculation based on the parties' gross incomes is unlikely to

[70] [1973] Fam. 72.

produce a realistic starting-point. A one-third calculation based on the parties' incomes *net* of income tax will produce a more reliable guide to an appropriate order. However, a more detailed net-effect calculation will still have to be made in many cases (see paragraphs 6–86 to 6–94 below).

6–83 *A starting point for children?*

The courts have never suggested a simple starting-point for assessing child maintenance comparable with the one-third starting point sometimes used for parties. Many courts will consider as a guide the personal allowances prescribed by the D.S.S. for income support purposes as the weekly require-ments of children of various ages. Provided his resources permit it, a father would normally be ordered to pay to his children an amount of maintenance at least equal to these allowances. The amounts prescribed as the normal require-ments for 1990–1991 are as follows:

Age	Weekly amount
under 11	£12.35
11–15	£18.25
16–17	£21.90
18 or over	£28.80

6–84 However, these amounts are obviously not generous, and, in view of the requirement in section 25(1) of the M.C.A. 1973, that the welfare of the children of the family must be the court's first consideration, most registrars and judges will want to order higher amounts than this where possible. An alternative and more generous guide is provided by the figures published annually by the National Foster Care Association (N.F.C.A.) as the minimum amounts recom-mended for payment by local authorities to foster parents. The recommendations for 1990–1991 are as follows:

Age	Weekly amount
0–4	£38.22
5–7	£44.59
8–10	£48.79
11–12	£53.06
13–15	£57.26
16–18	£76.37

(In the Greater London area these figures are increased by 15 per cent.)

Although these figures are intended to reflect the real cost of **6–85** bringing up children, the courts would not normally make orders as high as this. At the very least, deduction would be made for child benefit which is payable for all children, regardless of the custodial parent's means, but which is not paid to foster parents. Furthermore, the N.F.C.A. figures include an allowance towards household expenses, which a court might already have taken into account in assessing periodical payments to the custodial parent. In practice, a figure somewhere between the income support rate and the N.F.C.A. guideline will often produce an appropriate starting point.

The net effect approach **6–86**

The "one-third rule" was expressly disapproved of by the Court of Appeal in two cases in 1981, *Furniss* v. *Furniss*[71] and *Stockford* v. *Stockford*.[72] In these cases the court stressed the need to calculate the precise effect on both parties' finances of any proposed order. The essence of this "net effect approach" is to see how much money each party will actually have to live on, each week or each month, if a particular order is made. There are various ways of working this out, and some courts have adopted their own "net effect calculators" for use by practitioners in those courts. Any net-effect calculation must, however, entail taking the following five steps:

(1) Fix a proposed order to work with. This could be the **6–87** amount which the husband is offering to pay as part of the negotiations, or the amount which he is already paying voluntarily. Alternatively the one-third (of net incomes) starting point might be used. If there are children, proposed orders will have to be fixed for them too, on the lines suggested above.

(2) Calculate the gross incomes of both sides. The amount of the proposed maintenance orders should be included in the figures for the wife's household. In some cases it may be appropriate to include the income of third parties, such as a husband's second wife, or older children in employment.

(3) Calculate the net incomes of both sides. At this stage the income tax liability of each side must be calculated and National Insurance and pension contributions should also be deducted.

[71] [1981] 3 F.L.R. 46.
[72] [1982] 3 F.L.R. 58.

(4) Deduct all reasonable and necessary outgoings from each side's net income. This obviously includes housing costs, fuel bills, loan commitments and the cost of travel to work. The cost of the proposed maintenance orders should also be deducted from the husband's income. It may be better not to attempt deductions for items such as food and clothing, since these can vary widely from month to month between different families.

(5) Compare the net spendable income which remains to both sides for all other items—including food and clothes. Is there a wide disparity, bearing in mind the size of each party's household? If the proposed orders have produced an unacceptable disparity between the incomes of each side, new proposed orders must be taken and the whole process repeated.

6–88 By following these steps practitioners and the courts should be able to arrive at appropriate figures which will make adequate provision for the recipient and will not cripple the payer financially. The calculation does assume, however, that there is enough money available to be divided between the parties. There is generally no point in using this method unless the combined income of the parties is at least £12,000–£15,000 a year. Below this the court will often be compelled to take into account the availability of welfare benefits for one or both parties.

6–89 *Example of a net-effect calculation*

In this example of how a simple net-effect calculation might work, James has left his ex-wife, Susan, living in the former matrimonial home with one child of the family, Tom aged 11. James has married another woman who has one child, Linda, aged 9, but no income of her own. Linda's natural father is unemployed, and does not contribute to her maintenance. James' family receives ordinary child benefit (£7.25 per week per child). Susan's family also receives this, but in addition is entitled to one-parent benefit (£5.60 per week for the first child), hence the difference in the figures included as "Child Benefit." Susan has a part-time job and will pay the mortgage and other outgoings on her home. James is living in rented accommodation.

6–90 The proposed orders used in the calculation are reached in the following way:

1. James offers to pay Susan maintenance for herself of £1200 p.a.

2. Tom's maintenance is assessed at £35 per week, being roughly half-way between the D.S.S. and N.F.C.A. guidelines set out at 6–83 and 6–84, above. This gives an annual figure of approximately £1,800 proposed maintenance.

The income tax liability of each party must be calculated first, **6–91** so that the effect of the proposed orders on their *net* incomes can be assessed. The income tax treatment of maintenance payments is considered in detail in Chapter 7.

TAX MODEL

(The tax rate and allowances used in this calculation are those for the tax year 1990−1991.)

HUSBAND			WIFE		
		£			£
Statutory Income:		24,000	Statutory Income:		6,000
		24,000			6,000
Less:	£		Less:	£	
Mortgage:	—		Mortgage: (Interest relief at source)		
Pension:	1,200		Pension:	Nil	
Less maximum-qualifying maintenance payment:	1,720				
Less personal allowance:	4,725	7,645	Less personal allowance:	4,725	4,725
Taxable Income		16,355	Taxable Income		1,275
Tax at 25% =		4,088	Tax at 25% =		318

147

6–92

EFFECT OF PROPOSED ORDER

Proposed order for wife = £1,200 (p.a.)
Proposed order for child = 1,800 (p.a.)

	Husband's Family		Wife's Family	
	No. of adults: 2 No. of children: 1		No. of adults: 1 No. of children: 1	
GROSS INCOME		£		£
Earnings		24,000		6,000
Child Benefit		377		668
Maintenance for self				1,200
Maintenance for child				1,800
		24,377		9,668
NET INCOME	£		£	
Tax (see model)	4,088		318	
N.I.	1,638		540	
Pension	1,200			
		6,926		858
		17,451		8,810
OUTGOINGS				
Mortgage/Rent and Community Charge	3,500		2,500	
Fuel	600		500	
HP/Loans	500		300	
Maintenance for wife	1,200			
Maintenance for children	1,800			
Travel to work	600		300	
		8,200		3,600
		9,251		5,210
Approximate net spendable income for food, clothes, etc.		per month £770		per month £434

6–93 *Conclusions*

The net-effect calculation suggests that the proposed orders are not correct in the circumstances. The husband's family is, of course, left with substantially more net spendable income per month, but his family consists of two adults plus a child, while the wife is a lone parent. To test whether the discrepancy between the two families is reasonable, deduct from both sides the amount allowed for the maintenance of the children. Taking this to be £150 per month for each child (they are of similar ages), this leaves the husband's family with spendable income of £620, which, divided by two, gives £310 for each adult. Deducting the same amount from the wife's spendable income leaves her with £284. In view of this it would probably be argued that she should receive a rather higher amount than that proposed, and, if so, the calculation would have to be repeated using a higher figure.

It should be noted that, in any order embodying these figures, care should be taken to express the maintenance for the child, Tom, as being payable to Susan for his benefit and not to Tom direct. This will ensure that James gains the maximum tax relief available on the maintenance payments. (See Chapter 7 below for detail.) **6–94**

(iii) Assessing lump sum payments **6–95**
In *Wachtel* v. *Wachtel* Lord Denning suggested using the one-third starting point in relation to capital as well as income, and this suggestion was followed in subsequent cases.[73] It is, however, open to a similar objection to that already raised in maintenance cases, namely that it is liable to produce an unjust result if applied mechanically, without enough regard for the actual resources and requirements of the parties. This has led the Court of Appeal, in some of the later cases, to emphasise the importance of the statutory criteria in section 25 of the M.C.A. 1973, and, in particular, the need to balance one party's requirements against the other's ability to pay. Thus, for example, in *Potter* v. *Potter*[74] the Court of Appeal reduced a lump sum order from £23,900 to £10,000, because the judge, in using the one-third rule, had not sufficiently considered what the wife really needed to supplement her income, and what the husband could afford to pay. This case, like many of the reported cases concerning the assessment of a lump sum order, involved a husband who owned his own business, and in such cases the courts will normally wish to avoid ordering the husband to raise so much capital that he is forced to sell the business which represents his livelihood.

---

[73] *e.g.* *O'D.* v. *O'D.* [1976] Fam. 83. For a much later example, see *Bullock* v. *Bullock* [1986] 1 F.L.R. 372.
[74] [1982] 1 W.L.R. 1255.

6–96   In cases where the husband can afford to pay a very substantial amount of capital to the wife it will often be sensible to aim for a clean break order. This may involve first calculating what the wife might reasonably expect by way of periodical payments and then commuting those payments for a lump sum. The way in which this is done can vary, but, in general, it should not be assumed that the wife will simply live off the income from the lump sum; instead the capital should be gradually used up during her remaining lifetime. This in turn involves taking into account such variables as the wife's present age and life-expectancy, future rates of inflation and income tax, and the rates of income return and capital growth that can be assumed for the future. This approach was adopted, for example, in *Duxbury* v. *Duxbury*,[75] a case which has given its name to a particular form of the calculation required. Here the calculation resulted in the 45-year-old wife of a millionaire businessman receiving £540,000 to provide a net income of £28,000 per year.

6–97   It must be emphasised, however, that the appropriate level of income, and hence the lump sum required, will vary from case to case. In *B.* v. *B. (Financial Provision)*[76] a judge held that, while a *Duxbury* calculation is a useful tool in assessing a wife's needs, it must not supplant the wide discretion which the court exercises under section 25 of the M.C.A. 1973. This view was endorsed by the Court of Appeal in *Gojkovic* v. *Gojkovic*,[77] a case which is also significant for its emphasis on the fact that a lump sum awarded as part of a clean break order will sometimes have to do more than just provide for the reasonable maintenance of the wife. Here the wife had played an important part in building up the husband's hotel business, and now wanted to buy and run a small hotel of her own. The Court of Appeal upheld the award to the wife of £1 million on the ground that she should not merely receive what was reasonable for her maintenance. She was entitled to receive a share in the value of the business which (unlike Mrs. Duxbury) she had helped to build up, in order that she might now establish a business of her own.

6–98   Where the party who is seeking a lump sum is legally aided, it is also important to bear in mind the possible impact of the legal aid charge in assessing the amount to be paid. As pointed out at 2–27, lump sums up to £2,500 are exempt, but

---

[75] [1987] 1 F.L.R. 7.
[76] [1990] 1 F.L.R. 20.
[77] [1990] 1 F.L.R. 140.

the charge will bite on any surplus, and, of course, will do so immediately unless the money is to be used for the purchase of a home for the assisted party or his or her dependants. In some cases, if the costs have been high, it may be better to accept instead periodical payments (which are totally exempt).

(iv) Orders concerning the matrimonial home   6–99

The question of what is to be done with the former matrimonial home is often one of the most important and difficult questions the court has to deal with on marriage breakdown. However, a distinction must be drawn at the outset between those homes that have a capital value, and those that do not. Where the home is owned by one or both parties it will often have been regarded, not just as a shelter for the parties and their children, but also as a capital investment. This may well lead to a conflict between one party who wants to remain in the home, and the other who wants a sale and division of the proceeds. Where, on the other hand, the accommodation is rented, the question is simply one of deciding which, if either, party is to have the tenancy, and the courts' powers to decide this depend on the kind of tenancy involved. The possible solution to these problems will be considered in turn.

Homes with a capital value   6–100

There are three possible ways of dealing with homes that have a capital value

(i)   The home may be sold immediately and the proceeds divided between the parties.

(ii) The home may be made the subject of an order postponing sale until some future date.

(iii) The home may be transferred outright to one of the parties.

Immediate sale and division of the proceeds   6–101

This solution will often be appropriate where the parties have no children and both are working. Each party can receive a share of the equity and is then free to buy a new home of their own, probably with the aid of a new mortgage. An immediate sale will also sometimes be appropriate where the value of the house is such that it can be sold to provide each party with enough money to buy alternative accommodation.

There will be other situations in which a sale and division of the proceeds (not necessarily in equal shares) will be found appropriate. Now that the courts are under a duty to consider a clean break in every case, it is an option that should always be reviewed.

6–102 One special case in which an immediate sale and division of the proceeds will not be advisable is that in which the matrimonial home was formerly a council property, which had been bought by the parties from the local authority at a discount. Where such a home has been sold at a discount to the sitting tenants, and the home is then sold within three years of the purchase, a proportion of the discount must be repaid to the council.[78] This requirement does not apply to disposals made by virtue of an order under section 24 of the M.C.A. 1973, which are specifically exempted.[79] However, no such exemption exists in the case of an order for sale made under section 24A of the M.C.A., and in *R.* v. *Rushmoor Borough Council ex p. Barrett*[80] the Court of Appeal confirmed that in such circumstances a proportion of the discount will be repayable in the ordinary way. In this case the parties were divorced a year after buying their council home and by consent the court ordered that the house be sold and the proceeds divided equally between the parties. The local authority then successfully demanded repayment of 80 per cent. of the discount that had been allowed, which, in this case, meant that more than £10,000 had to be repaid. Clearly in cases such as this it would be preferable to make the house subject to an order for postponed sale so that the value of the discount is preserved, or perhaps alternatively, to obtain an order transferring the home outright to one party with a lump sum back to the other.

6–103 *Postponed sale*

An order which provides for the sale of the home to be postponed can take one of two forms. The home may either be made subject to a trust for sale, or to a charge in favour of the party out of occupation.

6–104 **Trust for sale.** This is the commoner of the two forms. The order provides that the property be transferred into the joint names of the parties, if it is not already jointly owned. It will

---

[78] Housing Act 1985, s.155(2), as amended by Housing and Planning Act 1986, s.2(3).
[79] Housing Act 1985, s.160(1)(*c*).
[80] [1989] Q.B. 60.

then provide that the parties are to hold the property on trust for sale, with sale postponed until whichever one of certain events first occurs; in the meantime one of the parties will be given sole rights of occupation in the home. The order must also provide for the sale and division of the proceeds when a "triggering" event occurs, and in particular must specify the proportion of the proceeds which each party is to receive.

This form of order is most frequently used where there are **6–105** children of the family living in the home, and provides a means of ensuring that the children have a secure home until they have grown up. In such cases the main "triggering" event may, therefore, be the date when the youngest child reaches a certain age (usually 17 or 18), or ceases full-time education if this happens earlier. Such orders are generally known as "Mesher orders" after the first reported case in which this device was used.[81]

Other events which may be included as "triggering" events, should they occur first, · are the death, remarriage or the voluntary departure of the party in occupation.

In some cases the order will contain no reference to the **6–106** children reaching a certain age—indeed there may be no children. In such cases the party in occupation, usually the wife, is in effect given a life interest in the house if she chooses to remain. This was done, for example, in *Martin* v. *Martin*[82] which, like *Mesher*, has given its name to this form of order. This might be appropriate where the husband is already adequately accommodated elsewhere, and so has no urgent need of capital, whereas an immediate sale would make the wife homeless, and, perhaps, leave her without enough capital to buy alternative accommodation.

The remarriage of the party in occupation is not always **6–107** included as a "triggering" event. It was not, for example, included in *Mesher* v. *Mesher* itself. Furthermore some registrars take the view that, to include the remarriage of the occupying spouse as a trigger for a sale, is contrary to the requirement that the children's welfare must be the first consideration in making orders for ancillary relief. It could lead to the children being turned out of the home on the custodial parent's remarriage, and possibly having to move into inadequate alternative accommodation. Nevertheless the party out of occupation may feel strongly that he should not

---

[81] *Mesher* v. *Mesher* (Note) [1980] 1 All E.R. 126 (decided in 1973).
[82] [1978] Fam. 12.

be kept out of his share of the capital if the other chooses to remarry, and, indeed a further clause is sometimes included to the effect that a sale shall take place if the wife cohabits with or becomes dependent on another man. Such clauses are probably best avoided, however, as they can easily lead to disputes as to whether their terms have been satisfied.

6–108 The voluntary departure of the party in occupation is normally included so that the home will be sold if, for example, the wife goes to live with another man or with relations, and leaves the house empty. In such circumstances it is clearly fair that the capital tied up in the home should be released. However, there will often be cases where the party in occupation wants to sell the home and buy another one somewhere else, perhaps for employment reasons or to be nearer relations. It may, therefore, be wise to provide in the order that the party in occupation shall be entitled, during the subsistence of the trust, to substitute an alternative property for the matrimonial home.

6–109 It will be appreciated that, where the sale of the home is not dependent on the children growing up, the party out of occupation may be kept out of his capital indefinitely. In *Harvey* v. *Harvey*[83] an attempt was made to compensate the husband for this by including in the order a provision that, when the children had grown up and the mortgage had been paid off, the wife should pay the husband an "occupation rent." This device does, however, give rise to several potential problems. Some of these are practical; for example, will the wife be able to pay the "rent" and how will the amount be fixed? Others are legal; for example, is the money taxable in the husband's hands and will the wife obtain security of tenure by the arrangement? Because of these problems such orders are rarely made.

6–110 **Deferred charge.** Under this form of postponed sale order, the home is transferred into the sole name of the occupying party, unless that party is already the sole legal owner. The party out of occupation is given a charge over the property representing their share of the capital, but this charge can be realised only when some "triggering" event occurs. The events specified will be of the same kind as these used in the trust for sale orders discussed previously. The court must decide on the size of the charge when making the order, but there are two ways of expressing this. The party out of

---

[83] [1982] Fam. 83.

occupation may be given a charge for a fixed proportion of the eventual net proceeds of sale,[84] or a charge for a fixed amount of money.[85] Normally that party will prefer the first arrangement, as this will allow him to benefit from house price inflation.

Where the charge is expressed to be for a proportion of the sale proceeds, the effect of this form of order is the same as where the home is made subject to a trust for sale. One factor that will decide which form of order should be made is the existing legal ownership. If the home is already in joint names, a trust for sale order will avoid the need for a fresh conveyance, whereas, if it is already in the sole name of the party who is to remain in occupation, creating a charge in favour of the other party will be simpler.

6–111

Outright transfer to one party

6–112

The main defect of both types of order postponing a sale, is that they provide only a temporary solution to the parties' housing problems. This is especially so in the case of the *Mesher* order, where the house has to be sold when the children have grown up. Such orders may cause unforeseen hardship if, for example, a middle-aged wife, with little or no earning capacity, finds herself forced to sell the home at a price which, after division of the proceeds, will leave her too little money to buy alternative accommodation.

This hardship can be avoided by giving the spouse in occupation the right to remain for life, but this, in turn, may cause hardship to the party out of occupation. Sometimes, therefore, a fairer solution will be to transfer the property to one spouse outright. It may be possible to compensate the party out of occupation by the award of a lump sum, which may be raised by a mortgage over the property. Additionally or alternatively, if the wife is to have the house, she may receive a reduced amount by way of periodical payments, or no periodical payments at all. However, the court will not normally order an outright transfer of the home to one party unless the other was adequate accommodation elsewhere. This does not necessarily mean that he should own other property. In *Hanlon* v. *Hanlon*,[86] for example, the matrimonial home was transferred to the wife absolutely, as the husband, a policeman, was living rent free in a police flat.

---

[84] See, *e.g. Browne* v. *Pritchard* [1975] 1 W.L.R. 1366.
[85] See, *e.g. Hector* v. *Hector* [1973] 1 W.L.R. 1122.
[86] [1978] 1 W.L.R. 592.

6–113   *Third-party interests*

An additional difficulty facing the court when making orders affecting ownership of the matrimonial home is the fact that third parties often have an interest in the outcome, and these third-party interests must be considered too. The third parties most likely to be involved are mortgagees of the property, other individuals claiming a beneficial interest in the property, and the creditors of one or both parties.

6–114   **Mortgagees.** Where the court orders an immediate sale of the property, the mortgagees can raise no objection. The only problem that may arise is that mortgage instalments are in arrears, but, as these will be paid off when the home is sold, the mortgagee will normally agree not to commence or pursue possession proceedings.

6–115   Where the court orders mortgaged property to be transferred from joint names into the sole name of one party, or where it orders a transfer from one party to the other, the mortgagee's consent will be required. The court has no power to compel the mortgagee to consent, nor can it release a party from the mortgage covenants. Orders can be made on the basis that a party will use his best endeavours to obtain the mortgagee's consent to the transfer and release, and, if this were not forthcoming, the terms of the order would have to be reconsidered. Clearly the best solution is to obtain the consents before the order is made. As a wife often has a relatively low income, the mortgagee may insist on someone else, for example, the husband, acting as a guarantor for the payment of the mortgage, if the house is to be transferred into the sole name of the wife.

6–116   **Other beneficial owners.** It is not unusual for someone besides the parties to the marriage to have contributed to the purchase of the home. One of the parties' parents may have paid the deposit, for example, or indeed may be sharing the accommodation and contributing to the mortgage. As mentioned at 6–30, above, where the court is contemplating an order for the sale of property in which a third party has a beneficial interest, the court must consider any representations that party makes. Furthermore, the Court of Appeal has held in *Tebbutt* v. *Haynes*[87] that, on an application under section 24 of the M.C.A. 1973, the court has got jurisdiction to determine the interests of third parties who have intervened

[87] [1981] 2 All E.R. 238.

in the suit. Thus, in this case, the court held that the judge had been entitled, on a section 24 application, to find that the entire beneficial ownership of a house, legally owned by the husband, was vested in the husband's aunt. This finding was not open to challenge by the wife in subsequent Chancery proceedings. The explanation for this decision is that a judge, faced with an application for the transfer of property, must be able to decide to whom the property really belongs before he makes an order.

Creditors. Difficult problems arise when, on the breakdown of   **6–117** the marriage, it emerges that the husband's creditors or his trustee in bankruptcy are claiming his share of the house. Even if the husband is not bankrupt, a creditor may have obtained judgment against him and been granted a charging order over the house as a means of enforcement. Such a creditor, or a trustee in bankruptcy, can seek an order for the sale of the home under section 30 of the L.P.A. 1925, under which "any person interested" may apply for an order compelling a sale of the property against the wishes of one or both trustees for sale (*e.g.* the parties to the marriage). The courts then have to decide between the competing claims of the creditors, who want their money, and the wife and children who need a home. Where the application is made by a trustee in bankruptcy, section 337(5) of the Insolvency Act 1986 provides that the court must make such order as it thinks just and reasonable, having regard to the interests of the bankrupt's creditors, to the conduct of the spouse or former spouse in contributing to the bankruptcy, to the needs and resources of the spouse or former spouse, to the needs of any children, and to all the circumstances of the case, other than the needs of the bankrupt. However, section 337(6) adds that, where the application is made a year or more after the bankruptcy, the court must assume that the interests of the creditors should prevail "unless the circumstances of the case are exceptional." Previous cases suggest that the courts will refuse to treat the predicament of a wife and children faced with eviction as "exceptional." In *Re Lowrie*,[88] for example, Walton J. described it as "a normal circumstance" and the "all too obvious result" of the way the husband had conducted his affairs. An example of an exceptional case (decided before the passing of the Insolvency Act) is *Re Holliday*,[89] where the Court of Appeal refused a sale, after the husband had

---

[88] [1981] 3 All E.R. 353.
[89] [1981] Ch. 405.

presented his own bankruptcy petition, apparently as a tactical move to avoid the wife's application for a transfer of property order.

6–118   Where, on the other hand, a wife has already started divorce proceedings, and applied for a property adjustment order before a creditor has sought a charging order over the home, the court is entitled to make the charging order subject to the outcome of the ancillary proceedings, and may then, in those proceedings, order the house to be transferred to the wife absolutely. This was done in *Harman* v. *Glencross*,[90] where the Court of Appeal held that the hardship that would be suffered by the wife if the house were sold, was an overwhelming factor which outweighed the creditor's interests. In many cases of this kind, however, it may be more equitable simply to postpone a sale while any children are being brought up in the home. This was done in *Austin-Fell* v. *Austin-Fell*,[91] a case in which *Harman* v. *Glencross* was distinguished, partly on the ground that in that case the judgment creditor had not asked the court to postpone enforcement of his charge.

6–119   A further difficulty is that section 39 of the M.C.A. 1973 provides that the fact that a transfer of property is made pursuant to an order under section 24, does not prevent its being treated as a transaction in respect of which an order under sections 339–340 of the Insolvency Act 1986 may be made. Under sections 339–340, certain transactions may be set aside if they were entered into at an undervalue by a bankrupt within five years prior to his bankruptcy. It would seem from this that a creditor might be able to take advantage of sections 339–340 by having the husband made bankrupt. In some cases, however, it could be argued that the transfer to the wife was not at an undervalue, if she had, for example, given up her claim for periodical payments in return for the house.

6–120   *The rented home*

Where the former matrimonial home is rented, the question of whether and how the tenancy can be transferred depends on the nature of the tenancy. Four categories must be distinguished. Contractual tenancies (which may be periodic or for a fixed term), secure tenancies under the Housing Act 1985,

[90] [1986] Fam. 81.
[91] [1989] 2 F.L.R. 497.

statutory tenancies under the Rent Act 1977 and assured tenancies under the Housing Act 1988. The extent to which the court can order transfers of these tenancies on marriage breakdown will be considered in turn.

Contractual tenancies These are regarded as "property" **6–121** within the meaning of section 24(1) of the M.C.A. 1973, and so the court has power to order that the tenant spouse should transfer the tenancy to the non-tenant, on or after divorce, nullity or judicial separation. This was done, for example, in *Hale* v. *Hale*[92] in which the Court of Appeal ordered the husband to transfer his weekly tenancy of the former matrimonial home to the wife—even though the landlord was the husband's father and objected to the transfer. The court held that, in the absence of any contractual or statutory prohibition against assignment, it could order a tenant to make any transfer which he could have made voluntarily.

Where a contractual tenancy is also a protected tenancy under **6–122** the Rent Act 1977 it can also be transferred on or after divorce, nullity or judicial separation by virtue of section 7 of and Schedule 1 to the M.H.A. 1983. The effect of an order under this Act is to vest the tenancy in the other spouse without the need for assignment by the tenant. As this avoids problems of enforcement, it may be preferable to obtain an order under this jurisdiction, rather than under section 24. Furthermore, since such orders do not entail assignment, the problems caused by leases which contain a prohibition on assignment should be avoided. However, the landlord is always entitled to a hearing before an order is made under Schedule 1 and the court may, of course, be reluctant to make an order contrary to his wishes. If an application is made under the M.H.A. 1983, rather than ancillary to the main suit, it is important to check that any legal aid certificate that may have been granted will cover the application.

Secure tenancies In general a secure tenancy under the **6–123** Housing Act 1985 (the main example of which is a local authority tenancy) loses its security if it is assigned. However, section 91(3) of the Act provides that such tenancies shall not cease to be secure if assigned pursuant to an order under section 24 of the M.C.A. 1973. The Housing Act does not prevent local authorities and other public sector landlords, from including a prohibition on assignment in their leases, so presumably, by analogy with *Hale* v. *Hale* (above), the court

---

[92] [1975] 1 W.L.R. 931.

would not order a transfer if the lease contained an absolute prohibition against assignment.[93]

Secure tenancies can also be transferred under section 7 of and Schedule 1 to the M.H.A. 1983, and, for the reasons outlined in 6–122, above, it may be preferable to use this provision where possible.

6–124   *Statutory tenancies* This is the name given to the tenancy which arises under the Rent Act 1977, when a protected fixed term or periodic tenancy comes to an end by, for example, effluxion of time or notice to quit. The tenant who remains in occupation has a statutory tenancy on the same terms as his former contractual tenancy, and can be lawfully evicted only when a court makes a possession order against him. The "tenancy" in this case is a right of personal occupation and not a right in property, and hence it cannot be the subject of a transfer of property order under section 24 of the M.C.A. 1973. It can, however, be transferred under section 7 of and Schedule 1 to the M.H.A. 1983. Even so it is important to bear in mind that the tenancy must still be in existence at the date of the application for transfer.[94] If a *sole* statutory tenant gives up occupation of the property, the tenancy will not lapse as long as his *spouse* remains in occupation.[95] On decree absolute, however, that protection is lost and the tenancy ends. It is vital, therefore, to apply for an order for the transfer of the statutory tenancy before the decree is made absolute.

6–125   *Assured tenancies* The Housing Act 1988 introduces into the private sector the assured tenancy and provides that as from January 15, 1989, new tenancies of dwellings shall not be subject to the Rent Act 1977. These assured tenancies (unlike statutory tenancies) are "property" capable of being transferred on divorce under section 24 of M.C.A. 1973. Like the other tenancies discussed above, assured tenancies can also be transferred on divorce under section 7 and Schedule 1 of the M.H.A. 1983. If a *sole* assured tenant gives up occupation of the property, the security of tenure which comes from having an assured tenancy will continue as long as his *spouse* remains in occupation. On decree absolute, although the contractual tenancy will continue, the security of tenure will cease. It is

---

[93] It could be argued, however, that the H.A. 1985, s.91(3), by implication, prevents public sector landlords from prohibiting assignment pursuant to the M.C.A. 1973, s.24.

[94] See *Lewis* v. *Lewis* [1985] A.C. 828.

[95] Because under s.1(6) of the M.H.A. 1983 the wife's occupation is deemed to be the husband's (and vice versa). See 9–14, below.

therefore essential that an application for a transfer is made before decree absolute.

2. Property Disputes Under the Married Women's Property Act 1882

THE NATURE OF THE JURISDICTION   6–126

A dispute between a husband and wife as to the ownership or possession of property may be resolved by either party making an application to the High Court or a county court under section 17 of the M.W.P.A. 1882. Under section 17 the court can declare the rights of ownership in the property which is in dispute. Although section 17 provides that the court may make "such orders as it thinks fit," this does not entitle the court to vary the existing property rights.[96] (The principles according to which existing property rights are established are considered in detail in Chapter 15, below.) The court does, however, have power to order the sale of the property in question.[97]

Applications under section 17 have usually concerned the   6–127
matrimonial home, but section 17 is not confined to real property. It could be used, for example, where the ownership of personal property, such as furniture or a car, was in dispute. Orders may also be made under section 17 in respect of property which is no longer in the other party's possession, and, if the original property has been sold, the order can extend to the proceeds of sale or to other property representing the original.[98]

At first, applications under section 17 could be made only by   6–128
a husband or wife. Nowadays, however, it can be used by parties who were only engaged (see 15–50, below), and by couples who were married, but whose marriage has been dissolved or annulled.[99] An application must in this case be brought within three years of the divorce or annulment. Although then an application could be made as an alternative to proceedings for property adjustment under the M.C.A. 1973, s.24, this is hardly ever done. The lack of any power to redistribute property under section 17 makes it unattractive

---

[96] *Pettitt* v. *Pettitt* [1970] A.C. 777 (H.L.) and *Gissing* v. *Gissing* [1971] A.C. 886.
[97] Matrimonial Causes (Property and Maintenance) Act 1958, s.7(7).
[98] *Ibid*. s.7.
[99] Matrimonial Proceedings and Property Act 1970, s.39.

both to the parties and to the courts, and the courts discourage applications under section 17 in cases where the jurisdiction under the M.C.A. 1973 is available.[1]

Nevertheless cases do occasionally arise in which an application for a declaration under section 17 is appropriate. These cases are considered below.

THE USES OF SECTION 17 OF THE MARRIED WOMEN'S PROPERTY ACT 1882

6–129 **(i) Where one spouse becomes bankrupt**
On bankruptcy, the property of the bankrupt vests in the trustee in bankruptcy. It is not possible therefore to apply under the M.C.A. 1973, s.24 for a property adjustment order against a bankrupt spouse as they no longer own any property. Even if the adjustment of property order is made prior to a spouse becoming bankrupt, it may be that any transfers of property made under such an order could be set aside by the court on the application of the trustee.[2]

The only remedy for the non-bankrupt spouse is to apply for an order under section 17 declaring her to be the owner of property in dispute rather than the bankrupt spouse. The court's decision will be based on ordinary property law principles.

6–130 **(ii) Capital gains tax**
If capital gains tax is likely to be a burden on the parties following a possible transfer of property order, a declaration as to ownership, as an alternative, will result in no liability to tax. This is because there has been no disposal of the property for capital gains tax purposes.

Example

Whilst they were married Harold and Beverley bought a second house as a holiday home. The house was bought from a legacy left to Beverley by her father, but the legal estate was conveyed to Harold. In this case a resulting trust will arise, in the absence of any contrary intention, so that the house is held by Harold on trust for Beverley.

Now the couple have been divorced, they agree that the matrimonial property should be re-distributed between them. As part of this Beverley is to have the holiday home. If a property adjustment

---

[1] See, *e.g. Kowalczuk* v. *Kowalczuk* [1973] 1 W.L.R. 930.
[2] See the M.C.A. 1973, s.39 and the Insolvency Act 1986, ss.339–340; see also 6–116, above.

order is made under section 24 of the M.C.A. 1973, capital gains tax will be payable as there will be a transfer of property to which the principal private dwelling house exemption will not apply (see 7–34). If, however, a declaration is obtained under M.W.P.A. 1882, s.17 that Beverley is the sole beneficial owner of the property, and always has been, then no transfer has taken place and no capital gains tax is payable.

(iii) Where it is too late for an application under the Matrimonial Causes Act 1973

6–131

It will be recalled that an application under the M.C.A. 1973 for property adjustment must be made before re-marriage by the applicant.

Example

Wendy was divorced by Fred because of her adultery with Stephen. Wendy did not defend the divorce and sought no legal advice on the proceedings. As soon as her decree absolute arrived she married Stephen. She now wishes to apply for a share of the matrimonial home which is in Fred's sole name. She will not be able to do so under the M.C.A. 1973.[3] If, however, she can establish some interest in the property in land law terms, she will be able to apply for a declaration under the M.W.P.A. 1882, provided that proceedings are brought within three years of decree absolute. After this period has elapsed, an application would have to be made for a bare declaration as to ownership.[4]

---

[3] M.C.A. 1973, s.28(3).
[4] The procedure is considered further at 15–50, below.

7. Tax

7–01   When considering the financial provision that must be made on marriage breakdown the impact of the relevant tax legislation cannot be ignored.

It is important, however, not to place too much emphasis on tax considerations as in many cases the tax consequences of an order are unavoidable. There is, nonetheless, scope for "tax planning" at a basic level, especially with regard to income tax. In particular, it should be remembered that tax saving is not only important in cases where the parties are well off. Indeed a saving of a few pounds will be of proportionately greater value in those cases where there is only just enough money to go round.

In this chapter income tax, capital gains tax, inheritance tax and stamp duty will be considered in turn.

1. Income Tax

PRELIMINARY POINTS

In Chapter 6 the net effect approach was considered. It was stressed that for a proper appreciation of the effect of a maintenance order on the parties it is necessary to calculate their income tax liability on any order that may be proposed. In Chapter 6 (at 6–91 and 6–92), in the context of a case study, examples of an income tax calculator and a net effect calculator can be seen.

Before considering the income tax implications of maintenance payments, it is necessary to set out and explain some of the basic terminology that we will be using in this chapter.

7–02   **(i) Statutory income, total income and taxable income**

    (i)   "Statutory income" consists of the taxpayer's income from all sources after deduction of any allowable expenses, as provided by the appropriate schedule or case in the I.C.T.A. 1988.

    (ii)   "Total income" is calculated by deducting "charges on income" from the taxpayer's statutory income. The charges on income with which we are primarily concerned are qualifying maintenance payments and the payment of interest on a loan for the purchase of a dwelling-house.

(iii) "Taxable income" is calculated by deducting the appropriate personal reliefs from the taxpayer's total income. The three which are of particular importance on marriage breakdown are the married couple's allowance, the personal allowance and the additional personal allowance.

7–03 **(ii) Independent taxation**
Until the end of the tax year 1989–90 the income of a married couple was aggregated and they were taxed together. This had two principal drawbacks: the wife had no freedom over her own tax affairs and the system of personal allowances meant that a married couple could be at a disadvantage compared to an unmarried couple. From April 6, 1990 a husband and wife have been taxed separately on their incomes and each has been entitled to their own personal allowances and to a full basic rate income tax band. Each has had to complete their own tax returns and each is liable to pay their own tax.

7–04 **(iii) Personal reliefs**

(i) The personal allowance.[1]

This is available to all individuals including minor children.

(ii) The married couple's allowance.[2]

This is given to a married man living with his wife for the whole or part of the year of assessment. This is given to him in addition to his personal allowance. Any part of the allowance not used by the husband may be transferred to his wife.

During the year of marriage only a proportion of the allowance will be given, depending on the date of marriage. During the year of separation the husband will continue to be entitled to the full married couple's allowance. Thereafter he will receive only the personal allowance, unless the additional personal allowance is also available (see below).

---

[1] I.C.T.A. 1988, s.257(1) as substituted by Finance Act 1988, s.33. The amount for the year 1990/91 is £3005.
[2] I.C.T.A. 1988, s.257A inserted by Finance Act 1988, s.33.

The husband and wife will be treated as being separated for income tax purposes if they are separated under an order of the court or by deed of separation, or they are separated in such circumstances that the separation is likely to be permanent.[3]

7–05 (iii) Additional personal allowance.[4]

This is also sometimes known as "single parent relief" and often plays an important part in the tax consequences of marriage breakdown. Its purpose, broadly, is to give the same personal relief in amount to a taxpayer with care of a child as is available to a married man.

It is available to a man who is not entitled to the married couple's allowance and who has a qualifying child living with him during the year of assessment. It is also available to a woman who has a qualifying child living with her during any part of the year of assessment when she is not married and living with her husband.[5] Where more than one qualifying child lives with the taxpayer (or with an unmarried couple) only one relief will be given.

7–06 (iv) Qualifying child[6]

This is defined as any child who is:

(a) born in, or is under the age of 16 at the commencement of, the year of assessment or, being over that age at the commencement of that year, is receiving full-time instruction at any university, college, school or other educational establishment; and

(b) a child of the claimant or, not being such a child, a child who is born in or is under the age of 18 years at the commencement of the year of assessment and who is maintained for the whole or part of that year by the claimant at his expense.

---

[3] I.C.T.A. 1988, s.282 as substituted by Finance Act 1988, Sched. 3, para. 11.
[4] I.C.T.A. 1988, s.259 as substituted by Finance Act 1988, Sched. 3, para. 5.
[5] I.C.T.A. 1988, s.259(1)(*a*), (4) as substituted by Finance Act 1988, Sched. 3, para. 5.
[6] I.C.T.A. 1988, s.259.

Example   **7–07**

*Peter and Jane have two children, Adam and James. Prior to their
separation Peter claimed the married couple's allowance and Jane
claimed the personal allowance. Following separation Adam went to
live with Jane and James went with Peter. The tax consequences (so
far as personal reliefs are concerned) are as follows:*
*—Peter is entitled to continue to claim the married couple's
allowance for the year of separation. From that time he will be
entitled to the personal allowance plus the additional personal
allowance for James.*
*—Jane can claim the personal allowance plus the additional personal
allowance in respect of Adam.*

MAINTENANCE PAYMENTS   **7–08**

The payment of maintenance is largely ignored for the
purposes of income tax. Limited compensation is available for
the payer in so far as he is allowed a special deduction in
computing his total income. The amount of his deduction is
the *lesser* of: either the figure which represents the amount of
the married couple's allowance or the amount of qualifying
maintenance payments.

The recipient does not pay tax on maintenance received.

A limited amount of tax can be saved by ensuring that the
payment qualifies for tax relief by being a qualifying
maintenance payment.

(i) Qualifying maintenance payments[7]   **7–09**
The payment must be made:

(a) under a court order, or by virtue of a written agreement
where the parties have separated. A purely voluntary
payment will not count; and

(b) to a spouse or former spouse who has not remarried.
Payments to the spouse, or former spouse, for the benefit
of the children will also count. Payments directly to the
child will not.

An example will help to explain the operation of these
principles.

(ii) Income tax example   **7–10**
The figures given in the following examples for personal
reliefs are the figures current for the tax year 1990/91.

---

[7] I.C.T.A. 1988, s.347B(1).

(a) Richard and Anita are happily married. They have a son Christian. They have no mortgage.

Their tax bills are as follows:

Richard's tax bill

TOTAL INCOME	£29,000
less married couple's allowance	£4,725
TAXABLE INCOME	£24,275

Tax thereon
first £20,700 @ 25% = £5,175
next £3,575 @ 40% = £1,430

| £24,275 | £6,605 |

Anita's tax bill

TOTAL INCOME	£8,000
less personal allowance	£3,005
TAXABLE INCOME	£4,995

Tax thereon
£4,995 @ 25% = £1,248.75

TOTAL TAX BILL = £6,605 + £1,248.75 = £7,853.75

7–11 (b) Anita leaves Richard (because he has neglected her for his work) and takes Christian with her. Richard voluntarily pays maintenance for Anita and Christian in the composite sum of £7,000 p.a. In the year of separation Richard will continue to receive the married couple's allowance. Anita will be entitled to her personal allowance and the additional personal allowance from the date of separation. In the following year the parties' tax position will be as follows:

Richard's tax bill

TOTAL INCOME	£29,000
less personal allowance	£3,005
TAXABLE INCOME	£25,995

Tax thereon
    first £20,700 @ 25% = £5,175
    next £5,295 @ 40% = £2,118
    ————————   ————————
    £25,995   £7,293

Anita's tax bill

TOTAL INCOME   £8,000
less personal allowance   £3,005
    plus additional personal allowance £1,720
                                     ————————
                                     £4,725
                                                     ————————
TAXABLE INCOME   £3,275

Tax thereon
    £3,275 @ 25% =   £818.75

TOTAL TAX BILL = £818.75 + £7,293 = £8,111.75

As can be seen, this figure is slightly higher than the total tax bill whilst they were married and living together. Although the personal reliefs are the same in amount in both situations, in the second example Anita pays tax at a lower marginal rate than Richard. For this reason the higher personal relief she receives is worth less than when Richard received it. However, looking at Anita's situation in isolation she clearly pays less tax.

For the year of separation Richard and Anita would be slightly better off as they would both be entitled to the higher personal relief.

(c) Anita now obtains a court order for periodical payments **7–12** for the sum of £4,000 for herself and £3,000 to herself for the benefit of Christian.

(Had the order provided for the periodical payments for Christian to be paid directly to him, Richard would not have lost any tax relief. This is because he is only entitled to a maximum tax allowance for maintenance of £1,720 and this is exhausted by the payments to Anita for herself. However, there may still be an advantage in expressing the periodical payments for Christian to be made to Anita for Christian's benefit. Should Anita's periodical payments order be reduced on an application for variation, because of an increase in her earnings, so that the order is lower than the maximum figure for tax relief available, Richard will still be entitled to obtain maximum tax relief. This is because Christian's periodical payments will be qualifying maintenance payments.)

The tax position is as follows:

Richard's tax bill

STATUTORY INCOME	£29,000
less qualifying maintenance payment	£1,720
TOTAL INCOME	£27,280
less personal allowance	£3,005
TAXABLE INCOME	£24,275

Tax thereon
first £20,700 @ 25% = £5,175
next £3,575 @ 40% = £1,430

£24,275   £6,605

Anita's tax bill

TOTAL INCOME	£8,000
less personal allowance plus additional personal allowance	£4,725
TAXABLE INCOME	£3,275

Tax thereon
£3,275 @ 25% =   £818.75

TOTAL TAX BILL = £818.75 + £6,605 = £7,423.75

7–13   As can be seen a total tax saving of £688 has been made by the simple device of obtaining a court order recording the voluntary payment. Clearly, although Richard is the direct beneficiary of this saving, it could be shared between him and Anita by increasing her periodical payments order.

If the parties should divorce, and Richard remarry, he will be entitled to the married couple's allowance for his second wife. If Anita should remarry, Richard will lose all of the special deduction in respect of his maintenance payments. As far as the periodical payments for Anita are concerned, of course, these will cease on her remarriage in any event. However, although the periodical payments for the benefit of Christian will continue[8], Richard will get no tax relief in respect of them.

(iii) Agreements and orders prior to March 15, 1988   **7–14**
The tax treatment of maintenance orders and agreements which were applied for before March 15, 1988 and made before June 15, 1988 was radically different than under the current system. This is also true for such orders or agreements which are varied after that date. Broadly, the tax treatment of such orders was more generous than now. For this reason, transitional relief is available for such orders or agreements, so that whatever tax relief was given in the tax year 1988/89 is frozen in amount and is available in subsequent years. The situation is further complicated by the fact that tax relief was given to both the payer and the payee. This was done, effectively, by treating the whole amount of the maintenance payment as a charge on income for the payer and the payee was entitled to a limited form of tax exemption as well.

An election can be made by the payer for the current tax system to apply if this will be more favourable than the old regime. The election should be considered when the current married couple's allowance is more than the amount of maintenance paid in the tax year 1988/89. In most cases it is unlikely that an election will be beneficial for some time, and once the election has been made it is final.

Example

In 1987 Saul was ordered to pay to his wife Ruth £1,500 p.a.

In the tax year 1988/89 Saul was entitled to deduct the £1,500 from his statutory income as a charge on his income and therefore he would not have paid tax on it.

[Although this would become income in Ruth's hands, she does not pay tax because this sum would have been less than her personal reliefs. In addition to the single personal relief, in 1988/89 she would have been entitled to an extra personal relief of £1,490.]

In April 1990 the order was varied to increase the amount to £1,700. If Saul does not elect for the current scheme to apply, his tax relief will be limited to £1,500. Under the current system his tax

---

[8] See 6–24 and 6–26.

relief is £1,700. (A maximum deduction of £1,720 is available for the tax year 1990/91.) Clearly, once the election is made, Ruth will not be charged to tax on the maintenance.

7–15 **(iv) Backdated maintenance orders**

Sometimes periodical payments orders are backdated to the date of application, although this is rare.[9] In the same way periodical payments orders are sometimes varied retrospectively. If voluntary payments have been made, the fact that the order is backdated to record the payments is ignored by the Revenue. The nature of the payment cannot be changed retrospectively, so that if, for example, at the time of the payment it was made voluntarily no tax relief is available.[10] However, if payment is made subsequent to a backdated order then in practice the Revenue will treat the money paid as being paid for that period and tax relief will be available.

7–16 **(v) Voluntary maintenance payments**

From what has been said above, it can be seen that voluntary maintenance payments are the least effective method of payment for tax purposes. Payments are treated as made voluntarily if they are not made under a binding agreement or a court order. Under the old tax regime a husband was entitled to continue to claim the married man's allowance if he wholly and voluntarily supported his wife even though they were living separate and apart. This is no longer the case, as has been explained above (see 7–04).

However, there is a form of transitional relief which applies where a couple ceased to live together before 1990/91 but remain married. In this case, providing the husband was entitled to the married man's allowance (because he was wholly and voluntarily maintaining his wife) in 1989/90, he will be able to claim the married couple's allowance for 1990/91 and thereafter. This will continue for as long as they remain married and he continues to maintain her voluntarily.[11]

7–17 MORTGAGE INSTALMENTS

It is now necessary to consider the best method of dealing with the payment of mortgage instalments in respect of the former matrimonial home. The court has no power to order these to be paid directly, but the obligation to pay them can

[9] See 6–17.
[10] *Morley-Clarke* v. *Jones* [1986] Ch. 311.
[11] I.C.T.A. 1988, s.257F inserted by Finance Act 1988, s.33.

arise by agreement or by an undertaking contained in the preamble of a court order. Assuming the mortgage payment is to be financed by the non-occupying spouse, it now falls to be considered whether, for tax purposes, it is better for the payment to be made direct to the lender or via an increased periodical payments order.

There may, of course, be considerations other than tax ones which must be borne in mind. For example, if the occupying spouse actually makes the payment, he or she will know that the payment has been made and will not be at the risk of eviction due to non-payment of which he or she was unaware.

7–18 From a tax point of view it is vital to ensure that the payment qualifies for mortgage interest relief. If this relief is available, the payment will be a charge on the payer's income, which will mean that the payer will be able to pay this from his statutory income before calculating his total income. The net result of this is that he pays it before he pays tax, thus achieving a saving at his marginal rate of tax. The tax relief will actually be given under M.I.R.A.S.[12] (mortgage interest relief at source) so that when the mortgage instalment is paid the payer can deduct an amount which is equivalent to tax at the basic rate. Higher rate relief must be claimed by the taxpayer as a charge on income.

(i) Qualifying conditions
7–19
Broadly speaking, mortgage interest relief can be claimed[13] where the following conditions are satisfied.

(a) The person claiming the relief has an estate or interest in the land[14]; and

(b) the loan is taken out to purchase an estate or interest in the land[14]; and

(c) the land is used as the taxpayer's only or main residence[15]; and

(d) the relief is only available on a loan or loans to the extent they do not exceed £30,000.[16]

---

[12] I.C.T.A. 1988, ss.369–379.

[13] I.C.T.A. 1988, ss.353–358.

[14] I.C.T.A. 1988, s.354(1).

[15] I.C.T.A. 1988, s.355(1).

[16] This limit applies to each residence (although it is possible to have a number of borrowers who have loans to purchase it). I.C.T.A. 1988, s.356A–356D inserted by Finance Act 1988, s.42(1).

7–20   *Example*

Harold, who owns the matrimonial home in his sole name, subject to a mortgage, leaves his wife Wilma in occupation of the property. If he continues to pay the mortgage, he will no longer be entitled to mortgage interest relief. If he ceases to pay the mortgage Wilma will be forced to pay the mortgage to stop repossession proceedings by the lender. To enable Wilma to obtain mortgage interest relief she must have either a legal or equitable interest in the property (see 7–19). It will probably be unclear whether she is entitled to a beneficial interest in the matrimonial home until this has been decided by the court. In practice it seems that in this situation the Revenue will allow her relief for the interest she pays.

7–21   In Chapter 6 it was explained that the orders relating to the matrimonial home broadly fall into one of three categories. The payment of mortgage instalments will be considered in relation to each category in turn.

7–22   *Immediate sale and division of the net proceeds of the property*

Should one of the parties buy the other's interest in the matrimonial home, assuming the other conditions are satisfied, the purchasing spouse will obtain interest relief on any loan taken out, as this is done to buy an interest in land.

7–23   *Outright transfer to one party*

In these circumstances the owning party must make the mortgage payments. Assuming it is the former wife to whom the property is transferred, if the former husband makes the payments he will not be entitled to mortgage interest relief as he will not have an estate or interest in the land.

7–24   *Retention of the home for one party to occupy*

As has been mentioned,[17] there are two methods which might be used in making such provision.

The trust for sale In this case the legal estate is held by both parties, therefore both would be eligible for the interest relief. It is essential for the party in occupation to make the payments. This will leave the other party free to utilise his full entitlement to £30,000 worth of loans on an alternative property.

The deferred charge In this type of order the occupying party has the property transferred into his or her name. Clearly it is essential that this party pays the mortgage instalments.

---

[17] See 6–103 *et seq.* above.

CHECK LIST   7–25

The following list summarises the main income tax points to
bear in mind when dealing with maintenance.

   (i)   Make sure any voluntary payment is embodied in an
      agreement or a court order.

  (ii)   Make orders relating to children payable to the spouse
      for the benefit of the child.

 (iii)   Ensure the mortgage is payable by the person in
      occupation of the property.

 (iv)   Reconsider the net effect of the above. If tax has been
      saved for the payer of the maintenance, the amount of
      the order should be increased to pass some of the
      benefit to the recipient.

2. Capital Gains Tax   7–26

On marriage breakdown, in many cases, capital has to be
divided between the parties. Frequently the matrimonial
home is the largest capital asset of the parties. The impact of
capital gains tax (C.G.T.) cannot be ignored because, if this is
payable on the disposal of the asset, it will alter the effect of
any negotiated settlement or court order.

Before considering the impact of capital gains tax on the
situations likely to be met on marriage breakdown, the
elements of the tax must be considered.

WHAT IS TAXABLE?   7–27

By virtue of section 1 of the C.G.T.A. 1979, C.G.T. is charged
on any "chargeable gains" which accrue on the disposal of
chargeable assets. The chargeable gain is assessed by
deducting allowable expenditure from the consideration for
disposal. This usually means deducting the original purchase
price (plus the cost of any improvement and the costs of
disposal) from the price obtained when the asset is sold.[18]
However, where the asset is disposed of by way of gift, the
consideration is taken to be the market value of the asset at
the date of disposal.[19] This is true of any disposal which is
not at arm's length. Disposals between "connected persons"

---

[18] C.G.T.A. 1979, s.32.
[19] C.G.T.A. 1979, s.29A.

fall into this category[20]; a husband and wife are "connected persons" and remain so until decree absolute.[21]

As will be seen, however, the incidence of C.G.T. can often be avoided or reduced on disposals between spouses, during marriage and on divorce, by use of the various exemptions and reliefs available.

7–28 REBASING

For assets owned on March 31, 1982 the chargeable gain may be computed on the basis that the asset was acquired in March 1982 at its then market value. This is known as rebasing and means that gains from 1965 to 1982 have been removed from the tax charge.

7–29 ANNUAL EXEMPTION

Where a chargeable gain is realised, C.G.T. is charged as if the gain were within the top slice of the taxpayer's income,[22] but an individual is entitled to an exemption on the first £5,000 of his gains in the tax year 1990–91. Any unused exemption is lost and cannot be carried forward to the next tax year.

7–30 INDEXATION ALLOWANCE

Where the increase in value of an asset is due solely to the effect of inflation, it is clearly unfair that the owner should be charged to tax on any "gain" made when it is sold. Accordingly the allowable expenditure (*e.g.* the original purchase price plus any costs incurred in enhancing the value of the asset) is linked to rises in the retail prices index,[23] with the result that C.G.T. should be paid only on the disposal of assets which have increased in value by more than the general rate of inflation.

In general, the indexation allowance is calculated by reference to the allowable expenditure actually incurred. However, if the asset was acquired before March 31, 1982, this expenditure is taken at its market value on that date (when indexation was first introduced) if this is greater.[24] This

---

[20] C.G.T.A. 1979, s.62.
[21] *Aspden* v. *Hildesley* [1982] 1 W.L.R. 264.
[22] F.A. 1988, s.98.
[23] Finance Act 1982, s.86.
[24] Finance Act 1988, s.96.

expenditure will then be indexed in line with inflation up to the date of disposal.

Example **7–31**

Henry buys a holiday cottage in 1980 for £15,000. In March 1982 its value has risen to £35,000. In March 1990 Henry disposes of the cottage for £60,000 (net of incidental costs).

Henry's acquisition cost is taken to be £35,000 (the value of the cottage in March 1982) and this amount is then indexed in line with the rise in the retail prices index between March 1982 and March 1990. Assuming this to produce a figure of £45,000,[25] this will be treated as his allowable expenditure, and his chargeable gain will be £60,000 − £45,000 = £15,000 (which will be further reduced by Henry's annual exemption). If indexation and rebasing had not been available, his chargeable gain would have been £60,000 − £15,000 = £45,000.

OTHER EXEMPTIONS AND RELIEFS **7–32**

Of the other exemptions and reliefs available, the following are those that are most likely to be applicable to disposals during marriage and on divorce.

(i) Disposals between spouses **7–33**
While a husband and wife are living together they are treated as one person for C.G.T. purposes. Thus any disposal between spouses is treated as having taken place for a consideration which gives rise to neither gain nor loss.[26] In other words, the inter-spouse disposal is ignored, and any liability to C.G.T. is postponed until the spouse to whom the disposal was made later disposes of the asset.

On separation, and regardless of whether they divorce, husband and wife become separate individuals for C.G.T. purposes. They remain "connected persons" until divorce, however, so that a disposal between spouses between separation and decree absolute is treated as being for market value, as noted at 7–27, above.

(ii) The main residence exemption[27] **7–34**
An individual is exempt from C.G.T. on any gain realised on the disposal of his only or main residence. A person who

---

[25] See the C.G.T.A. 1979, Sched. 5 for the method of calculation.
[26] C.G.T.A. 1979, s.44.
[27] C.G.T.A. 1979, ss.101–102. It is important not to confuse the conditions which apply here with the conditions of mortgage interest relief; see 7–19, above.

owns more than one residence can elect which of them shall be regarded as his main residence. If he does not do so, the Inspector of Taxes can decide for him.

To qualify for the exemption the individual must have occupied the property as his only or main residence throughout the period of his ownership. Periods of absence can lead to a proportion of the gain realised on disposal being charged to tax. The proportion is calculated according to the formula:

$$\text{Total gain} \times \frac{\text{period of absence}}{\text{period of ownership}}$$

However, certain periods of absence, including the last two years of ownership, are ignored, which may be particularly relevant on marriage breakdown.

7–35 *Example*

John buys a house in 1980 for £10,000. He subsquently marries Susan and the house becomes their matrimonial home. In 1982 John leaves Susan and never returns. In 1990, when the house is worth £60,000, the marriage is dissolved and John is ordered to transfer the house to Susan. Assuming that after indexation and rebasing John's allowable expenditure is taken to be £30,000, the proportion of his total gain of £30,000 which is chargeable is calculated as follows:

$$= \qquad £30,000 \times \frac{\text{8 years less 2 years}}{\text{10 years}}$$

$$= \qquad £30,000 \times \frac{6}{10}$$

$$= \qquad \text{Chargeable gain of } £18,000.$$

(This gain will then be subject to John's annual exemption, further reducing the C.G.T. due.)

7–36 In cases such as this it is sometimes possible to eliminate C.G.T. liability altogether by invoking Extra Statutory Concession D.6 (E.S.C. D.6). Under this concession, which applies only to disposals between separated or former spouses, the transferring spouse is deemed to have continued in occupation of the matrimonial home until the date of the transfer, so that the whole gain on disposal will be exempt.

However, two conditions attach to E.S.C. D.6

(i)   The spouse to whom the property is transferred must have continued to occupy the home as his or her only main residence.

(ii) The transferring spouse must not have elected to treat any other home as his or her only or main residence.

It is this second condition which will prove a stumbling block in many cases. Where the transferring spouse has bought a home of his own before the transfer, it will be necessary to calculate whether it is worth giving up the main residence exemption on that new home for the period prior to transfer of the former matrimonial home.

(iv) Other exempt assets   7–37
Various assets are specifically exempted from C.G.T. Those which are most likely to be relevant on marriage breakdown are sterling[28] (so that payment of a lump sum by one spouse to another is exempt), private motor vehicles,[29] and chattels worth not more than £6,000.[30]

CAPITAL GAINS TAX ON ORDERS DISPOSING OF THE   7–38
MATRIMONIAL HOME

As may already have been gathered, C.G.T. problems are most likely to arise on divorce on the disposal of the matrimonial home. Below the C.G.T. consequences of each of the possible orders that may be made in respect of the home are considered in detail.

(i) Immediate sale and division of the proceeds

House in one party's name   7–39

The court will normally order the owning spouse to pay the other a lump sum and this will be backed by an order for sale of the house. No C.G.T. will usually be payable on the sale of the house as the owning spouse will either still be in occupation or will have left within the last two years, so that the full main residence exemption is available. If, however, the owning spouse has been absent for more than the last two years of ownership, a proportion of the gain will be chargeable (7–34, above). No C.G.T. is payable on the lump sum (7–37, above).

---

[28] C.G.T.A. 1979, s.19(1).
[29] C.G.T.A. 1979, s.130.
[30] C.G.T.A. 1979, s.128.

7–40   *House in joint names*

Assuming the proceeds are to be divided equally, the court need only make an order enforcing the existing trust for sale. No doubt at least one spouse will have remained in occupation and can claim the full main residence exemption on their share of the proceeds of sale; a spouse out of occupation will again be able to claim a full or partial exemption depending on whether sale takes place within two years of separation.

Note that E.S.C. D.6 cannot be invoked on eventual sale in either case, as the disposal is not to an existing or former spouse.

7–41   **(ii) Outright transfer to one party**

Assuming that the husband is ordered to transfer his interest in the house to the wife, he will again be able to rely on the main residence exemption if the transfer takes place within two years of separation; otherwise a proportion of his gain will be chargeable. However, in this case he does have the option of invoking E.S.C. D.6 and would certainly exercise it if he has not in the meantime bought a home of his own on which he wishes to claim the main residence exemption.[31] Even if he has bought another home, he might decide that it was worth ultimately losing a portion of the exemption on that home for the benefit of avoiding an immediate charge to C.G.T. at a time when his resources are likely to be fully stretched.

7–42   **(iii) Retention of the home for one party to occupy**

This may be achieved in a number of ways, but the aim of all of them is to give one spouse an exclusive right to occupy the home until, for example, the children have grown up, while preserving for the other spouse some interest in the eventual proceeds of sale. In the following cases it is assumed that the wife remains in occupation.

7–43   *By trust for sale (e.g. Mesher v. Mesher,[32] Martin v. Martin[33])*

If the house is already in joint names the court need only vary the terms of an existing trust for sale and no immediate disposal occurs. If the house is in the name of one spouse only the court must order a transfer into joint names. The C.G.T. consequences of such a disposal will be the same as in 7–41, above. In either case a charge to C.G.T. is likely to arise

[31] See 7–34, above.
[32] [1980] 1 All E.R. 126.
[33] [1978] Fam. 12.

only when the house is eventually sold and the proceeds are divided. The wife's share of the proceeds will be covered by the main residence exemption, but a proportion of the husband's share will not (calculated as in 7–34, above). Although the husband's liability will be reduced by indexation, and by the annual exemption, it is still quite possible that a charge to C.G.T. will arise.

The only way in which this might be avoided is to argue that the effect of the order has been to create a settlement of the home. Under section 104 of the C.G.T.A. 1979, C.G.T. is not charged on the disposal by a trustee of a dwelling-house which during the period of the trustee's ownership has been *"the only or main residence of a person entitled to occupy it under the terms of a settlement."* Property to which two persons are "jointly absolutely entitled" is not settled property for C.G.T. purposes,[34] but it has been held that the word "jointly" denotes concurrent rather than successive interests.[35] "Concurrent" in this context means co-existent and of the same quality. It may, therefore, be argued that, as the wife under this order has a right to exclusive occupation of the property during the currency of the trust for sale, the parties' interests are not of the same quality and are, therefore, successive. If this is correct they are not "jointly absolutely entitled" and the property is occupied under a settlement to which the section 104 exemption can apply. The husband's prospects of gaining this exemption may be improved if the order expressly provides that the beneficial interests shall be *settled* on the terms set out in the order. He is also more likely to be successful where the terms of the trust for sale give the wife the sole right to occupy the house for life (as in *Martin* v. *Martin*), since this more arguably creates successive interests than an order which limits the wife's occupation to the date when the youngest child has grown up (as in *Mesher* v. *Mesher*). However, if the property is regarded as settled, a charge to Inheritance Tax may arise in certain circumstances. This is considered at 7–47, below.

7–44

By deferred charge (e.g. Browne v. *Pritchard*[36] *and Hector* v. *Hector*[37]*)*

7–45

Under this type of order the property is held in the sole name of the occupying spouse, but the other is given a charge over

---

[34] C.G.T.A. 1979, s.46.
[35] *Booth* v. *Ellard* [1980] 1 W.L.R. 1443.
[36] [1975] 1 W.L.R. 1366.
[37] [1973] 1 W.L.R. 1122.

the property. The charge may be for a fixed sum of money (as in *Hector* v. *Hector*) or for a proportion of the net proceeds of sale (as in *Browne* v. *Pritchard*).[38]

If the order involves a transfer of the property by husband to wife, the C.G.T. consequences will be as in 7–41, above. The consequences on eventual sale depend on the form of the charge. If it is for a fixed sum, the husband's share of the proceeds represents the repayment of a debt for which there is no charge to C.G.T.[39] If the charge is for a proportion of the net proceeds, however, it appears that the husband's share is not a debt, since it has been held that the term does not cover a liability to pay an unidentifiable sum at an unascertainable date.[40] Instead the charge represents an asset on the disposal of which C.G.T. will be payable. (Of course other reliefs such as the annual exemption and the indexation allowance will be available). Simply from a C.G.T. point of view, therefore, a charge for a fixed sum may be preferable, but any C.G.T. advantage would normally be outweighed by the fact that this form of charge gives the husband no benefit from future house-price inflation, which, if the house is not to be sold for a number of years, may be considerable.

7–46 ORDERS UNDER SECTION 17 OF THE MARRIED WOMEN'S PROPERTY ACT 1882

Although the courts discourage applications under section 17 on marriage breakdown, it should be remembered that, since such orders simply declare what existing property rights are and do not involve any transfer of property, there can be no charge to C.G.T. on them. This can occasionally prove useful.

Example

Wendy buys shares outright with money she has inherited, but they are bought in the name of her husband, Henry. The marriage breaks down shortly afterwards and they separate. Wendy now wants the shares to be transferred to her absolutely.

If this done by order under the M.C.A. 1973, s.24, Henry will be liable to C.G.T. on the disposal of the shares. No charge will arise, however, if an order is obtained under the M.W.P.A. 1882, s.17, declaring Wendy to be beneficially entitled to them.[41]

---

[38] For further details see 6–110.
[39] C.G.T.A. 1979, s.134.
[40] *Marren* v. *Ingles* [1980] 1 W.L.R. 983.
[41] See 6–128 for the court's attitude to the use of M.W.P.A. 1882, s.17 compared to the use of its powers under the M.C.A. 1973.

3. Inheritance Tax 7–47

As with income tax and capital gains tax, the inheritance tax impact of any negotiated settlement or court order must be borne in mind. Fortunately in the vast majority of cases the various exemptions usually mean that no inheritance tax liability will be incurred on marriage breakdown.

WHAT IS TAXABLE? 7–48

In general, the aim of Inheritance Tax (I.H.T.) is to tax certain gratuitous dispositions of wealth, whether made during an individual's lifetime, or on his death.

By virtue of section 1 of the I.H.T.A. 1984, I.H.T. is charged on a "chargeable transfer" which is defined by section 2 to mean "a transfer of value which is made by an individual but is not ... an exempt transfer."

INHERITANCE TAX ON MARRIAGE BREAKDOWN 7–49

There should rarely be any charge to I.H.T. as a result of transfers made on marriage breakdown, because such transfers will almost invariably be exempt. Transfers between spouses are always exempt and, for I.H.T. purposes, this exemption applies throughout marriage, regardless of whether the parties are living together or not.[42] (Compare the interspouse exemption for C.G.T. purposes, discussed at 7–33, above). On decree absolute the benefit of this exemption is, of course, lost, but it should still be possible to invoke one of the following exemptions and avoid any charge to I.H.T.

(i) Maintenance 7–50
The payment of maintenance is exempt under I.H.T.A. 1984, s.11, which provides that a disposition is not a transfer of value if made by one party to a marriage (or former marriage) for the maintenance of the other party or of a child of either party. The term "maintenance" is not defined, but clearly covers periodical payments. Section 11 is probably not wide enough to cover lump sum payments, nor property adjustment orders.

(ii) Capital and property adjustment 7–51
Whether a transfer of the home and other transfers of capital are exempt under section 11 or not, they will almost certainly

---

[42] I.H.T.A. 1984, s.18.

be exempt under section 10 of the I.H.T.A. 1984. This provides that a disposition is not a transfer of value if it was not intended to confer a gratuitous benefit, and was made in a transaction at arm's length between persons not connected with each other. To avoid any doubt about the application of this exemption to transfers on marriage breakdown, the Senior Registrar of the Family Division has, with the agreement of the Revenue, issued the following statement:

> "Transfers of money or property pursuant to an order of the court in consequence of a decree of divorce or nullity will, in general, be regarded as exempt from [Inheritance Tax] as transactions at arm's length which are not intended to confer any gratuitous benefit."[43]

7–52 **(iii) The effect of creating a settlement**
One possible exception to the general rule that orders made on divorce will not give rise to a charge to I.H.T. arises when an order is made settling the home on, for example, the wife for life, with a later sale and division of the proceeds (*e.g. Martin* v. *Martin*[44]).

This is of no consequence at the time when the order is made, as although the creation of a settlement is a chargeable transfer, no charge will arise owing to the absence of any gratuitous intent.

7–53 The wife has an interest in possession in the property and is, therefore, treated as its owner.[45] When her life interest comes to an end no charge will arise on the half share to which she or her estate becomes entitled. If the husband is still alive at this time, his half share will not be chargeable either, as it is covered by a provision which excludes property which, on termination of an interest in possession, reverts to the settlor.[46]

7–54 If, however, the husband dies before the property is sold (which is quite likely in the case of a *Martin* order), a double charge to I.H.T. will arise. The value of the husband's reversionary interest will form part of his estate on his death, and will be included in any charge to I.H.T.[47] Then, when the wife's interest under the settlement comes to an end, the revertor to settlor exemption cannot apply to the share that

---

[43] (1975) 119 S.J. 596.
[44] [1978] Fam. 12.
[45] I.H.T.A. 1984, s.50.
[46] *Ibid.* s.53(3).
[47] *Ibid.* s.48(1).

passes to the husband's estate, so that I.H.T. will be charged on it.

Nevertheless, as chargeable transfers up to a total of £128,000 (which is index-linked) are within the nil-rate band, any liability that does arise may well be small.

4. Stamp Duty   7–55

When property is conveyed under or by virtue of a separation deed, or a court order on divorce, the instrument effecting the conveyance is exempt from *ad valorem* duty, and, subject to certification by the transferor, from fixed duty as well.[48]

---

[48] Finance Act 1985, s.83, and the Stamp Duty (Exempt Instruments) Regulations 1987 (S.I. 1987 No. 516).

8. Welfare Law

8–01 INTRODUCTION

All matrimonial practitioners need to be familiar with the law governing welfare benefits. Even a client who has previously enjoyed a high standard of living may find it necessary to seek temporary assistance if, for example, she is suddenly deserted by her husband and left without financial support. In any case, as has been pointed out before (6–05, above), income support is often a better alternative to an order for maintenance pending suit. In the longer term it will also often be necessary to consider the welfare benefit implications of the various orders for financial provision and property adjustment. Since, on divorce, the parties' resources will normally have to be stretched to support two households instead of one, it is not uncommon for one of the parties, usually the wife, to have to have long-term resort to welfare benefits to supplement her income.

8–02 A solicitor can advise a client about the availability of welfare benefits under the Green Form scheme. Even if the client is also receiving advice and assistance in divorce or other matrimonial proceedings, it should be remembered that advice on welfare benefits will be treated as a separate matter which can be dealt with on a separate Green Form. The advice that can be given is not confined to the relevant law, but extends to checking the accuracy of an assessment regarding a benefit.

8–03 In this chapter the following benefits will be considered:

    (i)   child benefit and one-parent benefit.

    (ii)   income support.

    (iii) family credit.

    (iv) housing benefit.

    (v)   community charge benefit.

The emphasis throughout, however, is on the relevance of these benefits to the client with matrimonial or similar difficulties. It is beyond the scope of this book to provide a comprehensive guide to the law on welfare benefits.[1]

All the benefits considered in this chapter, other than child benefit and one-parent benefit, are income-related. In other words all of them require some form of means test as one of the conditions of eligibility. The law on income-related benefits was radically reformed by the Social Security Act 1986 (S.S.A. 1986), and detailed regulations made under that Act.[2] These reforms came into force in April 1988. The S.S.A. 1986 also introduced the so-called Social Fund out of which certain payments can be made to those in receipt of welfare benefits, and, in some cases, to other people as well. The workings of this Social Fund will be considered in more detail after the benefits themselves have been examined.

1. Child Benefit and One-Parent Benefit

CHILD BENEFIT

(i) Who can claim?   8–04

This benefit, governed by the Child Benefit Act 1975 and regulations made under it, is payable to a person who is responsible for a child. In practice this usually means a parent of the child, although the conditions prescribed by the Act[3] are that the claimant must either:

(a)   have the child living with him; or

(b)   be paying maintenance for the child at, at least, the current rate of child benefit.

Benefit will be paid only to one person.

If a dispute arises as to who is entitled to the benefit, it is resolved by reference to a series of rules governing priority which are contained in the Act.[4] These can be summarised as follows:

(a)   The person with whom the child lives takes priority over a person paying maintenance.

(b)   Subject to (a), where a husband and wife are living together, the wife takes priority.

---

[1] A very useful general guide is the *National Welfare Benefits Handbook* published annually by the Child Poverty Action Group.
[2] The S.S.A. 1986 has subsequently been amended in some respects by the Social Security Acts 1988 and 1989. References to the S.S.A. 1986 are to the Act as amended.
[3] Child Benefit Act 1975, s.3.
[4] *Ibid.* Sched. 2.

(c) Subject to (a) and (b), where a parent is living with a non-parent, the parent takes priority, and, where the parents are living together, the mother takes priority.

8–05 **(ii) Definition of "child"**
By virtue of section 2 of the Act, a child is a person under 16, or under 19 if still in full-time secondary education.

8–06 **(iii) The amount of benefit**
Payment of child benefit does not depend on any means test. It is payable to anyone responsible for a child at a fixed rate which is reviewed annually. For the year April 1990 to April 1991, the rate is £7.25 for each child. It is not subject to income tax, and is ignored in assessing a person's gross income for family credit purposes. It does, however, count as a resource for income support purposes.

8–07 **(iv) Claiming the benefit**
Claims are made on a form which can be obtained from post offices or local D.S.S. offices. The claim is then submitted to the D.S.S. If granted, child benefit is payable via a book of orders which must be cashed at a post office. Child benefit is normally payable once every four weeks, but lone parents and those on income support or family credit can choose to be paid weekly.

8–08 ONE-PARENT BENEFIT

Lone parents are entitled to an extra amount of child benefit, known as one-parent benefit.[5] This too is paid at a fixed rate, regardless of means, but, unlike ordinary child benefit, is paid only in respect of the first child and is unaffected by the number of children for whom the claimant is responsible. As from April 1990, it is payable at a rate of £5.60 per week.

8–09 The term "one-parent" is misleading in the sense that the claimant need not be a parent of the child at all. The conditions of eligibility are that the claimant must be entitled to child benefit and must

(i)   have no spouse, or not be living with a spouse, and

(ii) not be living with anyone else as a spouse.

Thus, for example, the widowed grandmother of a child who had taken over the sole care of the child could claim one-parent benefit, as well as ordinary child benefit. In practice,

---

[5] One-parent benefit is simply a special rate of child benefit payable by virtue of the Child Benefit and Social Security (Fixing and Adjustment of Rates) Regulations 1976 (as amended).

however, one-parent benefit will usually be claimed by separated or divorced mothers.

Where a claimant is married and is claiming one-parent **8–10** benefit following a separation, benefit will only be paid after at least 13 consecutive weeks of separation, and the separation must be likely to be permanent.[6] This rule does not apply if the court has granted a decree of judicial separation, nor does it apply to claimants who were formerly only cohabiting with a person to whom they were not married.

Like child benefit, one-parent benefit is not taxable and does **8–11** not count as a resource in calculating family credit. It is, however, a resource for income support purposes, which means that a person who is on income support will gain no advantage by claiming one-parent benefit.

Claims are made on a separate form to the D.S.S., but, if the claim is granted, the benefit will be paid with the ordinary child benefit.

2. Income Support

BACKGROUND **8–12**

Income support (I.S.) is a means-tested benefit which was introduced in 1988 to replace supplementary benefit. The general idea behind it is to supplement the incomes of those not in full-time work, who without it would be living below an income level defined annually by Parliament. As it is income-related, it is available to claimants according to their need, unlike benefits available under the national insurance scheme, which depend upon the claimant's record of contributions.

As mentioned above, the law on I.S. is contained primarily in the Social Security Act 1986 (S.S.A. 1986). The detailed workings of the scheme are governed by a series of regulations made under the Act, which are regularly revised.[7]

The scheme itself is administered by the D.S.S. through local offices situated throughout the country. Officials in the offices, known as adjudication officers, are responsible for deciding whether a claimant is entitled to I.S.

---

[6] Child Benefit (General) Regulations 1976, reg. 11 (as amended).
[7] The main regulations are the Income Support (General) Regs. 1987, S.I. No. 1967, as amended.

8–13 WHO CAN CLAIM INCOME SUPPORT?

The essential conditions that allow a person to claim I.S. are set out in the S.S.A. 1986, section 20(3). These conditions may be summarised as follows.

(i) The claimant must be present in Great Britain (though absences of up to four weeks are permitted).

(ii) He or she must be 16 or over (though 16- and 17-year-olds are eligible only in certain restricted circumstances, *e.g.* as a lone parent).

(iii) He or she must have no income, or their income must not exceed an "applicable amount." (This is considered in detail below.)

(iv) He or she must not be in paid employment for 24 hours or more a week, nor must any partner with whom the claimant lives (regardless of whether they are married to each other).

(v) He or she must be available for work. However, many categories of claimant are exempt from this condition, the main example for our purposes being a lone parent who has a dependent child aged under 16 living with her.

(vi) He or she must not be receiving full-time non-advanced education, (*i.e.* up to and including A-levels).

8–14 WHO WILL BE INCLUDED IN A CLAIM?

Obviously many claims for I.S. are made by people living alone. However, claims often include other people living with the claimant. Claims are made in respect of what the D.S.S. call "the family," and this may consist of the claimant, a partner and any dependent children.

8–15 **(i) Partners**
Where a man and a woman are living together as husband and wife they are treated as a couple and only one of them may make the claim on behalf of them both. Subject to the rule that neither partner must be in full-time employment, the parties are free to choose which of them shall be the claimant. If they cannot decide, the social security office will decide for them. It is irrelevant to the assessment whether the couple are

married or simply cohabiting, although the question of whether a man and a woman are cohabiting is not always easy to answer. The D.S.S. in its own guide to income support lists the following criteria as being those that are taken into account by adjudication officers.

(a) Both partners must be living in the same household and neither of them will usually have any other home where they normally live.

(b) There should be some evidence of an established relationship; living together as husband and wife clearly implies more than an occasional or very brief association.

(c) Usually one party will provide financial support for the other, though this is not an essential feature.

(d) Usually the parties will have a sexual relationship. However, the absence of such a relationship does not necessarily prove that the parties are not living as husband and wife, nor does its presence prove that they are.

(e) Where the parties are caring for a child or children of whom they are the parents, this is likely to imply that they are living as husband and wife.

(f) The way other people see the relationship is relevant. However, the fact that the parties wish to retain their separate identities publicly as single people does not mean that they cannot be regarded as living together as husband and wife.

(ii) Dependants   **8–16**
A claim for I.S. will generally include any child who is a member of the same household as the claimant, and for whom the claimant is responsible. This covers children up to the age of 16, but the claim can also cover young people who are receiving secondary education, and are under 19. It is immaterial that the claimant is not a parent of the child or young person in question.

CALCULATING ENTITLEMENT TO INCOME SUPPORT   8–17

As was seen in 8–13 above, entitlement to I.S. depends on whether a claimant's weekly income is below an "applicable amount." It is therefore necessary to calculate first the "applicable amount" for the family in question and then deduct from the total any relevant income that they may have. Assuming that the "applicable amount" is greater than the income, the shortfall will be met by way of I.S. payments.

8–18 **(i) The applicable amount**
The applicable amount has three component parts; personal allowances, premiums and housing costs. All claimants start off with a personal allowance. The amount of this allowance depends on their age, on whether they have children and on whether they are living with someone else. Thus, for example, a lone parent of 18 or over receives a higher personal allowance than a lone parent under 18. Where there are children in the household, additional personal allowances which increase with the age of the child will be added to the claimant's allowance. These personal allowances are by no means generous, but they are intended to meet the basic living expenses of the family, and indeed to allow some money to be saved to pay for the replacement of essential household items from time to time. Some idea of the amounts involved will be gathered from the list set out below. These are the weekly rates in force for the year April 1990–91.

	£
Lone parent – under 18	21.90
– age 18 or over	36.70
Couple – both under 18	43.80
– at least one aged 18 or over	57.60
Dependent children – age 0–10	12.35
– age 11–15	18.25
– age 16–17	21.90
– age 18	28.80

8–19 The premiums which are then added to these personal allowances represent amounts for extra needs which the family may have. Thus, for example, there is a family premium for all those with dependent children. This is at a flat rate, which remains the same regardless of the number of children in the family. On top of this there is also an additional lone-parent premium. This premium, as well as the family premium, will continue as long as any dependent child remains in full-time, non-advanced education.

8–20 Thirdly, certain housing costs can be included as part of the I.S. applicable amount. However, for this purpose "housing costs" are fairly narrowly defined. The most important example is mortgage interest. A new claimant for I.S. is not entitled to have all of his or her mortgage interest included within the applicable amount. As long as the claimant, and any partner, are under 60 the D.S.S. will take into account only 50 per cent. of the mortgage interest for the first 16 weeks of the claim. As only half the mortgage interest is included for the first 16 weeks, cases will arise in which a claimant will be denied I.S. completely for this period, although, had the full amount of mortgage interest been taken into account, some I.S. would have been payable immediately. In such cases it is important that an initial claim is made, even though it will fail, so that the 16-week period can start running. A second claim should then be made shortly before or very soon after the expiry of the 16-week period.

Example   **8–21**

Louise, who has two children, is separated from her husband. She is responsible for mortgage interest payments of £50 per week. This, added to her personal allowances and premiums, brings her applicable amount to £122 per week. Her income is £100 per week. Her normal I.S. entitlement is, therefore, £22 per week. However, as only half of her mortgage interest is included for the first 16 weeks of her claim, this reduces her applicable amount to (£122 − £25) £97 per week. Her income therefore exceeds her applicable amount for 16 weeks. Louise must reapply for I.S., preferably just before this period expires, to ensure that she receives her £22 per week benefit thereafter.

It will be noted that the capital element of mortgage   **8–22** repayments is never included as a part of a claimant's housing costs. A number of other housing costs are not included either. For example, there is no separate allowance for water rates and insurance, because it is intended that the basic personal allowances should include an amount for these items. Rent is never included as a housing cost for I.S. purposes, since this is covered by payments of housing benefit.

(ii) Income   **8–23**
In general, the weekly income of all members of the family will be added together in assessing the amount of I.S. that will be payable. The main items will be considered in turn.

Earnings   **8–24**

The earnings of the claimant and any partner will be included in the calculation, but the earnings of a dependent child are ignored, as long as the child is at school. Certain deductions are made from gross earnings in computing income. In particular, income tax and national insurance contributions are deducted, as is one-half of any contribution made towards an occupational or personal pension scheme. There is no deduction, however, for other work-related expenses, such as travelling and child-minding costs.

Once net earnings in the sense defined above have been calculated, an additional earnings disregard is deducted. This disregard is currently £5.00 from the earnings of the claimant plus a further £5.00 from the earnings of any partner. However, a lone parent is entitled to a higher earnings disregard of £15.00 per week.

8–25 *Maintenance*

Maintenance received from a spouse, or ex-spouse, or the father of any children will be taken into account in full. Maintenance usually takes the form of periodical payments, but it is immaterial whether it is paid under a court order or not. Payments of maintenance in the form of a lump sum may also be treated as income; the special rules affecting lump sum payments are considered in more detail at 8–32 to 8–43 below.

8–26 *Other welfare benefits*

Most other welfare benefits are taken into account in full as income. This applies, for example, to child benefit and one-parent benefit. If payments of family credit are being received, these too are taken into account in full. However, housing benefit (8–78 to 8–83, below) is not taken into account.

8–27 *Income from capital*

The capital of the claimant and any partner is added together. If the total exceeds £8,000 then no I.S. can be claimed. Any capital owned by a dependent child is not included for this purpose, but if the child has capital of more than £3,000 no claim can be made for that child. Certain capital items are complete disregarded in making the calculation. The main example for most people will be the value of the home in which they live.

8–28 Subject to the above rules, capital of £3,000 or less is completely ignored, as is any income from such capital. However, where the family has capital of between £3,000 and £8,000, it will be assumed that capital of more than £3,000 is producing a weekly income. Thus, although a claim will still be possible, the amount of I.S. payable will be reduced by the amount of the assumed weekly income. The amount of this so-called "tariff income" is £1 per week for each £250 (or part of £250) of capital in excess of £3,000. So, for example, a claimant with £5,000 in savings would be assumed to have income of £8 per week. It is irrelevant whether the capital is actually producing more or less income than this, as all interest received from capital is ignored in assessing income.

(iii) The passport effect

8–29

Once a person's entitlement to I.S. is established, he or she will be automatically entitled to certain other benefits as well. The value of these benefits may be as great, or even greater, than I.S. itself, and this means that a claim to I.S. may well be worth establishing and preserving, even if the amount of weekly benefit received is relatively small.

It is particularly important to bear this in mind when negotiating maintenance payments for a client on I.S. If the proposed maintenance is only just sufficient to take the client off benefit, it would probably leave her worse off overall than if she accepted a reduced amount of maintenance, preserved her entitlement to I.S., and took advantage of its passport effect.

The following are the main benefits to which I.S. is a passport:

(a) Free school meals.

(b) Exemption from N.H.S. charges for prescriptions, dental treatment and glasses.

(c) Free milk and vitamins for expectant and nursing mothers and pre-school children.

In addition, a person entitled to I.S. is automatically entitled to the maximum amount of housing benefit and community charge benefit (see 8–78 to 8–87 below). Claimants of I.S. are also able to receive payments out of the Social Fund (see 8–88 to 8–99, below).

(iv) Specimen calculation

8–30

Mary, aged 40, lives in a house which she owns jointly with her husband Tom. There are three children of the family, Anne (aged four), Belinda (aged 12) and Charles (aged 17). All three attend local schools. Two weeks ago Tom and Mary agreed to separate and Tom left Mary living in the home with the children.

Mary is responsible for paying the mortgage of £30 per week. She works 20 hours a week, for which she earns £20 (net of income tax). Tom pays her £25 per week maintenance.

Mary applies for I.S. and her entitlement is calculated as follows, using the benefit rates current for the year April 1990 to 1991.

APPLICABLE AMOUNT

Personal allowances	£
Mary	36.70
Anne	12.35
Belinda	18.25
Charles	21.90
Premiums	
Family premium	7.35
Lone-parent premium	4.10
Housing costs	
Mortgage interest	15.00
Applicable amount =	115.65

INCOME	
Maintenance	25.00
Earnings	5.00
Child Benefit (£7.25 X 3)	21.75
Income =	51.75

I.S. = £115.65 — £51.75
I.S. = £63.90 per week

8–31 *Explanatory notes*

(i) Although Charles is over 16 he is treated as a dependant as he is in full-time secondary education.

(ii) Mary, being under 60, has only half her mortgage interest allowed for the first 16 weeks of her claim.

(iii) As a lone parent, Mary qualifies for the extra earnings disregard of £15 per week.

(iv) As she is entitled to I.S., Mary will also be entitled to other benefits because of the passport effect (see 8–29, above).

196

THE SPECIAL RULES ON LUMP SUM PAYMENTS   **8–32**

As mentioned at 8–25, above, the treatment of lump sum payments requires special consideration, though it should be noted first that, if the lump sum represents a share in the proceeds of sale of a former home, it will be ignored for at least six months if the money is to be used to buy another home.

When, however, a lump sum is intended as a form of maintenance, it will be treated as income and may debar a claimant from benefit, or at least reduce the amount of benefit payable, for a period of time while the lump sum is used up. This prevents a claimant from accepting a lump sum from a spouse, an ex-spouse, or the parent of a dependent child, in lieu of periodical payments so as to avoid losing benefit. The rules according to which this is done may be summarised as follows.

(i) Lump sums to a claimant   8–33

Where a lump sum payment is made to a claimant, it is decapitalised according to the formula:

$$\frac{\text{Lump sum}}{\text{I.S.} + 2} = \text{number of weeks off benefit}$$

The effect of this formula is that the claimant is expected to use the money at her usual weekly rate of I.S., plus £2. It means that she will not receive any I.S. for this period, but will have £2 a week more income from the lump sum payment than she would have done if she had been relying solely on I.S.

Example   8–34

Linda who has two children and is separated from her husband, Ken, claims I.S. of £48 per week. She receives no maintenance from Ken, but one day he offers her £500 which she accepts. The lump sum will be decapitalised thus:

$$\frac{£500}{48 + 2} = 10$$

Linda will receive no further benefit for 10 weeks, during which time she is expected to live on the lump sum at just £2 per week above her normal level of I.S.

8–35   **(ii) Lump sums to a child**
If the lump sum is paid as maintenance for the benefit of a child only, it will not debar the claimant from I.S. but it will reduce the amount of benefit payable for a period of time. The claimant will be expected to spend the money at the same weekly rate as her usual personal allowance for the child, together with any premiums, (*e.g.* family or lone-parent premiums) relevant to that child.

8–36   *Example*

Susan's I.S. entitlement is £48 per week. Jeff, her husband, pays no maintenance but pays a lump sum of £500 to Mandy, their 10-year-old daughter who lives with Susan. In calculating her I.S., Susan has been entitled to a personal allowance for Mandy of £12.35 per week, plus family and lone-parent premiums which together total £11.45. Mandy therefore contributes a total of £23.80 to Susan's applicable amount. On receipt of the lump sum from Jeff, Susan's I.S. will be reduced by £23.80 per week for

$$\frac{£500}{23.8} = 21 \text{ weeks}$$

8–37   **(iii) Lump sum payments plus maintenance**
Where a lump sum payment is accompanied by periodical payments to a family on I.S., the amount of benefit payable will again be extinguished or reduced for a number of weeks while the lump sum is used up. The formulae according to which this is done depend on whether the *maintenance* is for the claimant or only for a child or children.

In the case of a claimant, the lump sum will be treated as extra income according to the formula:

$$(\text{I.S.} + 2) - M$$

Where I.S. = the amount of benefit payable if no maintenance
were paid
and M = the maintenance paid

8–38   *Example*

Jill, who has been receiving £48.00 per week in I.S., starts receiving £20.00 per week from her husband, Bill. (This reduces her I.S. entitlement to £28.00 per week). She then receives from Bill a lump sum of £600. The lump sum will be treated as extra income according to the formula in 8–37, above:

$$(48+2) - 20 = £30 \text{ per week}$$

This extra income temporarily extinguishes Jill's entitlement to I.S. Assuming rates of benefit, etc., remain constant, it will take Jill 20 weeks to use up her lump sum of £600 at the rate of £30 per week and no benefit will therefore be payable for 20 weeks.

Where the maintenance is paid *only* for a child or children, **8–39** but is less than the total of their personal allowances plus any premiums relating to them, (*e.g.* family and lone-parent premiums), any lump sum paid to the claimant or the child will be treated as extra income according to the formula:

$$(P.A. + P) - M$$

Where P.A. = Personal Allowance
P = Relevant Premiums
M = Maintenance

Example **8–40**

Carol is an unmarried mother with an I.S. entitlement of £50.00 per week. As she has a baby, Mark, her applicable amount includes £23.80 per week for him (personal allowance plus family premium plus lone-parent premium). Mark's father, Paul, then starts paying maintenance for Mark at the rate of £13.80 per week. This reduces Carol's I.S. to £36.20 per week. Paul then pays Carol a lump sum of £250. As the maintenance Paul pays for Mark is less than Mark's personal allowance plus premiums, the lump sum will be treated as extra income according to the formula in 8–39 above:

$$23.80 - 13.80 = £10.00 \text{ per week}$$

Assuming rates of benefit, etc., remain constant, it will take Carol 25 weeks to use up the lump sum of £250 at the rate of £10 per week and her benefit will be reduced by this amount, (i.e. to £26.20 per week) for 25 weeks.

It should be noted, however, that if maintenance payments **8–41** for a child equal or exceed the amount of their personal allowance plus any relevant premiums, any lump sum paid will be treated as capital and not as income. If, therefore, the lump sum took the family's capital to more than £8,000, I.S. would cease; and if it took their capital to between £3,000 and

£8,000, the tariff-income rules would apply. Possession of smaller amounts of capital can also affect entitlement to payments out of the Social Fund (see 8–85 to 8–89, below).

8–42 Of course, all the above examples assume that all other circumstances, such as rates of benefit and the claimant's income, remain the same throughout the period of dis-qualification or reduction. In practice, this will often not be the case, so that the period may be reduced or increased depending on how circumstances change.

8–43 A further complication that can easily arise in any of these cases is that a claimant is found to have spent a lump sum faster than the rules allow, possibly while she was awaiting a decision on her claim to I.S. In this case, adjudication officers are instructed not to apply the decapitalisation formulae if they are satisfied that the claimant has not deliberately deprived herself of the money in order to claim I.S.

8–44 THE DUTIES OF A LIABLE RELATIVE

Under section 26 of the S.S.A. 1986, a man is liable to maintain his wife and his children, and a woman is liable to maintain her husband and her children. No liability arises between ex-spouses, although the liability to maintain children is unaffected by divorce or annulment. The liability to maintain children arises only in respect of natural children; it is irrelevant that a party has merely treated children as children of the family. The significance of this provision is that if, for example, a wife is claiming I.S. in respect of herself and her children, the D.S.S. will inquire whether her husband and the father of the children is fulfilling his statutory duty to maintain the family and, if he is not, may take steps to obtain a contribution from him.

8–45 For this purpose a "liable relative officer" may interview the husband to investigate his means and to assess whether he is providing a reasonable amount of support for the family on I.S. As a starting point in this assessment, the officer will apply the "liable relative formula" to decide how much money the husband needs to live on.[8] This is done by taking the notional I.S. allowances and premiums relevant to the husband and any partner or dependants living with him, and adding to these an amount representing his reasonable

---

[8] There is no statutory basis for this formula. Its existence was first revealed in the Finer Report on One Parent Families. Cmnd. 5629 (1974).

housing costs, his community charge liability, and 15 per cent. of his net earnings. This is the amount he is entitled to keep. Any surplus net earnings are regarded as being available for the support of his family. If the husband is not paying at least approximately this amount he will be asked to do so.

If the husband fails to make a proper contribution, the D.S.S.   **8–46** can, under the S.S.A. 1986, s.24, take civil proceedings against him in a magistrates' court, which may result in an order being made requiring him to make payments in future to the D.S.S. This may cost the husband more than if he paid the money to the wife by agreement, or under an ordinary court order, because income tax relief is not available on payments to the D.S.S.[9] In the worst cases of failure to maintain, the D.S.S. can take criminal proceedings against the liable relative in a magistrates' court, under the S.S.A. 1986, s.26.

In proceedings brought under the S.S.A. 1986, a defendant   **8–47** cannot rely on a prior court order under which he was not ordered to pay maintenance. Thus, in *Hulley* v. *Thompson*,[10] a consent order made on divorce had contained no provision for the children of the family. The ex-wife claimed supplementary benefit (now I.S.) which included an amount for the children's requirements. The Divisional Court held that the father remained under a statutory duty to maintain the children, regardless of the court order, so that the magistrates were entitled to make an order against him. This is an important point to bear in mind when negotiating a consent order. It may be that a father, for example, is ready to make more generous capital provision than normal, on the basis that he will not be required to make periodical payments to the children. However, if a claim for I.S. which includes the children is made after the divorce, the father may find that he has to contribute to their maintenance after all.

It is, of course, possible for a wife who is in receipt of I.S. to   **8–48** take her own proceedings against a husband who is unreasonably failing to maintain her or his children.[11] In many cases, however, a wife will be reluctant to do so, because a maintenance order made in her favour will often not be sufficient to take her off benefit, so that her total income will remain the same. She will, also, have the

---

[9] *McBurnie* v. *Tacey* [1984] 1 W.L.R. 1019.
[10] [1981] 1 W.L.R. 159.
[11] See Chapter 14 below.

uncertainty of not knowing whether the husband is going to pay the maintenance regularly. Consequently, adjudication officers should not put pressure on wives to take proceedings of their own against a husband who is not providing proper maintenance. In any case, they have no power to insist on this as a condition of her receiving benefit. They may, however, legitimately point out to her the possible advantages of taking proceedings, namely that the maintenance order might be high enough to take her off benefit altogether, and, even if it did not, it could remain in force if the wife subsequently came off benefit as a result of a change in her circumstances.

8–49 THE DIVERSION PROCEDURE

Where a claimant (usually a wife or ex-wife) is receiving maintenance under a court order as well as I.S., it will sometimes be to her advantage to assign the benefit of the order to the D.S.S. Her benefit will then be increased proportionately, and the D.S.S. will receive the maintenance. This is particularly useful in cases where the husband is an unreliable payer, because it relieves the wife of the anxiety of wondering whether she will receive her maintenance each week.

8–50 *Example*

Under an order made on her divorce from Mark, Fiona receives maintenance of £20 per week. She is also entitled to I.S. of £30 per week. Mark proves to be a bad payer and Fiona frequently has to apply for extra benefit in those weeks when she receives no money from him. Fiona therefore signs her maintenance order over to the D.S.S., and becomes entitled to £50 per week in benefit, while the D.S.S. looks to Mark for payments of £20 per week.

8–51 The diversion procedure, as it is usually known, operates best in cases where the claimant's I.S. entitlement is greater than the maintenance payable, because in such cases the claimant will clearly be entitled to I.S. anyhow. Where the maintenance ordered is more than the I.S. entitlement, so that no I.S. is payable as long as the maintenance is paid, the D.S.S. will be reluctant to accept a signing over of the order. They will do so, however, if the husband has a bad record of making the payments, so that the wife is frequently forced to claim I.S.

8–52 The D.S.S. will only accept a signing over if the order has been made or registered in a magistrates' court, or if a county court attachment of earnings order has been made in respect of it. This means that the order should be easily enforceable, as the collection of the money is the responsibility of either the clerk of the magistrates' court, or the husband's employer. (Methods of enforcement are considered in more detail in Chapter 13, below.)

PROCEDURE

Applying for Income Support[12]   **8–53**
Claims for benefit must be made in writing, but this can be done quite easily by completing the short S.B.1 form, available at post offices and local D.S.S offices, or, for the unemployed, form B.1, available from unemployment benefit offices. Alternatively a letter claiming benefit can be written instead. The form or letter should be sent to the claimant's local D.S.S office. In urgent cases, a claimant can call at the office in person, or can telephone the office, but a written claim will still be required before benefit is granted.

Claimants will be required to provide detailed information   **8–54**
about their means. This is given on a form which the claimant completes and returns by post. Help in filling in the form can be obtained at the D.S.S. office or a home visit can be requested. The D.S.S. will require evidence of means such as payslips, bank statements and building society passbooks, as well as evidence of outgoings, such as mortgage payments.

Once an adjudication officer has decided whether I.S. is   **8–55**
payable, the claimant will be notified in writing of the decision. The claimant will also receive a short form showing how the decision was arrived at. The claimant is entitled to a detailed explanation of how the claim was decided, but this is only issued on request. It is well worth making this request if there is any reason to think that the claim has been wrongly decided, because the detailed calculation should reveal whether there are grounds for applying for a review of or for appealing against the decision.

If the claim is successful, I.S. may be backdated to the date   **8–56**
the claim was received by the D.S.S.

The way in which I.S. is paid depends on the category of   **8–57**
claimant. Claimants who are not required to be available for

---

[12] The rules are contained in the Social Security (Claims and Payments) Regs., 1987, S.I. No. 1968.

work (which includes many matrimonial clients) are paid by a book of orders which they cash each week at a post office. Unemployed people, on the other hand, are usually paid by girocheque, sent fortnightly by the unemployment benefit office.

8–58 (ii) Reviews and appeals[13]

In many cases in which a claimant wants to challenge a decision regarding benefit, it will be best to apply first for an internal review of the decision. An adjudication officer can review a decision if it was based on ignorance of, or a mistake about, a material fact, or if there has been an error of law, or if the claimant's circumstances have changed since the original decision was made. There is no time-limit within which a review must be sought, although one of the advantages of seeking a review is that it may result in the decision being altered much more quickly than if it is made the subject of an appeal.

8–59 If a review does not result in a satisfactory revision of the decision, the claimant can appeal against it to an independent Social Security Appeal Tribunal. Everyone can appeal as of right against any decision of an adjudication officer.

8–60 The appeal can be made by writing a letter to the adjudication officer at the local D.S.S. office, and should be lodged within three months of the decision. Where the claimant is out of time, a useful tactic is to apply for a review (for which there is no time-limit) and, if the review decision is unfavourable, the claimant will have a further three months to appeal against that. Alternatively, the chairman of the appeal tribunal has a discretion to hear an appeal that is out of time.

8–61 The appeal hearing itself, which may not take place for two months or more after the lodging of the appeal, is before a tribunal which normally consists of three members assisted by a clerk. The chairman is a lawyer. The proceedings are in public, unless the claimant requests otherwise, or the chairman considers that the hearing should be in private. There is no prescribed order that the proceedings must follow, but the claimant and an officer representing the D.S.S will be invited to speak, and may be asked questions by the tribunal. Legal aid is not available for these proceedings, so solicitors do not normally appear. A solicitor can, however, assist a claimant to prepare an appeal under the Green Form

---

[13] The rules are contained in the S.S.A. 1986, s.52 and the Social Security (Adjudication) Regs. 1986, S.I. No. 2218.

scheme. The claimant is entitled to be accompanied and represented by anyone (for example, an adviser from a Citizen's Advice Bureau) and statistics show that claimants who are represented have a better chance of success.

A few days after the hearing, the clerk sends both parties the tribunal's decision. This is on a standard form, setting out the decision and the reasons for it. Either side may then appeal to a Social Security Commissioner, but only on a point of law, and only with the leave of the chairman of the tribunal, or, if this is refused, with leave of the Commissioner himself. Social Security Commissioners are lawyers of at least 10 years' standing, who sit only in main regional centres. An appellant has three months from the date of the tribunal's decision in which to apply for leave to appeal, and, if leave is granted, another 42 days in which to lodge the appeal itself. The Commissioner can make his decision on the basis of written submissions, although the appellant may request an oral hearing. Legal aid is not available for the proceedings. **8–62**

Either side can appeal from the Commissioner's decision to the Court of Appeal, but, again, only on a point of law and only with leave of the Commissioner or the court. Ultimately an appeal to the House of Lords on a point of law is possible. Legal aid is, of course, available for proceedings in the ordinary courts. **8–63**

3. Family Credit

BACKGROUND **8–64**

Family credit (F.C.) was also introduced by the S.S.A. 1986 and replaced family income supplement.[14] The idea behind F.C. is to supplement the income of families in which the claimant or a partner is working full time. As a full-time worker cannot claim I.S., but might not be earning enough to keep the family above subsistence level, F.C. provides the top-up which is supposed to ensure that the family is at least as well off as a family on I.S.

Like I.S., F.C. is administered by the D.S.S. and decisions are taken by adjudication officers. As, however, there are far fewer claimants than for I.S., it is possible to administer it from a central office which is situated in Blackpool. Claims are not dealt with by local D.S.S. officers.

---

[14] The main regulations are the Family Credit (General) Regs. 1987, S.I. No. 1973, as amended.

8-65 WHO CAN CLAIM FAMILY CREDIT?

The claimant must be ordinarily resident in Great Britain and present here at the date of the claim. Besides this the essential conditions for eligibility, as set out in section 20(5) of the S.S.A. 1986, are as follows.

    (i) The claimant or a partner must be engaged in full-time work.

   (ii) The claimant or a partner must be responsible for at least one dependent child.

  (iii) The claimant's income must not exceed the applicable amount, or, if it does exceed it, must do so only by a certain defined margin.

Each of these conditions requires further explanation.

(i) Full-time work
The claimant or a partner must be working in paid employment for an average of at least 24 hours a week. This is, of course, the same definition of "full-time work" that is used for I.S. purposes.

8-66 (ii) A dependent child
Children are the key to getting F.C. The claimant may be a lone parent, or living as one of a couple, whether married or unmarried, but the number of adults in the family has in itself no bearing on the question of whether F.C. is payable, or on the amount of F.C. that will be paid.

8-67 To qualify for F.C. the claimant, or a partner if any, must be responsible for the needs of at least one child under the age of 16 (or under 19 if the child is in full-time education up to A-level or equivalent standard). Neither the claimant nor the partner need be a parent of the child concerned, provided the child is living with them as a member of their family.

8-68 (iii) Income below a prescribed level
A claimant's income is calculated in much the same way as for I.S., although there are several important differences. The same principle of aggregation applies, so, in general, the income of all members of the family is treated as being the income of the claimant. As with I.S. the earnings of the claimant or a partner are taken into account after deduction of income tax, national insurance contributions and half of any occupational pension contribution. However, unlike I.S. there are no other earnings disregards. Maintenance payments are treated as income in the same way as for I.S., but child

benefit and one-parent benefit are ignored. Furthermore the decapitalisation rules on lump sums do not apply to F.C. Capital is treated in exactly the same way as for I.S. In other words capital of more than £8,000 debars a claim entirely, and capital between £3,000 and £8,000 will be subject to the tariff income rules. Capital of £3,000 or less is ignored, as is any interest received from capital of any amount.

The amount of any F.C. payable is calculated by comparing the claimant's income with a set figure known as the "applicable amount." This applicable amount is quite different from that prescribed for I.S. purposes. It is simply a set figure which is revised annually. If the claimant's income is below or equal to this set amount, the family will receive the maximum amount of F.C. appropriate to their circumstances. If the claimant's income is above the set figure, the amount of F.C. payable will be the maximum amount reduced by 70 per cent. of the difference between the claimant's income and the applicable amount. **8–69**

CALCULATION OF FAMILY CREDIT **8–70**

The maximum amount of F.C. which can be awarded depends on the number and ages of the children in the family. The calculation begins with a single adult credit which is the same for lone parents and for couples. There is then an additional child credit for each child in the family, and the amount of this credit increases with the age of the child. For the year April 1990 to 1991 the maximum credits prescribed are as set out below.

Adult Credit	£36.35
Child Credit – Age 0–10	£8.25
– Age 11–15	£14.15
– Age 16–17	£17.80
– Age 18	£25.10

For 1990–91 the applicable amount prescribed is £57.60.
Using these rates we can see how F.C. is calculated.

Example 1 **8–71**

Alice is a lone parent with two children, Bobby aged 12 and Carol aged six. Her income for F.C. purposes is calculated as being £55 per week. This is below the prescribed applicable amount and she is therefore entitled to the maximum amount of F.C. for a person in her circumstances:

Adult Credit	£36.35
Bobby	£14.15
Carol	£8.25

F.C. = £58.75 p.w.

8–72 *Example 2*

Diane is a lone parent with two children, Edward aged 12 and Fiona aged six. Her income for F.C. purposes is calculated as being £100 per week. This is above the prescribed applicable amount and so Diane's maximum F.C. will be reduced by 70 per cent. of the difference.

Diane's maximum credit = £58.75
(the same as for Alice in Example 1)

Diane's income is £42.40 above the applicable amount
(*i.e.* £100 — £57.60)

£42.40 x 70% = £29.68
So Diane's F.C. = £58.75 — £29.68 = £29.07 p.w.

8–73 THE PASSPORT EFFECT

Entitlement to F.C. does not have the same passport effect as does I.S. In particular, households in receipt of F.C. will not be entitled to free school meals or free welfare milk and vitamins. Instead it is intended that the amounts allowed as child credits should include an element to reflect the average price charged for school meals by local authorities. Those in receipt of F.C. will, however, gain automatic exemption from N.H.S charges, in the same way as recipients of I.S.

8–74 MAKING A CLAIM[15]

In two-parent families it is the woman who must claim F.C., though lone parents can, of course, claim in their own right for their family.

8–75 The claim is made on form F.C.1 which can be obtained at any post office or local security office. The form is then sent

---

[15] See the Social Security (Claims and Payments) Regs. 1987, S.I. No. 1968.

by post to the central unit in Blackpool. If the claim is successful F.C. will be paid either by automatic credit transfer through, for example, a bank or building society account, or by a book of orders which can be cashed each week at the post office of the claimant's choice.

Once entitlement to F.C. has been established, it normally **8–76** remains payable at the same rate for 26 weeks, after which it will be reassessed. The fact that F.C. remains payable at the same level for 26 weeks, regardless of a change in circumstances, can work both ways. It might, for example, be wise to claim F.C. before applying for an increase in periodical payments, because once granted the amount of F.C. payable would not immediately be reduced if the maintenance were increased. On the other hand, the claimant cannot obtain an immediate increase in F.C. if her circumstances change for the worse. If, for example, her hours of work were reduced, this would have no immediate effect on her entitlement. In some cases, however, a claim for I.S. might then be possible.

REVIEWS AND APPEALS   8–77

A claimant who considers that F.C. has been wrongly refused, or that the amount awarded is too low, has the same right to request a review or to institute an appeal as does a claimant for I.S. The rules governing such reviews and appeals are set out at 8–58 to 8–63, above.

4. Housing Benefit

BACKGROUND   8–78

Housing benefit (H.B.) was also reformed by the S.S.A. 1986.[16] H.B. was originally a means of getting help with the payment of both rent and rates, but, with the introduction of the community charge in April 1990, housing benefit became restricted to a rent rebate or allowance, and ceased to be relevant to the owner/occupier. It does not assist with mortgage repayments, although, as seen above, a person may be able to have mortgage interest payments included as part of his housing costs for I.S. purposes. Although people claiming I.S. and F.C. will generally be entitled to H.B., it is

---

[16] The governing regulations are the Housing Benefit (General) Regs. 1987, S.I. No. 1971, as amended.

by no means confined to such people. Many people who do not qualify for I.S. or F.C. are able to claim H.B.

8–79   H.B. is administered by local authorities, not the D.S.S. The way in which a claimant receives the benefit depends on what kind of householder he is. Local authority tenants receive no money at all; instead they receive a *rebate* on the rent which they would otherwise have to pay. Private tenants, on the other hand, receive a rent *allowance*, which takes the form of a payment towards their rent, which they must still pay in full to their landlord.

8–80   HOW MUCH?

Calculation of H.B. begins by establishing a claimant's maximum housing benefit. If the claimant is on I.S. or if his income is not more than an applicable amount, he will be entitled to receive the maximum H.B. figure. However, if the claimant's income exceeds his applicable amount, then the maximum H.B. figure is reduced by a percentage of the difference. In making this calculation, "income" and the "applicable amount" mean very much the same as for I.S. purposes. There are some differences however. For example, a lone parent receives a higher premium in calculating the applicable amount for H.B. purposes than she does for I.S. The amount of capital which a claimant may have is higher too; a claim is barred only when the claimant has capital of more than £16,000.

8–81   In practice the effect of the calculation is that a person on I.S., or whose income does not exceed I.S. levels, will usually receive 100 per cent. of the rent actually payable. Where a claimant has income above I.S. levels, the maximum amount of H.B. will be reduced by 65 per cent. of the amount by which his income exceeds the applicable amount.

8–82   *Example*

Heather is a lone parent with one child. She works full time and does not receive I.S. or F.C. Her income for H.B. purposes is £150 per week and her applicable amount is £66 per week. Heather pays rent of £75 per week for a privately-rented flat. She claims H.B. which is assessed as follows:

100% of rent *less* [(income — applicable amount) x 65%]
= 75 — [(150 — 66) x 65%]
= 75 — [84 x 65%]
= 75 — 54.60 = £20.40 per week

APPEALS   **8–83**

There is no right of appeal to an independent body in respect
of decisions on housing benefit. There is, however, a right to
have a decision reviewed. There are two stages to the process;
first, an internal review, in which the original decision will be
reconsidered, and secondly, a hearing before a review board.
The review board is made up of a panel of three local
councillors and the claimant has a right to attend to put his or
her case in person. In general, the decision of the review
board is final although it might in some cases be possible to
challenge the decision by making an application to the High
Court for judicial review.

5. Community Charge Benefit

BACKGROUND   **8–84**

The community charge was introduced by the Local Government Finance Act 1988 to replace domestic rates. The 1988 Act
has made a number of amendments to the S.S.A. 1986 to
allow those on low incomes to claim relief from the
community charge in the form of a new welfare benefit
known as community charge benefit (C.C.B.).[17] Like housing
benefit, C.C.B. is administered by local authorities, and not
by the D.S.S.

CALCULATION OF C.C.B.   **8–85**

Entitlement to C.C.B. is calculated in a very similar way to
H.B. A maximum C.C.B. is calculated, and some claimants, in
particular those in receipt of I.S., will be entitled to receive
this maximum benefit. However, those claimants whose
income exceeds the applicable amount (these terms mean the
same as for H.B.) will be required to devote 15 per cent. of
the difference to meeting their community charge liability. In
other words, the formula to be applied will be very similar to
that illustrated above (see 8–82) with regard to H.B., with 15
per cent. being substituted for 65 per cent. in the equation.

There is, however, one important difference between C.C.B.   **8–86**
and H.B. This is that the maximum C.C.B. can never be more
than 80 per cent. of the full community charge which is
actually payable. This mean that all claimants, including those

---

[17] The detailed operation of this benefit is governed by the Community
Charge Benefits (General) Regulations 1989; S.I. No. 1321.

on I.S., must meet at least 20 per cent. of the charge out of their own resources. The theory behind this is that if everyone liable to pay the charge has to pay something out of their own pocket, this should act as a disincentive to high spending by local authorities. This could, of course, operate particularly harshly on those claimaing I.S., although an amount representing 20 per cent. of the average community charge should be included in the allowances that go to make up the I.S. applicable amount. Nevertheless, those living in areas where the community charge is above the national average will still suffer a shortfall.

8–87 Where entitlement to C.C.B. is established, it will normally be payable as a rebate, *i.e.* claimants will simply pay the local authority less than the full amount of the community charge bills.

6. The Social Fund

8–88 BACKGROUND

The social fund is a fund operated by the D.S.S. out of which loans and grants can be paid to those on low incomes.[18] Certain payments out of the fund are available only to those claiming a particular income-related benefit, but others are made to anyone who can establish a relevant need.

8–89 WHAT IS COVERED

There are five main areas of need covered by the fund.

  (i)   Maternity and funeral expenses.

  (ii) Cold weather payments.

  (iii) Community care grants.

  (iv) Budgeting loans.

  (v)   Crisis loans.

8–90 MATERNITY AND FUNERAL EXPENSES[19]

Where a claimant or his partner is getting I.S. or F.C., they may be entitled to a grant of a set amount (currently £85.00)

[18] The fund was established by the S.S.A. 1986, ss.32–35.
[19] The main regulations are the Social Fund Maternity and Funeral Expenses (General) Regs. 1987, S.I. No. 481.

out of the social fund towards the cost of having a baby. The full amount is only payable, however, where the claimant has capital of £500 or less. Where a claimant has capital of over £500, the grant will be reduced by the amount of the excess. This means, of course, that in some cases no grant is payable at all.

Payments are also available to help low-income families with the reasonable cost of a funeral for which they are responsible. A claimant or his partner must be in receipt of I.S., F.C. or H.B. (including community-charge rebate) at the date of the claim. There is no set amount for this payment, which may vary according to locality. Claimants with more than £500 capital are subject to the same limitations as affect maternity expenses, outlined above. It should also be noted that funeral costs are recoverable by the D.S.S. out of the dead person's estate whenever possible.   **8–91**

COLD WEATHER PAYMENTS[20]   **8–92**

Certain claimants of I.S. may be entitled to a cold weather payment out of the fund, when the average of the mean daily temperature for seven consecutive days remains equal to or below 0°C. Once again, capital of more than £500 can reduce or extinguish this benefit.

COMMUNITY CARE GRANTS   **8–93**

Community care grants are payable out of the fund to people who have "special difficulties arising from special circumstances." They can be paid, for example, to help people re-establish themselves in the community after, for example, a period in hospital or residential care. They are only available to those in receipt of I.S. or to those expecting to receive I.S. in the near future. Unlike the maternity and funeral expenses and cold weather payments discussed above, community care grants are not governed by regulations, but are subject to a much wider discretion on the part of the officers administering the fund. In theory this means that there is a great deal of flexibility in the way these payments are made. On the other hand they are subject to a fixed budget, and cases can arise in which no payment can be made because the budget has been exhausted. As they are grants, rather than loans, in general

---

[20] The governing regulations are the Social Fund Cold Weather Payments (General) Regs. 1988, S.I. No. 1724.

there is no question of a community care grant having to be repaid.

There is no maximum amount laid down for a community care grant, but claimants will be expected to use any savings they have in excess of £500 before a grant is payable.

8–94 BUDGETING LOANS

Budgeting loans are interest-free loans designed to meet intermittent expenses, such as the cost of furniture and other household equipment. They are only available to those on I.S., and, in general, the claimant must have been receiving I.S. continuously for the 26 weeks prior to the claim.

8–95 Like community care grants, budgeting loans are not subject to regulations, but are largely left to the discretion of the officers administering the fund. There is, however, a ceiling of £1,000 on the amount of any budgeting loan. As with community care grants, claimants are expected to use any savings in excess of £500 towards their needs before a budgeting loan will be payable. Thus, for example, if a claimant in receipt of I.S. had capital of £550, and needed a budgeting loan in order to buy a second-hand cooker costing £100, the claimant would be expected to put £50 of his or her own savings towards the cost and would receive a budgeting loan of only £50 to make up the balance.

8–96 One of the essential differences between a budgeting loan and a community care grant is that the loan will be repayable. Repayments are normally made by way of deduction from benefit, although there are limits on the proportion of benefit that can be deducted each week.

8–97 CRISIS LOANS

Crisis loans are also interest-free loans, which as their name implies are designed to meet expenses which arise as a result of a disaster or some other kind of emergency. They could, for example, be paid to the victims of a fire or flood, or to people who have lost money or had it stolen, and are temporarily left without any other means of subsistence. There is no general requirement that a claimant should already be entitled to any other welfare benefit.

8–98 Like community care grants and budgeting loans, crisis loans are not governed by detailed regulations, but, as with budgeting loans, there is a limit of £1,000 on the amount that may be paid. Crisis loans must also be repaid.

REVIEWS AND APPEALS   8–99

Claimants who wish to challenge decisions regarding maternity and funeral payments, and cold weather payments, can seek an internal review or appeal to a social security appeal tribunal in the same way as can claimants for I.S. (see 8–58 to 8–63 above). As, however, other payments out of the social fund are not subject to detailed regulations, but depend on the discretion of the officers administering the fund, it is not possible to appeal against their decisions to a tribunal. These decisions are subject only to review, first by a social fund officer, and then, if necessary, by a social fund inspector.

7. Welfare Benefits on Marriage Breakdown   8–100

In order to sum up the main welfare benefit implications of the various orders that may be made on marriage breakdown, a checklist of points is set out below. All of these points are considered in more detail elsewhere in the book, most of them in this chapter. The notes assume that the husband will be making payments and the wife will be receiving them.

MAINTENANCE   8–101

(i)   I.S. is often a better alternative to claiming maintenance pending suit.

(ii) Ensure that the wife does not receive periodical payments which only just keep her off I.S. She may be better off on benefit because of the passport effect.

(iii) If the wife receives periodical payments as well as I.S., consider signing the order over to the D.S.S. This is also worth doing where the husband is a consistently bad payer, so that the wife frequently has to resort to I.S.

(iv) The husband cannot generally rely on the availability of welfare benefits to the wife as a reason for not making proper periodical payments.

(v)   Where, however, the effect of making an adequate order for the wife would be to depress the husband below subsistence level, the availability of benefits to the wife will be taken into account.

(vi) Remember that a father remains a "liable relative" for his children after divorce, and may be compelled by the D.S.S. to pay maintenance for them, even if not ordered to do so by the divorce court.

8–102 LUMP SUMS

(i) If a lump sum is treated as capital, remember the capital limits for the income-related benefits, and remember also the tariff-income rules.

(ii) If a lump sum is to be treated as maintenance, remember the special decapitalisation rules for I.S. purposes. These rules do not apply to F.C., H.B. or C.C.B.

8–103 PROPERTY ADJUSTMENT

(i) The value of a home is generally ignored in assessing benefits.

(ii) Remember that I.S. housing costs do not include the capital element of mortgage repayments. Consider other ways of repaying capital.

9. Protection of Property

Although the topic of protecting property in which a spouse **9–01** may wish to claim an interest is dealt with at this stage of the book, it is important to realise that it is something that must often be considered at the first interview in a matrimonial case. It has been left to this stage so that the law relating to ancillary relief could be dealt with first, and this subject placed in context, before considering the procedure for seeking relief.

We consider first the possible registrations that might be made to prevent the sale of the matrimonial home or other land. The severing of a joint tenancy is then discussed, followed by the possibility of obtaining an injunction to prevent the respondent disposing of any item of property. Finally, where it is too late to prevent a transaction taking place, the possibility of obtaining an order to set it aside is considered.

All these are problems which might fall to be considered at any stage of the case. However, it should be stressed that prevention is better than cure, and that possible problems should be anticipated from the outset, and steps taken to stop the matrimonial property being disposed of by the other party.

1. Registration of Rights under the Matrimonial **9–02** Homes Act 1983

If one of the spouses does not have the legal title of the matrimonial home vested in his or her name, the property may be sold or mortgaged without his or her knowledge or consent.

It is imperative to prevent this by registering the non-owning spouse's rights of occupation, created by the M.H.A. 1983.

THE STATUTORY RIGHTS OF OCCUPATION **9–03**

Section 1 of the M.H.A. 1983 defines the rights of occupation as:

(i) a right not to be evicted or excluded from the dwelling house without the leave of the court;

(ii) if out of occupation, a right to enter and occupy the dwelling house with the leave of the court.

They arise, "where one spouse is entitled to occupy a dwelling house by virtue of a beneficial estate or interest or contract and the other spouse is not so entitled."[1]

It is worthwhile considering this provision in some detail:

9–04 (i) "A dwelling house"

The M.H.A. 1983[2] defines this to include "any building, or part thereof, which is occupied as a dwelling, and any yard, garden, garage or outhouse belonging to the dwelling-house and occupied therewith." It could not therefore include, for example, a caravan or a houseboat.

9–05 (ii) "Beneficial estate or interest"

These words clearly cover the spouse who owns the entire legal estate. If the "owning spouse" owns a beneficial interest in property, the legal estate of which is vested in separate trustees of the legal estate and there are no other beneficiaries under the trust[3] then the other spouse's rights of occupation will be a charge on the trustees' legal estate as well.

9–06 (iii) "The other spouse is not so entitled"

The spouse seeking to register must not have a legal estate in the property (*i.e.* he or she must not be a joint tenant). If a spouse does have a legal estate, protection comes from the fact that no dealing with the legal estate can take place without the consent of all joint owners (as to this see 9–18 below).

The "non-owning spouse" may be entitled to an equitable interest in the property, but this will not prevent that spouse from having and registering rights of occupation.[4]

9–07 (iv) The matrimonial home

The Act goes on to provide[5] that the statutory rights of occupation can only exist in respect of a property which has been the matrimonial home of one of the parties, and that only one home can be protected by the registration of a charge at any one time. Therefore, if the couple currently

---

[1] M.H.A. 1983, s.1(1).
[2] M.H.A. 1983, s.10.
[3] See, for the definition of "other beneficiaries," the M.H.A. 1983, s.2(2).
[4] M.H.A. 1983, s.1(11).
[5] M.H.A. 1983, s.1(10).

own, and have lived in, two houses, the non-owning spouse must choose which to protect by registration of the statutory rights of occupation. The other property could be protected by the registration of a pending action.[6]

REGISTRATION 9–08

Registration of the rights of occupation will ensure that any subsequent purchaser or mortgagee of the home takes it subject to those rights. It must, however, be remembered that, however quickly the rights are registered, they will not take priority over the rights of a mortgagee who lent the money with which the home was originally purchased.

Registration is effected in two different ways, depending on whether the title to the property is registered or unregistered.

(i) Registered title 9–09
The rights are protected by the registration of a "notice" which is placed on the charges register of the registered title. In order to do this it is necessary to know the title number of the registered title. This can be ascertained by effecting a Public Index Map search at the Land Registry. The form applying for such a search is sent, giving details of the address of the property[7] to the relevant District Land Registry for the area in which the property is situated. On the return of the form to the applicant, he will then be able to register his notice by filling in an application form (giving the title number) and sending this to the Registry with the appropriate fee.

(ii) Unregistered title 9–10
The rights are protected by the registration of a Class F Land Charge in the central land charges department against the name of the owning spouse. If the nature of the title is not known it may be ascertained by effecting a search of the Public Index Map against the property, as explained above.

EFFECTS OF REGISTRATION

(i) Failure to register the charge 9–11
This will mean that a purchaser for value or a mortgagee of the property will not be bound by the statutory rights of occupation.

---

[6] See 9–17, below.

[7] In country areas a plan of the boundaries of the property may also be required.

Nonetheless, if the non-owning spouse in occupation of the property has a beneficial interest in it, for example, by contribution to the purchase price, then a subsequent purchaser or mortgagee may take subject to their equitable rights.[8] However, this is not a safe principle on which to rely. In particular, it is not always clear whether or not a spouse has a beneficial interest (See Chapter 15, where this question is considered in detail). Furthermore, a non-owning spouse who has acquiesced in the obtaining of a mortgage may not be allowed to assert her rights against the mortgagee.[9]

9–12 **(ii) Notification of proceedings**
Regardless of whether she has registered her rights, it is open to the non-owning spouse to make payments of the current mortgage instalments, and such payments towards the arrears as would settle the debt within a reasonable period of time. Such payments must be treated by the lender as being made by the borrower.[10] The non-owning spouse who has registered her rights under the M.H.A. 1983 must be notified of any proceedings for possession brought against the owning spouse under the terms of the mortgage.[11]

The non-owning spouse may apply to the court to be made a party to the possession proceedings. The court must allow this if it does not see any special reason against it, and it is satisfied that the non-owning spouse is likely to be able to contribute sufficiently to affect the outcome of possession proceedings.[12] The court has power to refuse an order for possession, where it seems likely that the sums due can be paid within a reasonable period of time.[13]

It must be emphasised, however, that although a non-owning spouse who has registered her rights must be notified of any possession proceedings, there is no requirement that she should be told in advance of any arrears that may have arisen under the mortgage. Consequently she may be unaware of the state of the mortgage account until possession proceedings are brought.

9–13 TRUSTEE IN BANKRUPTCY

Whether or not the statutory rights of occupation are registered, they are binding on the owning spouse's trustee in

---

[8] See *Williams & Glyn's Bank* v. *Boland* [1981] A.C. 487; *Kingsnorth Trust Co. Ltd.* v. *Tizard* [1986] 1 W.L.R. 783.
[9] *Bristol & West Building Society* v. *Henning* [1985] 1 W.L.R. 778.
[10] M.H.A. 1983, s.1(5).
[11] M.H.A. 1983, s.8(3).
[12] M.H.A. 1983, s.8(2).
[13] Administration of Justice Act 1970, s.36.

bankruptcy. If, for example, the owning spouse becomes bankrupt, the non-owning spouse will be able to remain in the property, temporarily at least, despite the claims of the creditors. An application can, however, be made under section 1 of the M.H.A. 1983 for an order terminating the rights of occupation. Where such an application is made more than a year after the bankruptcy, the interests of the creditors will be paramount, except in exceptional circumstances.[14]

PROTECTION FOR A NON-TENANT   9–14

Where one spouse is the sole tenant of the home by virtue of a statutory tenancy under the Rent Act 1977 or a secure tenancy under the Housing Act 1985, or an assured tenancy under the Housing Act 1988, it is important that the non-tenant spouse should be protected against the tenancy lapsing or its security being lost. In normal circumstances a tenant loses his security if he gives up his occupation of the property. This would, however, leave a non-tenant spouse vulnerable to an action for possession if, for example, a wife were deserted by her tenant husband. Consequently section 1(6) of the M.H.A. 1983 provides that the occupation of the property by a spouse with rights of occupation is to be treated as if it were occupation by the tenant spouse. Thus, as long as the non-tenant remains in the home, the tenancy is unaffected.

TERMINATION   9–15

The rights of occupation will be ended by the death of the owning spouse or the granting of a decree absolute. In divorce cases the court will often not have made a property adjustment order by the date of the granting of the decree absolute. For a short period, the simplest solution, to avoid losing the protection of the registration, is for the petitioner to delay applying for the decree. However, after a further three months the respondent will be in a position to apply.[15] In any case, the petitioner may not want to delay, because, for example, she plans to remarry. In such cases, an application could be made to register a pending action. This is considered at 9–17, below. Alternatively, it is possible to make an application to the court before the decree absolute for an order continuing the rights of occupation beyond the

---

[14] See Insolvency Act 1986, s.336.
[15] See above, 4–82.

termination of the marriage.[16] This does, however, require further court proceedings and possibly an application for an extension of legal aid. Consequently, where possible, it will be better to register a pending action instead.

9–16   EXTENT OF PROTECTION

Even though the non-owning spouse's rights are registered, they are subject to challenge in certain limited circumstances. Section 1(3) of the M.H.A. 1983 provides that an application can be made to determine the occupational rights of spouses taking into account, *inter alia*, the conduct of the spouses and all the circumstances of the case.[17] Two factors call for particular consideration:

(i) Purpose of registration
It is important to appreciate that the purpose of registration is to protect a spouse's rights of occupation. In *Barnett* v. *Hassett*[18] the husband left the matrimonial home which was in his wife's name. He was a rich man and did not want to occupy the house. In an attempt to force his wife to agree to pay him a lump sum, he registered his rights of occupation against the matrimonial home. The court ordered the removal of the registration, holding that this was an abuse of the process.

(ii) Circumstances of a purchaser
One object of registration is to protect the non-owning spouse against the sale of the property to a purchaser. Clearly, in most cases the purchaser will discover the existence of the registration from his pre-completion search and will not continue with his purchase. (This may incidentally result in dire consequences for the vendor, who may then find himself liable to pay damages to the prospective purchaser for his inability to give vacant possession of the property.)[19]

In exceptional circumstances, however, a purchaser may complete the purchase of the property subject to the rights of the non-owning spouse. Even so, it does not automatically follow that the spouse will always be able to enforce her rights against the purchaser.

In *Kashmir Kaur* v. *Gill*[20] the purchaser completed a purchase with the husband without the existence of the wife's

---

[16] M.H.A. 1983, s.2(4).
[17] See 20–29 where the criteria are fully set out.
[18] [1982] 1 All E.R. 80.
[19] *Wroth* v. *Tyler* [1974] Ch. 30.
[20] [1988] 3 W.L.R. 39.

registration being revealed to him. The reason for this was that there had been some confusion over the result of the purchaser's pre-completion search. However, the registration was perfectly valid and was binding on him. The wife, who was living elsewhere, applied for an order allowing her to re-occupy the property. The court held that it was right to consider all the circumstances of the case including the circumstances of the purchaser. The purchaser was blind and had bought the house with his special needs in mind. The court therefore found for the purchaser and refused to allow the wife to enforce her rights against him.

2. Pending Land Action   9–17

Once proceedings have been commenced in relation to unregistered land, (for example, by filing a petition for divorce including a prayer for "property adjustment" or by making a similar application in Form 11) it is possible to register a pending action to prevent any dealing with the property.[21]

If the title to the land is registered, the correct method of protection would be by registration of a caution. Again, if the nature of the title is not known, or the title number of registered land is required, a Public Index Map search will have to be effected.

Registration of a pending action is a particularly useful way of protecting an interest in property which has never been the matrimonial home, so that it is not covered by the M.H.A. 1983. It can also be used to protect a second home, as indicated at 9–07, above. Even in cases where rights of occupation have been registered, it will often be wise to register a pending action as soon as an application for property adjustment has been made. This will guard against the danger of the rights of occupation lapsing on decree absolute, as explained at 9–14, above.

3. Severing a Joint Tenancy   9–18

If the property is in joint names, the legal estate will be held by the parties as joint tenants. The equitable interest will be held either as beneficial joint tenants, or as tenants in common. The property cannot be sold or mortgaged without the consent of both parties, so that no steps need be taken to prevent an adverse dealing with the property.

---

[21] See *Perez-Adamson* v. *Perez-Rivas* [1987] 3 W.L.R. 500.

If the equitable interest is held in joint names, then the right of survivorship means that on the death of one of the joint tenants the other will succeed to the deceased tenant's interest. This cannot be altered by a will. It is, however, possible to guard against such a succession by converting the equitable joint tenancy into a tenancy in common (to which the right of survivorship does not apply). This may be done by the service of a notice (usually in the form of a letter) by one of the joint tenants to the other indicating that the tenancy is severed.[22]

The fact of severance should be recorded in the correct manner to protect the interests of the severing party. In the case of unregistered land this will be done by placing a memorandum of the severance on the conveyance to the parties. If the title is registered a restriction must be placed on the proprietorship register.

In deciding whether to effect a severance it is impossible to avoid the element of chance. If the joint tenancy is severed and the client's spouse then dies, the client may fail to inherit his or her spouse's property. On the other hand if severance is not effected and the client dies then his or her spouse will succeed to the property automatically, which may be the last thing the client wanted.

Clearly, there may be cases where there are special circumstances which affect the decision. For example, where one of the spouses is much older than the other it is probable that that spouse will die first, but even so this could be a dangerous gamble. Although ultimately it must of course be the client's decision, severance does at least prevent the other spouse from succeeding to the whole property and does not prevent the court from making such subsequent orders for property adjustment as may be appropriate.

9–19 4. Obtaining an Injunction to Prevent a Disposition

If the property in dispute does not consist of land in this country, it may be necessary to obtain an injunction to prevent the respondent from disposing of it. This injunction can be granted under section 37(2)(a) of the M.C.A. 1973. This provides that, where proceedings are brought for financial

---

[22] As to other methods of severance see any standard work on Land Law. Severance will not be implied from the filing of a petition (*Harris* v. *Goddard* [1983] 1 W.L.R. 1203): *cf.* proceedings under the M.W.P.A. 1882, s.17; see *Re: Draper's Conveyance, Nilian* v. *Porter* [1969] 1 Ch. 486. See Law of Property Act 1925, s.36(2).

relief,[23] the court may make such order as it thinks fit to restrain the respondent from making a disposition of the property.

However, the court must be satisfied: "that the other party is, with the intention of defeating the claim for financial relief, about to make any disposition or to transfer out of the jurisdiction or otherwise deal with any property."

There must therefore be evidence before the court that the respondent intends to make the disposition for the purpose of preventing or reducing an order for financial relief or for impeding the enforcement of such an order.[24] This means that it cannot be used just as a precaution in case the respondent attempts to dispose of the property.

The term "disposition" is extremely widely defined to include **9–20** any conveyance, assurance or gift of any property whether made in writing or otherwise.[25] An injunction under section 37 may be applied for *ex parte* in urgent cases, but an *inter partes* hearing should follow shortly. The application should be supported by an affidavit.

Example **9–21**

Susan has filed a petition for divorce and has made an application for financial provision and property adjustment. She discovers her husband, Paul, is about to withdraw some money from his building society account and transfer the money abroad.

Susan's solicitor may make an application for an injunction under section 37. Once the injunction is granted it is important to notify the building society of that fact.

5. Setting Aside a Disposition **9–22**

Even if it is too late to prevent a disposition of property being made, it may still be possible to have it set aside by applying for an order to this effect under section 37(2)(*b*) of the M.C.A. 1973. This allows the court to set aside a disposition if it is satisfied that, if this were done, financial relief, or different financial relief, would be granted to the applicant.

Such an order can only be made if the disposition[26] is a **9–23** reviewable disposition. This is defined by section 37(4) as:

---

[23] This is widely defined by the M.C.A. 1973, s.37(1) to include relief under ss.22, 23, 24, 27, 31 (except subs. 16) and 35.

[24] M.C.A. 1973, s.37(1). This intention is presumed to exist where the court is satisfied that the disposition would have this consequence. M.C.A. 1973, s.37(5).

[25] s.37(6); but it does not include a provision in a will or codicil.

[26] Disposition here has the same meaning as in 9–20; see s.37(6).

> "a disposition not made for valuable consideration (other than marriage) to a person who, at the time of the disposition acted in relation to it in good faith and without notice of any intention on the part of the other party to defeat the applicant's claim for financial relief."

If the disposition took place less than three years before the date of the application, it will be presumed that the respondent made it with the intention of defeating the claim if that was in fact the effect of the disposition.[27] The burden will then be on the respondent to rebut this presumption.

9–24 *Example*

Wilma having commenced proceedings for ancillary relief against her husband, Ted, discovers that he transferred £10,000 worth of his British Airways shares into the name of his mother a year ago. His mother gave no consideration for the shares. Wilma's solicitor can apply to the court for an order setting aside the disposition.

9–25 6. Dispositions Made to Prevent Enforcement

If a "reviewable disposition" is made with the intention of preventing enforcement of an order for financial relief that has already been granted, then it may be set aside under section 37(2)(*c*) of the M.C.A. 1973. The conditions under which such a disposition may be set aside are the same as those considered above for setting aside a disposition made with the intention of defeating a claim for financial provision.

---

[27] M.C.A. 1973, s.37(5).

226

10. Ancillary Relief—Procedure

This chapter describes the way in which orders for ancillary **10–01** financial and property relief are obtained. The procedures outlined apply to applications made in proceedings for divorce, nullity or judicial separation, although the great majority of applications are, of course, made in divorce proceedings. It will be assumed throughout that the parties to the application are being divorced.

In this chapter, unless the contrary is stated, the word "applicant" will refer to the applicant for ancillary relief. The word "respondent" will refer to the opponent to the application, irrespective of that person's standing in the divorce suit.

Outline of Procedure   10–02

In order to put this topic in perspective, it is best to start with a simple outline of the procedure. The detailed points are then dealt with below.

(i) Obtain legal aid
Clearly it is possible that the applicant may not be legally aided. If this is the case all the following references to the legal aid documentation will be irrelevant. The topic of legal aid has been considered above.[1] The legal aid application is likely to have been made at an early stage of the proceedings, probably at the initial interview, or in any event as soon as it became clear that a claim for ancillary relief was going to be necessary. It is only after the legal aid certificate is received that any step in the proceedings can be taken.

(ii) File

Notice. The precise nature and contents of this document are dealt with below, but essentially it is the document which starts the process to obtain a hearing date. A copy must also be filed.

---

[1] See 2–09.

Affidavit of means. This sets out details of the applicant's income and capital and raises any other issues relevant to the case.

Legal aid certificate

Notice of Acting (if relevant). This will only be necessary where there has been a change of representation. This usually arises because the applicant was in receipt of Green Form advice and assistance for the divorce and was therefore acting in person. Now legal aid has been obtained for the ancillary relief claim the applicant will be represented by solicitors and their name must be placed on the court file as acting for the applicant.

Court fee[2]

(iii) Receive from court

Copy notice

Automatic directions order (from some courts). As these applications tend to run to a pattern, in most cases similar directions as to the further conduct of the application will usually have to be given by the court, so that it is common for standard directions to be issued at the outset. These regulate such things as the filing of further affidavits, the giving of oral evidence at the hearing and valuations of the parties' assets. These directions will be received in duplicate.

(iv) Serve on the respondent by post

The copy notice

A copy of the affidavit of means

The copy of the order for directions

A Notice of Issue of legal aid. This document is required to be served on the other party to inform them that legal aid has been granted to the applicant. A copy should be sent to the court to show that this has been done.[3]

Notice of acting (if relevant)

(v) The respondent's affidavit of means

This should be filed and a copy served on the applicant. There are cases where the affidavit may not be forthcoming and steps may have to be taken to force the respondent to produce it. This is dealt with below.

---

[2] Currently £15.
[3] Civil Legal Aid (General) Regulations 1989, reg. 50.

(vi) Affidavit in answer

The applicant may file a further affidavit in answer and serve a copy on the respondent. In theory, a number of further affidavits by either party may be filed. These should be avoided if possible because it is important to keep costs to a minimum.

(vii) Discovery and inspection

If this does not take place automatically then a letter may be written requesting this.

(viii) Further details

A letter may be written by either party requesting further information.

(viii) Orders for directions

At any stage applications may be made for orders for directions about the further conduct of the case. These are likely to cover such matters as:

— discovery;

— interim maintenance;

— penal notice to enforce compliance with directions.

— valuation of property

(ix) Hearing date

Eventually, when both parties are ready for trial it will be necessary to apply for a hearing date.

(x) Hearing

This takes place before the registrar in chambers.

We can now consider each of these main steps in the procedure in more detail.

2. The Application

MAKING THE APPLICATION[4]   10–03

The way the initial application is made is primarily determined by the applicant's status in the divorce proceedings.

The applicant may be either:

[4] M.C.R. 1977, r. 68.

(i) The petitioner, in which case the application should be made in the prayer of the petition; or

(ii) A respondent who is defending, in which case the application should be in the answer; or

(iii) A respondent who is not defending, when the application will be made on a separate form, *i.e.* notice of application (Form 11).[5]

10–04 PROCEEDING WITH THE APPLICATION

Once the application has been made, a hearing date must be obtained to enable the court to consider the application. The way this is done will again depend on the status of the applicant.

(i) If the applicant falls into either category (i) or (ii) above, the application has already been made. In order to start the process of obtaining a court order a notice of intention to proceed (Form 13)[6] must be filed.

(ii) If the applicant is a non-defending respondent (*i.e.* within category (iii) above), then in order to trigger the ancillary application the notice of application referred to in that paragraph must be filed. This notice of application in Form 11 is effectivly two steps in one. Not only has the application now been technically made, it is also being proceeded with.

Apart from the name of the forms, there is little else to distinguish them. The forms are referred to together hereafter as Form 11/13, although, clearly, only the relevant form would be used in each case.

10–05 WORDING OF THE FORM 11/13

In so far as applications for financial provision or maintenance pending suit are concerned there seems to be no need for the Form 11/13 to do any more than merely repeat the relevant form of words (*e.g.* it might ask for periodical payments and a lump sum, or even just for "financial provision").

---

[5] This refers to the number of the form in Appendix 1 of the M.C.R. 1977.
[6] This refers to the number of the form in Appendix 1 of the M.C.R. 1977.

However, the rules[7] provide that, in the case of applications for property adjustment orders, the Form 11/13 should state briefly the nature of the adjustment proposed. This rule is often not complied with, and such applications usually ask simply for "a property adjustment order."

Indeed it is often impractical for anything more specific to be stated at this early stage, as the applicant may well not be fully informed of the respondent's true financial circumstances. However, where the application in Form 11/13 seeks a property adjustment order in respect of land, it must:

(i) identify the land,

(ii) state whether the title is registered or not, and if registered give the title number, and

(iii) give particulars of any mortgage.[8]

TIMING OF THE APPLICATIONS 10–06

Section 26(1) of the M.C.A. 1973 states that proceedings for any order under sections 22–24 of the M.C.A. 1973 may be begun at any time after the presentation of the petition.

The stages at which the court can hear particular applications for particular forms of ancillary relief and the dates on which particular orders take effect have been referred to at 6–17 and 6–23 (above). It may be useful now to see the stages of an application in diagrammatic form.

Application for financial provision and property adjustment orders can be *made*.

Orders for financial provision and property adjustment can be *made*.

Petition | Decree Nisi | Decree Absolute

Orders for M.P.S. and financial provision for children can be *made and take effect*.

Orders for financial provision and property adjustment can *take effect*. M.P.S. ends.

---

[7] Appendix 1 Form 11, *ibid*.
[8] *Ibid*. r. 74(2).

10–07 However, other factors also influence exactly when a particular Form 11/13 is filed in any given case. For example if legal aid is required to finance the application, this cannot be filed until the legal aid certificate has been issued.[9] Further, many county courts have long waiting periods before an application can be heard, making an early filing of the Form 11/13 advisable.

Apart from these considerations, there are three further factors which make it desirable, or even essential in some cases, to make the application in good time, and certainly before the decree absolute is granted.

10–08 **(i) Leave may be required**

Under the M.C.R. 1977, r. 68, an application which should have been made in the petition or answer may be made subsequently:

(i) by leave of the court by notice in Form 11 (notice of application) or at the trial, or

(ii) where the parties are agreed upon the terms of the proposed order without leave by notice in Form 11.

When leave is required, it should not generally be difficult to obtain. The Court of Appeal has said[10] that leave should be given if the applicant has a seriously arguable case and a reasonable prospect of obtaining the relief claimed. Leave is only likely to be refused if there has been some serious unwarranted delay, or where it would be unjust or oppressive to the respondent to make the order. Nevertheless, it is obviously sensible to include a prayer for all forms of relief in the petition or answer in all appropriate cases, to avoid any risk of leave being refused at some later stage.

It is sometimes difficult to explain to a husband petitioner who is working and fully fit that he ought to include a claim for periodical payments against his wife. However, circumstances may change, he may find himself unable to work at some time in the future and his wife may become rich. Alternatively the parties or the court may ultimately decide on a clean break order and this can only be properly achieved if both parties have applied for periodical payments so that their applications can be formally dismissed; see 6–71 above.

---

[9] See 6–05 for comparison of maintenance pending suit with income support.
[10] *Chatterjee* v. *Chatterjee* [1976] 1 All E.R. 719.

(ii) The remarriage trap

10–09

Section 28(3) of the M.C.A. 1973 provides that, *"if after the grant of a decree . . . either party . . . remarries, that party shall not be entitled to apply . . . for a financial provision order in his or her favour, or for a property adjustment order . . . "*

This section can obviously pose a trap for the unwary. It could, for example, catch a petitioner who failed to apply for a property adjustment order in the petition and who then remarried having obtained a decree absolute. However, the problem is more likely to arise where a petitioner obtains the decree absolute in an undefended divorce suit. In these circumstances it is not normally necessary for the respondent to file any forms in which the application would be made. Should he or she then remarry, without taking the deliberate step of filing a Form 11, it would not be possible to obtain, for example, a property adjustment order in respect of the matrimonial home.

Example

Henry files a petition for a divorce. His wife, Wendy, is pleased by this as she is anxious to remarry. Immediately the decree absolute is pronounced she remarries. On the way to her honeymoon she stops off at her solicitor's office to instigate proceedings for a property adjustment order.

Her solicitor will have some bad news for her. As she did not make an application for this relief prior to her remarriage she will be unable to make the claim now.[11]

(iii) Backdating

10–10

As seen at 6–17, (above), the court has power to backdate orders for periodical payments to the date on which they were applied for. It obviously follows that the earlier the application is made, the larger the backdated order may be. In practice, however, orders are not normally backdated unless the respondent has the means to pay the backdated amount as the effect of such an order will be to impose immediate arrears.

SERVICE OF THE APPLICATION

10–11

Once the Form 11/13 has been filed in duplicate, the court will stamp both copies with the court stamp. In some courts a return date will be inserted for the hearing. In many courts, however, no fixed hearing date is given and the parties are

[11] See *Nixon* v. *Fox* [1978] Fam. 173.

notified that they can only apply for a date when both are ready for trial.

When the court returns one copy of Form 11/13, duly stamped, it must be served on the respondent within four days.[12] Service, by the applicant's solicitor, is by post to the address for service, which unless subsequently altered will be as stated in the divorce petition.[13]

In an application for a property adjustment order the Form 11/13 must also be served on any mortgagee mentioned in the affidavit.[14] This step must not be overlooked. Many applications are adjourned at the hearing, because it transpires that this step has not been taken. The registrar may also direct that the documents be served on "other persons."[15] For example, in relevant cases the registrar will direct that landlords of the property which is the subject-matter of the application should be served with the documents.

10–12 2. The Affidavit of Means

Generally the primary evidence in ancillary applications is given by way of affidavits from both parties.

10–13 CONTENTS OF THE AFFIDAVIT

Broadly speaking the contents of the affidavits filed by applicant and respondent are similar. They should give full particulars of the party's property and income.[16] The style of the affidavit varies in practice. There is a standard form affidavit, in the style of a questionnaire, which was introduced in an attempt to encourage uniformity of presentation of the relevant information. Many practitioners do not use this form. Where a conventional narrative style affidavit is used, a Practice Direction[17] requires that the information be presented in the same order as that in which the questions appear on the standard form.

Where the application is for a transfer or settlement of property order, the rules go on to provide that the affidavit of means filed by the applicant should additionally contain details of:

[12] M.C.R. 1977, r. 74(4) and (5).
[13] *Ibid.* r. 74(4).
[14] *Ibid.* r. 13(1).
[15] *Ibid.* r. 119.
[16] *Ibid.* r. 73(2) and (3).
[17] [1973] 1 W.L.R. 72.

(i) the property in respect of which the application is made; and

(ii) the property to which the respondent to the application is entitled either in possession or reversion.[18]

FILING AND SERVICE OF THE AFFIDAVIT OF MEANS   10–14

When the Form 11/13 is filed, it must be accompanied by the court fee and the applicant's affidavit of means. When the stamped copy of the Form is served on the respondent, a copy of the affidavit of means must be served as well.

Although any mortgagee must be served with a copy of the application there is no need to serve him with a copy of the affidavit. He may, however, request a copy within 14 days of being served with the application, although in practice this is unlikely to happen.

3. Directions   10–15

Under the M.C.R. 1977, r. 77(6) the registrar may at any stage of the proceedings give directions as to the filing and service of pleadings and as to the further conduct of the case. Acting under this jurisdiction, many county court registrars now issue a form of automatic directions, usually as soon as the Form 11/13 has been filed. Two copies will be returned to the applicant's solicitor with the copies of the Form 11/13. One of these will be served on the respondent with the application and affidavit.

The content of these directions varies from court to court, but they will usually deal with such matters as the filing and service of subsequent affidavits, the discovery and inspection of documents, the need for the parties to attend the hearing and give oral evidence and the valuation of the matrimonial home. The directions will usually further provide that the hearing date will be given on application by the parties.

In those courts where automatic directions are not issued there will often be a return date inserted in the notice of application for a hearing for directions. (See 10–22, below). At this hearing the parties' solicitors will attend and similar orders will be made as in the automatic directions order referred to above. Obviously, it will be possible with this type of procedure for the directions to be tailored to fit the needs of the case.

---

[18] M.C.R. 1977, r. 74.

In some cases more than one order for directions will be required as the case develops. For example, an order for directions may be given and then the respondent may fail to comply with a particular direction. A further order must then be sought to ensure his compliance. As can be imagined this can often lead to such matters becoming extremely protracted. A further explanation of the use of orders for directions to obtain evidence in this way can be seen below at 10–22.

10–16 4. Discovery and Inspection

Strictly speaking, mutual discovery should take place 14 days after the last affidavit has been filed and, unless otherwise agreed, inspection should take place seven days later.[19] An order to this effect may be included in an automatic order for directions. If discovery has not been ordered, it can be triggered by writing a letter under rule 77(4), (see 10–21 below). In the event of non-compliance it can be enforced by an order made on an application for directions. In many cases the applicant will not bother with an order for general discovery and instead will apply for an order in relation to specific documents, (see 10–22 below).

Discovery takes place by one party's solicitor preparing a list of all his client's documents which relate to the case. They are divided into three categories: those which are available for inspection, those that are no longer in his possession, custody or power, and those which are privileged, (e.g. solicitor and client correspondence).

This list is then sent to the other party's solicitor who selects those (if any) which he wishes to inspect. Arrangements are then made for inspection. This usually consists of photocopies being sent through the post.

If he has reason to believe that there are other documents which have not been disclosed then discovery of these documents can be enforced by a letter under rule 77(4) (see 10–21, below) followed by an order made on an application for directions.

10–17 5. Obtaining Evidence

It is not uncommon for parties who are in the throes of a divorce to be as unco-operative as possible at this stage. Quite often the repressed bitterness which builds up throughout the breakdown of their relationship and marriage is first released

[19] Practice Direction [1981] 2 All E.R. 642.

in the proceedings for ancillary relief. In trying to salvage as much of their financial investment in the marriage as possible, either or both parties may now seek to be as obstructive and deceptive as possible.

In these circumstances either party can conceal matters from the other, but the commonest problem that arises is that the respondent refuses to disclose full details of his income and capital.

OBTAINING THE RESPONDENT'S AFFIDAVIT   10–18

The first problem that often arises is that the respondent fails to file an affidavit of his means. Under the rules he is required to file an affidavit in reply to the application within 14 days of being served with it. He is told this by the wording of the Form 11/13. Furthermore, this is usually repeated in the automatic directions issued to both parties.

If, despite this, no affidavit is received from the respondent it will be necessary to take further steps to enforce the order.

(i) Penal notice   10–19
If the party refuses to obey the order it may be reissued with a penal notice attached.[20] This, if disobeyed, may result in the offending party being committed to prison for contempt of court. This is a procedure which is available to compel any person to comply with an order of the court and might be used at any stage of the proceedings.

(ii) Interim orders   10–20
The registrar has power[21] to make an interim order upon such terms as he thinks fit. This power may be used to make a temporary order whilst awaiting the finalisation of some detail (*e.g.* the valuation of an asset). Sometimes, however, the power is used to force the husband to supply evidence on which a final order can be based. For example, if a wife files her Form 11/13 together with an affidavit of means and the husband fails to file his own affidavit, the wife may apply for an interim order for periodical payments. The registrar may then make an order based on information as to the husband's means supplied by the wife in her affidavit. The resultant

---

[20] See 20–55 (below), where penal notices are explained. Essentially they warn the respondent that he may be committed to prison for disobedience. They must be served personally on the respondent. If necessary the registrar can request the assistance of certain government departments to trace him. See Practice Direction [1989] 1 All E.R. 765.
[21] M.C.R. 1977, r. 78.

order may be for an amount which the husband cannot easily afford, thereby encouraging him to file his own affidavit speedily, in order to expedite the final hearing.

10–21 RULE 77 LETTER

Even when an affidavit has been obtained, it will often be found that the information it contains is incomplete. The first step that is usually taken to obtain details of matters which are not disclosed by one of the parties in his or her affidavit is to write to that party seeking the information. The letter is written by virtue of the M.C.R. 1977, r. 77(4) which provides:

"Any party to an application for ancillary relief may by letter require any other party to give further information concerning any matter contained in any affidavit filed by or on behalf of that other party or any other relevant matter, or to furnish a list of relevant documents or to allow inspection of any such document."

This provision thus enables 'further and better particulars" (as they would be called in civil procedure) to be obtained. Some solicitors, rather than writing a specific letter, will use a more general form of questionnaire to ask for such information. In the same way, if documents are believed to be in the possession of the other party and discovery of them has not taken place, then this letter or questionnaire can ask for such documents to be produced.

This provision allows one party to request, for example, copies of the other's pay slips, building society pass book, or bank statements.

10–22 APPLICATION FOR DIRECTIONS

If the rule 77(4) letter is not complied with, an application should be made to the registrar, under rule 77(5), for directions. The registrar will usually then order that the other party must disclose the information or produce the document required. The other party will usually be ordered to pay the costs of the application. If such an order is disobeyed it can be enforced by either reissuing the order, endorsed with a penal notice, and/or an interim order. These have been considered above.

In such cases it is unlikely that an application would be made for an order for formal, general, discovery and inspection of documents. Further, if such an order has been made (perhaps in an automatic order for directions) it is unlikely that any attempt will be made to enforce it. Obviously this is a matter for the judgment of the individual solicitor but in many cases no practical benefit will accrue from such an order. It is likely to be difficult to enforce in practical terms because it relates to general matters only, and even if complied with this may only be done half-heartedly.

As was explained at 10–15 above, it may be necessary at this application for directions to make other directions for the further conduct of the case, particularly if no other directions have yet been given as, for example, in courts where automatic orders for directions are not issued.

ORDERING FURTHER AFFIDAVITS AND ATTENDANCE OF WITNESSES 10–23

Rule 77(5) goes on to provide that the registrar may at any stage of the proceedings order the attendance of any person for the purpose of being examined or cross-examined, and may order the discovery and production of any document or require further affidavits. This seems to give wide powers to the registrar. However, the rule has been restrictively interpreted.

Quite often the income and capital resources of, for example, **10–24** the woman with whom the husband is living, are thought relevant by the wife.[22] The problem is how to obtain such evidence from that third party. In one case[23] the court held that rule 77(5) does not enable the registrar to order an affidavit from a third party. In another case[24] it was held that the court has no power to order third parties who have not given evidence in chief to attend for cross-examination only. This means that third parties can only be ordered to attend and be examined in chief by the solicitor who requested their attendance. Although this prevents the third party being asked leading questions by the solicitor, many registrars will put their own leading questions to such witnesses at the hearing. In any case it is not a leading question to ask: "How much do you earn?" The court has also held that rule 77(5) does not give the court power to order a third party to produce documents. If this is wanted, an ordinary witness summons must be sought.

---

[22] See 6–45 (above, for relevance of third party's means in such applications.
[23] *Wynne* v. *Wynne* [1980] 1 W.L.R. 69.
[24] *W.* v. *W. The Times*, March 21 and 27, 1981.

10–25 This is a summons which can be obtained in any civil case in the county court compelling the attendance of a witness at the hearing. It can be extended to compel the witness to produce documents (*e.g.* the accounts of a firm). In the High Court a similar procedure is possible although leave to issue the document is required[25] and the document is called a *subpoena*.

10–26 **6. The Hearing**

Neither party need attend the hearing, unless there is an order for them to attend and give oral evidence. This order is fairly common and will be found in most courts' standard directions.

The evidence will be contained primarily in affidavits, and, if the parties do attend, it will be largely to enable them to be cross-examined on these. Witnesses may also give evidence, either by affidavit or orally. Examples of these witnesses might be: a third party, *e.g.* a male respondent's present wife; or an expert, *e.g.* a valuer of the property.[26] The hearing will normally be before a registrar in chambers. It will be informal and in many courts will be conducted around a table with the parties and their solicitors seated.

The procedure adopted at the hearing is fairly flexible in most courts but usually the applicant's solicitor will open.[27] He will outline the matter, and then call his client and any witnesses, who will be cross-examined by the respondent's solicitor and then possibly re-examined by the applicant's solicitor. The respondent's solicitor will then put his case in the same way. The respondent's solicitor will then make his closing speech followed by the applicant's solicitor. Finally the registrar will make orders deciding the matter and relating to costs.

10–27 **7. Transfer to the High Court?**

In a small proportion of cases the registrar might decide not to deal with the case himself. He does have a discretion, at any stage of the proceedings, to order that applications for ancillary relief be transferred to the High Court. If the matter is one which is likely to be transferred, an early application for directions is advisable, as otherwise a transfer may be

---

[25] R.S.C., Ord. 32, r. 7; See W. v. W. (1981) Fam. Law 247.

[26] See *Brent* v. *Brent* (1978) 9 Fam. Law 59. The court has no power to bind the parties to accept one valuer's valuation.

[27] In some courts, especially in London, the parties are more often represented by counsel than by solicitors.

ordered at the hearing. The exercise of this discretion is governed by a Practice Direction[28] which requires the registrar or judge to consider whether the complexity, difficulty or gravity of the issues demands a transfer. In particular he is required to have regard to the following factors:

(i) The capital values of the assets involved and the extent to which they are available for, or susceptible to, distribution or adjustment;

(ii) any substantial allegations of fraud or deception or non-disclosure;

(iii) any substantial contested allegations of conduct.

8. Negotiating   10–28

The above outline of the procedure assumes that the application is not resolved at some earlier stage by the parties reaching agreement. Not every applicant or respondent to a claim for financial provision is embittered or reluctant to reach some compromised solution to the matter. In many cases agreement is fairly easy. In others it comes after protracted bargaining. In too many cases agreement is only reached at the "door of the court" when the imminence of the hearing serves as an encouragement to settle. This topic is considered further in Chapter 11 (below), which deals with Consent Orders.

9. "Calderbank Letters"[29]   10–29

At some stage during negotiations, one of the parties may feel that they have offered a solution which would be as good as, or even better than that which would be ordered by the court. Unfortunately the other side may still not be prepared to settle the case. There is no alternative then, but to proceed to take the matter to court and incur more expenditure.

In these circumstances it is usual to try to protect the position of the party making the offer against future orders for costs by writing a so-called "Calderbank letter." This is a "without prejudice" letter, which concludes with a paragraph specifically reserving the right to produce the letter to the court on any question of costs which might arise in the future. A copy of this letter should be filed at court[30] although

---

[28] [1988] 1 W.L.R. 560. This Practice Direction is also discussed at 1–06.

[29] See *Calderbank* v. *Calderbank* [1976] Fam. 93.

[30] See County Court Rules 1981, Order 11, r. 10 (inserted by the County Court (Amendment) Rules 1986).

it should not, of course, be seen by the registrar until the end of the hearing.

The letter can be referred to when asking the court to order that the applicant should bear the costs of the proceedings from, say, 14 days after the date of the letter, assuming, of course, that the applicant does not succeed in obtaining more than was offered.

It should be stressed that this will not always be effective. Costs in matrimonial litigation cannot always be dealt with in the same way as in other forms of civil litigation. (See 10–30, below). Although the existence of a "Calderbank letter" may influence the registrar, he does have a complete discretion as to costs.

10. Costs

10–30 ORDERS AS TO COSTS

The general principle of civil litigation is that orders as to costs are always in the discretion of the court. This usually means that the successful party obtains an order for costs against the unsuccessful party.

However, in matrimonial cases it is often difficult to describe one party as successful and the other as unsuccessful. For example, a wife may obtain an outright transfer of the former matrimonial home, but be ordered to pay the husband a lump sum in return. Consequently, registrars and judges quite often make no order as to costs at the end of a contested case. Furthermore, a large proportion of matrimonial clients are legally aided, and, in general, orders for costs are unlikely to be made against legally aided parties.[31] The court usually orders only that the costs of the assisted party shall be subject to legal aid taxation. It is occasionally possible, however, for a successful unassisted *respondent* to obtain an order that his costs be paid out of the Legal Aid Fund in cases where the applicant was legally aided.[32] The court can only make such

---

[31] Under the Legal Aid Act 1988, s.17(1), the amount of costs which a legally aided party can be ordered to pay must not "exceed the amount (if any) which is a reasonable one for him to pay having regard to all the circumstances, including the financial resources of all the parties. ... " "Financial resources" can, however, include a lump sum awarded to a party in the proceedings; *McDonnell* v. *McDonnell* [1977] 1 W.L.R. 34. See also 2–17 above.

[32] See Legal Aid Act 1988, s.18 and 2–17 above.

an order, however, if it is satisfied that the unassisted party will suffer severe financial hardship unless the order is made. It must also, of course, be satisfied that the respondent would have been entitled to an order for costs against the applicant if that party had not been legally aided.

Finally the question of costs cannot be considered in isolation from the substantive orders that the court makes on the basis of the net effect calculation. For example, if the effect of a lump sum order has been carefully calculated, and the court were then to make an order for costs against the payer, this could radically alter the net effect of the financial provision order.[33] The courts have stressed on a number of occasions that it is important to keep costs to a minimum wherever possible. It is particularly important not to complicate procedural matters where little benefit can be achieved.[34] For example, if the husband's business cannot be sold as it provides his sole means of livelihood, an accurate valuation (at a cost of several thousands of pounds) may not be justified.[35]

The operation of the statutory charge has been explained earlier.[36] When acting for a legally aided client it is important to remember the impact of the charge, and to attempt to obtain orders for costs against the other side whenever possible. Otherwise, where lump sum orders, or orders under sections 24 or 24A of the M.C.A. 1973 are obtained, the charge may reduce their value. **10–31**

11. Case Study **10–32**

To attempt to illustrate some of the procedural points made in this chapter there follows, in tabular form, a simple case study.[37] The letter "A" represents the solicitors instructed by the applicant and "R" represents the respondent's solicitors.

---

[33] Furthermore, it has been held that a judge should not increase the size of a lump sum order to take account of the fact that he cannot make an order for costs against the payer: see 2–31 above.

[34] *Evans* v. *Evans* (1990) *The Independent*, February 6.

[35] See, for example, *P.* v. *P.* [1989] 2 F.L.R. 241 and *B.* v. *B. (Financial Provision)* [1989] 1 F.L.R. 119. There will, of course, be cases where such a valuation is essential because the asset can properly be sold or money raised as security: see, *e.g. Gojkovic* v. *Gojkovic* [1990] 1 F.L.R. 140.

[36] See 2–21 *et seq.*, above.

[37] Note that this is just a limited example of what may happen in the course of one application. In particular it does not include any legal aid documentation that may have to be filed if either or both parties are legally aided. For details of this documentation see 2–13, above.

(1) *A*, acting for the petitioner, files Form 13 (applying for a periodical payments order, lump sum order and a property adjustment order) and a copy, the court fee, and an affidavit of means.

(2) The court returns the copy of the Form 13 stamped with the court seal and attaches its automatic directions order in duplicate.

(3) *A* serves the copy of Form 13, a copy of the applicant's affidavit of means and the automatic directions order on *R*.

(4) *R* files an affidavit in reply and serves a copy on *A*.

(5) *A* writes a letter under rule 77(4) requesting details of the respondent's shareholding in certain companies and of the financial position of the respondent's new wife.

(6) The respondent fails to supply these details.

(7) *A* files and serves an application for directions asking for an order that the respondent give details of shareholdings and that the respondent's new wife attend at the hearing and give oral evidence.

(8) The registrar makes the order and serves it on both parties.

(9) The respondent fails to supply details of his shareholding.

(10) *A* files and serves an application for the order made at (8) above, to be endorsed with a penal notice and for an interim periodical payments order.

(11) The registrar makes this order and serves it on both parties.

(12) The respondent supplies the information. Other matters dealt with in the order for directions are complied with: valuations obtained, discovery and inspection completed. Both parties are now ready for the hearing and *A* indicates this to the court giving an estimate of how long the hearing should take.

(13) The court notifies both parties of the hearing date.

(14) The hearing takes place before the registrar. He reads the affidavits filed on behalf of the parties, hears oral evidence and submissions from the parties' solicitors

(or counsel). He then makes orders for financial provision and property adjustment and costs. The order is served on the parties following the hearing.

11. Consent Orders

11–01 In many cases the parties do not continue to contest the question of financial provision to the bitter end and they manage to compromise the ancillary relief application. This agreement will usually be recorded in a consent order, which will be submitted to the court for approval. As so many cases are settled, with obvious advantages to all concerned, significant skills are required of the family practitioner in drafting consent orders. At the end of this chapter some draft orders are set out, together with a check-list of points to be remembered when drafting.

11–02 ## 1. Advantages and Disadvantages of Negotiating a Settlement

There are clearly several advantages in negotiating a compromise of the application for ancillary relief. The costs will be lower, the matter will be settled more quickly and there will be less bitterness between the parties. It is often said that it is better to obtain a lower consent order, with which the payer will comply, than to impose on him a higher order which may be difficult to enforce.

However, there are also some disadvantages in settling a case. The obvious one is that the negotiated compromise may be for substantially less than the court would have ordered, which may have unfortunate consequences for the advisers, as they may be liable in negligence. There is no doubt also that some clients want their "day in court" and excessive pressure brought to bear on such clients may be counter-productive. However, they must be carefully warned of their possible liability in costs[1] and in legal aid cases the Legal Aid Board may have to be informed.[2]

It is equally important to ensure that a client, who is apparently anxious and willing to settle a case, is not emotionally vulnerable, and therefore prepared to accept a

---

[1] See 10–30 as to liability for costs.
[2] See 2–13 for the duty of solicitors to keep the Legal Aid Board informed in such situations.

disadvantageous offer. Such clients should clearly be given more time to reflect on the suggested settlement. If they still insist on accepting a patently disadvantageous offer, it is important that the solicitor should obtain clear written instructions to this effect to preclude the possibility of a subsequent action for negligence.

2. The Need to Obtain Full Information   11–03

It is important to ensure that all the relevant information is obtained before agreeing to the terms of a settlement. For this reason many solicitors insist on affidavits of means being exchanged prior to settling a case. There is, however, a duty of full and frank disclosure imposed on parties in such matters regardless of whether affidavits are exchanged. In *Livesey* v. *Jenkins*,[3] for example, the House of Lords held that a consent order, which had not been preceded by an exchange of affidavits, was invalid as the wife had not disclosed to her husband, or to the court, her intention to remarry.

3. The Extent to which the Settlement is Binding   11–04

Once the parties have reached an agreement, the court will not automatically force them to comply with it. The court retains its unfettered jurisdiction to make orders for ancillary relief applying only those factors contained in sections 25 and 25A of the M.C.A. 1973. However, the existence of the agreement will be one of the "circumstances of the case" within the M.C.A. 1973, s.25(1) and might well affect the court's discretion.

In one case[4] the wife entered into a separation agreement   **11–05** with her husband under which she was paid a lump sum. In return for this she agreed not to claim against her husband in divorce proceedings for a property adjustment order or a lump sum. This agreement was entered into against the advice of her solicitors. Following the divorce, she did claim against her husband and at first instance the judge, declining to give effect to the agreement, awarded her £670,000. The Court of Appeal, however, held that the fact of her agreement, on which she had received legal advice (albeit against the agreement), was to be taken into account under section 25 of the M.C.A. 1973. They, therefore, dismissed her claim for a lump sum in its entirety and allowed the

---

[3] [1985] A.C. 424. For setting aside orders generally, see 12–03 *et seq.* below.
[4] *Edgar* v. *Edgar* [1980] 1 W.L.R. 1410 (C.A.).

husband's appeal. It is unlikely, however, that the court would take such a view if an agreement had been entered into without legal advice.[5]

Conversely, it is also true that the parties cannot compel the court to make an order simply because they are agreed upon its terms. On an application for a consent order the court must be supplied with all the necessary information as to the income and outgoings of the parties, so that it can ensure the suggested order is fair.

11–06 4. The Procedure for Obtaining a Consent Order

Obviously agreement may be reached at any stage of the application for ancillary relief, or even prior to formal proceedings being commenced. Provided the jurisdiction of the court has been invoked by the filing of a Form 11 or 13, an application for a consent order may be made at any time. As a matter of practice, however, it may be better to wait until a decree nisi has been granted in the divorce proceedings before lodging a consent order with the court for its approval. This is because a valid order containing provisions for a party to the marriage cannot be made until a decree nisi has been granted, and if, by oversight, the order is made before this it will be void.[6]

11–07 To apply for a consent order, the M.C.R. 1977, rule 76A provides that two documents must be filed. These are:

(i) a draft of the proposed order signed by the respondent to the application, or his solicitors, to signify his agreement; and

11–08 (ii) a statement of information. This must be comprehensive and contain information about:

> (a) the ages of the parties and the children and the duration of the marriage;
>
> (b) the income and capital resources of the parties and the children as at the date of the statement;
>
> (c) the net equity in any property concerned and the effect of its proposed distribution;
>
> (d) the arrangements intended for future accommodation;
>
> (e) any intention to remarry or cohabit;
>
> (f) whether, if relevant, any mortgagee of property which is proposed to be transferred by the suggested order has been served with notice of the application; and

[5] *Backhouse* v. *Backhouse* [1978] 1 W.L.R. 243.
[6] See *Board* v. *Checkland* [1987] 2 F.L.R. 257.

(g)   any other especially significant matters.

Rule 76A does not require the statement of information to be signed by or on behalf of both parties, but a Practice Direction[7] suggests that it is nevertheless appropriate for this to be done.

Where the application is for a consent order varying an order **11–09** for periodical payments, all that is required of the statement of information is that it should contain an estimate of the income referred to in (b) above. This is also the only information required on an application for a consent order for interim periodical payments.

Where a consent order is designed to achieve a clean break **11–10** between the parties, it is common practice to take advantage of section 15 of the Inheritance (Provision for Family and Dependants) Act 1975 and to insert in the draft order a clause excluding either party from subsequently seeking provision out of the estate of the other. Rule 76A does not require any additional information in such cases. However in *Whiting* and *Whiting*[8] the Court of Appeal held that, before it could decide (as required by section 15) whether it would be just to exclude future applications for provision out of a deceased spouse's estate, it had to have evidence of what that estate was likely to consist of and information about those whom the applicant considered to have a prior claim on the estate. In practice it will often be difficult to provide such information, however, and the extent to which it is insisted upon appears to vary widely from court to court.

There are many cases where the parties manage to settle the **11–11** application in the court waiting-room prior to the hearing. The imminent danger of a court appearance often has an amazing power to focus the parties' minds, and many seemingly impossible cases are compromised at the last minute.

To facilitate such "door of the court" settlements, rule 76A goes on to provide that, if the parties attend the hearing of the application for ancillary relief, the court may dispense with the necessity of lodging a draft consent order and the statement of information. Instead the court has power to give directions that the order be drawn up, and may also give

---

[7] [1986] 1 W.L.R. 381. The current version of the form to be used is set out in [1990] 1 W.L.R. 150.
[8] [1988] 1 W.L.R. 565.

directions as to the provision of details[9] which would otherwise have to be given in a statement of information.

11–12   *Example*

Paul and Samantha were not able to resolve their financial affairs. They and their solicitors attended at court for a hearing of the application for ancillary relief. In the waiting-room, after much discussion, the parties were able to reach agreement. Their solicitors attended before the registrar who was told of the terms of the agreement. As the affidavits of means were out of date, the registrar was also told of the changed financial circumstances of the parties. He agreed with the terms of the settlement and he gave directions that a detailed order be drafted by the parties and submitted to him within 14 days. He further ordered that a brief statement of information should be filed by the parties bringing up to date the information contained in their affidavits.

11–13   5. Drafting a Consent Order

This can be an extremely difficult task, requiring the solicitor to draft an order covering not only all the current provisions that should be made, but also anticipating changes that may occur in the future. This is especially important in view of the fact that orders for a lump sum and property adjustment cannot be varied (see 12–20).

Owing to the vast number of possible permutations of the provisions of consent orders, the drafting of them will be dealt with first by a series of general points, followed by three examples of the most common types of order.

11–14   GENERAL DRAFTING POINTS

It is important to distinguish the substantive part of the order from the preamble. The substantive part of the order can only contain those provisions which the court has power to order. The preamble, however, can record the agreement of one or both parties to comply with provisions which it is outside the court's powers to order. The usual method of dealing with this type of provision is by means of an undertaking to the court contained in the preamble. For example it is usual to provide in a *Mesher* type of order[10] for the party in occupation

---

[9] The rule provides that the statement may be "in more than one document." In cases where all the information is before the court in affidavits, there would seem to be no objection to these affidavits constituting the "statement of information."

[10] See draft order at 11–22.

of the matrimonial home to pay the mortgage and other outgoings in respect of that property. This cannot be ordered by the court, as it has no power to do so. It is usual, therefore, to deal with this by an undertaking to make the payments, given by the spouse in occupation, and recited in the preamble to the order.

An undertaking can be enforced in the same way as a term of **11–15** the order, since a breach of an undertaking to the court amounts to contempt. However it should be borne in mind that, in the case of a consent order, the undertaking will not normally have been given to the court in person. It would therefore be prudent to ensure that the party giving the undertaking signs the draft order as well as his solicitor, and acknowledges that he has had the consequences of a breach of the undertaking explained to him. This should avoid any doubts arising in the future about the enforceability of the undertaking.

As an alternative to an undertaking, the order could provide **11–16** in the preamble that it is made, "on the basis that [for example] the petitioner shall discharge all outgoings and expenses on the property ... " If the petitioner then failed to do this, it would presumably be possible to apply to the court under the liberty to apply clause for the outstanding sum to be paid from that party's share of the sale proceeds.

CHECKLIST **11–17**

The following is a checklist of points that should be considered when drafting consent orders:

(i) Periodical payments orders:
   by whom;
   to whom;
   from when;
   until when;
   period by reference to which calculated (*e.g.* £12,000 per annum);
   period by reference to which payable (*e.g.* payable at £1,000 per month);
   in advance or in arrear.

(ii) Lump sum orders: **11–18**
   by whom;
   to whom;
   how many sums;
   when payable;
   interest?

11–19   **(iii) Property adjustment orders:**
Generally:

legal estate—who is to have it;
beneficial interest
date for compliance (*e.g.* of execution of transfer into joint
names).

Where the house is retained for one party to occupy:

who is to occupy;
triggers for sale;
shares on sale;
other terms (*e.g.* outgoings).

11–20   **(iv) Clean break orders:**
Periodical payments for spouse:

dismiss both sides' applications; *or*
limit duration, with prohibition on extension of term.

Dismiss any "spare" applications.
Exclude section 2 of the Inheritance (Provision for Family
and Dependants) Act 1975;

(v) Liberty to apply[11]

(vi) Costs/legal aid taxation

11–21   SPECIMEN ORDERS

It is difficult to generalise about the terms of consent orders
as, of course, within the limits of the court's powers, anything
is possible. Broadly, however, orders relating to the matrimonial home fall into three types. These are: orders retaining
the property for one spouse to occupy, orders for transfer of
property, and orders for transfer of property with lump sum
back or sale in default.

To illustrate the points which must be covered when
drafting such orders, three specimen orders are set out below.
These are not intended to be exhaustive precedents; for
example the order deferring sale of the house is in the form of
a *Mesher* order rather than a *Browne* v. *Pritchard* order.

---

[11] This term enables either party to apply for a "working out" of a minor
incidental matter which was not dealt with at the time of the drafting of the
order. For example, the appointment of a particular firm of solicitors to deal
with the conveyancing of the matrimonial home. See Practice Direction
[1980] 1 All E.R. 1008.

Furthermore, the way in which an order for immediate sale would be drafted can be gathered from the order for a lump sum with sale in default.

Case study A   11–22

Order retaining property on trust for sale for one party to occupy

Simon (respondent) and Jane (petitioner) jointly own a three-bedroomed house. They have two children aged five and seven. The parties obtain a divorce and it is agreed that the house will be retained for Jane to live in with the children, until both children are 18 or cease full-time education, whichever is the later. During that time Simon will pay Jane periodical payments, and out of these Jane will pay the mortgage and other outgoings on the house. When the house is sold the net proceeds will be divided, one-third to Simon and two-thirds to Jane. Simon will not be liable to pay any further periodical payments to Jane after then, as she will be in a position to maintain herself.

Draft order   11–23

[Heading as in main suit]

BY CONSENT and upon the petitioner UNDERTAKING to discharge fully all outgoings of the former matrimonial home known as [address] (hereinafter referred to as the property), other than structural repairs and, in particular, to discharge fully the instalments falling due under the mortgage secured on the property without extending the term thereof AND UPON the respondent and petitioner UNDERTAKING to contribute equally towards the cost of any structural repairs to the property.

IT IS HEREBY ORDERED THAT:

1. The respondent shall pay or cause to be paid to the children of the family [names] periodical payments at the rate of £00 each per month, payable monthly in advance on the first day of each calendar month, the first payment to be made on the [insert date]; until they shall attain the age of 18 or until further order.

2. The respondent shall pay or cause to be paid to the petitioner, periodical payments at the rate of £00 per month, payable monthly in advance on the first day of each calendar month, the first payment to be made on [insert date]. These payments to continue until:

    (i)   either the petitioner or respondent shall die; or

    (ii)   the petitioner shall remarry; or

    (iii) all the children of the family [names] have attained the age of 18 or ceased full time education if later;

whichever shall first apply. It is hereby directed that the petitioner shall not be entitled to apply under section 31 of the Matrimonial Causes Act 1973 for this order to be varied by extending the term.[12]

3. The property shall be retained by the petitioner and the respondent as trustees for sale[13] but the beneficial interests shall be settled[14] as hereinafter provided.

4. The terms of the said settlement shall be:

    (i)   That the petitioner shall have the sole use, occupation and benefit of the property and the income therefrom until sale. It is intended that the property shall be used as a home for the petitioner and her dependants.[15]

    (ii) That the trust for sale shall not be enforced without the consent of the petitioner[16] until:

        (a)   all the children of the family [names] attain the age of 18 years or cease full-time education if later; or

        (b)   the petitioner shall die or remarry or, subject to clause 4(iv) hereof, voluntarily leave the property; or

        (c)   further order of the court;
        whichever shall first apply.

    (iii) That the trustees shall have full powers to deal with the property or the proceeds of sale thereof as if they were an absolute beneficial owner.[17]

---

[12] The court's powers to order limited term maintenance and in appropriate cases to include this provision were discussed at 6–21. It is unlikely in practice that this "total bar" would be used, but it is included here for the purpose of illustration.

[13] If the property was currently held in the name of one of the parties only, then the property should first be transferred into the joint names of both of them. If one party was likely to be unco-operative, it could be transferred into the names of separate trustees.

[14] The C.G.T. advantages of a settlement have been discussed at 7–44.

[15] This phrase is essential to ensure postponement of the statutory charge. See 2–28.

[16] This method of delaying the sale, *i.e.* by requiring the consent of the wife, is the only means of restricting the power of sale of trustees for sale. See s.26 of the L.P.A. 1925.

[17] The powers of the trustees of sale are limited, therefore it is wise specifically to extend their powers.

(iv) That to enable the petitioner to move to another home (hereinafter called the new home) during the subsistence of this trust:

    (a) the trustees for the time being shall if so required by the respondent sell the property and apply the proceeds either:

        (aa) in the purchase of a freehold dwelling; or

        (bb) in taking the grant or assignment of a leasehold dwelling, provided that at least 75 years of such leasehold term remains unexpired at the date of the contract for purchase;
as she shall direct for her occupation.

    (b) the costs of and incidental to such sale and purchase shall be borne by the petitioner;

    (c) the new home shall be held upon the same trusts as the property, and the trustees shall have full power, as if they were beneficial owners thereof, to execute such mortgage deed as may be necessary to enable the purchase thereof to be completed, subject to the proviso that the term for repayment of the loan secured by such mortgage deed shall not exceed the term then remaining for repayment of the loan secured by the mortgage now secured on the property;

    (d) if the purchase price of the new home shall be less than the sale proceeds of the property, the difference shall be divided as to one-third to the respondent and two-thirds to the petitioner.

    (e) the removal from the property by the petitoner in accordance with these provisions shall not constitute a voluntary removal within 4(ii) (b) hereof.

(v) That upon sale (save in accordance with clause 4(iv) hereof) the proceeds shall be applied in discharging the mortgage secured thereon, and the costs of and incidental to the sale, and in dividing the balance then remaining as to one-third to the respondent and two-thirds to the petitioner.

5. That the applications of the parties hereto for a lump sum order in the prayer of the petition and the notice of application filed herein shall stand dismissed.[18]

---

[18] A notice of application should be filed by the respondent so that this may be dismissed.

6. That there be liberty to each party to apply.[19]

7. That the respondent do pay £00[20] towards the petitioner's costs of this application and that there be legal aid taxation[21] of the petitioner's costs.

[Dated and signed by the solicitors for both parties.]

11–24 **Case study B**

Transfer of property order

Kevin (respondent) and Joan (petitioner) have divorced. They are both working and self-supporting. Kevin has substantial capital and has agreed, in settlement of Joan's claims on him, to transfer the matrimonial home to her. All other applications are to be dismissed.

11–25 *Draft order*

[Heading as in main suit]

BY CONSENT and upon the petitioner UNDERTAKING to indemnify the respondent against any future liability under the mortgage in favour of the A.B. Building Society, secured on the former matrimonial home, known as [description of the property] (hereinafter referred to as the property) and to use her best endeavours to procure his release from his covenants thereunder.[22]

IT IS HEREBY ORDERED THAT:

1. The respondent shall on or before the   day of   199   [23] execute such document as may be necessary to transfer and release unto the petitioner all his legal and equitable interest in the property and in the proceeds

---

[19] See 11–20 and note 7.

[20] Or costs to be taxed. This formula might be preferable from the husband's point of view as it limits the extent of his indebtedness.

[21] As to the legal aid charge see 2–18.

[22] If the mortgage contains a clause prohibiting transfer without consent, the building society's consent must be obtained before this application is made. The court cannot order their consent nor would it wish to prejudice their interests in the property. So far as the release of the respondent of his covenants under the mortgage is concerned, it would be advisable to obtain consent prior to the application.

[23] It is essential to insert a date for enforcement purposes.

of sale thereof and in the contents thereof. Such document to be prepared by the petitioner's solicitors and at her expense.[24]

2. Upon compliance with the order in clause 1 hereof the remaining applications of the parties hereto in the prayer of the petition and the notice of application filed herein shall stand dismissed and the court hereby directs that each party shall not be entitled to make a further application in relation to the marriage for an order under section 23(1) (*a*) or (*b*) of the Matrimonial Causes Act 1973.[25]

3. Pursuant to section 15 of the Inheritance (Provision for Family and Dependants) Act 1975 neither party shall be entitled on the death of the other to apply for an order under section 2 of that Act.[26]

4. Liberty to apply.[27]

5. There be no order as to costs.

[Dated and signed by the solicitors for both parties.]

Case study C

11–26

Order for transfer of property with lump sum back or sale in default.

The marriage of Ronald (petitioner) and June (respondent) broke down after a year. They have no children and they have recently divorced. They own their house in joint names and it was intended to sell this and divide the proceeds equally. June has now offered to buy Ronald's half share which has been valued at £7,000. It has also been agreed that June will take over the existing mortgage and extend this by £7,000. Neither Ronald nor June is legally aided.

Draft order

11–27

[Heading as in main suit]

BY CONSENT and upon the respondent UNDERTAKING to indemnify the petitioner against any future liability under the mortgage in favour of Z.X. Building Society secured on the former matrimonial home known as [description of the

---

[24] Should the party refuse to sign the document recourse may be had to s.39 of the Supreme Court Act 1981 and s.38 of the County Courts Act 1984 to obtain an order empowering a third party (usually the registrar) to sign on their behalf.

[25] See note 18 above, and also 6–75.

[26] See 6–71.

[27] See 11–20 and note 11.

property] (hereinafter referred to as the property) and to use her best endeavours to procure his release from his covenants thereunder.

IT IS HEREBY ORDERED THAT:

1. The respondent shall pay or cause to be paid to the petitioner the following lump sum:

    (i)   £7,000 on or before the   day of 199   [28]; or if not paid on or before that date;

    (ii) a sum equivalent to £7,000 plus interest thereon from the   day of   199 until payment at the rate of   per cent per annum[29] or, if not paid by the   day of   199 [30] then,

    (iii) a sum equivalent to one half the net proceeds of sale as provided by clause 3 hereof.

2. The petitioner shall upon payment of the lump sum execute such document as may be required to transfer and release to the respondent all his legal and equitable interest in the property and in the proceeds of sale thereof, such document to be prepared by the respondent's solicitors and at her expense.

3. If the lump sum shall not be paid by the   day of 199 [30] then the property shall be sold and the proceeds of sale (after redemption of the mortgage and the payment of the costs of and incidental to such sale) shall be divided equally between the petitioner and the respondent.

[Clauses 4., 5. and 6. are the same as clauses 2., 3. and 4. in draft order B, above.]

7. There be no order as to costs.

[Dated and signed by the solicitors for the parties.]

[28] It is essential to insert a date for enforcement purposes. At a time of rising house prices this date should be fairly soon (e.g. three months' time).
[29] The limitations on the court's powers to award interest are considered at 6–12.
[30] This is a long-stop date. In times of rapidly rising house prices the sum specified may soon become too small a figure to represent a half of the sale proceeds even taking into account the conveyancing costs of sale. If the respondent has been unable to obtain a further mortgage after, say, six months it will be unlikely that she will be able to do so. Once this date has passed, then the sale provisions of the order are triggered, and it may be necessary to go back to court, under the liberty to apply provision, for further directions as to the conduct of the sale, if the respondent is dilatory.

12. Appeals, Setting Aside and Variation

There are three ways in which a party may seek to have the **12–01**
provisions for an order for ancillary relief altered. He may be
able to appeal against the order, usually as soon as it is made,
or he may subsequently apply to have it set aside or varied.
This chapter deals with the scope of the courts' powers to
make such changes.

1. Appeals   12–02

Any party may appeal as of right to a judge against any order
made by a registrar. However rule 124 of the M.C.R. 1977,
which governs appeals from county court registrars in
matrimonial proceedings, provides that notice of appeal
should be filed within five days of the order.[1] This is an
unrealistically short period, bearing in mind that in many
cases appellants will need time to take advice on whether an
appeal would be worthwhile, and may need to obtain an
amendment of their legal aid certificates to cover the appeal.
It is therefore often necessary to apply to the judge for leave
to appeal out of time, but such leave is normally granted.

The appeal is heard in chambers and takes the form of a
rehearing of the case. This means that the judge can hear
evidence which was not put to the registrar, and is completely
unfettered by the registrar's decision. A further appeal lies to
the Court of Appeal, with leave of either that court or of the
judge.

2. Setting Aside   12–03

A party may sometimes seek to have an order set aside on the
ground that it was tainted by some fundamental irregularity
which invalidates the whole order. An application to have an

---

[1] Where the appeal is from a district High Court registrar the period is seven
days: R.S.C., Order 58, r. 3(2).

order set aside can be made on appeal, but should preferably be made separately to a judge at first instance, because difficult issues of fact may have to be resolved on such applications.[2] The application is not, of course, subject to any prescribed time limits, and may be made several years after the original order. A further advantage of an application to set aside is that it allows the court to change any of the terms of the original order, and not only those which can be varied under section 31 of the M.C.A. 1973, set out at 12–13 (below).

12–04 However, any application to set aside can succeed only on certain narrow grounds, the scope of which is not entirely certain. The case law shows that orders may be set aside on the following grounds, which to some extent overlap.

12–05 NON-DISCLOSURE OF MATERIAL EVIDENCE

This clearly covers cases where a party fails to divulge the full extent of his assets. It also covers the case of a spouse who fails to divulge an intention to remarry. Thus, in *Livesey* v. *Jenkins*[3] a consent order had been made under which the wife received the matrimonial home in return for the dismissal of her applications for financial provision. Before the order was made the wife had become engaged, although she did not reveal this fact to the husband. Two days after the husband had transferred his share of the house to the wife, in pursuance of the order, the wife remarried. The House of Lords held that the order should be set aside, because of the wife's failure to make a full and frank disclosure of all material facts to the husband, and to the court. Unless such disclosure is made, it is impossible for the court to exercise its discretion properly under section 25 of the M.C.A. 1973 and take into account all the relevant facts affecting the case. The House of Lords emphasised that this duty to make a complete disclosure of all material facts applies just as much to cases where the order is made by consent, as where the proceedings are contested.

12–06 However, in *Livesey* v. *Jenkins*, Lord Brandon also emphasised that it is not every failure of full disclosure which will justify setting an order aside. A party applying on this ground will have to show that the absence of disclosure has led to an order being made which is substantially different from the order which would otherwise have been made.

---

[2] *Robinson* v. *Robinson* (*Practice Note*) [1982] 1 W.L.R. 786.
[3] [1985] A.C. 424.

FRAUD 12–07

No doubt a failure to divulge material evidence might often be treated as a fraud on the other party, but, of course, fraud in the sense of a deliberate misrepresentation about, for example, the size of a party's assets, has also been recognised as a ground on which an order can be set aside.[4]

MISTAKE 12–08

There are dicta in a number of cases accepting that mistake constitutes a ground for setting aside,[5] but, except in so far as the victim of fraud, or material non-disclosure, may be said to have acted under a mistake, there are no clear guidelines as to the scope of this ground. No doubt a party who felt that he could not prove fraud could sometimes claim that he had acted under a unilateral mistake, but the mistake would have to be as to a matter of fundamental importance before it would justify setting an order aside. The facts of *Thwaite* v. *Thwaite*[6] provide a possible example of an order based on mistake. Here the husband had been ordered, by consent, to transfer his interest in the matrimonial house to the wife. The husband had agreed to this on the understanding that the wife intended to remain in the home with the children. However, before the conveyance was completed, it transpired that the wife intended to make her home in Australia. The Court of Appeal held that the county court judge had got jurisdiction to set the order aside on the basis of this fresh evidence of the wife's intention, although the judge had not found her guilty of any "deliberate calculated deceit."

SUBSEQUENT EVENTS

The courts are understandably reluctant to set aside orders 12–09 because of events that have occurred after the order was made. This could encourage aggrieved parties to apply to have orders set aside (including orders which are incapable of variation under section 31 of the M.C.A. 1973, discussed below), and much undesirable uncertainty would result. However, in *Barder* v. *Barder (Caluori intervening)*[7] the House

---

[4] See, *e.g. de Lasala* v. *de Lasala* [1980] A.C. 546 and *Allsop* v. *Allsop* (1981) 11 Fam. Law. 18.

[5] *e.g. de Lasala* v. *de Lasala* (above), and *O'Dougherty* v. *O'Dougherty* [1983] 4 F.L.R. 407.

[6] [1982] Fam. 1.

[7] [1988] A.C. 20.

of Lords accepted that there could be circumstances in which subsequent events so radically affected the assumptions underlying the original order, that the only just solution would be to set the order aside. In this case the husband had been ordered, by consent, to transfer the matrimonial home to the wife within 28 days. Before he could do so the wife killed both children of the family and committed suicide. Under her will, the wife's estate went to her mother. The husband therefore sought leave to appeal out of time against the order. The House of Lords held that he should succeed. Clearly it had never been contemplated at the time the order was made that the wife's mother should have the benefit of the property, which had really been intended as a home in which the children could be brought up. At the same time, the court was clearly concerned not to encourage applications to set aside in future by discontented parties seeking to use unexpected subsequent events as a ground for challenging orders. The court therefore laid down a series of stringent conditions which must be met before such applications can succeed.

These conditions are:

(i)   the subsequent events must have invalidated the basis on which the order was made;

(ii) those events must have occurred within "a relatively short time," (*i.e.* usually a matter of months);

(iii) the application must be made reasonably promptly;

(iv) the granting of leave must not prejudice the rights of a bona fide purchaser for value of the property in question.

12–10 Perhaps predictably, despite the conditions laid down by the House of Lords, there have been subsequent unmeritorious attempts to have orders set aside on the ground that events occurring since the order was made have invalidated the basis of that order. Thus in *Rooker* v. *Rooker*[8] the Court of Appeal refused to set aside a consent order because of the husband's delay in complying with an order for the sale of the matrimonial home. The order had been made in 1984 and the wife was to receive £20,000 out of the proceeds. However, the sale did not take place for two years and by then, argued the wife, the lump sum was inadequate to buy appropriate accommodation. The court held, however, that the husband's

[8] [1988] 1 F.L.R. 219.

delay did not constitute a supervening event which invalidated the basis of the order—after all, the wife could have taken steps to enforce the order and had failed to do so.

Rooker v. *Rooker* was itself distinguished, however, in *Hope-Smith* v. *Hope-Smith*.[9] In this case the former matrimonial home had originally been valued at £116,000 when the sale was ordered in the ancillary proceedings on divorce. Out of this money the wife was to receive £32,000. The husband, however, managed to avoid selling the property for over two years, by which time the house was estimated to be worth £200,000. The wife then sought to appeal out of time for the order to be set aside. The Court of Appeal held that in this case the wife should succeed, because her failure to enforce the order was almost entirely due to the delaying tactics of the husband, and not to any lack of diligence on her part. The Court of Appeal, therefore, substituted a percentage figure of the proceeds of sale for the lump sum of £32,000 which had originally been ordered. (It should be noted, incidentally, that the difficulty which arose in this case could have been completely avoided if a percentage figure had appeared in the original order.)

12–11

OTHER GROUNDS

12–12

It is not clear whether other irregularities could justify setting an order aside. In *Tommey* v. *Tommey*[10] Balcombe J. held that undue influence was not a ground for doing so, but in *Livesey* v. *Jenkins*,[11] Lord Brandon, with whom all members of the court agreed, said that he was "not persuaded that Balcombe J.'s decision on the question was necessarily correct." Even if undue influence (*e.g.* in the form of taking advantage of a party's emotional state, or lack of legal advice) were not regarded as sufficient, presumably pressure amounting to duress would be accepted as a ground for setting an order aside.

Nevertheless the courts will certainly remain reluctant to set orders aside unless there are strong reasons for doing so, because the need to achieve an end to litigation between the parties must be set against the desire to ensure that justice is done between the parties. This applies especially to those cases where the order was designed to achieve a clean break.

---

[9] [1989] 2 F.L.R. 56, C.A.
[10] [1983] Fam. 15.
[11] See note 3, above.

3. Variation

12–13 ORDERS THAT CAN BE VARIED

The orders for ancillary relief that can be varied are listed in section 31(2) of the M.C.A. 1973. They are:

(a) orders for maintenance pending suit and interim maintenance;

(b) periodical payments orders;

(c) secured periodical payments orders;

(d) orders for the payment of lump sums by instalments;

(e) orders for a settlement of property or a variation of a settlement made under section 24 of the M.C.A. 1973 (but only where the original order was made on or after the grant of a decree of judicial separation and the application for variation is made in proceedings for rescission of that decree, or in proceedings for divorce);

(f) orders for the sale of property under section 24A of the M.C.A. 1973.

12–14 POWERS OF VARIATION

Under section 31(1) of the M.C.A. 1973 the court has wide powers to vary the orders listed above. These powers apply to orders made by consent as well as to orders made after a contested hearing.

The court can both vary and discharge orders, and may also suspend provisions temporarily and subsequently revive them. In addition, under section 31(2A), where the court has made any kind of maintenance order, it has power to remit any arrears due under the order. In practice, most applications made under section 31 are for the variation of periodical payments orders, either upwards or downwards. There are, however, two restrictions on the courts' powers to vary orders for periodical payments, both secured and unsecured.

12–15 **(i) Limited term maintenance**
In general, where the court has made an order limiting the term for which periodical payments are to be made to a party to the marriage, that party can apply under section 31 for an extension of the term, provided the application is made before the term has expired. However, the court does have power,

under section 28(1A) of the M.C.A. 1973, to prevent this, by
including in the order a direction that no application for an
extension is to be made.

(ii) Capital orders as a means of varying maintenance orders   **12–16**
The court cannot make a property adjustment order as a
means of varying an order for periodical payments.[12] This
applies to orders made for both parties and children. Nor can
the court make a lump sum order as a means of varying an
order for periodical payments for a party to the marriage.[12]
This type of variation is, however, permitted in the case of a
child.

The reason for these restrictions is that it is not considered
generally appropriate to redistribute capital and property once
the parties have regulated their affairs according to the terms
of the original order.

The exception, whereby a lump sum may be awarded to a
child as a means of varying a periodical payments order, may
be justified on the basis that lump sums can in any case be
awarded to children at any time after divorce (see 6–10,
above).

There is one way in which the court may circumvent the ban   **12–17**
on awarding a party a lump sum by way of varying a
periodical payments order. This is illustrated by *S.* v. *S.*[13]
Here the wife of a famous pop star applied for a variation of a
periodical payments order of £23,000 per year, which had
been made on divorce. The judge held that he was prepared
to increase the payments to £70,000 per year, but, if the
husband were to pay the wife a lump sum of £400,000 the
periodical payments order would be discharged. The judge
clearly had no power under section 31 to make an order for
the payment of the lump sum, but was prepared to discharge
the maintenance order under section 31 upon the husband
giving a satisfactory undertaking to make the capital payment.[14]

The opportunity to terminate a continuing obligation to pay
maintenance by making a lump sum payment might appeal to
many husbands who have the necessary capital, but it must
be borne in mind that any income tax relief available on the
periodical payments will be lost, and, of course, a lump sum

---

[12] M.C.A. 1973, s.31(5).
[13] [1986] Fam. 189.
[14] In fact the husband chose not to give the undertaking; see [1987] 2 All E.R.
312. The Court of Appeal refrained from expressing any opinion as to the
validity of the approach adopted by the judge at first instance.

will immediately attract the statutory charge if the recipient was legally aided, unless the money is to be used to purchase a home for the assisted party. A husband might also want to consider whether his former wife is likely to remarry in the foreseeable future, before commuting the periodical payments for a lump sum.

12–18 Where the court makes an order varying or discharging a periodical payments order, it also has power to postpone the variation or discharge for a specified period of time,[15] thus giving either party an opportunity to adjust to the eventual change. On the other hand, the court can also backdate a variation order, even beyond the date of the variation application.[16] However, since income tax relief is no longer restrospectively available, the incentive for seeking to have the order backdated has largely disappeared.

12–19 The powers of variation contained in section 31(1) are exercisable by the High Court, and those county courts with matrimonial jurisdiction. Where, as often happens, a periodical payments order has been registered in a magistrates' court for enforcement purposes (see 13–10, below), the magistrates' court has power to vary it instead.[17] Magistrates' powers to vary orders which have been registered are limited to varying the amounts of the payments specified in the order. This means that applications to suspend or discharge the order must still be dealt with by the court that made the order, and, in exceptional cases, even an application to vary the amount of the payments may be referred to the original court by the magistrates.[18]

12–20 ORDERS THAT CANNOT BE VARIED

It will be gathered from the list of orders that can be varied (12–13, above), that, in general, lump sum orders and property adjustment orders cannot be varied. This is in accordance with the general principle, already mentioned, that the distribution of capital and property on divorce should not normally be open to subsequent adjustment. The parties should be entitled to make plans for the future on the assumption that the original distribution is permanent.

---

[15] See M.C.A. 1973, s.31(10) (inserted by the M.F.P.A. 1984).
[16] See, *e.g. MacDonald* v. *MacDonald* [1964] P. 1. and *Morley-Clarke* v. *Jones* [1986] Ch. 311.
[17] Maintenance Orders Act 1958, s.4.
[18] See *Gsell* v. *Gsell* [1971] 1 W.L.R. 225n.

The general principle is, however, subject to certain qualifications.

(i) Lump sums by instalments

12–21

As has been seen, a lump sum order may be varied, but only where payment by instalments was ordered. It has been held,[19] however, that this power can even be used to order the complete discharge of the remaining instalments, so that the actual sum paid may be substantially smaller than originally ordered.

(ii) Property adjustment orders

12–22

There are very limited powers to vary settlement of property orders where the original order was made in proceedings for judicial separation (see 12–13, above), but, in general, property adjustment orders are not capable of variation under section 31.

The courts have also made it clear that they will not connive at attempts to obtain variations of property adjustment orders by indirect methods. So, for example, they will not give leave to appeal out of time against such orders when the application is made several years after the original order, and is obviously an attempt to have that order varied. Similarly, a party who has already received one type of property adjustment order will not normally be allowed to make subsequent applications for another type of property adjustment order or a lump sum order, if it is clear that the original order was designed to deal comprehensively with the distribution of capital assets between the parties.

12–23

Both these points can be illustrated by reference to *Carson* v. *Carson*.[20] Here a wife had applied for a property adjustment order on divorce, which resulted in a *Mesher* order being made. Under the order the wife was to have sole occupation of the former matrimonial home until the youngest child of the family reached 18. Some six years later the wife sought to forestall the sale of the house by applying for:

(a)   a transfer of the home to her absolutely; and

(b)   leave to appeal out of time against the original order.

The Court of Appeal dismissed both applications. Although the wife had originally applied in general terms for a property

---

[19] *Tilley* v. *Tilley* (1979) 10 Fam. Law 89.
[20] [1983] 1 W.L.R. 285. The decision was approved by the House of Lords in *Dinch* v. *Dinch* [1987] 1 W.L.R. 252. See also *Sandford* v. *Sandford* [1986] 1 F.L.R. 412.

adjustment order, the making of a settlement of property order had effectively disposed of that application. The wife was not entitled to a second property adjustment order in respect of the same asset. Furthermore, the court held that it would be wrong to grant leave to appeal out of time against a six-year-old order, when the position of both parties had radically changed since the making of the order.

12–24 Although it is not possible to obtain a postponement of sale beyond the time originally envisaged, it may sometimes be possible to obtain a sale earlier than any of the dates contained in the original order for a deferred sale. This is by making an application under the M.C.A. 1973, s.24A, for a sale of the property. Orders for sale can be made (*inter alia*) at any time after the court has made a property adjustment order. Therefore, once the court has made a *Mesher* order, it is open to either party to make a subsequent application for a sale of the property, even though none of the events which would trigger a sale under the order have yet occurred.[21] Of course, the power to order a sale is entirely discretionary, and in many cases the court would, no doubt, reject the application on its merits. There will, however, be some circumstances in which an earlier sale may be justified, as where, for example, it is the spouse in occupation who is seeking the sale against the wishes of the non-occupying spouse.[22]

12–25 Given the general principle that capital orders cannot be varied, it seems odd that orders for the sale of property are included in the list of orders that are capable of variation under section 31. It is, however, possible to think of cases where a power to vary such orders might be useful. For example, where the order for sale was made as a means of enforcing the payment of a lump sum order, the court could discharge the order for sale if the respondent found other ways of raising the money.

12–26 THE PRINCIPLES ON WHICH VARIATION IS ORDERED

The principles on which a variation order is based are really the same as those on which the original order was made (see 6–34 *et seq.*, above). Under section 31(7) of the M.C.A. 1973 (as amended by the M.F.P.A. 1984) the court is required to

---

[21] See *Thompson* v. *Thompson* [1986] Fam. 38 and *Taylor* v. *Taylor* [1987] 1 F.L.R. 142, C.A.
[22] See *Thompson* v. *Thompson* (above).

"have regard to all the circumstances of the case, first consideration being given to the welfare while a minor of any child of the family who has not attained the age of 18." Section 31(7) provides that the phrase "all the circumstances of the case" includes any change in the matters which the court was required to consider when making the original order. Where the party against whom the order was made has died the phrase "all the circumstances of the case" also includes the changed circumstances resulting from his death.[23] This is likely to be relevant only where the application is for variation of an order for secured periodical payments.

The increased emphasis which is nowadays placed on achieving a clean break between the parties is relevant to variation as well as to original applications. The court can, of course, discharge a periodical payments order completely under section 31(1), but where it is simply considering a variation of a periodical payments order made in favour of a party in divorce or nullity proceedings, it must consider whether the term of such payments could be limited without causing undue hardship to the payee.[24]   **12–27**

As was seen in Chapter 6 (see 6–76, above) the courts are notoriously reluctant to impose a clean break on a payee without her consent. In fact several of the cases discussed in Chapter 6 were variation applications in which the court refused to dismiss the wife's order for periodical payments outright. The courts' narrow approach is further illustrated by *Fisher* v. *Fisher*,[25] a case in which the parties had been divorced 10 years previously, at which time the husband had been ordered to pay the wife a lump sum and periodical payments. Some three years after this the wife had borne a child by another man. However, she found that she was unable to obtain maintenance from the child's father and subsequently sought an increase in her periodical payments from her ex-husband. The husband cross-applied for a reduction or a discharge of the periodical payments, arguing that the wife should not be entitled to rely on a reduction in her earning capacity which had come about as a result of her voluntary action in having another man's child. The Court of Appeal rejected this argument, however, in upholding the   **12–28**

---

[23] See s.31(7)(*b*).
[24] See s.31(7)(*a*); see also *Morris* v. *Morris* [1985] 6 F.L.R. 1176 in which it was held that a judge's failure to consider the hardship that would be caused to a wife by terminating a periodical payments order in five years' time, vitiated the order.
[25] [1989] 1 F.L.R. 423.

registrar's decision that the periodical payments should be increased. The court confirmed that the wife's responsibilities towards the child which she had had by another man must be taken into account under section 31(7) with its reference to "all the circumstances of the case."

12–29 Finally, it is important on variation applications to pay close attention to the totality of the original order. That order should have represented a fair "package deal" for the parties (see 6–80, above). For example, a wife who received a better than average capital settlement may have received lower than average periodical payments. If she now applies for an increase in those payments, it is important that the court should be reminded of the circumstances in which the order was made, otherwise the balance that was achieved by the original order is in danger of being upset by the variation.

12–30 PROCEDURE ON VARIATION APPLICATIONS

The party seeking a variation of an order for ancillary relief applies by notice on Form 11.[26] No leave is required for the application. A copy of the application must be served on the respondent within four days of filing.[27] Unlike the original application, an application for variation need not be accompanied by an affidavit of means. The applicant need file an affidavit, setting out particulars of property and income and the grounds for the application, only if ordered to do so by the registrar.[28] In practice, however, an affidavit will usually be filed anyway, and in this case the respondent must file an affidavit in reply within 14 days of being served with the applicant's affidavit.[29]

12–31 A variation order may, of course, be made by consent, in which case rule 76A of the M.C.R. 1977 applies and the application must be accompanied by a draft order and a statement of information (see 11–07 to 11–09, above). However, the information required on an application to vary periodical payments is confined to an estimate of the net income of each party and any minor child of the family.

---

[26] M.C.R. 1977, r. 68(3).
[27] M.C.R. 1977, r. 70.
[28] M.C.R. 1977, r. 75 (as substituted by the Matrimonial Causes (Amendment) Rules 1984).
[29] M.C.R. 1977, r. 75 (as amended by the Matrimonial Causes (Amendment No. 2) Rules 1985).

13. Enforcement

Once an order for ancillary relief has been obtained, it may be **13–01** necessary to consider how best this order can be enforced. This chapter is primarily concerned with the enforcement of county court orders ancillary to divorce. The matter may, in a few cases, be transferred to the High Court,[1] in which case essentially the same methods of enforcement will apply. Methods of enforcement of magistrates' courts' orders are dealt with at 14–59, below.

1. Preliminary Considerations

AFFIDAVIT OF SUMS DUE

Before any order for the payment of money can be enforced, the applicant must file an affidavit setting out the amount of arrears due under a periodical payments order, or the balance outstanding under a lump sum order.[2] This is because payment of these orders is made direct between the parties, so that there is no independent record of payments.

ORAL EXAMINATION   **13–02**

Should there be any doubt as to the extent of the debtor's assets, and, therefore, the best method of enforcement, an application might be made for the debtor to be orally examined about his financial circumstances. This is usually undertaken by the registrar, and should be a thorough cross-examination of the severest kind.

However, in the majority of cases the applicant will have, by this stage of the proceedings, a reasonably accurate knowledge of the extent of the respondent's financial assets. It is only where some time has passed since the proceedings for ancillary relief that the need for an oral examination will be likely to arise.

---

[1] See 10–27, above.
[2] M.C.R. 1977, r. 86(1).

LEGAL AID CONSIDERATIONS

Certain legal aid considerations must be borne in mind when contemplating enforcement proceedings.

(i) When legal aid is granted for the purpose of obtaining an order for ancillary relief, it will not cover enforcement proceedings unless this is specifically mentioned. It will usually be necessary, therefore, to obtain an amendment to the certificate.

(ii) It is usual for the amended certificate to specify one type of enforcement proceedings. If it does not it will be regarded as covering one application for enforcement only.

(iii) In the case of periodical payments orders *to* a child, these can only be enforced by the child acting by his next friend or guardian *ad litem*.[3] As the parent's certificate cannot be amended to provide for this, a separate legal aid application will have to be made by the child. This does not apply, fortunately, to applications to register such an order in the magistrates' court for enforcement (see 13–10). Such an application is regarded as part of the process of obtaining the order rather than an application for enforcement.

This problem does not, of course, apply to periodical payments orders which are expressed to be to a party for the benefit of a child, although it appears that in both situations the certificate may still need to be amended to cover the registration procedure.[4] In practice it is likely that the wording of the original certificate will cover registration in a magistrates' court.

TRACING THE RESPONDENT

There are cases where, before enforcement proceedings can be started, it is necessary to trace the respondent. It may be that enquiry agents will have to be employed. In some cases it may be appropriate for the applicant to ask the registrar to request disclosure of the respondent's address by various government departments, *e.g.* the D.S.S.[5]

[3] *Shelley* v. *Shelley* [1952] 1 All E.R. 70.
[4] See *Legal Aid Handbook* 1990, p. 63.
[5] Practice Direction [1989] 1 All E.R. 765.

2. Methods of Enforcement of Lump Sum Orders

ORDER FOR SALE OF ASSETS   **13–03**

By section 24A of the M.C.A. 1973 the court has power to
order the sale of property when it has made an order for (*inter
alia*) a lump sum. This section has been considered at 6–27,
above. If the possibility of non-payment by the respondent
was considered by the court at the time of the original order,
provision may have been made for an order for sale of the
asset at that time.

   If this was not ordered at the time the lump sum order was
made, an order for sale under section 24A might be made
later, containing a direction that a sum of money be paid to
the petitioner.

Example

*Simon is ordered to pay Felicity £25,000 which represents her share
of the matrimonial home. If the problem of enforcement was
considered at the time the order was made, the order could have gone
on to provide that, if the payment was not made within six months,
the house should be sold and net proceeds divided equally.*

   *Assuming that the question of enforcement was not considered
when the order was made, then, if the money is not forthcoming
within the six-month period, a later application may be made for an
order for sale under section 24A.*

   Should the respondent refuse to co-operate with the order,
directions may be made for the conduct of the sale, and for
the registrar to execute the conveyance or transfer. This is
considered further at 13–12, below.

WARRANT OF EXECUTION   **13–04**

This is the county court equivalent of the High Court writ of
fieri facias (*fi. fa.*). It can be obtained on application to the
court and does not involve a hearing. It empowers the county
court bailiff, or in the High Court the sheriff, to seize and sell
certain goods belonging to the payer to the value of the lump
sum.

GARNISHEE PROCEEDINGS   **13–05**

An order can be made to secure payment from a third party
who owes money to the debtor. For example, if the
respondent has a building society or bank account in which

there is a sum of money invested, this account may be "garnisheed" and the bank or building society ordered to pay the applicant the money due. The procedure involves two hearings before the registrar, one on the application for the order, which freezes the account, and the second which orders payment to the applicant.

13–06 CHARGING ORDER

An order can be applied for to charge land (or certain securities) with the debt. The procedure is similar to the garnishee procedure (involving two stages, at the second of which the order may be made absolute). However, it is even more protracted, as it involves a further application for an order to sell the asset if the lump sum remains unpaid. Clearly the applicant would be better advised to apply for an order for sale under section 24A of the M.C.A. 1973. (See 13–03, above.)

13–07 JUDGMENT SUMMONS

In some cases an application might be made for a judgment summons. This will provide that the respondent must attend before the judge and be examined as to his means, and the judge will make an order as to the payment of the lump sum by such date or by such instalments as he thinks fit. There is power to commit the payer to prison for non-payment but it will normally be suspended initially, so that only if the payment is not made will the payer be committed to prison. Once reason why this method is rarely used is that legal aid is not available for this procedure in the county court.[6]

13–08 **3. Enforcement of Orders for Periodical Payments**

If arrears are owed under a periodical payments order, they might be enforced by one of the methods considered above for the enforcement of a lump sum.

Leave will be required to enforce arrears that are more than 12 months old.[7] The application for leave is made separately from any application to enforce the order, except where an application is being made for a judgment summons or an attachment of earnings order, when the application will incorporate an application for leave. As the court is often

---

[6] Legal Aid Act 1988, Sched. 2, Part II para. 5.
[7] M.C.A. 1973, s.32.

minded to allow the payer a fresh start, it may well refuse leave to enforce the arrears and may go further and remit the arrears in whole or in part.[8]

The current instalments (and arrears in instalments) of a periodical payments order might be enforced by one of the methods outlined below.

ATTACHMENT OF EARNINGS ORDER[9]   13–09

Under the terms of this order the payer's employer will be ordered to deduct a specified sum from his pay. This sum will represent the amount of maintenance, plus possibly a proportion of the arrears. This sum is known as the "normal deduction rate." The order will also specify a "protected earnings rate" below which the debtor's pay must not be reduced, to cater for fluctuations in his earnings. This rate should not normally be less than subsistence level for income support purposes.[10] The employer must forward this money to the court. The order cannot be applied for until the maintenance order is in arrears (unless the payer makes the application).

The drawback with this method of enforcement is that it can only be used where the payer is an employee.[11] Even then, because of the administrative burden of such orders, if the payer constantly changes his job, it may be difficult in practice to recover payments, even though the payer and his new employer are required to inform the court of any change of job.

REGISTRATION IN THE MAGISTRATES' COURT[12]

(i) Effect of registration   13–10
As has been mentioned (at 13–01, above), payment of an order in the High Court or county court is made direct between the parties, and this has two drawbacks. First, there is no independent record of payments, and, secondly, there is constant contact between the parties which may well reinforce any bitterness between them. In some cases these drawbacks

---

[8] M.C.A. 1973, s.32(2).

[9] Attachment of Earnings Act 1971. In theory payment of a lump sum order can be enforced by attachment of earnings too, but in practice this would usually be an unsatisfactory method of enforcement unless the lump sum was small.

[10] cf. Billington v. Billington [1974] Fam. 24.

[11] Although it is possible for a payer's pension to be attached.

[12] Maintenance Orders Act 1958, Pt. 1.

may be overcome by arranging for the order to be paid by standing order from the payer's bank account. However, this is not always possible or acceptable, and a better option may be to register the order in a magistrates' court. This can be done as soon as the order has been made.

Once registered, payment of the order in the magistrates' court is to the clerk to the justices, who then forwards the payment to the recipient. Thus a record is kept of payments and there is no contact between the parties over the payment of maintenance.

Enforcement proceedings can be taken by the clerk to the justices at the request of the recipient. The powers of the magistrates include a power of committal to prison. Magistrates' powers of enforcement are considered in detail at 14–59 (below). Once the order has been registered, an application to vary the amount of the payments ordered is usually dealt with by the magistrates' court.[13]

13–11 **(ii) Procedure**[14]

The application for registration is made to the county court registrar, usually at the same time the original order is made, or on an application to vary it. An application may, however, be made at any time. In all cases application is made on a prescribed form which contains (*inter alia*) the names and addresses of payer and payee, details of any arrears and the reason for seeking registration. This will usually be because the respondent is in arrears with the payments.

The attitude of registrars when dealing with such applications varies, but some take the view that, owing to the administrative burden on the courts, there should be some arrears under the order to establish that the magistrates' powers of enforcement are needed. A Practice Direction[15] makes it clear that nominal orders should not be registered, and interim orders and orders for maintenance pending suit should only be registered in exceptional circumstances.

13–12 **4. Enforcement of Property Adjustment Orders**

Should one of the parties fail to comply with an order which requires them to execute documents, then the court has

---

[13] Maintenance Orders Act 1958, s.4, as amended. The magistrates may refer an application for variation to the court which originally made the order in exceptional circumstances, *Gsell* v. *Gsell (Note)* [1971] 1 W.L.R. 225.

[14] See C.C.R., Ord. 36, r. 8. The procedure for registering a High Court order is similar. See R.S.C., Ord. 105, rr. 7–12.

[15] [1980] 1 W.L.R. 354.

power to order the document to be executed by another person, usually the registrar, on their behalf.[16]

Example

An order has been made requiring Christopher to transfer his interest in the matrimonial home to his wife, Denise. Christopher then leaves the country and refuses to answer letters requesting that he sign the appropriate documents. In these circumstances the court can order the registrar to sign them instead.

If the court feels that the drafting of a document requires the assistance of conveyancing counsel then there is power to refer the matter to him. The court can go on to direct that the granting of a decree be deferred until the document has been executed.[17]

5. Enforcement Prevented by the Disposal of Assets 13–13

If enforcement proceedings are hindered because the respondent has disposed of assets after an order for financial relief has been made, the disposal can be set aside by the court in certain circumstances. This is dealt with at 9–25, above.

●

---

[16] Supreme Court Act 1981, s.39 (High Court), County Courts Act 1984, s.38.
[17] M.C.A. 1973, s.30.

14. Financial Provision During Marriage

14–01　This chapter deals with the various forms of financial relief which are available to one party to a marriage against the other without instituting proceedings for any other form of relief. A wife, for example, may wish to obtain an order for maintenance for herself and her children without taking divorce proceedings, at least for the time being. Such financial relief is available in the magistrates' court under the D.P.M.C.A. 1978, and in the county court under section 27 of the M.C.A. 1973. It is also possible for the parties to enter into a maintenance agreement or a separation agreement, under which provision is usually made for maintenance. These forms of relief will be considered in turn. In all cases, for ease of reference, it is assumed that the husband is the party making the payments, although everything that is said would apply equally if the wife were the payer.

It should also be noted at the outset that many clients in urgent need of financial support will, in the first instance, have to resort to welfare benefits, and, for reasons similar to those outlined when discussing maintenance pending suit (Chapter 6, at 6–05), it may be felt that no advantage is to be gained by taking proceedings for a court order.

14–02　## 1. Financial Relief under the Domestic Proceedings and Magistrates' Courts Act 1978

Under Part I of the D.P.M.C.A. 1978 there are three ways of obtaining financial provision from a magistrates' court. (When section 92 of the Children Act 1989 comes into force, magistrates hearing these applications will constitute a "family proceedings court.")

　(i)　By making a complaint and obtaining an order for periodical payments or a lump sum under section 2.

　(ii)　By obtaining a consent order for periodical payments and/or a lump sum under section 6.

　(iii)　By obtaining an order under section 7 for periodical payments only, based on prior voluntary payments made after the parties have separated.

The magistrates' court has no power to make orders for secured periodical payments or property adjustment.

ORDERS UNDER SECTION 2 OF THE DOMESTIC PROCEEDINGS AND MAGISTRATES' COURTS ACT 1978

(i) The grounds   14–03

There are four grounds on which either party to a marriage may apply to a magistrates' court for an order under section 2. The grounds, which are set out in section 1, are as follows:

(i)   the failure of the other party to provide reasonable maintenance for the applicant;

(ii)   the failure of the other party to provide, or to make a proper contribution towards, reasonable maintenance for any child of the family;

(iii)   the fact that the other party has behaved in such a way that the applicant cannot reasonably be expected to live with the respondent;

(iv)   the fact that the other party has deserted the applicant.

Failure to provide reasonable maintenance: section 1(a) and (b)   14–04

The Act provides no definition of what constitutes "reasonable maintenance," and this will, of course, vary from case to case. However, the court is clearly supposed to consider what an appropriate level of maintenance would be, taking into account all the factors which are relevant to the making of a financial provision order (see D.P.M.C.A. 1978, s.3 discussed at 14–18 to 14–23, below). If the other party is not paying as much as the court considers appropriate, an order will be made against him.

The court may find a complaint of failure to maintain proved   14–05
even though the failure did not arise out of any neglect on the part of the respondent. He may have been unaware of the shortfall in income from which the applicant was suffering. Normallly, though, it would be sensible to approach the respondent first for increased maintenance, which could, with his agreement, be made the subject of a consent order under section 6 (see 14–24 to 14–28, below). Only if the respondent

refuses to co-operate should proceedings for a section 2 order be necessary.

14–06 As noted above, the failure to maintain may relate to a child of the family as well as to a party to the marriage, The term "child of the family" is defined by section 88(1) of the D.P.M.C.A. 1978[1] in almost exactly the same way as it is defined by section 52 of the M.C.A. 1973 for the purposes of that Act. In other words, the child must be either a natural child of both parties to the marriage, or a child, other than an officially fostered child, who has been treated by both parties as a child of their family.

14–07 *Behaviour: section 1(c)*

The wording of the behaviour ground is identical to that of the behaviour fact on which a divorce petition may be based, contained in section 1(2)(*b*) of the M.C.A. 1973 (see 3–23 *et seq.*, above). In *Bergin* v. *Bergin*[2] the Divisional Court confirmed that the magistrates' approach to this ground should be the same as that of the divorce court to section 1(2)(*b*). In other words, the court should consider whether any right-thinking person would conclude that the respondent had behaved in such a way that the applicant could not reasonably be expected to live with him, taking into account the characters and personalities of the parties. In one sense, however, this ground is broader than in divorce cases, because adultery, which is not a specific ground for an order under section 2, would have to be pleaded under this head.[3]

14–08 *Desertion: section 1(d)*

The respondent's desertion, the fourth ground for complaint, also has a parallel in divorce law under section 1(2)(*c*) of the M.C.A. 1973 (see 3–31 *et seq.*, above). The only difference is that, under the D.P.M.C.A. 1978, there is no requirement that the desertion should have run for at least two years, or any other minimum period.

14–09 **(ii) Choice of grounds**

Since the only object of proceedings for an order under section 2 of the D.P.M.C.A. 1978 is to obtain an order for financial provision, the most likely ground of complaint will be failure to maintain. Complaints based on behaviour or

---

[1] As amended by the Children Act 1989, Sched. 13, para. 43(*b*).
[2] [1983] 1 W.L.R. 279.
[3] Although a single act of adultery might not always be regarded as sufficient to constitute behaviour in terms of the D.P.M.C.A. 1978, s.1(*c*).

desertion need only be made where the applicant is receiving adequate voluntary payments, but wants the added security of a court order. Although it is unlikely to be an influential factor in the choice of grounds, a possible advantage of obtaining an order on the basis of behaviour or desertion is that the order may be used as proof of either of those facts in subsequent divorce proceedings.[4]

(iii) Time-limits

14–10

Section 127 of the Magistrates' Courts Act 1980 provides that any complaint to a magistrates' court must be made within six months from the time when the matter of complaint arose. This provision has only limited relevance to complaints made under section 1 of the D.P.M.C.A. 1978. Failure to maintain and desertion are continuing matters to which section 127 cannot apply; even if they had ceased less than six months before the complaint was made, the complaint would still fail, because there would be no grounds for making an order.[5] Section 127 could, however, apply to a complaint based on behaviour, so that the magistrates could not hear a complaint based solely on incidents which had occurred more than six months earlier.

(iv) The section 2 orders

14–11

Where the applicant satisfies the court of any of the grounds in section 1, the court may, under section 2, make any of the following orders:

(i) an order that the respondent make periodical payments to the applicant;

(ii) an order that the respondent pay the applicant a lump sum (which cannot exceed £1,000[6]);

(iii) an order that the respondent make periodical payments, either to the applicant for the benefit of a child of the family, or to the child direct.

(iv) an order that the respondent pay a lump sum (not exceeding £1,000[6]) to the applicant for the benefit of a child of the family, or to the child direct.

---

[4] See the M.C.A. 1973, s.4.

[5] Questions can, however, arise as to whether a failure to maintain really has ceased. A complaint of failure to maintain might be upheld in the case of a respondent who had a poor general record of paying maintenance, even though he was paying it at the time.

[6] D.P.M.C.A 1978, s.2(3), and Magistrates' Courts (Increase of Lump Sums) Order 1988 (S.I. 1988 No. 1069).

These powers to order periodical payments and lump sums must now be considered in more detail.

14–12 (v) The power to order periodical payments
There is no statutory maximum imposed on the amount the court can order under section 2, but magistrates are not usually regarded as being very generous in this respect.

14–13 Where periodical payments are ordered for a child it will often be sensible for the order to provide that the payments are to be paid to the mother for the benefit of the child. As with orders made in divorce proceedings, this may allow the payer to treat the payment as a "qualifying maintenance payment," and thus make a reduction in respect of it in computing his taxable income. (The income tax treatment of maintenance payments is considered in detail in Chapter 7 above.)

14–14 (vi) The power to award lump sums
The amount which magistrates can award by way of a lump sum under D.P.M.C.A. 1978, s.2 is currently limited to £1,000.[7] The same limit applies to orders for both parties and children, but there is nothing to prevent the court from making orders which in total exceed £1,000 (*e.g.* £1,000 to a wife and a maximum of £1,000 to each child of the family).[8]

14–15 Although there are no restrictions on the purpose for which a lump sum may be awarded, section 2(2) specifically provides that one purpose for which such an order may be made is to meet liabilities or expenses incurred for the maintenance of the applicant or children before the order was made.

14–16 The lump sum may be ordered to be paid by instalments. There is no provision in the D.P.M.C.A. 1978 to this effect,[9] but section 75 of the Magistrates' Court Act 1980 provides that, where a magistrates' court orders a sum of money to be paid, payments may be ordered by instalments. The same section also allows the court to give the respondent a period of time in which to make payment of a lump sum. The fact that payment can be ordered by instalments allows the court to order a lump sum even when the respondent has no

---

[7] Under the D.P.M.C.A. 1978, s.2(3) the Secretary of State can raise the maximum by statutory instrument. The current order is the Magistrates' Courts (Increase of Lump Sums) Order 1988 (S.I. 1988 No. 1069).

[8] See *Burridge* v. *Burridge* [1983] Fam. 9.

[9] Although the D.P.M.C.A. 1978, s.22 deals with variation of a lump sum paid by instalments.

capital assets; the money can be paid out of income instead. This happened in *Burridge* v. *Burridge*,[10] where the husband not only had no capital, but was also out of work at the time the order was made. As he hoped to find a new job within six weeks, the magistrates ordered him to pay lump sums to his wife and children by instalments, the first payment to be made in six weeks' time. Anthony Lincoln J. held that in principle the order was sound, although the magistrates should not have ordered payment to start until the husband was actually earning. Normally, however, where a respondent has only income rather than capital, a periodical payments order would be more appropriate.

Lump sum orders in magistrates' courts are not regarded as **14–17** "once and for all orders" in the way that they are in proceedings ancillary to divorce. A party to a marriage can receive only one lump sum order in ancillary proceedings,[11] but this restriction does not appear to apply in the magistrates' court. Section 20(7) of the D.P.M.C.A. 1978 (dealing with variation of orders) provides that *"the court may make an order for the payment of a lump sum ... notwithstanding that the person required to pay the lump sum was required to pay a lump sum by a previous order. ...."* Although the Act does not say so, it is presumably possible for the court to order the respondent to pay a second or subsequent lump sum to the same person.

(vii) Matters the court must consider in making section 2 **14–18**
orders
The matters which the court must consider in an application for an order under section 2 are set out in D.P.M.C.A 1978, s.3 (as amended by the M.F.P.A. 1984). They are almost identical to the factors which the court is required to take into account on an application for ancillary relief under the M.C.A. 1973 and which are set out in section 25 of that Act (see 6–35 *et seq.*, above).

General duty **14–19**

Under section 3(1), where the court is considering making any order under section 2, it must "have regard to all the circumstances of the case, first consideration being given to the welfare while a minor of any child of the family who has not attained the age of eighteen."

---

[10] See note 8, above.
[11] See *Coleman* v. *Coleman* [1973] Fam. 10.

14–20 *Specific factors relevant to a party to the marriage*

Under section 3(2), the court is required to have particular regard to a list of factors when considering making periodical payments and lump sum orders for a party to the marriage.

(i) The income, earning capacity, property and other financial resources which each of the parties to the marriage has or is likely to have in the foreseeable future, including, in the case of earning capacity, any increase in that capacity which it would in the opinion of the court be reasonable to expect a party to the marriage to take steps to acquire.

(ii) The financial needs, obligations and responsibilities which each of the parties to the marriage has or is likely to have in the foreseeable future.

(iii) The standard of living enjoyed by the parties to the marriage before the occurrence of the conduct which is alleged as the ground of the application. (It will be seen that the wording here differs from that used in the corresponding paragraph in M.C.A. 1973, s.25(2), which refers instead to the standard enjoyed before the breakdown of the marriage).

(iv) The age of each party to the marriage and the duration of the marriage.

(v) Any physical or mental disability of either of the parties to the marriage.

(vi) The contributions which each of the parties has made or is likely in the foreseeable future to make to the welfare of the family, including any contribution by looking after the home or caring for the family.

(vii) The conduct of each of the parties, if that conduct is such that it would in the opinion of the court be inequitable to disregard it. (The magistrates' courts will no doubt continue to follow the divorce court in taking conduct into account only in cases where one spouse's conduct can be clearly identified as the cause of the breakdown,[12] or where, at any rate, one

---

[12] As, *e.g.* in *Robinson* v. *Robinson* [1983] Fam. 42 where a wife refused to live with her soldier husband on his return from abroad. Compare *Vasey* v. *Vasey* (1984) 5 Fam. Law. 159 where the Court of Appeal held that magistrates had been wrong to take a wife's desertion into account without balancing it against the needs and resources of the parties. (These cases were decided before s.3 was amended by the M.F.P.A. 1984.)

spouse's behaviour has been in some way much more blameworthy than the other's.)

It will be seen from this list that one other respect in which it **14–21** differs from M.C.A. 1973, s.25(2), is that it omits any reference to the value of any benefit which a party will lose the chance of acquiring by reason of the dissolution or annulment of the marriage. This, of course, simply reflects the fact that magistrates' orders cannot affect the status of the marriage.

Factors relevant to children of the family **14–22**

Under section 3(3) the court is required to have particular regard to a list of factors when considering making a periodical payments or lump sum order in favour of a child of the family.

  (i)   The needs of the child.

  (ii) The income, earning capacity (if any), property and other financial resources of the child.

  (iii) Any physical or mental disability of the child.

  (iv) The standard of living enjoyed by the family before the occurrence of the conduct which is alleged as the ground of the application.

  (v) The manner in which the child was being and in which the parties to the marriage expected him to be educated or trained.

  (vi) The matters mentioned in relation to the parties to the marriage in section 3(2)(*a*) and (*b*), above (resources and needs respectively).

Section 3(4) then adds a further list of matters to be **14–23** considered in the case of a child of the family who is not the natural child of the respondent.

  (i)   Whether the respondent assumed any responsibility for the child's maintenance and, if he did, the extent to which and the basis on which he assumed that responsibility and the length of time during which he discharged that responsibility.

  (ii) Whether in assuming and discharging that responsibility the respondent knew that the child was not his own.

(iii)   The liability of any other person to maintain the child.

"CONSENT ORDERS" UNDER SECTION 6 OF THE DOMESTIC PROCEEDINGS AND MAGISTRATES' COURTS ACT 1978

14–24   **(i) The scope of section 6 orders**
By virtue of section 6 of the D.P.M.C.A. 1978 (as substituted by section 10 of the M.F.P.A. 1984) either party to a marriage may apply to a magistrates' court for an order on the ground that either the applicant or the other party to the marriage has agreed to make the financial provision specified in the application. The term "financial provision" means the same provision as the court can order under section 2,[13] *i.e.* periodical payments and lump sums for a party and a child of the family. The only difference is that under section 6 the court can make lump sum orders for any amount if the parties are agreed.[14]

14–25   The availability of a limited amount of tax relief on payments made under a court order explains why a party is allowed to apply for an order against himself under section 6. This avoids the problem which would otherwise arise where one spouse is prepared to make maintenance payments, but the other is not prepared to apply for the order that would give the payer tax relief on those payments.

14–26   **(ii) The factors the court must consider**
The matters listed in section 3 as being relevant to orders under section 2 (see 14–18 to 14–23, above) are not expressly relevant on a section 6 application. Section 6 does, however, refer to certain matters which the court must consider.

The fact of the agreement

Under section 6(1)(*a*) the court must be satisfied that the payer has agreed to make the provision referred to in the order. This poses no problem where the applicant is to be the payer. The ways in which a respondent's consent to the order may be provided are considered in 14–55, below.

---

[13] D.P.M.C.A. 1978, s.6(2).

[14] A close reading of section 6 shows that, although a respondent must have agreed to make the *provision* now being applied for, he need not have consented to the making of an *order* in those terms. Nevertheless, in practice, orders under s.6 will invariably have been agreed to by the respondent, and they will be referred to as "consent orders" throughout.

The interests of justice

Under section 6(1)(*b*) the court must have no reason to think it would be contrary to the interests of justice to make the order. Under this heading the court is presumably meant to consider whether the order contains provisions broadly in line with those which the court might have ordered if there had been no agreement. In this respect it will be relevant for the court to have regard to the factors set out in section 3.

Provision for children

Where the order contains financial provision for a child of the family, the court must be satisfied, under section 6(3), that it provides for, or makes a proper contribution towards, the financial needs of the child.

(iii) Alternative provision to that originally agreed 14–27
Under section 6(5), if the court decides that the agreed order would be contrary to the interests of justice or that it does not make proper provision for a child, but that some other order would satisfy these criteria, then the court can make the order in those alternative terms instead, provided both parties agree to this.

(iv) Compromised section 2 applications 14–28
A party who has already applied for an order under section 2 may apply for a section 6 order instead at any time before the section 2 application is determined.[15] The section 2 application is then treated as withdrawn. This provision is most likely to be used where the parties to a contested hearing reach agreement just before, or even during, the hearing of the section 2 application.

Where an order for periodical payments is made under section 6, following the withdrawal of a section 2 application, the order can be backdated to the date of the section 2 application.[16] This is contrary to the normal rule that payments cannot be backdated beyond the date on which they were applied for.

ORDERS BASED ON PRIOR VOLUNTARY PAYMENTS: SECTION 7 OF THE DOMESTIC PROCEEDINGS AND MAGISTRATES' COURTS ACT 1978

(i) The scope of section 7 14–29
Under section 7 of the D.P.M.C.A. 1978, a magistrates' court can make an order for periodical payments (but not a lump

---

[15] D.P.M.C.A. 1978, s.6(4).
[16] *Ibid.* s.6(8).

sum) in favour of a party to the marriage and any children of the family.

14–30 **(ii) The grounds for the application**
In order to obtain an order under section 7, the applicant must establish two things.[17]

   (i) "That parties to the marriage have been living apart continuously for more than three months, without either party being in desertion." This condition would be satisfied in cases where the parties had agreed to live apart, but there could be other reasons why desertion was not running (*e.g.* the spouse allegedly in desertion might have just cause for living apart).

   (ii) That the other party has been making periodical payments for the benefit of the applicant or a child of the family.

14–31 **(iii) The amount that can be ordered**
The respondent need not have been paying maintenance throughout the whole of the three-month period immediately preceding the application, but, when applying, the applicant must specify the aggregate amount of the payments made during that period.[17] The court cannot then make an order under section 7 which would require the respondent to make payments exceeding this aggregate over any future three-month period.[18]

14–32 *Example*

Wanda and Harry agreed to live apart in January. Wanda stayed in the matrimonial home with the two children of the family. Over the past three months Harry has been very erratic in the maintenance payments he has voluntarily provided for Wanda and the children.

   February: *Harry sent Wanda £400.*
   March: *Harry sent Wanda £300.*
   April: *Harry sent Wanda £200.*

   If Wanda now applies for an order under section 7, she must specify £900 as the aggregate amount paid over the past three months and (assuming that the court wants to order payments to be at a

---

[17] *Ibid.* s.7(1).
[18] *Ibid.* s.7(3)(*a*).

uniform rate each month) the court cannot order Harry to pay more than £300 per month in future.

If the court considers that the amount of maintenance which could be ordered on the basis of this calculation is more than it would have ordered under section 2 of the Act (*e.g.* on a complaint of failure to maintain), the court must reduce the amount ordered under section 7 accordingly.[19]

14–33

Conversely, if the court considers that the maximum amount which it can order under section 7 would not provide reasonable maintenance for the applicant or a child of the family, it must not make any order under section 7, but may instead treat the application as if it were made for an order under section 2. This, of course, also entitles the court to order lump sum payments of up to £1,000.

(iv) Factors to be taken into account

14–34

Besides the considerations relating specifically to the amount that can be ordered, the court is also required to take into account the same factors set out in section 3 of the Act which apply to applications for an order under section 2 (see 14–18 to 14–23, above). The only qualification to this is that the reference in section 3(2)(*c*) to the standard of living enjoyed by the parties before the conduct complained of, is altered to refer to the standard of living before the parties started to live apart.[20]

In cases where an order is sought in favour of a child of the family against a respondent who is not the natural parent of that child, the court must further consider whether it would have made an order had the application been made for an order under section 2, and only make the order if it considers that it would have done.[21]

(v) Is an application worthwhile?

14–35

The idea behind the introduction of section 7 was to cater for cases where one party was paying adequate maintenance to the other and to any children, and was not guilty of any unreasonable behaviour or of desertion, so that an application for an order under section 2 was not possible. At the same time the payer spouse might be unwilling to agree to the payments being made under a consent order, so that an application under section 6 would also not be feasible.

---

[19] *Ibid.* s.7(3)(*b*).
[20] *Ibid.* s.7(5).
[21] *Ibid.* s.7(3)(*c*).

14–36 However, although section 7 does in theory provide a remedy for a spouse who would like the added security of a court order but cannot use sections 2 and 6, it seems that, in practice, it is very rarely used. This is probably because those clients who do want to use the magistrates' court to get a maintenance order, generally find that sections 2 or 6 provide the remedy they want. It is also worth bearing in mind that an application to the court for an order against a party who is already making maintenance payments could result in an order for a lower amount than was being paid voluntarily.

14–37 CUSTODY AND MAINTENANCE ORDERS

A unique feature of the D.P.M.C.A. 1978 is that, whenever an application is made for an order under sections 2, 6 and 7, the court must automatically consider whether to make an order under section 8 for the custody of or access to any child of the family under 18.[22] This custody jurisdiction is considered in more detail at 16–28 to 16–32 below. At this point, however, it should be noted that where the court does exercise its custody jurisdiction under section 8 (or where, instead, it commits a child to the care of a local authority under section 10[23]), it has certain additional powers to order financial provision in favour of the child. These powers are set out in section 11 of the Act.[24] The salient features of section 11 are as follows:

(i) Where the court awards actual custody to the applicant, on an application for an order under section 2, it can order the respondent to make periodical payments and lump sum payments in respect of the child *even though the applicant's complaint is dismissed* (section 11(1)).

(ii) Where the court awards actual custody to the *respondent* to an application for an order under section 2 or 7, it can order the *applicant* to make periodical payments and lump sum payments in respect of the child (section 11(2)).

(iii) Where the court awards actual custody *to a party who has agreed to make financial provision* on an application for a consent order under section 6, the court can

---

[22] When the Children Act 1989 comes into force, s.8 will be amended to require the court to consider instead whether to exercise any of its powers under that Act with respect to the child. (Sched. 13, para. 36.)

[23] s.10 will be repealed by the Children Act 1989: Sched. 15.

[24] s.11 will be repealed by the Children Act 1989: Sched. 15.

order *the other party* to make periodical payments and lump sum payments in respect of the child (section 11(2A)).

(iv) Where the court awards legal custody to *a parent of the child who is not a party to the marriage*, the court can order *either or both parties to the marriage* to make periodical payments and lump sum payments in respect of the child (section 11(3)).

(v) Where the court makes a *care order* under section 10 the court may order *either or both parties to the marriage* to make periodical payments (but *not* lump sum payments) in respect of the child (section 11(4)).

THE DURATION OF ORDERS

(i) Parties to the marriage   14–38
The rules about the duration of orders for parties to the marriage are set out in section 4 of the D.P.M.C.A. 1978 and apply to all orders for periodical payments, whether made under sections 2, 6 or 7. The rules are the same as those that apply to orders for ordinary periodical payments under the M.C.A. 1973, section 28 (see 6–17 to 6–18, above). Thus the order cannot take effect earlier than the date of application (though it may be backdated to this date), and cannot extend beyond the death of either party. The order also ceases to have effect (subject to any arrears) on the remarriage of the payee. This takes account of the fact that the maintenance order can continue in force, notwithstanding the subsequent dissolution or annulment of the marriage.

(ii) Children of the family   14–39
As with parties, the rules about the duration of orders under section 2, 6, or 7 in favour of children, which are contained in section 5 of the D.P.M.C.A. 1978, are the same as those that apply to orders made under the M.C.A. 1973, s.29. Thus a periodical payments order may run from the date of the application, but should not normally be made to extend beyond the age of 17 in the first instance. In any event it must cease when the child reaches 18, unless the child is receiving some form of instruction or training, or special circumstances (such as a disability) justify the extension. Similarly the court can only make a periodical payments or a lump sum order in favour of a child who has already reached 18 if one of these exceptions applies. A periodical payments order must, in any event, cease on the death of the payer.

291

14–40 INTERIM ORDERS

Under section 19 of the D.P.M.C.A. 1978 the court has power to make an interim maintenance order on an application for an order under sections 2, 6, or 7. This is the broad equivalent of an order for maintenance pending suit in the divorce court, but payments can be ordered both to a party and to children of the family under 18. Payments can run from the date of application for an order, and subject to any shorter term that may be specified in the order itself, will cease on the date a final order is made or the application is dismissed, or three months from the date the order was made, if a final decision has not been made after this time. If, however, the order does expire before a final decision has been made, it may be renewed for further periods up to a total of three months. Apart from this, only one interim maintenance order can be made on an application for an order under sections 2, 6 or 7. However, in practice, the court would almost certainly have made a final order within the six-month period allowed. No appeal lies against a magistrates' court's decision in respect of an interim order.

14–41 THE EFFECTS OF COHABITATION

Some periodical payments orders made under the D.P.M.C.A. 1978 may be affected by the continued or resumed cohabitation of the parties. The rules about this are set out in section 25 of the Act and may be summarised as follows:

(i) Any order (including an interim order) made on a section 7 application ceases to have effect as soon as the parties resume living with each other (section 25(3)).[25] As, of course, section 7 orders are based on the fact that the parties have separated, no such order could be made if the parties were cohabiting at the time of the hearing.

(ii) Orders for periodical payments under sections 2 and 6 can be made and are enforceable even though the parties are living with each other at the time the order is made. However orders made in favour of a party to the marriage (whether for the benefit of the party *or* a child of the family) cease automatically if the parties

---

[25] For the purposes of the Act, "living with each other" means "living with each other in the same household" (s.88(2)). For discussion of the equivalent provision in s.2(6) of the M.C.A. 1973, see 3–41, above.

continue to live with each other, or resume living with each other, for a continuous period of more than six months (section 25(1)).

(iii) Orders made under sections 2 and 6 which require periodical payments to be made directly *to* a child of the family are unaffected by the continuing or the resumed cohabitation of the parties for any length of time, unless the court directs otherwise (section 25(2)).

The purpose behind allowing orders under sections 2 and 6 to **14–42** remain in force, at least for a time, when the parties are cohabiting, is to avoid prejudicing the prospects of a reconciliation. If, for example, a wife knew that her maintenance order would lapse as soon as she agreed to an attempt at reconciliation, she might decide the attempt was not worthwhile. As it is, she can resume cohabitation for up to six months, or for any number of separate periods none of which exceeds six months, and the order will remain enforceable.

PROCEDURE FOR OBTAINING ORDERS

(i) Which court? **14–43**

The rules governing the jurisdiction of magistrates' courts under Part I of the D.P.M.C.A. 1978 are contained in section 30 of the Act. These rules concern both the national jurisdiction of magistrates' courts generally, and the jurisdiction of an individual court to hear a particular case.

(ii) General jurisdiction[26] **14–44**

A magistrates' court in England and Wales has jurisdiction if at the date of the application:

(i) *both parties* reside in England and Wales;

or

(ii) the *applicant* resides in England and Wales, the respondent resides in Scotland or Northern Ireland, *and* the parties last ordinarily resided together as man and wife in England and Wales;

or

---

[26] D.P.M.C.A. 1978, s.30(3).

(iii) the applicant resides in Scotland or Northern Ireland and *the respondent* resides in England and Wales.

It is irrelevant whether either party is domiciled in England and Wales.[27]

Where an application is made under section 20 of the D.P.M.C.A. 1978 for variation or revocation of an order, these jurisdictional rules are modified by section 24(1). In this case a magistrates' court in England and Wales can hear the application even though one party (who may be either the applicant or the respondent) is residing anywhere outside England and Wales, whether in the United Kingdom or not. it will, however, still be necessary for the other party to be resident in England and Wales, because of the rules concerning the jurisdiction of individual courts referred to next.

14–45 **(iii) Individual jurisdiction**[28]

A magistrates' court has jurisdiction to hear an application under Part I of the Act if, at the date of the application, either the applicant or the respondent ordinarily resides within the commission area of that particular court. This means that one of the parties must live in the country in which the court is sitting, or in the case of the London courts, in a London commission area or the City of London.[29]

However, where the application is for an order under sections 2, 6 or 7 of the Act the rules have been relaxed to give a court jurisdiction in cases where neither party now lives within the court's commission area, provided this is where the parties last ordinarily resided together as man and wife.[30]

14–46 **(iv) Legal aid and assistance by way of representation**

It is rarely necessary to seek legal aid for an application under the D.P.M.C.A. 1978, since such applications are covered by the scheme for A.B.W.O.R. Under this scheme, a client, who qualifies for advice under the Green Form, may then be represented under the Green Form. The solicitor, having established the client's eligibility for Green Form advice and assistance,[31] must apply to the legal aid committee for

---

[27] *Ibid.* s.30(5).
[28] *Ibid.* s.30(1).
[29] See the Justices of the Peace Act 1979, ss.1 and 2.
[30] Magistrates' Courts (Matrimonial Proceedings) Rules 1980, r. 11.
[31] Note, however, that the capital limit of eligibility for A.B.W.O.R. is higher than that for ordinary Green Form advice, so that a client may qualify for the former but not the latter.

approval for assistance by way of representation. If approval is given the client may then be represented in court under the Green Form and the normal two-hour limit on the amount of costs that can be incurred without prior authority is removed. A.B.W.O.R. is considered in more detail at 2–35 (above).

It will be necessary to apply for legal aid instead of A.B.W.O.R. only in those occasional cases where the client's means disqualify her from A.B.W.O.R., but not from legal aid.

(v) Making the application

14–47

All applications for orders under Part I of the D.P.M.C.A. 1978 are made by laying a complaint,[32] the precise form of which depends on the order being sought.

Orders under section 2

The Magistrates' Courts (Matrimonial Proceedings) Rules 1980, rule 3 require applications for an order under section 2 to be made in writing. The rules contain a form (Form 1) which may be used for this purpose, although this is not essential. However, whatever form the complaint takes, it must state the ground or grounds on which it is based, and, where behaviour constitutes a ground, the complaint must give brief details of the circumstances relied on.

Consent orders under section 6

Rule 4 of the 1980 Rules also requires applications for consent orders to be made in writing. Again an optional form (Form 3) is provided,[33] but again certain particulars must always be given. These are the types of financial provision which have been agreed on, the amounts of the payments to be made and the term of any periodical payments.

Where an application has already been made for an order under section 2 and this has been compromised, so that an order under section 6 is wanted instead, rule 4(1) provides that the application can be made orally instead of in writing.

Orders for periodical payments under section 7

Rule 5 of the 1980 Rules requires a complaint for an order under section 7 to be in writing, and also requires the complaint to be in the form prescribed by the rules (Form 6). In particular the complaint must set out the aggregate amount

---

[32] D.P.M.C.A. 1978, s.30(2).
[33] As substituted by the Magistrates' Courts (Matrimonial Proceedings) (Amendment) Rules 1986.

of payments already made over the past three months (see 14–31 above).

14–48 **(vi) The summons to the respondent**
Contrary to the procedure adopted on applications for ancillary relief, once a complaint has been laid, the court, rather than the solicitor, normally serves a summons by post on the respondent to the application. The form of the summons is prescribed by the 1980 Rules,[34] according to whether the application is being made under sections 2, 6 or 7.

There are three methods of service of the summons, prescribed by rule 20 of the 1980 Rules.

(i)   Delivery to the respondent (*i.e.* personal service).

or

(ii) Leaving it for him with some other person at his last known or usual place of abode.

or

(iii) Sending it to him by post at his last known or usual place of abode, or at an address given by him for the purpose of service.

Where the summons relates to an application for an order under section 2, the respondent can acknowledge service by returning to the court a tear-off slip at the bottom of the summons. He should indicate on this whether or not he will contest the application. No time-limit is prescribed for the return of the acknowledgment of service.

14–49 **(vii) Notice of the court's powers regarding children**
As mentioned above (at 14–37) the court has extensive powers to make orders for the maintenance of children of the family, when applications are made under sections 2, 6 or 7. By virtue of rule 8 of the 1980 Rules, the court must give notice to the parties to the marriage of these powers in cases where children are involved. This notice (Form 10) is given to the applicant when the complaint is laid, and is served on the respondent with the summons.

14–50 **(viii) The hearing**
As proceedings under Part I of the D.P.M.C.A. 1978 are "domestic proceedings" within the meaning of section 65 of

---

[34] The form of the summons for use in s.6 cases is the one substituted by the 1986 Rules, referred to above.

the Magistrates' Courts Act 1980, they must be dealt with by a domestic court. A domestic court must be composed of not more than three justices of the peace and should, if possible, include both a man and a woman.[35] The magistrates who sit in a domestic court have to be members of a domestic court panel.[36] Members of such panels are selected because they are considered suitable for the work involved, and periodically receive certain special training to help them carry it out.

Hearings in domestic proceedings are not open to the public, and, in practice, the only people present will be those directly concerned with the case.[37] If the applicant appears but the respondent does not, the court can proceed in his absence, provided it is satisfied that the summons was served on him within a reasonable period of time before the hearing.[38] If the court adjourns, instead of proceeding in the respondent's absence, and the complaint has been substantiated on oath, a warrant for the respondent's arrest may be issued,[39] but this is rarely done. The court is more likely to adjourn the hearing to allow time for the summons to be reserved on the respondent, and then to make an order at the adjourned hearing whether the respondent appears or not.

(ix) Evidence of means   14–51

The magistrates will require evidence of the parties' means before making an order for financial provision. Even when the order is being made by consent under section 6, the court needs information about means so that it can judge whether the order is acceptable.

Affidavit evidence is not used in magistrates' courts, so that evidence of means will generally be given orally on oath. Such evidence may, however, need to be supported or supplemented by documentary evidence. This may take a number of different forms.

A statement of means from a party   14–52

Where an application is made for an order under sections 2 or 7 both parties may be asked to complete a statement of means. This is an abbreviated equivalent of the affidavit of

---

[35] Magistrates' Courts Act 1980, s.66. Special rules apply to courts in inner London.
[36] Magistrates' Courts Act 1980, s.67(2). When s.92 of the Children Act 1989 comes into force domestic proceedings will be known as "family proceedings" and the domestic panel will be known as the "family panel".
[37] *Ibid.* s.69.
[38] *Ibid.* s.55(1) and (3).
[39] *Ibid.* s.55(2).

means used in the higher courts, but is not made under oath. The form should be brought to the hearing together with evidence of income in the form of pay-slips or trading accounts or evidence of social security payments. The court may also want to see evidence of rent or mortgage paid, evidence of current loan repayments and a recent bank statement.

14–53 *Evidence of an employer*

By virtue of section 100 of the Magistrates' Courts Act 1980, a statement of wages signed by or on behalf of a party's employer must be accepted as evidence of the facts stated in it. Some courts will write to a respondent's employer for this evidence, although the court has no power to compel its production. Either party may, of course, voluntarily produce such a statement in support of their own case.

14–54 *Probation officer's report*

By virtue of section 72 of the Magistrates' Courts Act 1980, once the court has found a complaint proved, it can direct a probation officer to report to the court the result of any investigation into the parties' means which he may have been asked to make. Such a direction would be necessary only when it had not been possible to obtain the evidence in any other way.

14–55 *Evidence in consent order cases*

If the respondent to an application under section 6 of the D.P.M.C.A. 1978 is present or is legally represented at the hearing, his consent to the order and evidence of his financial resources can be given orally. If, however, he is not present and not represented, documentary evidence will be required. The 1980 Rules[40] prescribe a form (Form 5) on which both the respondent's consent and evidence of his means must be given. The respondent's signature on this form must be witnessed by a justice of the peace, a justice's clerk or a solicitor. There is no objection to its being witnessed by the respondent's own solicitor. The Rules also require a similar form (Form 5A) to be supplied giving evidence of the financial

---

[40] As amended by the Magistrates' Courts (Matrimonial Proceedings) (Amendment) Rules 1986.

resources of a child of the family, where the proposed order makes provision for that child.

(x) Orders and costs

14–56

As mentioned above (at 14–37), the court must not make a final order under sections 2, 6 or 7 without first considering whether to make a custody order in respect of any children of the family.[41] Where the application is for an order under section 2, the court must also consider whether there is any possibility of a reconciliation between the parties before making an order.[42] If a reasonable possibility of reconciliation does exist the court can adjourn the proceedings, and may request a probation officer or other person to attempt to effect a reconciliation.[43]

The 1980 Rules[44] prescribe a form (Form 13) on which the court's order under sections 2, 6 or 7 will be given.

The court's powers to make orders for costs are governed **14–57** principally by the Magistrates' Courts Act 1980, s.64. This gives the court a discretion to award such costs as it thinks just and reasonable against an unsuccessful party, whether it be the applicant or the respondent. In addition, however, where the application was for periodical payments, the court may order either party to pay the other's costs, whatever adjudication it makes—in other words, a successful party may be ordered to pay the costs.

Where costs are ordered in favour of a client who has **14–58** received A.B.W.O.R. under the Green Form, the solicitor has a first charge over those costs for the payment of his fees, to the extent that these are not covered by any contribution the client may have been required to make under the Green Form.[45] In practice, however, the solicitor usually assigns his charge to the Legal Aid Board, which enables him to receive payment in full out of the Legal Aid Fund relatively promptly. The other side will then pay the costs to the clerk of the magistrates' court, who will transmit them direct to the Legal Aid Board. The solicitor also has a charge over any property recovered or preserved in the proceedings to the extent that

---

[41] When the Children Act 1989 is in force, the court will have to consider instead whether to exercise any of its powers under that Act with respect to the child. (Sched. 13, para. 36.)

[42] D.P.M.C.A. 1978, s.26(1).

[43] *Ibid.* s.26(2).

[44] Rule 14.

[45] Legal Aid Act 1988, s.11(2)(*a*). Note that this is a separate charge from that belonging to the Legal Aid Board in cases where legal aid is granted. For details on the statutory charges, see 2–18 *et seq.* and 2–34, above.

his fees are not covered by either the client's contribution or costs obtained from the other side.[46] Since, however, periodical payments and the first £2,500 of any lump sum are exempt,[47] the only order made under the D.P.M.C.A. 1978 that could attract this charge would be a lump sum order made by consent under section 6. In practice, of course, the costs of such an application would be relatively small.

ENFORCEMENT OF ORDERS

14–59 **(i) The methods available**
Section 32(1) of the D.P.M.C.A. 1978 (as amended by the F.L.R.A. 1987) provides that an order for the payment of money under Part I of the Act shall be enforceable as a magistrates' court maintenance order. This means that there are four methods of enforcement available:

    (i)   an attachment of earnings order[48];

    (ii) committal to prison[49];

    (iii) a warrant of distress[50];

    (iv) registration of the order in the High Court for enforcement in that court.[51]

These methods will be considered in turn. Remember that, although orders under the D.P.M.C.A. 1978 are not frequently sought, magistrates' powers of enforcement also apply to orders made in the county court which have been registered in a magistrates' court (see 13–10, above).

It should also be noted at the outset that, under section 95 of the Magistrates' Courts Act 1980, on the hearing of a complaint for enforcement, the court has power to remit the whole or any part of the sum due. Magistrates follow the practice of the higher courts in generally not enforcing arrears which are more than 12 months old.[52]

14–60 *Attachment of earnings*

The way in which this method of enforcement works has already been considered in relation to orders made in the

---

[46] Legal Aid Act 1988, s.11(2)(*b*).
[47] Legal Advice and Assistance Regulations 1989, Sched. 4.
[48] Attachment of Earnings Act 1971, s.1(3)(*a*).
[49] Magistrates' Courts Act 1980, s.76.
[50] *Ibid.* s.76.
[51] Maintenance Orders Act 1958, s.2.
[52] See *Ross* v. *Pearson* [1976] 1 W.L.R. 224.

higher courts (see 13–09, above). It is undoubtedly the best method to use if it is available, but it must be borne in mind that it cannot be invoked until the respondent defaults, and is, of course, not available against a debtor who is self-employed or unemployed. In practice it may also be difficult to use against an employed debtor who frequently changes his job. The court can make an attachment of earnings order only if the debtor's default is due to his wilful refusal or culpable neglect.[53]

Committal to prison   **14–61**

This is obviously a drastic and possibly counter-productive method of enforcement, although it may be that magistrates, with their familiarity with the criminal jurisdiction, will be readier to exercise it than county court judges and registrars.

The conditions which must be satisfied before the debtor can be sent to prison are set out in section 93(6) of the Magistrates' Courts Act 1980. They are as follows:

(i)   the court must inquire, in the debtor's presence, as to whether the default was due to his wilful refusal or culpable neglect, and impose imprisonment only if satisfied that this was the case; and

(ii) the court must be satisfied in cases where attachment of earnings would be possible, that it is not appropriate; and

(iii) the debtor must be present when imprisonment is imposed.

Section 93(7) imposes an overall maximum of six weeks as the   **14–62**
period of imprisonment, although the actual maximum may be less than this, depending on the amount of the arrears that have accrued.[54] The fact that the debtor serves a term of imprisonment does not discharge the arrears,[55] but arrears do not continue to accrue while he is in prison, unless the court directs otherwise.[56] A debtor can obtain release from detention by paying the amount due or can reduce the period of detention by paying a proportion of what is due.[57] Once he has been imprisoned a debtor cannot be committed again for the same debt.

[53] Attachment of Earnings Act 1971, s.3(5).
[54] See Magistrates' Courts Act 1980, s.76(3) and Sched. 4.
[55] *Ibid.* s.93(8).
[56] *Ibid.* s.94.
[57] *Ibid.* s.79.

14–63 In many cases a better option than immediate committal to prison will be the threat of committal if the money is not paid. Under section 77(2) of the Magistrates' Courts Act 1980 the magistrates have power to postpone the issue of a warrant of committal until such time and on such conditions as they think fit. Using this power a magistrates' court could, for example, order the debtor to resume payments under the order and to pay off the arrears within a certain period of time or go to prison in default.

14–64 *Warrant of distress*

A warrant of distress orders the police to seize property belonging to the debtor, so that it may be sold and the proceeds used to pay the debt. It is hardly ever used as a means of enforcing a magistrates' order, most obviously because it is not an appropriate means of enforcing an obligation to make regular payments of money. Furthermore the resale value of much of the property that might be seized (*e.g.* household chattels) is often low, making this form of enforcement cumbersome and inefficient.

14–65 *Registration in the High Court*

As the powers of enforcement available to the High Court are wider and more sophisticated than those of the magistrates (see Chapter 13, above), a person entitled to payments under a magistrates' order is allowed to apply to have the order registered in the High Court. Such applications would be very rare indeed, however, as registration would not be worthwhile unless the debt were very substantial.

14–66 **(ii) Procedure for enforcement**

A magistrates' order (or a higher court order which has been registered in the magistrates' court) normally provides for payments to be made to the clerk of the court, unless the payee requests otherwise.[58] The advantages of this are that the clerk will keep an accurate record of the payments that are made, and if the payer defaults the clerk must notify the payee of this.[59] The payee can then authorise the clerk to take enforcement proceedings on her behalf. The clerk must then

---

[58] *Ibid.* s.59.

[59] The duty to notify the payee of a default arises once the payments are in arrears to an amount equal:

   (a) in the case of payments to be made monthly or less frequently, to twice the sum payable periodically; or

   (b) in any other case, to four times the sum payable periodically. (Magistrates' Courts Rules 1981, r. 40).

take the proceedings in his own name, unless he considers it would be unreasonable to do so. The payee, however, remains liable for any costs.

The enforcement proceedings themselves are begun by complaint, regardless of whether they are brought by the clerk or by the person entitled to the payments. The defendant will usually be served with a summons requiring his attendance at the hearing of the complaint, although the magistrates have power to issue a warrant for his arrest whether or not a summons has been issued.[60]

(iii) The diversion procedure   **14–67**
Where a magistrates' order is being paid through the clerk of the court, a payee who is entitled to income support from the D.S.S. may be able to take advantage of the "diversion procedure." This procedure, whereby the payee assigns her order to the D.S.S. and in return receives higher payments of benefit, is considered in detail at 8–49 *et seq.*, above. Once the order has been assigned, the payee will be asked by the D.S.S. to authorise enforcement proceedings should the payer default.

VARIATION

(i) The scope for variation   **14–68**
Orders for periodical payments made under sections 2, 6 or 7 of the D.P.M.C.A. 1978 can subsequently be varied or revoked by a magistrates' court, under section 20 of the Act. The power to vary includes a power to suspend an order temporarily and subsequently revive it.[61] Orders for periodical payments made under section 11 (14–37, above) can similarly be varied or revoked,[62] as can interim orders (14–40, above) provided the term of the order is not extended.[63]

(ii) The forms of variation   **14–69**
The usual form of variation sought will be an increase or decrease in the rate of periodical payments. However, unlike a court dealing with a variation application under section 31 of the M.C.A. 1973 (12–16, above), the magistrates' court can, in certain cases, order the payment of a lump sum as a means of varying a periodical payments order.

[60] Magistrates' Courts Act 1980, s.93(5).
[61] D.P.M.C.A. 1978, s.20(6).
[62] *Ibid.* s.20(4).
[63] *Ibid.* s.20(5).

Where the original order was made under section 2 of the D.P.M.C.A. 1978, the court can order payment of a lump sum of up to £1000 to the applicant or a child of the family.[64] Where the original order was a consent order under section 6, the court can similarly order the payer to make a lump sum payment to the other party or a child of the family.[65] There is no need for the payer under the consent order to agree to the variation, unless a lump sum in excess of £1000 is wanted, in which case his agreement must be obtained.[66]

The fact that the court has already ordered a person to make a lump sum payment under the D.P.M.C.A. 1978 is no bar to their being ordered to make further such payments.[67]

Periodical payments orders under section 11 may also be varied by the award of a lump sum of up to £1000 in cases where the original order could have included such an award.[68]

There is no power to vary an order under section 7 by ordering payment of a lump sum, since section 7 orders are restricted to periodical payments.

14–70   **(iii) The factors to be taken into account**
The factors which the court must consider on an application for variation are dealt with in section 20(11) of the D.P.M.C.A. 1978. The court must first consider any agreement reached by the parties, and must give effect to this if it seems just to do so. If it does not appear just or if there is no agreement, the court is in effect required to have regard to the same factors that apply to an application for an order under section 2. Section 20(11) provides that the court shall consider all the circumstances of the case, first consideration being given to the welfare while a minor of any child of the family who has not attained the age of 18. The "circumstances of the case" include any change in the matters set out in section 3 (see 14–18 to 14–23, above).

14–71   **(iv) The application**
Section 20(12) of the D.P.M.C.A. 1978 sets out a list of those who may apply for the variation or revocation of an order. Either party to the marriage may apply. In the case of a periodical payments order in favour of a child, applications

---

[64] *Ibid.* s.20(1) and (7), and Magistrates' Courts (Increase of Lump Sums) Order 1988 (S.I. 1988 No. 1069).
[65] *Ibid.* s.20(2).
[66] *Ibid.* s.20(8).
[67] *Ibid.* s.20(7).
[68] *Ibid.* s.20(4), and see 14–37, above.

may also be made by a parent who has legal custody of the child but who is not a party to the marriage, a local authority to whose care the child has been committed, or the child himself, once he is 16.[69]

In addition, by virtue of section 20A,[70] where a periodical payments order for a child has ceased to have effect between the child's sixteenth and eighteenth birthdays, the child may apply for its revival.

A variation order under section 20 may be backdated to the date on which it was applied for.[71]

(v) Discharge of magistrates' orders by a higher court   **14–72**
Magistrates' orders for financial provision and custody are not automatically terminated by a divorce decree. However, it is often desirable for the divorce court to make fresh orders in divorce proceedings. In this case the county court and the High Court have power under the D.P.M.C.A. 1978, s.28 to discharge magistrates' orders, other than orders for a lump sum.

No additional application to the magistrates for a discharge of the order is then necessary. The same power is available in proceedings for nullity and judicial separation.

2. Financial Relief under section 27 of the Matrimonial Causes Act 1973—Failure to Maintain

THE GROUNDS FOR AN APPLICATION   **14–73**

Under M.C.A. 1973, s.27, as amended by the D.P.M.C.A. 1978, section 63, either party to a marriage may apply to a divorce county court[72] for an order on the grounds that the respondent has failed to provide reasonable maintenance for the applicant, or has failed to provide, or make a proper contribution towards, reasonable maintenance for any child of the family.[73] Behaviour and desertion do not constitute grounds for an application as they do under the D.P.M.C.A. 1978, section 1.

---

[69] When the Children Act 1989 is in force, applications to vary a periodical payments order for a child will be restricted to a party to the marriage or the child himself once he is 16. (Sched. 13, para. 38.) This is consequent upon the repeal of s.11 of the D.P.M.C.A. by the Children Act 1989.
[70] Added by the F.L.R.A. 1987. A revised version will be inserted by the Children Act 1989, Sched. 13, para. 39.
[71] *Ibid.* s.20(9).
[72] M.C.R. 1977, r. 98(2).
[73] M.C.A. 1973, s.27(1).

In practice, applications under section 27 are becoming increasingly rare. In 1988, a total of only 71 applications were made.[74]

14–74 THE ORDERS THAT MAY BE MADE

Under section 27 the court can make orders for periodical payments, secured periodical payments and lump sums.[75] Orders may be made in favour of the applicant or a child of the family. In the case of a child, the order may be for payment to a person for the benefit of the child, or to the child direct.

The court's powers under section 27 are wider than those of the magistrates' court under the D.P.M.C.A. 1978 in so far as they include a power to order secured payments, and there is no ceiling imposed on the amount of any lump sum. As with the D.P.M.C.A. 1978, there is no power to make property adjustment orders.

14–75 THE RELEVANT FACTORS

In deciding whether the respondent has failed to provide reasonable maintenance, and in assessing what order, if any, to make under section 27, the court is required to have regard to all the circumstances of the case, including most of the matters set out in section 25[76] (see 6–35 *et seq.*, above). In other words the court will adopt the same approach to the assessment of orders under section 27 as it does to orders in ancillary proceedings on divorce.

14–76 THE DURATION OF ORDERS

The rules governing the duration of periodical payments orders under section 27 are the same as those governing the duration of orders made on divorce. These are contained in M.C.A. 1973, s.28 (parties) and section 29 (children) and are dealt with at 6–17 *et seq.*, above.

14–77 INTERIM ORDERS

Under section 27(5) the court can make interim orders for maintenance in favour of the applicant, if it appears that

---

[74] Judicial Statistics 1988 (Cm. 745 (1989)), Table 5.8.
[75] M.C.A. 1973, s.27(6).
[76] *Ibid.* s.27(3), (3A) and (3B).

either the applicant, or any child of the family, is in immediate need of financial assistance, but it is not yet possible to decide what, if any, final order should be made. Unlike the D.P.M.C.A. 1978, s.19, section 27 imposes no restriction on the duration or renewal of such orders. On the other hand, it should be emphasised that the only form an *interim* order can take under section 27 is payment to an applicant.

PROCEDURE

(i) Which court?   14–78
The application may be made to any divorce county court.[77] The court has jurisdiction to hear the application on the same grounds as those which apply to the hearing of a divorce; *i.e.*:

  (a) the applicant or the respondent is domiciled in England and Wales on the date of the application;

or

  (b) the applicant has been habitually resident here throughout the period of one year ending on that date;

or

  (c) the respondent is resident here on that date— regardless of the length of that residence.[78]

It can be seen from this that the applicant has, at least in theory, a wider choice of venue than the applicant for an order under the D.P.M.C.A. 1978 (see 14–44 and 14–45, above). In practice, however, most applicants would choose to make their application to their nearest divorce county court.

(ii) Legal aid   14–79
Eligible clients can be advised under the Green Form scheme, but the proceedings themselves are covered by legal aid.

(iii) The application   14–80
A party applies by originating application, which must comply with Form 19 in the M.C.R. 1977. This simply gives the names of the parties, states the ground for the application and asks for the appropriate form of relief. The application must be supported by an affidavit, containing particulars similar to those in a divorce petition and giving particulars of

---

[77] M.C.R. 1977, r. 98(2).
[78] M.C.A. 1973, s.27(2).

the respondent's failure to maintain, as well as particulars of the parties' property and income.[79] One copy of both the application and the affidavit must be filed as well, and these are served on the respondent together with a notice of the application and acknowledgment of service. The respondent should acknowledge service within eight days and file an affidavit in reply within a further 14 days.[80]

14–81 **(iv) The hearing**
The application would normally be heard by a registrar and the hearing takes the same form as the hearing of an application for ancillary relief (see 10–26, above).

14–82 VARIATION

Applications for the variation or discharge of orders under section 27 are governed by the M.C.A. 1973, s.31, and are thus treated in the same way as applications to vary orders made in ancillary proceedings (see 12–13 *et seq.*, above).

14–83 CHOICE OF FORUM

As the grounds for an application under section 27 correspond so closely with the grounds on which an application for an order under the D.P.M.C.A. 1978, s.2 is most likely to be made, the question naturally arises as to which forum should be chosen.
Some of the factors that may influence the choice have already been referred to and may be summarised as follows:

 (i) Secured payments and unlimited lump sums are available under section 27, but not under the D.P.M.C.A. 1978.

 (ii) Interim orders under section 27 are not subject to restriction in time, but, unlike orders under the D.P.M.C.A. 1978, can only be made to the applicant.

 (iii) The jurisdiction of the county court is wider than that of the magistrates' court.

14–84 However, other facts have a bearing on the choice of forum too. The most important question in many cases will be whether legal aid can be obtained for an application under section 27. Where an equivalent remedy can be obtained in

---

[79] M.C.R. 1977, r. 98(2) and (3).
[80] *Ibid.* r. 98(5).

the magistrates' court, the area committee may expect that jurisdiction to be used on the ground that it will be cheaper.[81] An application for legal aid, might, therefore be refused and the client left to seek assistance by way of representation. This does have the advantage for the client of being generally much quicker to obtain than a legal aid certificate, as the full legal aid assessment of means is avoided.

3. Separation Agreements   14–85

Sometimes, when a marriage breaks down, the parties are able to settle their affairs by agreement. If they want to record the terms of their agreement prior to divorce then a separation or maintenance agreement will commonly be used to do so. Before going further it is necessary to consider the difference between these two types of agreement.

TERMINOLOGY

(i) Separation agreement   14–86
This term is used to describe an agreement which may provide for maintenance to or for a spouse or child, custody,[82] and for the disposition of the matrimonial home. However, the essence of a *separation* agreement is that it also contains a clause which provides that the parties agree to separate.

(ii) Maintenance agreement   14–87
This document may contain the same provisions as a separation agreement, except for the agreement to separate. It would be used where, for example, one party is in desertion and the other party wishes to preserve their right to proceed for divorce on this basis once two years have elapsed.

Hereafter, in accordance with common practice, the term "separation agreement" will be used to include a maintenance agreement.

THE ADVANTAGES AND DISADVANTAGES OF USING A SEPARATION AGREEMENT

(i) Tax   14–88
A written separation agreement will be tax effective, in that provisions for maintenance payments to a spouse for their own benefit, or for the benefit of a child, may be "qualifying maintenance payments" which can be deducted from the

---

[81] See generally *Legal Aid Handbook* 1990 Notes for Guidance, No. 11.
[82] See 16–11, for the effect of agreements as to custody.

payer's taxable income up to the annual limit.[83] Making payments under a separation agreement is, therefore, clearly better for the payer than making them voluntarily.

14–89 **(ii) Speed**

A separation agreement can usually be concluded speedily, as, by definition, the bulk of the terms will have been agreed by the parties, leaving their solicitors[84] to work out the details. It is therefore quicker and cheaper than a consent order. As it does not require the court's approval, it may be less stressful for the client than an application for a consent order.

14–90 **(iii) Flexibility**

Anything can be agreed, even matters which the court could not order under the M.C.A. 1973. So, for example, the husband could agree to pay the outgoings on the home in which the wife remained living. The court has no power to order such payments directly. It is unlikely, however, that the parties will wish to provide for much that is beyond the scope of the divorce court's powers. Nonetheless, if the jurisdiction of the M.C.A. 1973 is not, or cannot, be invoked, this is the only realistic alternative to enable the parties to provide for the disposition of the matrimonial home.

14–91 **(iv) Enforceability**

A consent order can be enforced in the same way as any other court order. A separation agreement can only be enforced as a contract. Therefore, although it may be made orally or in writing, there must be some consideration. In some cases there may be no consideration given by the payee under an agreement.[85] For this reason agreements are usually made in the form of a deed.

The remedies for breaking this contract are limited to the usual remedies for such breach. For example, if an agreement provides for the payment of maintenance, and this is not met, the payee could sue to recover the arrears then outstanding as a debt. Even when the payee has obtained judgment in her

---

[83] See 7–09, above.
[84] As a separation agreement, like any contract, could be set aside for mistake, misrepresentation, duress, etc., it is wise to ensure that each party receives independent legal advice.
[85] A promise by the payee not to apply to the court for financial provision is void and therefore not consideration. *Hyman* v. *Hyman* [1929] A.C. 601. The fact that both parties to a separation agreement are releasing each other from the duty to cohabit is sufficient consideration, but this consideration will be lacking where the agreement is a maintenance agreement rather than a separation agreement.

favour, she may still be faced with the prospect of having to enforce that judgment in order to get her money. This is hardly an adequate means of enforcement against a constantly bad payer.

(v) Finality   **14–92**

A separation agreement can never be a final solution. This can only be achieved, in limited circumstances, by a court order. The court will, however, take into account any agreement which exists between the parties when considering the terms of its order.[86]

(vi) Conclusion   **14–93**

In conclusion, a separation agreement is only likely to be used:

   (i)   prior to divorce; and

   (ii) where the parties are in full agreement.

STATUTORY PROVISIONS   **14–94**

Although separation and maintenance agreements are private contracts between the parties, the M.C.A. 1973 does contain some provisions concerning them. In particular the courts are given powers to vary the terms of certain agreements under sections 35 and 36.

The agreements to which these sections apply must fall within the definition of "maintenance agreements" under section 34(2) of the M.C.A. 1973. This definition includes any written agreement containing financial arrangements, or any written agreement to separate which does not contain any financial arrangements (where no other document exists which does contain such arrangements.)

COURT'S JURISDICTION   **14–95**

Section 34(1) of the M.C.A. 1973 provides that any provision in a maintenance agreement which purports to oust the court's jurisdiction to make orders for financial provision shall be void. However this does not invalidate any financial provisions contained in such a document.[87]

---

[86] See 11–04 to 11–05, above.
[87] M.C.A. 1973, s.34(1); *cf.* an oral maintenance agreement: *Sutton* v. *Sutton* [1984] Ch. 194. See 11–04 above, for the extent to which the courts will take into account the terms of a separation agreement on an application for ancillary relief.

14–96 VARIATION

As has already been mentioned, the enforcement powers of the court are severely limited in scope, so that it would seem generally pointless to apply for an increase in periodical payments under an agreement when the payer will not agree to such a variation.[88] It is only where capital provisions are sought that such an application might be made, and only then when divorce or similar proceedings are not contemplated in the near future.[89]

14–97 For completeness, however, the powers of the courts to vary agreements are summarised below.[90]

  (i) A divorce county court can vary or revoke any financial arrangement or insert a financial arrangement for the benefit of one of the parties of the family.

  (ii) A magistrates' court can vary or revoke only periodical payments or insert a provision for periodical payments if no such provision has been made.

  (iii) The court can only vary the agreement if it is satisfied that there has been some change in circumstances such that it should be altered, or if proper financial arrangements have not been made for any child of the family. The court may then make such order as it thinks just having regard to all the circumstances.[91]

  (iv) The usual rules governing the duration of periodical payments orders will apply.[92]

  (v) The varied agreement takes effect as if made by an agreement between the parties for valuable consideration.[93]

14–98 Under the M.C.A. 1973, s.36, the High Court and county courts are given similar powers of variation in respect of maintenance agreements which provide for payments to continue after the death of one of the parties. An application

---

[88] Clearly, if agreement can be reached, the original separation agreement can be amended without application to the court.

[89] In these circumstances an application for an order would be made in the divorce proceedings in the usual way, with all the advantages of such an order.

[90] See M.C.A. 1973, s.35.

[91] M.C.A. 1973, s.35(2).

[92] M.C.A. 1973, s.35(4) and (5).

[93] M.C.A. 1973, s.35(2).

for such variation must normally be made by either the surviving party or the personal representatives of the deceased party within six months of representation being taken out in respect of the estate.[94]

4. Financial Provision for Children   14–99

It should be noted that under the Guardianship of Minors Act 1971 the courts have wide powers to make financial provision orders against parents for the benefit of children, independently of any other orders. (These powers are to be replaced by very similar ones under the Children Act 1989.) They are considered in detail in Chapter 15 below, in the context of the unmarried family, because they are most likely to be invoked by parties who are not married to each other. However, they are equally available to married partners. In particular they allow a party to seek transfer and settlement of property orders for the benefit of children, and no such powers exist under the other legislation considered in this chapter. There will be few cases in practice, however, where a court would be likely to make such orders during the subsistence of the marriage.

[94] M.C.A. 1973, s.36(1) and (2).

15. The Unmarried Family: Maintenance and Property Orders

15–01 Family law practitioners nowadays are increasingly being consulted by clients who have never married, although they have often lived in a stable relationship with a partner, sometimes for many years. When a non-marital relationship breaks down, the problems which arise are very similar to those that arise on marriage breakdown. However, the solutions which English law offers are by no means the same. In general, the remedies available to couples outside marriage are much more restricted than those available to parties on divorce.

This chapter is concerned with the extent to which an unmarried partner may be able to obtain maintenance orders and orders dealing with property acquired during the relationship. When the Children Act 1989 comes into force the law relating to the financial provision for children set out in paragraphs 15–03 to 15–06 and 15–11 to 15–15 below will be repealed and re-enacted in a revised version. The revised law is set out at paragraphs 15–16 to 15–23 below. Disputes about children and remedies for domestic violence are considered in later chapters.

15–02 1. Financial Provision for Children

There is no obligation between unmarried partners to support each other either during the subsistence of their relationship, or following its breakdown. However, the courts do have wide powers to make orders for the benefit of the children of unmarried couples, and inevitably these orders will sometimes indirectly benefit the party with whom those children are living. The relevant law is to be found in the Family Law Reform Act 1987, Part II, which amended the Guardianship of Minors Act 1971 (G.M.A. 1971), which now contains wide powers of financial relief for all children. The Act deliberately draws no distinction between children born to married couples and those born to unmarried couples. However, the G.M.A. 1971 provides only relief for children. When a

314

relationship breaks down between a married couple, the parties will usually be seeking wider forms of relief (*e.g.* divorce, maintenance for themselves, property adjustment orders, etc.). Therefore, the G.M.A. 1971 is likely to be used mainly to provide for the children of unmarried partners.

POWERS OF THE COURT UNDER THE GUARDIANSHIP OF MINORS ACT 1971 (AS AMENDED)   **15–03**

Section 11B of the G.M.A. 1971[1] differentiates between the powers of the court, depending on whether the proceedings were taken in the High Court, county court or magistrates' court. Proceedings under the G.M.A. 1971 can be taken in any of these courts.

(i) Powers of the High Court and county courts   **15–04**

The court may, on the application of either parent of a child, make:

  (i) an order requiring one parent to make to the other parent for the benefit of the child, or to the child, such periodical payments, and for such term as may be specified in the order;

  (ii) an order requiring one parent to secure to the other parent for the benefit of the child, or to secure to the child, such periodical payments, and for such term, as may be so specified;

  (iii) an order requiring one parent to pay to the other parent for the benefit of the child, or to the child, such lump sum[2] as may be so specified;

  (iv) an order requiring either parent to transfer to the other parent for the benefit of the child, or to the child, such property as may be so specified, being property to which the first-mentioned parent is entitled, either in possession or reversion;

  (v) an order requiring that a settlement of such property as may be so specified, being property to which either parent is entitled, be made to the satisfaction of the court for the benefit of the child.

---

[1] Inserted by the F.L.R.A. 1987, s.12.
[2] This may be paid by instalments; G.M.A. 1971, s.12B(5).

15–05   **(ii) The powers of the magistrates' court**

The magistrates' court has the power to make only those orders specified in (i) and (iii) above, and the amount of any lump sum order is limited to £1,000.[3]

15–06   These powers are reminiscent of the powers of the divorce court to make provision between the parties following a decree, and of the powers of the magistrates' court to make financial provision during marriage. Of course, the main distinction is that here the orders can only be made for the benefit of the child. Nonetheless the powers are extremely wide, and their possible uses are considered further at 15–13 and 15–14 below.

15–07   WHO IS THE FATHER?

In some cases the father of the child may, of course, admit paternity. In the absence of such acknowledgment, however, it will not always be easy to establish the truth. There is no formal requirement that the mother's evidence as to paternity must be corroborated, but courts will naturally often be reluctant to accept the bare assertion of the mother alone.

15–08   In cases of dispute, resort may be had to section 20 of the F.L.R.A. 1969 (as amended by the Children Act 1989). Under section 20 the court has power to order blood tests to be taken from the mother, child and the alleged father, in an attempt to discover who is the father of the child. The value of blood tests in establishing paternity has been much enhanced by the introduction of so-called "DNA profiling," which can indicate with a very high degree of certainty whether a particular individual is the father of the child in question. The Blood Tests Regulations 1989[4] now make DNA profiling available for use in court-directed tests under section 20.

15–09   Section 23 of the F.L.R.A. 1987 contains provisions designed to amend section 20 of the F.L.R.A. 1969 by enabling the court to order scientific tests on any bodily samples taken from the parties to the case. However, this provision has not yet been brought into force. When it is implemented it will

---

[3] G.M.A. 1971, s.12B(2), and Magistrates' Courts (Increase of Lump Sums) Order 1988 (S.I. 1988 No. 1069).
[4] S.I. 1989 No. 776.

enable DNA profiling to be carried out on a much wider range of bodily samples, but as noted above, such profiling can be carried out perfectly satisfactorily on blood samples, provided such samples are made available.

Section 21 of the F.L.R.A. 1969 makes it clear that blood **15–10** samples can only be taken from the parties with their consent, or, in the case of a child under 16, the consent of the party having care and control. However, section 23 of the same Act provides that, where any person fails to comply with a blood test direction, the court may draw such inferences from that refusal as appear proper in the circumstances. So, for example, the refusal of a man to comply with a blood test direction is capable of being evidence which in itself corroborates the mother's evidence of paternity.[5]

DURATION OF ORDERS   **15–11**

Section 12 of the G.M.A. 1971 provides that periodical payments or secured periodical payments ordered under section 11B may be backdated to the date of the application, and continue for the same period as orders in favour of a child following divorce proceedings. This is considered fully at 6–23 to 6–26, above, but means essentially until the child is 17, or in some cases 18. Payments may also continue beyond 18, until the child ceases to be in education or undergoing training for a trade, profession or vocation. Orders for periodical payments or secured periodical payments can be varied and discharged, suspended and revived, in the same way as orders made on divorce. (See Chapter 12, above.)

MATTERS TO WHICH THE COURT IS TO HAVE REGARD   **15–12**
IN MAKING ORDERS FOR FINANCIAL RELIEF

Section 12A of the G.M.A. 1971 provides that the court is to have regard to all the circumstances of the case including:

(i)   the income, earning capacity, property and other financial resources which the mother or father of the child has or is likely to have in the foreseeable future;

(ii)   the financial needs, obligations and responsibilities which the mother or father of the child has or is likely to have in the foreseeable future;

---

[5] *cf. McVeigh* v. *Beattie* [1988] Fam. 69 (decided under the former law of affiliation.)

(iii)   the financial needs of the child;

(iv)   the income, earning capacity (if any), property and other financial resources of the child;

(v)   any physical or mental disability of the child.

These factors again are very similar to the matters the divorce court takes into account when making orders for children (see 6–68 above). It is interesting to note, however, that there is no general directive here, as there is on divorce, requiring the court to give first consideration to the welfare of the child.

15–13   USE OF THE ORDERS

English law has never imposed an obligation on a man or woman to maintain the partner with whom he or she cohabits outside marriage. However, as has been seen above, the court has wide powers to order (*inter alia*) the transfer of property between parents for the benefit of a child, and to order the settlement of property for the benefit of a child.

It may be that the court will use these powers to provide for children of an unmarried family in a similar way as on divorce. If this happens, some of the common law doctrines considered below, relating to express and non-express trusts and licences, may have less impact, because, in a sense, in providing for the child, the courts will also be providing for the custodial parent. It is too early yet to say exactly how these powers will be used, but the example below indicates what might be ordered.

15–14   *Example*

Mandy and Fred have lived together without being married for six years. Their daughter Deborah was born two years ago. They bought a house, which was put into their joint names four years ago. Their relationship has now ended. They both agree that Deborah should stay with Mandy. Mandy has applied to the county court for financial provision for Deborah.

The county court orders Fred to make periodical payments to Deborah. As there is insufficient equity in the house for it to be sold and the net proceeds divided to enable Mandy to provide a new home for Deborah, the court orders the house to be settled on the parties to provide a home for Deborah until she is 18. Obviously, Mandy will also live in the property to look after Deborah.

Apart from the fact that no periodical payments can be ordered between Mandy and Fred, this is similar to the order

318

that might have been made had they been married. It is worth noting that no recourse has had to be made to the common law and equitable principles considered below.

PROCEDURE   **15–15**

The detailed procedural rules for the making of applications under the Act are outside the scope of this book. Essentially, the procedure to be followed will depend on the court in which proceedings were commenced, and will be exactly the same as the procedure to obtain a custody order under the G.M.A. 1971 described in outline at 16–38 to 16–41, below.

FINANCIAL PROVISION FOR CHILDREN UNDER THE   **15–16**
CHILDREN ACT 1989

The Children Act 1989 repeals in its entirety the G.M.A. 1971. The powers to order financial provision for the benefit of children contained in the G.M.A. 1971 (as amended) therefore disappear, and are replaced by comprehensive provisions contained in section 15 of and Schedule 1 to the 1989 Act. These provisions, which are broadly similar to the powers contained in the G.M.A. 1971, are summarised below. It should be noted that, although the court's powers under the Children Act to make orders for the benefit of children are generally as extensive as those contained in the M.C.A. 1973 and the D.P.M.C.A. 1978, the powers contained in those two latter Acts remain unaffected by the new law.

An application for an order under Schedule 1 to the 1989 Act   **15–17**
may be made by a parent or guardian of a child, or by any person in whose favour a residence order is in force with respect to the child. Proceedings may be taken in the High Court, county court or magistrates' court. However, the powers of the higher courts are more extensive than those of the magistrates'.

(i) Powers of the High Court and county courts   **15–18**
The higher courts may at any time make the following orders:

  (a) an order requiring either or both parents of a child to make to the applicant for the benefit of the child, or to the child himself, such periodical payments, for such term as may be specified in the order;

(b) an order requiring either or both parents of a child to secure to the applicant for the benefit of the child, or to secure to the child himself, such periodical payments, for such term, as may be specified;

(c) an order requiring either or both parents of a child to pay to the applicant for the benefit of the child, or to the child himself, such lump sum as may be specified;

(d) an order requiring a settlement to be made for the benefit of the child, and to the satisfaction of the court, of property to which either parent is entitled (either in possession or in reversion) and which is specified in the order;

(e) an order requiring either or both parents of a child to transfer to the applicant, for the benefit of the child, or to transfer to the child himself, such property to which the parent is, or the parents are, entitled (either in possession or in reversion) as may be specified in the order.

15–19 **(ii) The powers of the magistrates' court**

The magistrates' court has the power to make only those orders specified in (a) and (c) above, and, under Schedule 1, paragraph 5(2), the amount of any lump sum order is limited to £1,000.

15–20 DURATION OF ORDERS

By virtue of Schedule 1, paragraph 3, to the 1989 Act, an order for periodical payments made in favour of a child may begin with the date of the making of an application for the order or any later date. Such orders should not in the first instance be made to extend beyond the child's 17th birthday unless the court thinks it right in the circumstances of the case to specify a later date. In any event the order should not extend beyond the child's 18th birthday, unless the child is to receive further education or undergo training for a trade, profession or vocation, or there are other special circumstances which justify extending the order. These provisions are of course the same as those that apply to maintenance orders made on divorce. Again, as with orders on divorce, ordinary periodical payments must cease on the death of the payer, although secured periodical payments can continue beyond this date. One further express limitation which applies here, is not, however, to be found in the divorce legislation. This is that a periodical payments order will cease if a parent making the payments resumes cohabitation for a period of more than six months with the parent to whom the payments are being made.

MATTERS TO WHICH THE COURT IS TO HAVE REGARD **15–21** IN MAKING ORDERS FOR FINANCIAL RELIEF

By virtue of Schedule 1, paragraph 4, to the 1989 Act, the court, in deciding whether to exercise its powers to make orders for financial relief, must have regard to all the circumstances of the case. These circumstances include:

(a) the income, earning capacity, property and other financial resources which any parent, the applicant and any other person in whose favour the court proposes to make the order, has or is likely to have in the foreseeable future;

(b) the financial needs, obligations and responsibilities which any parent, the applicant and any other person in whose favour the court proposes to make the order, has or is likely to have in the foreseeable future;

(c) the financial needs of the child;

(d) the income, earning capacity (if any), property and other financial resources of the child;

(e) any physical or mental disability of the child;

(f) the manner in which the child was being, or was expected to be, educated or trained.

This latter factor is new in so far as it was not included as a relevant factor under the G.M.A. 1971. Apart from this it will be seen that the factors are very similar, both to those under the G.M.A. and to those which are relevant to ancillary orders made on divorce. There is no express requirement in Schedule 1 that the court should give first consideration to the welfare of the child in deciding whether to exercise its powers.

However, it should be remembered that, by virtue of section 1(5), the court should not make any order under the 1989 Act unless satisfied that it is better for the child to make the order than to make no order at all.

15–22 VARIATION OF ORDERS

The court's powers to vary periodical payments orders, whether secured or unsecured, are very similar to those that exist in relation to orders made on divorce. Under Schedule 1, paragraph 1(4), such orders may be varied or discharged on the application of either the payer or payee. In addition, under paragraph 6(4), a child of 16 or over can himself apply for the variation of a periodical payments order made in his favour. The power to vary an order includes a power to suspend it temporarily and to revive a provision which has been suspended. The courts also have powers, under paragraph 5(6), to vary lump sum orders where these are payable by instalments. The court can vary the number of instalments payable, the amount of any instalment, and the date on which an instalment shall be paid.

15–23 ALTERATION OF MAINTENANCE AGREEMENTS

The courts now have powers to alter maintenance agreements made between parents (regardless of whether they are married to each other) in favour of their children. These powers were originally introduced by the Family Law Reform Act 1987, sections 15 and 16, and in future are to be found in the Children Act 1989, Schedule 1, paragraphs 10 and 11. These provisions do not affect the powers to vary maintenance agreements between spouses which exist under section 35 of the M.C.A. 1973, which are discussed in Chapter 12, above. Under the Act, the High Court, county court and magistrates' court have power to alter agreements, although the jurisdicion of the magistrates' court is more limited than that of the higher courts. The powers of alteration are limited to written agreements which contain financial arrangements for a child of the parties. The courts have power to vary or revoke these financial arrangements either on the ground that circumstances have changed since the original agreement was made, or on the ground that the agreement does not contain proper financial arrangements with respect to the child. The powers of magistrates' courts under the Act are limited to inserting provision for periodical payments to be made for the maintenance of the child, or, where such a provision already exists, to increasing or reducing the rate of those payments, or terminating them altogether.

2. The Home

OWNERSHIP   **15–24**

A dispute about the ownership of property between un-married partners must be dealt with under general property law. The matrimonial legislation and the wide powers of the court under sections 24 and 24A of the M.C.A. 1973 are irrelevant.[6]

The task of the court is not to consider the question "to whom should the property be given?" but rather "to whom does it belong?" The item of property which is likely to lead to the most complex problems is the home, although the general principle discussed below can be applied to other kinds of property too.

(i) An express trust   **15–25**

It is very common, for a variety of reasons, for the home to be bought in joint names if a couple live together in a permanent relationship. In this case the conveyancing documents should contain an express declaration as to the nature of the parties' beneficial interests.[7] Their beneficial interests might be held jointly or as tenants in common; in the latter case the extent of their share should be specified (*e.g.* equally, or one-third to two-thirds). If their interests are declared, this will be conclusive except in very exceptional circumstances, such as where there has been fraud or mistake.[8]

However, this declaration merely indicates the entitlement of the parties to a share of the proceeds of sale. It may be that only one of the parties wants a sale. This problem is considered below, at 15–37.

(ii) A non-express trust   **15–26**

Where the property is in the sole name of one of the partners, and the other partner wishes to claim some right in the property, that partner will usually have to establish a non-express trust (*i.e.* an implied, resulting or constructive trust),

---

[6] See *Mossop* v. *Mossop* [1988] 2 W.L.R. 1255.
[7] *Walker* v. *Hall* [1984] F.L.R. 126. The Court of Appeal pointed out that the courts might soon have to consider whether a solicitor acting for joint purchasers would be negligent if he did not include such a declaration.
[8] *Goodman* v. *Gallant* [1986] Fam. 106.

in their favour. These terms are not easily distinguishable, and indeed some writers treat implied and resulting trusts as synonymous.[9] In essence, they arise through the presumed intentions of the parties. A simple example arises where property is put into the name of the other party, but the purchase price is provided by the other. The legal owner then holds the property on an implied or resulting trust for the other. A constructive trust, on the other hand, is one that is imposed because otherwise an inequitable result would be produced.

For our purposes it does not matter which label is applied as the results are the same. Indeed the courts frequently do not distinguish between them,[10] because, unlike an express trust, none of them need be created in writing.[11]

If the legal estate is held in joint names, but the conveyancing documents are silent as to the beneficial interest, similar principles are applied in order to establish the extent of the beneficial interests.

15–27 When considering the existence of a non-express trust, the courts are primarily concerned with ascertaining the intention of the parties. No doubt the best evidence of a common intention that the parties should own the property jointly would be an express agreement to this effect. However, it would be very rare for an express agreement to have been made. In the majority of cases where the courts have found evidence that the parties intended joint ownership, it has been in the form of contributions to the acquisition or improvement of the home. Such contributions may be direct or indirect.

15–28 *Direct contributions*

These may take the form of a contribution to the purchase price, such as payment of the initial deposit or the subsequent mortgage instalments. They could also take the form of paying for substantial improvements, such as central heating. Where the party claiming a share in the beneficial ownership of the property has made a substantial direct contribution to the acquisition or improvement of the property, the court would almost certainly hold that the legal owner holds the property on trust.

---

[9] See Philip H. Pettit, *Equity and the Law of Trusts* (5th ed., 1984), p. 54.
[10] Lord Diplock in *Gissing* v. *Gissing* [1971] A.C. 886 at p. 905. *cf.* the judgment of Lord Denning in *Hussey* v. *Palmer* [1972] 1 W.L.R. 1286 at p. 1291 with that of Lord Justice Phillimore at p. 1291.
[11] L.P.A. 1925, s.53(2).

Indirect contributions **15–29**

These may take the form of paying household expenses. If it can be shown that there is a connection between the ability of the legal owner to buy the house and the indirect contributions made by the other partner, the court may treat the contributions as evidence of the required common intention. The more crucial the indirect contributions were to the legal owner's ability to buy the home, the more likely it is that they will be treated as evidence that joint ownership was intended.

This means, however, that where the parties are unmarried, the court may hold that one party has no rights of ownership in a home they have occupied for many years. So, for example, in *Burns* v. *Burns*,[12] the Court of Appeal decided there was no common intention that the woman was to have any share in the home. In this case the woman (who was not married to the man), had shared the house with him for 17 years, and had brought up two children that she had had by him. She had spent her earnings (when she was able to work) on household expenses. However, there was no evidence that the defendant had asked her to make these payments and they did not affect his ability to buy the property. As she had not contributed substantially to the property the court did not award her any share in it. Of course, if the parties had been married, the plaintiff's contributions would have been taken into account under section 25 of the M.C.A. 1973, and the court could have made a property adjustment order in her favour under section 24.

However, in some cases a plaintiff may be able to point to **15–30** further evidence of a common intention that the house should be jointly owned, quite apart from the contributions. In *Grant* v. *Edwards*[13] this further evidence took the form of an assertion by the defendant, at the time of the purchase, that the plaintiff's name should not be included in the title, because it would prejudice matrimonial proceedings which were then taking place between the plaintiff and her husband. In the light of this, the plaintiff's contributions to household expenses could be seen as having been made on the understanding that she was to share in the beneficial interest, and this justified the imposition of a constructive trust to give effect to that understanding.

---

[12] [1984] Ch. 317.
[13] [1986] Ch. 638.

15–31   Contributions towards the acquisition of the home by labour
have been held to entitle the labouring partner to a share of
the equity. In *Cooke* v. *Head*,[14] for example, Mr.
Head bought a plot of land, and he and Miss Cooke built a bungalow on it.
Miss Cooke used a sledgehammer to demolish old buildings,
worked a cement mixer and did other heavy work, as well as
painting and decorating. The Court of Appeal held that she
was entitled to a third of the net equity.

Similarly in *Eves* v. *Eves*[15] (a case involving cohabitants
despite the name), Ms. Eves worked hard to improve the
house and increase its value. However, Mr. Eves had also
practised a deception, in that he had told Ms. Eves that the
house was to be put in his name alone, as she was too young
(being under 21) to own property. Lord Denning held that
Mr. Eves's behaviour, coupled with Ms. Eves's contributions
to the house, justified the imposition of a constructive trust
under which Ms. Eves was entitled to a quarter share in the
property. The other two members of the court concurred in
this result, but did so by the application of the resulting trust
principle. Their approach was to say that the only sensible
explanation for the work the woman had done on the
property was that there was an arrangement between her and
the man that they should share the beneficial ownership.

15–32   Although the approach of the majority in *Eves* v. *Eves* accords
more closely with orthodox principles (and indeed very little
has been heard lately of the constructive trust approach
favoured by Lord Denning), it will often be very difficult to
persuade the court that the only sensible inference to be
drawn in such cases is that the parties had a common
intention that ownership should be shared. Compare, for
example, *Thomas* v. *Fuller-Brown*.[16] In this case the parties
lived together in a house bought in the woman's sole name.
The man was unemployed and was supported by the woman,
but the woman obtained an improvement grant and agreed
with the man that he would carry out the work on the house
in return for his keep. The work needed was substantial, but
when completed the relationship broke down. The man now
claimed a two-thirds share of the equity. The judge held,
however, that it was not possible to say on the facts of this
case that the only reasonable inference was the parties
intended joint ownership. The judge believed that the parties
simply intended that the man should go on occupying the

---

[14] [1972] 1 W.L.R. 518.
[15] [1975] 1 W.L.R. 1338, and note *Hussey* v. *Palmer* [1972] 1 W.L.R. 1286.
[16] [1988] 1 F.L.R. 237.

house as a licensee, doing odd jobs in return for his board and lodging. The Court of Appeal refused to interfere with this finding, Slade L.J. saying: "Under English law the mere fact that A expends money or labour on B's property does not by itself entitle A to an interest in the property."

(iii) Estoppel

15–33

Although most ownership disputes between unmarried couples have been dealt with on the principles of resulting and constructive trusts, the case of *Pascoe* v. *Turner*[17] revealed the possibility of a partner achieving the same (or a better) result by invoking the doctrine of proprietary estoppel.

In *Pascoe* v. *Turner* Mrs. Turner and Mr. Pascoe cohabited for several years. Mr. Pascoe left to live with another woman and said to Mrs. Turner: "The home is yours and everything in it." Mrs. Turner then spent a small amount of money on repairs and improvements, on the assumption that it was her property. This was with the knowledge and the encouragement of Mr. Pascoe. Mr. Pascoe then brought an action for possession. The Court of Appeal found that there was insufficient evidence to justify the imposition of a constructive trust, but that, having made his promise, Mr. Pascoe was estopped from going back on it, as Mrs. Turner had acted to her detriment with his acquiescence and encouragement. To perfect the gift the Court of Appeal (somewhat surprisingly) ordered him to transfer the property to Mrs. Turner.

15–34

Pascoe v. *Turner* should probably be regarded as exceptional in the degree of generosity which the court showed to Mrs. Turner. It might well be that, in general, where the doctrine of estoppel can be invoked to protect a person's occupation of the home, that person could expect to be given no more than a life interest in the property.[18]

15–35

The difficulty of establishing a proprietary estoppel in cases such as this is well illustrated by *Coombes* v. *Smith*.[19] In this case the plaintiff and the defendant became lovers and the woman became pregnant. She then left her husband and moved into a house owned by the man. She gave up her job to have the baby, but the man never moved into the house. When the woman asked the man what security she and the child would have, the man replied with words to this effect:

15–36

---

[17] [1979] 1 W.L.R. 431.
[18] *cf. Greasley* v. *Cooke* [1980] 1 W.L.R. 1306. But see also *Grant* v. *Edwards*, referred to at 15–30 above.
[19] [1986] 1 W.L.R. 808.

"Don't worry. I have told you I will always look after you."
When later on the relationship broke down, the woman
brought an action based (*inter alia*) on proprietary estoppel for
an order that the property be conveyed to her absolutely. The
action failed, however. The judge held that the woman:

(i) had not believed that she was acquiring any interest
in the property on the strength of the man's promise;

(ii) the woman had not acted to her detriment in
becoming pregnant, leaving her husband, giving up
her job, and looking after the house and child.
Obviously much here depends on one's interpretation
of the word "detriment." Nevertheless, the result was
that the essential conditions necessary to give rise to
an equity in the woman's favour were lacking.

15–37 WILL THE COURT ORDER A SALE?

Once the party claiming a beneficial interest has established
the existence of a trust, express or implied, there may then be
a dispute as to whether or not the property should be sold.
"Any person interested" in the property may apply to the
court for an order for sale under section 30 of the L.P.A. 1925,
and the court is empowered to make "such order as it thinks
fit."

In reaching a decision, the courts will have regard to the
"underlying purpose" of the trust. If there are no children
living in the home when the relationship ends, the court is
likely to order a sale.[20] If, however, as in *Re Evers Trust*[21]
there are children present, then the court is likely to refuse to
order an immediate sale, leaving it open to the applicant to
apply again for an order for sale at some later date
(presumably when the youngest child is 18).

15–38 Where the court is willing to postpone the sale, it may make
the order subject to certain conditions. In one case,[22] sale was
postponed on condition that the man paid the woman £6,000
within four months. This is, of course, reminiscent of a lump
sum order on divorce. In another case,[23] the sale was
postponed to allow the woman six months to move to suitable
alternative accommodation.

[20] *Jones* v. *Challenger* [1961] 1 Q.B. 176.
[21] [1980] 1 W.L.R. 1327.
[22] *Bernard* v. *Josephs* [1982] Ch. 391.
[23] *Cousins* v *Dzosens*, (1984) 81 L.S.Gaz. 2855.

Where a sale is refused, the court may order the party in **15–39** occupation to make regular payments to the other party. Thus, in *Dennis* v. *McDonald*,[24] the parties owned a property jointly as tenants in common in equal shares. They cohabited for 12 years. Then Miss Dennis left Mr. McDonald because of his violence. Mr. McDonald continued to live in the house with three of their children. Miss Dennis moved out with the two younger children. The court refused to order an immediate sale, as the property was still being used to provide a home for some of the children. They did, however, order Mr. McDonald to pay Miss Dennis a periodical sum of money to compensate her for being unable to exercise her right to occupy the joint home. The basis of the court's jurisdiction to make this order is not entirely clear. It appears to be derived from the power to order a trustee to pay compensation to a beneficiary for the exclusive enjoyment of trust property.

THE SIZE OF THE SHARE   15–40

It will have been gathered from the cases already discussed, that the fact that the court declares that the home is jointly owned does not necessarily mean that it is owned in equal shares. The size of each party's share depends on their respective contributions.

Where these contributions have been direct, the apportionment of the proceeds should be relatively straightforward. This is because the parties' shares will follow the proportions in which the purchase money was provided, in the absence of a contrary intention. Where, however, the beneficial interest is based on indirect contributions it is much more difficult to see how the courts have decided on the division of the proceeds. What is clear is that there should be no automatic equal division, as was emphasised by the Court of Appeal in *Bernard* v. *Josephs* (above).

Another problem which has arisen in the past has been that **15–41** of deciding the date at which the parties' shares should be valued. However, in *Turton* v. *Turton*,[25] the Court of Appeal held that, in the absence of an express agreement to the contrary, the relevant date for the valuation of the shares is the date of the sale and not the date of separation. What is often really in issue is the question of whether both parties

---

[24] [1982] 2 W.L.R. 275.
[25] [1988] Ch. 542.

should share the benefit of house-price inflation. For example, a half-share valued at last year's prices may well be very different from the same half-share valued at today's prices. However, separation should in itself have no effect on the valuation of the parties' shares, since the beneficial interests continue to be held under a trust for sale regardless of the separation, and therefore can only be valued at the time of sale.

15–42 One further point that must be borne in mind in considering the value of a share in the property is the possible incidence of the legal aid statutory charge. This charge, which attaches to property recovered or preserved by a legally-aided party, may greatly reduce the real value of a share. In particular, it must be remembered that the £2,500 exemption available in respect of lump sum and property adjustment orders after divorce does not apply to unmarried couples. The potentially disastrous effect of this is illustrated by *Cooke* v. *Head (No. 2)*[26] in which the legally-aided Mr. Head, having previously been awarded two-thirds of the proceeds of sale of the bungalow, ended up with £98.

15–43 It must also be borne in mind that the Legal Aid Board has no discretion to postpone the charge generally. The discretion to postpone the charge is available only where the proceedings are taken under certain defined statutes, of which the L.P.A. 1925 is not one. The fact that there is no discretion to postpone the charge where proceedings for an order for sale are taken under the L.P.A. 1925 will undoubtedly lead to hardship in certain cases. It will be irrelevant that a legally-aided party's share of the proceeds is destined to be used for the purchase of new accommodation, and the charge will bite immediately, possibly leaving the assisted party without sufficient money to buy alternative accommodation after all.

OCCUPATION OF THE HOME

15–44 (i) Licence to occupy
A cohabitant who has no proprietary interest in the home is bound to have at least some sort of licence to occupy the premises. Licences can be broadly divided into at least two categories: bare licences and contractual licences; arguably a third category of licence exists, in the form of an equitable licence.

---

[26] [1974] 1 W.L.R. 972.

Bare licence **15–45**

At the very least a cohabitant will have occupied the home as a bare licensee, which means that the licence can be terminated "on reasonable notice." What is reasonable obviously depends on the circumstances of the case, but it would probably be generally agreed that 28 days should be regarded as a minimum period of notice.

Contractual licence **15–46**

In general, a cohabitant who wants to establish more than a bare licence is going to have to show the existence of a contract under which he or she occupied the home. This involves establishing all the ordinary ingredients of a contract:

(a) Clear terms of agreement.

(b) Intention to create legal relations.

(c) Consideration.

This third ingredient is perhaps the hardest to establish and there are few cases where it has been successfully done. One case in which sufficient consideration was found, however, was *Tanner* v. *Tanner*.[27] In this case the woman had been the tenant of a rent-controlled flat. This meant that the rent was extremely low and could not be increased.

When she had twins by Mr. Tanner (to whom she was not married), she agreed to give up the tenancy and move into his house. She also took his name. Some time later Mr. Tanner married another woman and sought possession. The Court of Appeal held that a contract could be inferred whereby Mr. Tanner had granted the woman a licence to occupy so long as the children were of school age. The consideration for the contract was the woman's surrendering of the tenancy of the rent-controlled property. In many cases, however, consideration will be lacking and it will not be possible to establish a contractual licence.[28]

Equitable licence? **15–47**

There is some authority to suggest the existence of a licence created by equity where there is insufficient evidence to establish a contract. Indeed, in *Tanner* v. *Tanner* (above) the language used by Lord Denning, as distinct from that of the other two members of the Court of Appeal, suggests that he

---

[27] [1975] 1 W.L.R. 1346.
[28] See *Horrocks* v. *Forray* [1976] 1 W.L.R. 230 and *Coombes* v. *Smith* [1986] 1 W.L.R. 808.

saw the court as imposing terms on the parties, rather than enforcing terms agreed by them.

15–48 **(ii) Protection from violence and molestation**
Where one unmarried partner seeks protection against the other as a result of being subjected to violence or molestation, it will generally be necessary to apply for exclusion and non-molestation injunctions under the D.V.M.P.A. 1976. By section 1(2) of the Act, its provisions apply to a man and a woman who are living with each other in the same household as husband and wife, in the same way as they apply to married parties. The provisions of the Act are considered in detail in Chapter 18, below.

15–49 **3. Joint Bank Accounts**

It is common for unmarried couples in a stable, long-term relationship, to have joint bank or building society accounts. Subject to the exceptional circumstances considered below, they will each be treated as equally entitled to the money.[29]

The exceptional circumstances may be summarised as follows:

(i) If the account was fed solely by one of the parties, it may be possible to show an intention that all the money should belong to that party (*i.e.* it is held on a resulting trust). Sometimes an account is opened in joint names simply for the convenience of enabling the non-contributing partner to draw money from the account. In these circumstances it is likely that the court will hold that the money belongs solely to the contributing partner.[30]

(ii) Property purchased with money withdrawn from a joint account belongs, *prima facie*, to the purchasing partner[31] unless it can be shown that the property purchased was intended for the parties' joint ownership.[32]

15–50 **4. The Procedure for Determining Disputes**

The matrimonial legislation is, of course, inapplicable to disputes between unmarried partners. Normally, in the case of land, an application is made to the High Court to grant a

---

[29] *Jones* v. *Maynard* [1951] Ch. 572.
[30] *Thompson* v. *Thompson* (1970) 114 S.J. 455; *Re Figgis (dec'd.)* [1969] 1 Ch. 123.
[31] *Re Bishop (dec'd.)* [1965] Ch. 450.
[32] *Jones* v. *Maynard* (above).

declaration of ownership. Section 22 of the County Courts Act 1984 gives the county court the same power as the High Court to grant such declarations, though restricted to land the rateable value of which does not exceed £1,000 per annum.[33] It is, of course, also possible in appropriate cases to apply to these courts for an order for sale under section 30 of the L.P.A. 1925.

Where the value of the property necessitates an application to the High Court, the proceedings are likely to be costly, both in time and money. There is, however, an alternative procedure available to unmarried couples who had formerly agreed to marry, provided they apply for such orders within three years of the termination of the agreement. Such parties can use section 17 of the M.W.P.A. 1882, which enables the county court to declare the ownership of property irrespective of its value. This provision was originally confined to husbands and wives in disputes about the ownership or possession of any property, but was extended to formerly engaged couples by the Law Reform Act 1970, s.2. Applications may be brought before the High Court as well, in which case they are assigned to the Family Division.[34]   **15–51**

The M.P.W.A. 1882, s.17 is essentially a procedural section under which the court can only declare existing rights of ownership. Thus the principles on which the dispute is resolved will be those outlined above.

---

[33] As at March 31, 1990. When the Courts and Legal Services Act 1990 comes into force jurisdiction based on rateable values will disappear.

[34] Administration of Justice Act 1970, s.1(2) and Sched. 1 (as amended).

PART III

CHILDREN

16. Custody and Access

The third section of this book is devoted to that most emotive **16–01** of all topics—children. The Children Act 1989 provides a completely new framework of concepts, principles and procedure for the law relating to children. This new law is so radical that it is impossible to incorporate the changes within a section dealing with the current law. However, the Act is not yet in force, nor is it expected to be until, at the earliest, October 1991. Therefore we deal with the existing and the new law in two separate sections. In this chapter, consideration is given to disputes between a couple over custody or access under the current law. Chapter 17 deals with substantially the same area, but on the assumption that the Children Act 1989 has been brought into force.

Chapters 18 and 19 examine how a child may be protected from either or both its parents, or from third parties. Chapter 18 deals with the current law, Chapter 19 with the law under the Children Act 1989.

In short, if the reader is studying this subject prior to the implementation of the Children Act 1989, the chapters to read are this one and Chapter 18. Once the Act is in force the reader is directed to Chapters 17 and 19.

In this chapter a number of general matters are considered first, then the three jurisdictions under which custody disputes are usually resolved are examined in detail.

1. Terminology

CUSTODY AT COMMON LAW

The word "custody" has long been used at common law, but has proved difficult to define satisfactorily. In its broader sense it covers:

(i) physical control over a child; and

(ii) the "bundle of rights and powers" exercisable in respect of a child, including control of his education and religious upbringing, the right to consent to the child's marriage and to surgical operations on the child and the right to apply for a passport on the child's behalf.

Sometimes, however, it becomes necessary to differentiate between the meanings in (i) and (ii) above. In this case the phrase "care and control" is used to designate the physical control referred to in (i) and the word "custody" is reserved for the rights, powers and duties referred to in (ii). Thus the meaning of the word "custody" at common law depends on the context in which it is used. Where it is necessary in this chapter to distinguish between the two meanings of custody we have used the expression "custody in its broader sense" to refer to both (i) and (ii) above, and in its "narrow sense" to refer to just (ii) above.

16–02 THE DEFINITIONS IN THE CHILDREN ACT 1975

The matter is further complicated by the Children Act 1975 (C.A. 1975), which introduced some alternative terminology.

(i) Parental rights and duties
These are defined by section 85 of the C.A. 1975 to be "all the rights and duties which by law the parents have in relation to a legitimate child and his property."

(ii) Legal custody
This is defined by section 86 of the C.A. 1975 as "so much of the parental rights and duties as relate to the person of the child (including the place and manner in which his time is spent)." This is similar to "custody" in its broader common law sense, referred to above. However certain rights are probably not included in legal custody, as they do not relate to the "person" of the child. For example, the right to change the child's name, or his religion. Certainly the right to control any property the child may possess is not included.

(iii) Actual custody
This is defined by section 87 of the C.A. 1975 as "actual possession of the person of the child." This is the same as "care and control" at common law, referred to above.

16–03 WHICH TERMINOLOGY SHOULD BE USED?

As will be seen below, two of the jurisdictions under which custody disputes can be resolved use the C.A. 1975 terminology. These are the jurisdictions contained in the

D.P.M.C.A. 1978 and the G.M.A. 1971. However, in the most commonly used jurisdiction of all—that contained in the M.C.A. 1973, under which custody disputes on divorce are dealt with—the common law terminology is still used. It is also used in wardship proceedings, which are considered in the next chapter.

ACCESS   16–04

This term has never been statutorily defined. It refers to the extent to which a person, who does not have actual custody of a child, is allowed to see that child. It can take different forms.

(i) Reasonable access   16–05
Where access is granted by a court it is usually granted in this form, at least initially. It is then for the parties to agree between themselves how the access arrangements should operate.

(ii) Defined access   16–06
Where it proves impossible for the parties to co-operate, the court may make an order for defined access, specifying when and where access shall take place.

A party who is refused reasonable access by the custodial parent should apply for an order for defined access rather than seek to have an order for reasonable access enforced. An order for reasonable access cannot by its very nature be enforced. In practice, however, even an order for defined access is extremely difficult to enforce because the court would be very reluctant to commit an unco-operative custodial parent to prison for contempt.[1]

(iii) Staying access   16–07
Access, whether defined or not, can in some cases extend to short periods during which a child stays with the non-custodial party; for example, weekends or short holidays.

CUSTODIANSHIP[2]   16–08

Courts administering the D.P.M.C.A. 1978[3] and the G.M.A. 1971[4] are also able to make a custodianship order. If a third

---

[1] *Re L. (Minors) (Access)* [1989] Fam. Law 433.
[2] C.A. 1975, Part II. For the circumstances where this might be used see 16–29 and 16–35, below.
[3] D.P.M.C.A. 1978, s.8(3).
[4] C.A. 1975, s.37(3).

party, (e.g. a step-parent, relative or foster parent) wishes to apply for care of a child, the court in these jurisdictions is not able to make a custody order in their favour, but only a custodianship order. In practice this is only likely to happen rarely.

The custodianship order is revocable by the court[5] but while it lasts, the right of any other person to legal custody is suspended.

An order of custodianship vests legal custody of the child in the custodian, but the legal status of the child, as the child of his natural parents, is not affected. Therefore, for example, his right to succeed on their intestacy is not affected.

16–09 2. Custody Rights in the Absence of a Court Order

At a very early date the common law recognised the natural duties of a father to protect and maintain his legitimate minor children. These duties carried with them the right to custody, as, without this right, it would have been impossible to perform them. The mother, since she had none of these duties, had no corresponding right to custody at common law. The position was changed by section 1(1) of the Guardianship Act (G.A. 1973) which provides that "In relation to the legal custody or upbringing of a child ... a mother shall have the same rights and authority as the law allows to a father. ... " Section 1(1) goes on to provide, in respect of legitimate children, that either parent may exercise any parental right without the other parent. This, however, only applies so long as the other parent has not "signified disapproval of its exercise or performance in that manner."[6]

16–10 In the case of illegitimate children, the mother alone has the parental rights. However, the law relating to illegitimate children was changed by the F.L.R.A. 1987. This has done much to remove the legal disadvantages of illegitimacy, but it is still necessary for the father of a child born outside marriage to take proceedings if he wishes to acquire parental rights.[7] In particular, section 4 of that Act gives the father a right to apply for an order allowing him joint parental rights and duties with the mother.

[5] C.A. 1975, s.35.
[6] C.A. 1975, s.85(3).
[7] If paternity is disputed the court may order scientific tests on blood samples to establish this: s.20 of the F.L.R.A. 1969, see 15–08, above. An application for a declaration as to paternity may be made without the need for any other proceedings: F.L.R.A. 1987, s.56.

Certain statutes specifically require the consent of both **16–11** parents in certain matters; for example, the adoption or marriage of their children. If the parents disagree, the G.A. 1973, ss.3 and 3A[8] enables either of them to apply to the court for directions. These provisions also allow either parent to apply to the court for directions in any case where they disagree about a matter affecting the child's welfare.

An agreement by one parent to assign the custody of his child to the other is contrary to public policy, as it would militate against the unity of the family and is, therefore, normally void. However, by virtue of section 1(2) of the G.A. 1973, an agreement may be valid if it is to operate only during the period when the parents are not living in the same household. Even then a court will refuse to enforce the agreement if it considers that it would not be for the benefit of the child.

3. The Principles Applied when a Court Order is **16–12** Sought

The principles which a court applies whenever custody or access is in dispute are the same regardless of the jurisdiction under which an order is sought. Section 1 of the G.M.A. 1971 provides that in any proceedings, "The court ... shall regard the welfare of the child as the first and paramount consideration. ... " The meaning of these words was considered by Lord MacDermott in the case of *J.* v. *C.*[9]

> "I think they connote a process whereby, when all the relevant facts, relationships, claims and wishes of the parents, risks, choices and other circumstances are taken into account and weighed, the course to be followed will be that which is most in the interests of the child's welfare as that term has now to be understood. That is the first consideration because it is of first importance and the paramount consideration because it rules on or determines the course to be followed."

It is clear from this passage that, in a sense, the child's welfare is the only consideration in these cases. It is not just the first matter to be considered in a list of others; the court must have the child's welfare in mind first, last and all the time. It should be satisfied that, whatever course it finally chooses to adopt, this is the best that can be done from the child's point of view.

[8] Inserted by the F.L.R.A. 1987, s.5.
[9] [1970] A.C. 668.

Obviously, the question of what is "best for the child" is an extremely complex one. The trial judge is given, therefore, a wide discretion within the ambit of these words. Indeed the Court of Appeal is reluctant to interfere with the view of the judge below and will only do so if the court's discretion was exercised on wrong principles or the decision is plainly wrong.[10]

Although, in a sense, the child's welfare is the only consideration, a large number of more specific factors may have a bearing on the matter. They have arisen from case law and are grouped under convenient headings below. Clearly, in any given case, other factors may arise which do not fall under one of the following headings. It is important to appreciate that the following do not constitute a "points system," so that the more factors in one party's favour, the more likelihood of their obtaining custody. There are some which carry far greater weight than others.

16–13 STATUS QUO

In the vast majority of cases the court is extremely reluctant to interfere with existing arrangements that have been made for the children's welfare, provided these are working satisfactorily. In most cases the parents agree that the children should remain with the mother and, as the court is usually merely confirming this arrangement, this may be the basis of the commonly held belief that mothers invariably obtain custody.[11] However, certain studies have been made[12] which indicate that there is little automatic bias in favour of mothers. The bias is towards the existing arrangement, and, if the child is currently with the father, it is likely that the court will confirm this arrangement.[13] It would appear that in only a very small percentage of cases[14] does the court alter the

[10] G. v. G. [1985] 1 W.L.R. 647.
[11] See Law Commission Working Paper No. 96, *Review of Child Law: Custody (1986)* and supplement *Custody Law in Practice in the Divorce and Domestic Courts* by J. A. Priest and J. C. Whybrow. This indicates that in only approximately 10 per cent. of all cases (whether contested or not) custody was granted to the father.
[12] See J. Eekelaar and E. Clive with K. Clarke and S. Raikes, *Custody After Divorce* (1977), and S. Maidment, "A Study in Child Custody" (1976) 6 Fam. Law 195 and 236, and J. Eekelaar [1982] *Oxford Journal of Legal Studies* 63.
[13] See for example, B. v. B. (1985) 15 Fam. Law 119—child of 11 months left with father for two years. Court accepted evidence that both mother and father competent parents, child allowed to remain with father.
[14] In less than 4 per cent. of the disputed custody cases studied by J. Eekelaar and Clive *et al.*, *op. cit.*

status quo. If the status quo is in favour of a person who is not a natural parent then, as a principle, it may be less significant. The Court of Appeal[15] has said that "The best person to bring up a child is the natural parent ... provided the child's moral and physical health are not endangered." In one case[16] the court took the child from his uncle and aunt, with whom he had lived since his mother had died, and awarded custody to his father (who had not been married to the mother). However, in another case,[17] the Court of Appeal upheld the status quo in favour of an uncle and aunt against the child's mother, where the child had been with them for three years.

For this reason the party seeking custody is often advised to stay with the children if custody is likely to be contested by the other party. In some cases this may lead a wife to stay in the matrimonial home, even though she is facing actual or threatened violence, as she may have nowhere to take the children. This often leads to an application for an injunction to oust the husband which, if granted, will increase the prospect of the wife's obtaining a custody order. Conversely, if a person is seeking custody of a child who is not living with him, he must pursue the application with all speed to reduce the amount of time the child remains settled with the other party.[18]

As the status quo is such an important consideration it is unlikely that the following factors will be relevant in any but a small proportion of cases.

AGE AND SEX OF THE CHILD   16–14

It is well accepted that young children are often better looked after by their mother[19] and this seems to extend to older girls as well.[20] There may be some preference for awarding custody of older boys to their father.[21] This, taken in conjunction with a further principle that the courts will not

---

[15] *Re K.D.* [1988] A.C. 806.

[16] *Re K.* (1989) *The Times*, December 4.

[17] *Re R.* (1989) *The Times*, June 12.

[18] See *Allington* v. *Allington* (1985) 15 Fam. Law 157, where 10 weeks was held to be insufficient time to establish a status quo, and the child was transferred from the father's care to the mother's.

[19] See *Allington* above. The court was clearly of the view that there was a presumption in favour of the mother. See also *Re C. (A.) (an infant), C.* v. *C.* [1970] 1 All E.R. 309; see also *Re T.* [1989] Fam. Law 233.

[20] *Pinch* v. *Pinch* (1973) 3 Fam. Law 171 (C.A.).

[21] *Re C. (A.) (an infant), C.* v. *C.* [1970] 1 All E.R. 309.

generally separate siblings, means that in some cases mothers have been able to persuade the courts to award them custody of their children, even though they may not have looked after them for some time.[22] Obviously other factors in such cases may be relevant; in particular the reason why the mother did not look after the children for this time. If, for example, this was because of lack of accommodation, or the fact that they had been taken from her against her will, her lack of recent contact with the children may not count against her.

16–15 WISHES OF THE CHILD

As will be seen, the court has power to make custody orders until the child is 18. However, it is difficult to conceive of a court awarding custody of a 16 or 17-year-old child to a parent against that child's wishes. Indeed, in practice, custody orders are rarely made in any case in relation to children over 16.[23]

So far as younger children are concerned, the extent to which the court will take account of their wishes will depend on their maturity. The court can ascertain their wishes or feelings from a variety of sources. Examples of these are social workers, teachers, parents, letters they may have written. One must be careful to distinguish, as far as possible, the child's own feelings from those suggested, either directly or indirectly, by one or both of its parents. It is open to the judge to interview the child in private, although this should not be done if the child is younger than eight years old.[24] Many judges would not interview a child unless he was 12 or more. It would seem that magistrates cannot interview children in private at all.[25] Where the child is consulted, it is important to ensure that he is not made to feel that he is being asked to choose between his parents.

16–16 OTHER BACKGROUND INFORMATION

The court will want to hear evidence from parents and prospective step-parents, to form some view as to their personalities. Any physical or mental disability suffered by the parties or the child must be considered. If the child is

---

[22] Re D.W. (a minor) (Custody) (1984) 14 Fam. Law 17 (C.A.). The facts of this case were exceptional. The period of separation from the mother was eight years.

[23] Making orders against the wishes of an older child can be futile: see M. v. M. (Minors: Custody Appeal) [1987] 1 W.L.R. 404.

[24] Ingham v. Ingham (1976) 73 L.S.Gaz. 486.

[25] Re T. (a minor) (1974) 4 Fam. Law 48.

suffering from illness or disability, a medical report will be ordered. If the child is attending a child guidance clinic, a report from the clinic will be ordered. The accommodation offered by the parties and other material advantages may be relevant, but the welfare of the child should not be equated with the wealth of the parent. Obviously, however, if one party has no suitable accommodation to offer the child, this may be of decisive importance.

The religious convictions of the parents and child will not usually be significant, particularly if the child is young. However, if the child has deep religious beliefs, the continuity of his religious upbringing may be of vital importance if any break would cause emotional disturbance. Consequently, custody of the child would probably be granted to the parent most likely to ensure such continuity.[26] Similar considerations will apply to the country or cultural background from which the parents and child come.

Such background information will usually be obtained by means of a welfare report which is nearly always ordered in disputed cases. The report will usually conclude with an opinion of the welfare officer regarding the custody of the child. The judge may, of course, follow this opinion, but he is in no way bound to do so.

ACCESS   16–17

It follows from section 1 of the G.M.A. 1971, quoted above, that the welfare of the child is the first and paramount consideration in determining questions of access as well as of custody. Judges usually consider it to be in the child's best interests for contact to be maintained with both parents, so it is unusual for access to be refused altogether.[27] Cases where access has been refused have been either cases where the parent has been shown to be unfit to have contact with the child (for example, by ill-treatment[28]) or cases where access is opposed by the child, or has at least had a detrimental effect on the child's health.

Although in this latter type of case the parent refused access may naturally feel aggrieved, since they may have

[26] Re M. [1967] 3 All E.R. 1071.
[27] M. v. M. [1973] 2 All E.R. 81, recognises access as the right of the child. However in Re K.D. (a Minor) (access: principles) [1988] 2 F.L.R. 139, the House of Lords held that a natural parent had a "right" to access.
[28] There is no settled principle that access should be refused in cases where the father has abused the child and each case must be considered on its merits. See L. v. L. [1989] 2 F.L.R. 16.

treated the child well, the courts justify the refusal by emphasising that the welfare of the child is of paramount importance. If the child shows positively, by words or conduct, that he does not want to see the non-custodial parent, it would be wrong to make an access order.

16–18 However, where a child is merely reluctant to have access, perhaps because he has not seen the parent for some time or because he has been encouraged by the custodial parent to think ill of the other party, the court sometimes tries to encourage contact by ordering supervised access. This takes place under the supervision of a third party, sometimes a social worker or a mutual friend. Unfortunately such visits are often not successful, but in some cases sufficient improvement in the relationship is achieved to allow normal access to be enjoyed in the future.

As mentioned above, if access is refused by the custodial parent, enforcement can be extremely difficult. Although committal for disobedience of an access order is possible, it is likely to be contrary to the child's interests for its parent to be sent to prison.

In fact, in many cases distress is caused to the child by the unwillingness of the non-custodial parent to avail himself of the access which he is allowed. There is, of course, no way to compel a parent to see his child, despite the courts' suggestion in some cases that access is the child's right.

16–19 4. The Jurisdictions

In this section three of the jurisdictions under which custody orders may be made are considered.
These are:

(i) the jurisdiction of the divorce court under section 42 of the M.C.A. 1973;

(ii) the jurisdiction of magistrates' courts under section 8 of the D.P.M.C.A. 1978;

(iii) the jurisdiction of the High Court, county courts and magistrates' courts under the G.M.A. 1971.

The Family Law Act 1986 lays down detailed rules governing the jurisdiction of the courts to make custody orders. These may be briefly summarised as follows.

The jurisdiction of the divorce court depends on the court's having jurisdiction to deal with the petition itself. (These jurisdictional rules are considered at 4–02 to 4–10 above).

The jurisdiction of the other courts in proceedings under the D.P.M.C.A. 1978 and G.M.A. 1971 depends on the child concerned being:

(i)   habitually resident in England and Wales,

or

(ii) present in England and Wales and not habitually resident elsewhere in the United Kingdom.[29]

Even if one of these conditions is satisfied, jurisdiction may still be excluded if divorce proceedings involving the child's parents are in progress in Scotland or Northern Ireland.[30]

In addition, an English court which does have jurisdiction to make a custody order may still refuse to do so if the matter has already been decided, or is currently being decided, in proceedings outside England and Wales.[31]

ORDERS UNDER SECTION 42 OF THE MATRIMONIAL CAUSES ACT 1973

(i) Powers of the court   16–20
Section 42 of the M.C.A. 1973 provides that, in proceedings for divorce, nullity or judicial separation, the court can, at any time, make an order regarding the custody of a child of the family who is under 18. This, of course, includes orders relating to access. The definition of a child of the family was considered earlier at 3–69. A custody order can be made even if the petition is dismissed.[32]

Section 42 also gives the court power to make custody orders on an application for maintenance under section 27 of the M.C.A. 1973 (failure to provide reasonable maintenance). In this case, however, a custody order can be made only if an order for financial provision is made, and the custody order will remain in force only for as long as the financial provision order.

---

[29] See the Family Law Act 1986, ss.2 and 3.
[30] *Ibid.* s.3(3).
[31] *Ibid.* s.5.
[32] The application for a custody order must be made on or before the dismissal of the petition.

Once a custody order is made it will continue (subject to further orders of the court) until the child attains the age of 18 or until the custodial parent dies. In the latter case the surviving parent normally has the right to custody of the child.

16–21 It is, however, provided in section 42(3) of the M.C.A. 1973 that the court may declare that the other party is unfit to have custody of any child of the family. This means that he will lose his automatic right to custody of the child on the death of the custodial parent. Such orders are extremely rare and will not be made unless there are strong reasons for so doing.[33]

16–22 The divorce court may make split or joint custody orders. A "split order" is an order whereby care and control is given to one party, but custody in the narrow sense is given to the other.[34] Such orders are today considered undesirable.[35] It is clearly unfair, and impracticable, for the party who has the responsibility for the day-to-day welfare of the child to be denied the right to decide on matters such as his education and religious upbringing. Only in the most exceptional case should a split order be made nowadays; for example, where it is necessary for the child's general welfare that one parent should have care and control, but that parent would refuse consent to a blood transfusion on religious grounds. In such a case the other parent might be granted custody so that the necessary consent could be given without delay.

A "joint order" is an order whereby one parent has care and control, but custody in the narrow sense is shared by both parties. Such orders used to be extremely rare until recently, but are now recognised as desirable in cases where the parties are prepared to co-operate in deciding the broad questions concerning a child's upbringing.[36]

It is arguable, however, that joint orders are unnecessary. Even where the court has awarded custody, care and control solely to one parent, the other retains certain rights. Subject to any court order, these include reasonable access, the right not to have the child's surname changed without his consent

---

[33] For example, where the father had been guilty of ill-treatment of the child. See also *B.* v. *B.* (1979) 3 F.L.R. 187.

[34] *Wakeham* v. *Wakeham* [1954] 1 All E.R. 434 (C.A.).

[35] See *Dipper* v. *Dipper* [1981] Fam. 31.

[36] In *Caffell* v. *Caffell* [1984] F.L.R. 169 (C.A.), the Court of Appeal held that, despite an acrimonious relationship between the parents, a joint custody order was desirable and might ease the bitterness between the parties. This case may encourage the making of joint custody orders where the parties do not get on.

and the right to veto adoption. Besides this, in *Dipper* v. *Dipper*,[37] two members of the Court of Appeal said that a non-custodial parent must also be consulted about such broader issues as the child's religion and education, thus enabling him to bring the matter before the court to resolve any dispute. It seems, therefore, that an order for joint custody only makes obvious, rights which are implied already. Nevertheless such an order will often reassure a non-custodial parent who is worried about losing contact with his children.

Exceptionally the court may make care orders (considered below, at 18–38) or supervision orders, placing a child under the supervision of a welfare officer or local authority. A supervision order might be made if there is some risk of harm to the child, or where the parent is being given care after some lengthy period of separation from the child. **16–23**

(ii) Procedure **16–24**
The petitioner seeking custody should apply for it in the petition. The same applies to a defending respondent who should apply in the answer. Failure to so apply, however, is no bar to a subsequent application to the court at any time.

If custody is not in dispute, it is likely that the judge will deal with this at the children appointment. This has been considered in the chapter on divorce procedure (see 4–78, above). Otherwise the procedure is as follows.

File notice of application and supporting affidavit plus court fee To instigate custody proceedings by either party where there is a dispute, a notice of application for custody on the general form of notice[38] and one copy should be sent to the court. The notice will usually be supported by an affidavit or affidavits.

Serve copies on the respondent When the copy notice of application is returned by the court, it should be served on the other party by post together with a copy of the affidavit or affidavits that were filed at court.

Affidavit in reply by respondent On receipt, the other party will file an affidavit or affidavits in reply and serve a copy on the applicant. Further affidavits may then be filed by either side.

---

[37] [1981] Fam. 31.
[38] Notice under C.C.R. 1981, Ord. 13, r. 1. This should not be confused with notices on Form 11 or 13, which are restricted to applications for financial provision.

Welfare report ordered In a contested case the court will usually decide that a welfare report should be prepared (see above, at 16–16). An application should be made to the registrar for such an order.

Application for a hearing date Once the report has been prepared, and the parties are ready, the case will be set down for a hearing before the judge.[39]

The hearing The judge will wish to hear oral evidence from all parties, step-parents, witnesses and, in some cases, the child. The order will then be made. The same procedure is followed if the dispute relates to access.

The topic of conciliation was discussed at 1–08 *et seq.* In a small number of courts a conciliation hearing may be fixed. In the Principal Registry this will be immediately after the notice of application is filed. This is attended by the parties and their advisers and any child over ten. The appointment is before a registrar, attended by a court welfare officer. The parties and their advisers are given the opportunity of having a private consultation with the welfare officer to attempt to reach an agreement. If the meeting is successfully concluded the registrar will then make the order agreed.[40] If not then the matter proceeds as normal.

16–25 **(iii) Link between declarations as to satisfaction under section 41 of the Matrimonial Causes Act 1973 and custody orders**
In view of the difficulties often experienced in understanding the connection between section 41 declarations and custody, there now follows a case-study to illustrate how these are linked in disputed cases. (For undisputed matters, see 4–78 and for the detail on section 41 declarations, see 3–63 to 3–73.

Example

Mandy and Fred have one child, Simon, who is aged 12. They are both seeking sole custody of Simon. Mandy left Fred six weeks ago, having decided that their marriage was over. She has committed adultery with John, whom she first met over a year ago, and has moved into John's house. Fred has refused to allow Simon to join his mother, and is about to petition for divorce on the basis of her adultery. The steps for resolving the dispute are set out below:

---

[39] A registrar may make orders for custody or access where there is no dispute between the parties. The only contested matter with which he may deal is a dispute as to the amount of access.

[40] See Practice Direction [1982] 1 W.L.R. 1420. Note also Practice Direction [1984] 3 All E.R. 800.

("*F*" represents Fred's solicitor, "*M*" represents Mandy's solicitor.)

1. *F* files the petition and supporting documents. The petition includes a claim for custody of Simon.

2. A copy of the petition and the statement of arrangements and Form 5 and 6 are served on *M*. Copies of petition and Form 5 and 6 are served on John.

3. John and *M* return the acknowledgments of service to the court, showing no intention to defend. *M*'s acknowledgment indicates an intention to apply for custody, and admits the adultery.

4. *M* files at the court a notice of application for custody and one copy, supported by affidavits from Mandy and John.

5. On return of the copy notice of application from the court, *M* serves it and copies of the affidavits on *F*.

6. *F* applies for directions for trial for the divorce, and files an affidavit in support of the petition and an affidavit in answer to the application for custody. He serves a copy of the custody application and affidavit on *M*.

7. The registrar sets down the petition in the special procedure list, but gives no date for a section 41 children appointment.[41]

8. Decree Nisi pronounced.

9. *M* writes to *F* requesting consent to a welfare report being ordered.

10. *F* writes giving consent.

11. *M* makes *ex parte* application (files notice of application supported by letter) to registrar with a copy of *F*'s consent to order.

12. Registrar orders a welfare report.[42]

---

[41] As to the possibility of applying for a children appointment and the powers of the court in such circumstances, see 4–72, above.

[42] A welfare report can be requested by the court of its own motion: M.C.R. 1977, r. 95(1). Alternatively the procedure illustrated can be followed, whereby one, or both, of the parties applies to the registrar for a welfare report: M.C.R. 1977, r. 95(2).

13. The welfare officer reports to the court; a copy is sent to *F* and *M*.

14. *M* contacts *F* for confirmation of readiness for trial and applies for a hearing date by writing to court with a time estimate.

15. At the hearing, the judge reads the affidavits, hears oral evidence from Fred, Mandy and John, reads the welfare report and sees Simon in private.
Simon confirms he wishes to live with his mother. The welfare report is in the mother's favour. The judge feels that John would make an excellent stepfather and orders custody to the mother.
The judge then makes a section 41 declaration stating that he is satisfied with the arrangements for Simon.

16. Decree Absolute is applied for and granted.

16–26 **(iv) Removal from jurisdiction**
Having decided who should have custody, the court will ensure that certain other terms are included in the order.

Permanent removal

Rule 94(2) of the M.C.R. 1977 provides that, unless otherwise directed, the order shall provide for the child not to be removed from England and Wales without leave of the court. An application for such leave should only be refused if the interests of the child and those of the parent with custody are incompatible.[43]

Therefore, for example, if the parent is considering emigrating to Australia with the child, and suitable arrangements have been made for the child's education and welfare, the court's leave is likely to be forthcoming. Of course, the non-custodial parent is likely, in such circumstances, to lose all direct contact with the child.

Temporary removal

Rule 94(2) of the M.C.R. 1977 allows the court to specify the terms on which a child may be removed temporarily from the jurisdiction. Clearly this will be relevant in the case of

---

[43] *Chamberlain* v. *De la Mere* [1983] 4 F.L.R. 434 (C.A.). Note also *Tyler* v. *Tyler* [1989] 2 F.L.R. 158 where leave was refused because of the children's close bond with the non-custodial parent.

holidays. The order will usually provide that one parent may remove the child, without leave, upon lodging at court the written consent of the other party, together with an undertaking to return the child at the end of an agreed period. If the other parent is not prepared to consent, an application for leave must be made to the court.

(v) Changing the child's name
16–27

Rule 92(8) of the M.C.R. 1977 provides that the order should contain a provision that the parent shall not, without the written consent of the other parent, or leave of a judge, take any step which will result in the children being known by a new surname before they are 18 (or, if female, before marrying under that age).

In contested cases, as in all disputes relating to children, the child's welfare is the first and paramount consideration. There are two possible views, however, of the matter.

It is often argued that a child should be encouraged to identify with his new family. This will ease the distress caused by his parents' marital breakdown. Where the child remains with his mother, his natural father has little contact with him and his mother has remarried, it is likely that changing the child's name will avoid the embarrassment which he will suffer if his surname remains that of his natural father.

However, in the case of W. v. A.,[44] the Court of Appeal rejected this approach. The court took the view that the child's name is a vital part of his identity and an invaluable aid in reinforcing the link with his natural father. In W. v. A. the court, whilst allowing the child to emigrate to Australia with his mother and stepfather, refused to allow a change of name. (It would be interesting to know what happened to the child's surname once the family reached Australia.)

ANCILLARY TO AN ORDER UNDER THE DOMESTIC PROCEEDINGS AND MAGISTRATES' COURTS ACT 1978

(i) Powers of the court
16–28

The magistrates' court must always consider the question of custody whenever an application is made for financial provision under sections 2, 6 or 7 of the D.P.M.C.A. 1978. (This has been considered earlier in Chapter 14.) The court can make orders for custody and access on such applications, irrespective of whether it makes an order for financial

---

[44] [1981] Fam. 14.

provision under these three sections. As has already been mentioned, magistrates' courts use the Children Act terminology of "legal" and "actual" custody and "parental rights and duties."

Section 8 enables the magistrates' court to make orders as to legal custody of a child of the family who is under 18. By section 8(4), legal custody can only be granted to one person, but the court can order that the party who is not given legal custody shall retain such parental rights and duties (other than actual custody) as it may specify, in which case these will be held jointly with the person having legal custody. A "split order" giving legal custody to one party and actual custody to the other is, therefore, not possible.

If the court wishes to award legal custody to a person other than one of the parties to the marriage, it may do so if that person is the natural parent.[45] For example, where a wife has a child by her first husband and takes proceedings against her second husband for financial provision, the court has power to award legal custody to the child's natural father.

16–29 Should the court be minded to award legal custody to some person other than a party to the marriage, or a parent of the child (*e.g.* a relative or foster parent), it can do so only by directing that he be treated as an applicant for a custodianship order.[46]

16–30 The court can order access in favour of the non-custodial parent. Additionally the court can order access in favour of grandparents, once an order for legal custody has been made.[47] This is occasionally useful, as the custodial parent may seek to isolate herself, not only from her spouse, but also from his family. This may cause distress to children who have formed a close attachment to their grandparents.

A custody order may be made even though the parents are living in the same household. This may be useful if they are about to separate. The custody order will continue even if, after separation, they resume living together. If, however, they live together for a continuous period exceeding six months, the order will cease to have effect.[48]

Like the divorce court, the magistrates may make care or supervision orders.[49] Periodical payments can be ordered from

---

[45] D.P.M.C.A. 1978, s.8(3).
[46] D.P.M.C.A. 1978, s.8(3) and C.A. 1975, s.33, and see 16–08, above.
[47] D.P.M.C.A. 1978, s.14.
[48] *Ibid.* s.25.
[49] *Ibid.* ss.9 and 10.

either party to the marriage to support the child. (This is dealt with earlier, at 14–37).

(ii) Procedure 16–31

Custody orders under section 8 are made ancillary to an application for financial provision. This procedure has been dealt with at 14–43 to 14–58, above.

Two further points should be noted:

Notice of the proceedings should be given to a parent who is not a party to the proceedings. The parent (including the father of an illegitimate child) is entitled to appear and be represented.[50]

Interim orders for custody or access may be made if special circumstances make this desirable; for example, where an adjournment is requested by one of the parties to apply for legal representation. Only one interim order can be made, and it will last for a maximum period of three months. It can however be extended for a further period of three months.[51] Such a power might be useful, for example, to allow the parties to attempt a reconciliation.

(iii) Removal from jurisdiction 16–32

The court may direct that no person may remove the child from the United Kingdom without leave of the court.[52] However, unlike orders made by the divorce court, such a direction will not be included automatically but only on an application being made for its inclusion.

GUARDIANSHIP OF MINORS ACT 1971 16–33

The original importance of this Act was that it introduced a jurisdiction to enable parents, whose only dispute related to the custody of their child, to apply to the court under section 9 of the G.M.A. 1971 for an order determining that question. Under this jurisdiction "the court" may be the High Court, the county court or the magistrates' court.

Unlike the other jurisdictions available to the parties for the determination of custody disputes, the G.M.A. 1971 can be used by the parents of children whether or not those parents are married to each other. Indeed, section 9 is rarely used by

---

[50] *Ibid.* s.12.
[51] *Ibid.* s.19.
[52] *Ibid.* s.34 as amended by the Family Law Act 1986, s.35.

parties to a marriage, because they usually want some further relief, such as divorce, or financial provision, for themselves.

16–34 **(i) The powers of the court**

Custody and access

Under section 9, the court has power to make orders as to legal custody and access in respect of the child on the application of either parent. It is immaterial whether the parents are married or not.

The court cannot make "split orders" under this jurisdiction. Section 11A of the G.M.A. 1971 prevents the court from awarding legal custody to one parent and actual custody to the other in terms very similar to those used in section 8(4) of the D.P.M.C.A. 1978, referred to in 16–28, (above).

Under section 9, the court can give legal custody of a child only to its mother or father. However, if the court considers that some other person should have legal custody, it can make a custodianship order in favour of that person.[53] The court can make access orders in favour of the non-custodial parent. It can also award access to a grandparent, once an order for legal custody has been made, in the same way as the magistrates can under the D.P.M.C.A. 1978 (see 16–30, above). Under the G.M.A. 1971, however, the court can also make an access order in favour of a grandparent if the child of that grandparent (being the natural parent of the child) is dead.[54]

As under the D.P.M.C.A. 1978, a custody order may be made under the G.M.A. 1971 even if the parents are still living together, although the order will lapse if they marry each other or remain or resume living together for a continuous period exceeding six months after the order is made.[55]

As under the previous jurisdictions, the court may, in exceptional circumstances, make supervision and care orders in respect of a child on an application under section 9.[56]

16–35 *Financial provision and property adjustment*

Under section 11B of the G.M.A. 1971 (inserted by the F.L.R.A. 1987), either parent of a child may apply to the court

---

[53] C.A. 1975, s.37(3).
[54] G.M.A. 1971, s.14A.
[55] G.A. 1973, s.5A.
[56] G.A. 1973, s.2(2), as amended.

for an order against the other parent for various forms of financial relief in favour of their child.

Magistrates' courts can make orders for:

   (i)   ordinary periodical payments;

   (ii) lump sums of up to £1,000.

The High Court and county courts can make orders for:

   (i)   ordinary periodical payments,

   (ii)   secured periodical payments,

   (iii) lump sums of any amount,

   (iv)   transfer of property to the child,

   (v)   settlement of property on the child.

Applications for this financial relief might well be made at the same time as a custody application under section 9, but orders under section 11B do not depend on a custody order having been made as well. Furthermore, section 11B can be invoked by the mother of a child born outside marriage who is seeking support for the child from the putative father. (Chapter 15, above, is devoted to the question of financial provision for the "unmarried family.")

As with custody orders under the G.M.A. 1971, orders for periodical payments can be made even if the parties are still living together, but will lapse if they marry each other, or cohabitation continues or is resumed for a continuous period exceeding six months after the order is made.[57]

(ii) Procedure   16–36

This varies depending on the court in which the proceedings are brought. In general, it will follow the usual procedure in that type of court.

Magistrates' court   16–37

Here the proceedings will be by way of complaint. A summons will be issued by the court and served on the respondent. As is usual with the magistrates' court, no

---

[57] G.A. 1973, s.5A.

affidavit or other written evidence will be filed; evidence will be given orally at the hearing. A welfare report or report of a probation officer may be requested and usually will be, in contested cases. The proceedings must be dealt with by a domestic court.

16–38 *County court*

All county courts have jurisdiction under the G.M.A. 1971; there is no need to proceed in a divorce county court. An originating application is made and served on the respondent. This will usually be supported by an affidavit from the applicant, and an affidavit in reply will be filed by the respondent. A welfare report will usually be ordered in contested cases. At the hearing oral evidence will usually be given as well.

As with the procedure ancillary to divorce, a judge, not a registrar, will deal with contested custody matters.

16–39 *High Court*

The application is by originating summons filed by the plaintiff. Affidavit evidence will be given with oral evidence at the hearing. A welfare report will normally be ordered. As in the county court, a judge will deal with contested custody summonses.

An interim order may be made pending the final determination of the application.[58]

16–40 **(iii) Removal from jurisdiction**
The order may contain a direction, on an application being made, that the child shall not be removed from the jurisdiction, as in the magistrates' court under the D.P.M.C.A. 1978.[59]

16–41 SUPPLEMENTAL POWERS

The Family Law Act 1986 contains certain provisions which increase the powers of the courts in the above jurisdictions to enable further directions to be given in custody proceedings. Section 33 gives all courts the power to require any person to disclose information relating to the whereabouts of a child.

---

[58] G.A. 1973, s.2(4).
[59] G.M.A. 1971, s.13A. See also 16–32 above.

Further, where the court orders that a child should be delivered to another person (*e.g.* from the father to the mother), section 34 empowers the court to authorise an officer of the court or a constable to take the child and deliver him as directed.

5. Choice of Jurisdiction   16–42

In certain circumstances only one jurisdiction will be available to deal with the question of custody. For example, if the parents are not married and the father seeks custody, he can only instigate proceedings under the G.M.A. 1971, unless he is prepared to take wardship proceedings (as to which, see Chapter 18).

However, in the vast majority of cases, all the jurisdictions will be available. The question of choosing the most appropriate jurisdiction then arises. Most of the factors that will influence this choice have already been referred to in this chapter, and for convenience these are summarised in the comparison chart[60] set out below. (The chart includes a reference to wardship,[61] which is discussed in Chapter 18).

Besides the factors summarised in the chart, the availability of legal aid may also be an important factor. Two points in particular must be borne in mind.

(a) The fact that the Legal Aid Board, in its *Legal Aid*   16–43
Handbook, emphasises the need to avoid a multiplicity of actions.[62] If, for example, an application has already been made under the D.P.M.C.A. 1978 for periodical payments, custody should be dealt with under this jurisdiction as well.

(b) The fact that the Legal Aid Board encourages the use of   16–44
the magistrates' court where possible, presumably because it is the least expensive forum. Consequently, if proceedings under the G.M.A. 1971 are contemplated and

---

[60] The chart is not comprehensive and does not, for example, include any reference to custody orders made in proceedings brought under M.C.A. 1973, s.27.

[61] In the wardship jurisdiction, custody of the ward is vested in the court which means that the court can only make orders for care and control and access. See 18–03, where this matter is considered further.

[62] (1990), p. 59. A.B.W.O.R. rather than legal aid, will normally be sought where proceedings are taken in the magistrates' court.

legal aid is required, the proceedings should normally be taken in the magistrates' court.

	M.C.A. (decree)	D.P.M.C.A.	G.M.A.	Wardship
Spouses can instigate proceedings for custody and access re. child of the family	*	*	*	*(for care & control)
Unmarried parents can instigate proceedings for custody and access			*	*(for care & control)
Any person can instigate proceedings				*(for care & control)
The court uses the concepts of parental rights and duties and actual and legal custody		*	*	
The court uses the concepts of custody care and control	*			*
The court can make care and supervision orders on an application for custody	*	*	*	*
The court can make orders for periodical payments for the child	*	*	*	*
The court can make orders for periodical payments and lump sums for the child	*	*	*	
The court can make orders for property adjustment for the child	*		*	
The court can make further orders for financial provision for the applicant	*	*		

	M.C.A. (decree)	D.P.M.C.A.	G.M.A.	Wardship
The court can make further orders for property adjustment for applicant and grant a decree	*			

17. Orders made under the Children Act 1989 in Family Proceedings

17–01 1. Introduction

The Children Act 1989 is not expected to come into force until, at the earliest, October 1991. It is recommended that this chapter is ignored, for practical purposes, until the Act is in force, the existing law being contained in Chapter 16.

For a full appreciation of the impact of the Children Act, particularly on procedure, we will have to wait for regulations to be published under the Act. Again, these are not expected for some time.

In the tradition of commentaries on Acts of Parliament which have been passed but are not yet in force, we have stated the new law as if it is in force and have used the present, rather than the future, tense throughout.

17–02 THE EFFECT OF THE ACT

The law relating to the obligations towards, rights over, and overall care for children was inconsistent, fragmented and covered by a variety of statutory and common law provisions. Much of the variety of the possible orders relating to children can be seen from Chapter 16. The Children Act, which repeals most of the old law and reforms the principles of the law relating to children, has been described by the Lord Chancellor as "the most comprehensive and far reaching reform of child law which has come before Parliament in living memory."[1]

The Act is deceptive. At first glance it seems as if all that has been done is that the terms "custody" and "access" have been replaced by "residence" and "contact" orders (otherwise known as section 8 orders). Of course this is partly true, but it is only when the full meaning of such new concepts as parental responsibilities and the exact effect, and full range, of

[1] H.L.Deb. Col. 488, December 6th, 1988.

362

section 8 orders is appreciated that one begins to see just how true are the words of the Lord Chancellor (quoted above).

Perhaps one of the most difficult things that parents, practitioners and the courts have to come to terms with is that no orders are to be made automatically in relation to children when families break up. It is only where the specific need arises that the court will make, for example, a contact order, and this will stand alone; there will be no need for a residence order first.

DEFINITION OF FAMILY PROCEEDINGS   17–03

The courts are able to make orders relating to children in "family proceedings." The Act[2] defines family proceedings as:

(i) Proceedings under the inherent jurisdiction of the High Court in relation to children. This will include wardship proceedings.[3]

(ii) Proceedings under Parts I, II, and IV of the Act. Parts I and II will be dealt with in this Chapter. Part IV deals with Care and Supervision orders and will be covered in Chapter 19.

(iii) Proceedings under the Matrimonial Causes Act 1973.

(iv) Proceedings under the Domestic Violence and Matrimonial Proceedings Act 1976.

(v) Proceedings under the Adoption Act 1976. These are outside the scope of this book.

(vi) Proceedings under the Domestic Proceedings and Magistrates' Courts Act 1978.

(vii) Proceedings under the Matrimonial Homes Act 1983, sections 1 and 9.

(viii) Proceedings under the Matrimonial and Family Proceedings Act 1984, Part III. This deals with financial orders following a foreign decree.

As can be seen, broadly speaking, in any proceedings where   17–04
children might be involved the Act will apply. Whilst the principles which govern orders in relation to children under all these jurisdictions will be considered together, the

---

[2] C.A. 1989, s.8(3) and (4).
[3] This does not include proceedings by local authorities under C.A. 1989, s.100(3), for leave to invoke the courts' inherent jurisdiction.

procedural implications will be considered separately at 17–31 to 17–35 below.

17–05 2. General Principles

NON-INTERVENTION

One of the most innovative principles contained in the Act is the so-called non-intervention principle. Section 1(5) provides:

> "Where a court is considering whether or not to make one or more orders under this Act with respect to a child, it shall not make the order, or any of the orders, unless it considers that doing so would be better for the child than making no order at all."

The Law Commission[4] was of the view that, where a child already had a good relationship with both parents, the court should not make orders unnecessarily as this could disturb that relationship. Parents do not cease to be parents because they are divorced and the parental responsibility of both parents is seen to be a continuing responsibility.

17–06 It is certainly true that under the old law and procedure the tendency was for courts always to make orders for custody and access whenever a family case came before it. An example of this can be seen in divorce proceedings. Under the old procedure, after *decree nisi* there was usually a children appointment at which custody and access orders were often made and the judge would grant a declaration as to his satisfaction with the arrangements for the children. This was always done even where there was no dispute regarding the children, so these orders were, arguably, totally unnecessary. The non-intervention principle introduced by the C.A. 1989 means that in future, where there is no dispute regarding the children on divorce, the court will make no orders at all in respect of them. (The Act continues the safety net of reviews of the arrangements for the children but no order may be necessary see 4–93, above.)

This principle continues into care orders, as to which see 19–06 to 19–19 below.

17–07 WELFARE OF THE CHILD

The Act maintains the principle that it is the child's interests that are effectively the only governing factor that will

[4] Report on Guardianship and Custody (No. 172 (1988)).

determine his upbringing. Section 1(1) provides: " ... The child's welfare shall be the court's paramount consideration." This re-enacts the provision of section 1 of the Guardianship of Minors Act 1971. Under that Act the child's interests were the "*first and* paramount consideration." The omission of the word "first" is not intended to change the law. It is a recognition of the fact that the word was unnecessary and added nothing to the meaning of the provision. (See 16–12 above where the meaning of this expression is considered more fully.)

There is no change, however, to the determination of other **17–08** disputes relating to the breakdown of the relationship between the parties, even though they may involve the interests of the children. For example, there is no change to the factors to be considered by the courts when contemplating making an order excluding a parent from the matrimonial home or making an order for ancillary relief on divorce.

Under the old law there were no statutory guidelines to help **17–09** the court apply the welfare principle. A large body of case law had been developed which identified certain principles to be applied in determining disputes relating to a child. Some of these principles have now been introduced into the Act as statutory guidelines. Section 1(3) provides that, where the court is considering making, varying or discharging a section 8 order in contested proceedings or where it is considering making a care or supervision order under the Act, it shall have particular regard to:

(a) the ascertainable wishes and feelings of the child concerned (considered in the light of his age and understanding);

(b) his physical, emotional and educational needs;

(c) the likely effect on him of any change in his circumstances;

(d) his age, sex, background and any characteristics of his which the court considers relevant;

(e) any harm which he has suffered or is at risk of suffering;

(f) how capable each of his parents, and any other person in relation to whom the court considers the question to be relevant, is of meeting his needs;

(g) the range of powers available to the court under this Act in the proceedings in question.

There is no attempt to give any guidance as to the relative importance of the factors.

17–10 The Law Commission saw the list as providing greater consistency and clarity in the law. However, it is extremely unlikely that this list will produce any change in the way that cases are decided and therefore the old case law will continue to be very relevant. The attitude of the courts to questions of custody and access can be seen at 16–12 to 16–18, above.

17–11 PARENTAL RESPONSIBILITY

This concept replaces the old ideas of "rights and authority of a parent" under the Guardianship Act 1973 and "parental rights and duties" in the Children Act 1975.[5] It is defined by section 3(1) as: *"all the rights, duties, powers, responsibilities and authority which by law a parent of a child has in relation to the child and his property."* This is similar to the definition in the Children Act 1975 and is not particularly helpful. It is designed to be as broad as possible and it is clear that the exact extent of parental responsibility will depend on the nature of the circumstances and the age of the child.[6]

Where a child's father and mother were married to each other at the time of his birth, they each have parental responsibility for the child. Where the parents were not married when the child was born the mother has sole parental responsibility. Adopted children and children whose parents marry subsequent to their birth are treated as if their parents were married at birth.[7] Where more than one person has parental responsibility at the same time, each may act alone.

17–12 An unmarried father may acquire parental responsibility by agreement (in a prescribed form) with the mother or by court order.[8] Parental responsibility can be acquired by an unmarried father or a non-parent in other ways under the Act, for example, where a residence order is made.[9]

In practical terms the person with parental responsibility has (in the absence of any order to the contrary) the legal

---

[5] See 16–02 and 16–09.
[6] See *Gillick* v. *West Norfolk and Wisbech Area Health Authority* [1986] 1 A.C. 112.
[7] Family Law Reform Act 1987, s.1, and Legitimacy Act 1976 ss.1 and 10.
[8] C.A. 1989, s.4.
[9] C.A. 1989, s.12.

authority to decide such matters as education, medical treatment, where the child is to live, what name he is to have and all other aspects of his upbringing and welfare.

(i) Loss of parental responsibility   **17–13**
It is not possible for someone who has parental responsibility to surrender or transfer it.[10] Therefore it cannot be lost or given away by a parent, and this is true even if the child is taken into care. In the same way, the person with parental responsibility will not cease to have it solely because another person subsequently acquires it,[11] for example, where a residence order is made in favour of a non-parent.

However, it will be lost in the following circumstances:

(a) if an adoption order is made; or

(b) if parental responsibility has been obtained by agreement or court order (for example, by an unmarried father), it may be terminated by court order.

(ii) Delegation of parental responsibility   **17–14**
Although the primary responsibility for a child cannot be transferred, it can be delegated,[12] for example to a babysitter or a school. The person with parental responsibility would, however, still incur liability under the civil or criminal law if the child suffered harm as a result of his failure to satisfy himself that the arrangements for temporary care of the child were adequate.[13]

3. Section 8 Orders   **17–15**

The old law was a complex tangle of differing terminologies and concepts which caused much confusion and many inconsistencies. In particular there were limitations on the orders available dependent on the status of the applicant. All this has been swept away so that, broadly, in all proceedings the same orders are available and the same terminology is used. These new orders, which are collectively known as "section 8 orders," replace custody, access and guardianship orders and can be made in matrimonial and other proceedings.

Section 8(1) defines the new orders and they will be considered in turn.

---

[10] C.A. 1989, s.2(9).
[11] C.A. 1989, s.2(6).
[12] C.A. 1989, s.2(9).
[13] C.A. 1989, s.2(11).

17–16   RESIDENCE ORDER

This is defined as:

"an order settling the arrangements to be made as to the person with whom the child is to live."

Clearly this is a very similar concept to the old order for "care and control." On marriage breakdown the court is able to make residence orders in favour of both parents, which would not have been the case under the old law.[14] In this case the court can specify the time to be spent in each household.[15] Residence orders will not remove parental responsibility but, where one is made in favour of a party who would not otherwise have parental responsibility, (for example, an unmarried father) the residence order will confer parental responsibility on that party.[16]

17–17   The end result of this seems to be that although, in the majority of situations, one party will have possession of the child, both parents will have a say in questions of its upbringing, for example, where it goes to school or what religion it follows. This is similar, in the context of divorce, to a joint custody order in favour of the parties, care and control being given to one of them.[17] Where the concepts differ is that under the Act both parents have parental responsibility, therefore they can take unilateral decisions regarding such matters without referral to the other parent. Although the position was uncertain under the old law, joint custody probably meant that major decisions had to be made jointly.

The effect of this, then, is that the parent who has *de facto* possession of the child can take major decisions without referral to the other parent. If the other parent does object, he could apply for a specific issue order (see 17–20, below).

17–18   *Example*

Adam and Eve have a son, Cain. Following divorce there is a dispute between the parties over where Cain is to live. The court makes a residence order in favour of Eve. By arrangement Cain stays with Adam periodically. Eve decides which school Cain will attend and, although it is hoped that she will consult Adam, there is no

---

[14] *Riley* v. *Riley* [1986] 2 F.L.R. 429.
[15] C.A. 1989, s.11(4).
[16] C.A. 1989, ss.12(1) and (2).
[17] See 16–22. It would seem to follow the principles laid down in the case of *Dipper* v. *Dipper* [1981] Fam. 31.

*obligation on her to do so. Indeed if Adam wishes to object to her
decision he must apply to the court for a specific issue order.*

*During a visit to his father Cain falls and breaks his arm. Adam
takes Cain to hospital where an operation is required to reset the
arm. Adam can give consent without reference to Eve.*

*The Act does, however, provide that nothing may be done in the
exercise of parental responsibility in a way which is incompatible
with a court order relating to the child.*[18] *If Adam refuses to return
Cain to Eve then she will be able to enforce her order. (See 17–29,
below for enforcement powers.)*

CONTACT ORDER

17–19

This is defined as:

> "an order requiring the person with whom the child
> lives, or is to live, to allow the child to visit or stay with
> the person named in the order, or for that person and the
> child otherwise to have contact with each other."

This is very similar to the old access order and would seem to
embrace the old orders for defined access and staying
access.[19] It enables the court to be very explicit in its order
and would cover any form of contact, for example, telephone
calls or letters where one of the parties was living abroad.

Presumably it would be possible for the court to order
"reasonable contact" in the same way that it used to order
reasonable access. However, in view of the non-intervention
principle (see 17–05, above), in the majority of cases where
such an order would be appropriate the court may be minded
to make no order feeling that the parties should be left to
make arrangements between themselves.

SPECIFIC ISSUE ORDER

17–20

This is defined as:

> "an order giving directions for the purpose of determin-
> ing a specific question which has arisen, or which may
> arise, in connection with any aspect of parental respon-
> sibility for a child."

This will enable either parent (or others, see 17–32) to ask the
court to resolve some particular problem or dispute. It would

---

[18] C.A. 1989, s.2(8).
[19] See 16–06 and 16–07.

probably arise after the making of a residence or contact order, although it is not limited to use in that way.

17–21 *Example*

In the above example, Adam wishes to contest Eve's decision to send Cain to a local state school. He would like, and is prepared to pay for, Cain to attend a private boarding school some miles away, believing that this would provide a better education for Cain. Adam could apply for a specific issue order for the court to decide.

17–22 PROHIBITED STEPS ORDER

This is defined as:

> "an order that no step which could be taken by a parent in meeting his parental responsibility for a child, and which is of a kind specified in the order, shall be taken by any person without the consent of the court."

This power is seen as a means of reducing the circumstances in which it would be necessary to make a child a ward of court. This is considered at 19–02 to 19–04 below. Unlike wardship where no important step can be taken without the court's leave, under this provision the court would specify the prohibited step.

17–23 *Example*

John and Juanita separate with a view to divorce. John becomes concerned that Juanita may take their son Manuel to Mexico to live with her parents. One option available to John is to obtain a prohibited steps order to attempt to prevent this.

17–24 ## 4. Miscellaneous Provisions

WELFARE REPORTS

The court is given power to request a welfare report from the local authority or a probation officer in all proceedings under the Act.[20] This is designed to eliminate all the previous different pieces of legislation which authorised the provision of welfare reports. The court is entitled to take account of any statement in a report regardless of any rule of law which would otherwise prevent it, for example, the rule against hearsay evidence.

---

[20] See 16–26.

REMOVAL FROM THE JURISDICTION   **17–25**

Section 13 of the Act provides that where a residence order is in force a child may not be removed from the United Kingdom without either the consent of every person who has parental responsibility, or leave of the court. This is similar to, but not precisely the same as, the old automatic provision that was endorsed on custody orders on divorce under the old law.[21] There is no reason to suppose that the attitude of the courts to such cases will be any different than under the old law. This has been covered at 16–26.

There is a further provision to deal with temporary removals. Under section 13(2) the restriction on removal does not apply to temporary removals of less than one month. This is to facilitate foreign holidays.

CHANGE OF NAME   **17–26**

Section 13 also provides that no person may cause a child to be known by a new surname where a residence order is in force. A change is permitted only by court order or with the consent of every person who has parental responsibility. Again, it would seem that the old case law is still relevant and this has been dealt with at 16–27 above.

It is worth noting that both the above provisions only apply where a residence order has been made. If either problem should arise where a residence order has not been made, it will be necessary to apply for a prohibited steps order.

DIRECTIONS   **17–27**

Section 11(7) enables the court to give directions as to how an order is to be carried into effect. This may be particularly useful where there is to be a change in the existing arrangements.

Example

Sandra and Philip's relationship has broken up and Sandra has for many months forbidden her daughter, Tina to see her father. Tina has grown to distrust Philip as her mother has constantly blamed him for leaving them. The court on making a contact order may give directions so that the relationship builds up gradually over a period of time. Contact may be ordered once every three weeks at first for an hour at some neutral location, e.g. the grandparents' house, then this

[21] C.A. 1989, s.7(1).

would increase to every two weeks for two hours, then weekly at Philip's house.

17–28 CONDITIONS

Section 11(7) also enables the court to impose conditions when it makes a section 8 order. This could enable the court to deal with problems that may have arisen at the time the order is applied for. For example, the court could attach a condition to a residence order that the child should attend a particular school.

17–29 ENFORCEMENT

The court may order any person who may have information as to the child's whereabouts to disclose it to the court.[22] Where a person fails to hand over a child in breach of a section 8 order, the court can authorise an officer of the court or a constable to collect the child and take him to the person in whose favour the section 8 order is made.[23]

If a person is in breach of a residence order made by the High Court or a county court, then the person in whose favour the order was made may enforce it by proceedings for contempt. In a magistrates' court the order may be enforced, under section 63(3) of the Magistrates' Courts Act 1980, as if it were an order requiring the person in breach to produce the child to the person with the residence order. This enables the court to fine or imprison the person in breach.[24]

17–30 DURATION

Subject to the provisions below, orders last until the child's 18th birthday, unless they are discharged earlier by the making of another order.

(i) Section 8 orders will cease to have effect when the child is 16 unless the court orders otherwise, which it can only do if the circumstances of the case are exceptional.[25]

(ii) Residence and Contact orders will automatically cease to have effect if the parents live together for a continuous period of six months.[26]

[22] Family Law Act 1986, s.33.
[23] Family Law Act 1986, s.34, as amended by C.A. 1989, Sched. 13.
[24] C.A. 1989, s.14.
[25] C.A. 1989, ss.9(6) and (7) and ss.91(10) and (11).
[26] C.A. 1989, s.11(5) and (6).

5. How to Obtain a Section 8 Order   17–31

THE PROCEEDINGS

The court can make a section 8 order either in the course of "family proceedings" or on a separate application by virtue of section 10(2) of the Act.

(i) In family proceedings[27]
"Family proceedings" were defined in 17–03 above and, as can be seen, they are very comprehensive. Thus, for example, the court can make section 8 orders whenever an application is made for a divorce; for financial provision during marriage under the Domestic Proceedings and Magistrates' Courts Act 1978; or for an injunction under the Domestic Violence and Matrimonial Proceedings Act 1976.

(ii) On an application under section 10(2)
If a party wishes to apply for an order without taking other proceedings, an application can be made under section 10(2) for a section 8 order. It is worth noting that the old procedure under the Guardianship of Minors Act 1971 section 9[28] has been abolished.

WHO CAN APPLY?   17–32

The Act distinguishes between those people who can apply as of right and those who need leave. A further distinction is made between residence and contact orders, and the other orders under section 8.

(i) Those entitled to apply as of right for all orders[29]

(a) Any parent or guardian of the child. This would include the unmarried father of the child.

(b) Any person in whose favour a residence order is in force with respect to the child.

(ii) Those entitled to apply as of right for residence and contact orders only

(a) Any party to a marriage (whether or not subsisting) in relation to whom the child is a child of the family. This would clearly cover step-parents.

---

[27] C.A. 1989, s.10(1).
[28] See 16–33.
[29] C.A. 1989, s.10(4).

(b) Any person with whom the child has lived for a period of at least three years.[30] This would cover most of the people entitled to apply for a custodianship order under the old law (foster parents for example).[31]

(c) Any person who has the consent of each of the persons in whose favour a residence order has been made, or, if the child is in care, has the consent of the local authority, or in any other case has the consent of each person (if any) with parental responsibility.

(iii) Those who need leave
Anybody who does not fall within the above categories can apply for a section 8 order with leave.

17–33 *Example*

Grania is concerned about the way that her son, Stephen and her daughter-in-law, Daphne are treating her grandson, Eric. Grania could obtain leave to apply for a prohibited steps order preventing them taking him to a third-world country on holiday; a specific issue order requiring them to ensure he attends a certain school; a contact order enabling her to see him; or a residence order providing for Eric to go and live with her.

Obviously her prospects of obtaining leave to apply for some or all of these orders would not be strong,[32] but under the old law her only hope of achieving any of these things would have been by taking wardship proceedings in the High Court.

Finally, it is worth noting that the court has power to make a section 8 order if it considers that the order should be made, even though no application has been made.

17–34 **WHEN THE COURT CANNOT MAKE AN ORDER**

Section 9 contains some further restrictions on making section 8 orders.

(i) Only a residence order can be made in favour of a child who is in the care of a local authority. This enables anyone to apply for a residence order in favour of a child in care

---

[30] C.A. 1989, s.10(10) provides that this period need not have been continuous but must have begun not more than five years ago or ended more than three months before applications.
[31] See 16–08.
[32] See C.A. 1989, s.10(9) for factors to be considered on granting leave.

and if the court makes a residence order this will discharge the care order.[33]

(ii) A local authority cannot apply for a residence order or a contact order. This means that a local authority has no alternative route to enable it to take a child into care.[34]

(iii) Some local authority foster parents cannot apply for leave to apply for a section 8 order without the consent of the local authority.[35]

6. Control of Procedure by the Court   17–35

Section 1(2) provides that the court should have regard to the general principle that any delay in determining any question relating to the upbringing of children is likely to prejudice the welfare of the child.

In order to limit the delay that is inevitable, the Act[36] contains the following provisions.

(a) The court is instructed to draw up a timetable with a view to determining the question without delay.

(b) The court must give such directions as it considers appropriate for the purpose of ensuring, so far as is reasonably practicable, that the timetable is adhered to.

(c) Rules of court may specify periods within which specified steps must be taken and make other provision for the purpose of ensuring that any questions are determined without delay.

(d) The court is also given power to make interim section 8 orders.

It is not possible to know precisely how these provisions will operate, and how they will affect the procedure on divorce or under the other relevant jurisdictions, until the rules of court have been published.

7. Family Assistance Orders   17–36

There are undoubtedly occasions when the breakdown of a family requires the assistance of an outside agency to help the parties and children come to terms with the new situation. If the court is concerned for the protection of children then it

---

[33] See 19–13 below.
[34] See 19–07 below.
[35] See C.A. 1989, s.9(3) and (4).
[36] C.A. 1989, s.11.

can make a supervision order, which is considered below at 19–14. If the court feels that some temporary assistance is required then it can make a family assistance order under section 16 of the Act, although it can only do this if the parties consent and the circumstances are exceptional.

A family assistance order requires either a probation officer or an officer of the local authority to "advise, assist and (where appropriate) befriend any person named in the order."

It is not necessary for a section 8 order to have been made before a family assistance order is made, although this would seem the most likely situation. The order will only last for six months and a shorter term might be imposed, although presumably a second order could be made. It is possible for the officer to apply for the section 8 order to be varied or discharged during the term of the family assistance order.

17–37 *Example*

Alan and Sarah, who are unmarried, have a daughter, Gloria. Alan is an alcoholic and has been violent to Sarah and Gloria. Sarah has been granted an injunction under the D.V.M.P.A. 1976. At the same time the court made a residence order in favour of Sarah because both parties wanted Gloria to live with them. Subsequently Sarah refused to allow Alan to visit Gloria and Alan applied for a contact order. The court felt that the circumstances were such that a contact order should be made, but that a family assistance order would help the parties come to terms with the situation. Both parties agreed to the family assistance order and the orders were made.

After a number of disastrous visits with Alan, the social worker felt that for the time being Alan should not see Gloria. The social worker is able to apply for the contact order to be discharged.

17–38 **8. Transitional Provisions**

The transitional provisions of the Act are comprehensive and detailed.[37] For our purposes, the broad effect of these can be summarised as follows:

(a) Existing orders regarding custody, legal custody, care and control and access continue to have effect.

(b) Pending proceedings will continue unaffected by the new law.

(c) Existing orders may be discharged by the court, either on application or of its own motion in family proceedings. They also terminate if the court makes a residence or a care

---

[37] C.A. 1989, Sched. 14.

order, otherwise the existing order will continue subject to the section 8 order.

9. Financial relief

17–39

The Act does not affect the courts' power in matrimonial proceedings or under the Domestic Proceedings and Magistrates' Courts Act 1978 to make orders for the financial relief of children. This is because under those proceedings the provision for the parties is so inextricably linked with provision for the children that it would be wrong to separate them.

However, in other family proceedings, the court has extensive powers to provide financial relief for children. These powers are contained in Schedule 1 of the Act.

Orders for financial relief under Schedule 1 can be made:

(a) On application.[38] As proceedings under Schedule 1 are deemed to be family proceedings, the court can also make, for example, section 8 orders on an application under Schedule 1.[39]

(b) At any time by the court.[40] In many cases they would probably be made, on application, when one of the parties is applying for a residence order, but even if no application is made they can be made by the court of its own motion when the court makes a residence order.[41]

In the vast majority of cases the financial powers of the court under Schedule 1 will only be relevant where the parties are unmarried. For this reason these powers are dealt with at 15–16 to 15–20.

Example

In the example at 17–37 above, Sarah could also apply for an order for financial relief for Gloria under Schedule 1 when seeking her injunction under the D.V.M.P.A. 1976 and her residence order in relation to Gloria.

---

[38] C.A. 1989, Sched. 1, para. 1(1).
[39] C.A. 1989, Sched. 1 is within Part II of the Act, see C.A. 1989, s.15.
[40] C.A. 1989, Sched. 1, para. 1(3).
[41] C.A. 1989, Sched. 1, para. 1(6).

18. Protection of Children

18–01 In this chapter we consider three aspects of the law concerning the protection of children. First, the wardship jurisdiction, which is very broad and available in most circumstances when no other jurisdiction can be used. It generally enables the court to intervene in any circumstances when the interests of the child require it.

Secondly, ways of preventing the removal of a child who is about to be taken from the country are considered. If the child has already been taken out of the jurisdiction, the powers of the court to secure the child's return are also discussed.

Finally, the public law powers of local authorities over children where they are "at risk" are considered in outline.

This aspect of the law relating to children will be radically affected by the Children Act 1989 when it comes into force. Please see Chapter 19 for the new law.

1. Wardship

18–02 INTRODUCTION

The general object of the wardship jurisdiction is the protection of the person or property of a minor. It originated as a prerogative duty of the Crown which has nowadays come to be exercised chiefly by the Family Division of the High Court. The Supreme Court Act 1981, s.41 provides that "no minor shall be made a ward of court except by virtue of an order to that effect made by the High Court." Wardship proceedings, once started, may be transferred to a county court,[1] though this is likely to happen only in the more straightforward cases,[2] and only the High Court can order that a minor cease to be a ward.

[1] M.F.P.A. 1984, s.38(2).
[2] See Practice Direction [1988] 2 All E.R. 103.

CONSEQUENCES OF WARDSHIP   **18–03**

The effect of an order making a minor a ward is to vest custody in the narrow sense of that term (see 16–01, above) in the court, so that all important decisions affecting the child can be taken only by the court. Thus, for example, the court's consent will be required before the ward can get married or be taken out of the jurisdiction, and the court must be consulted about any important decision affecting the child's education or general upbringing. Of course, the court must also decide where the ward is to live and can grant care and control of the ward to anyone; for example, a parent, grandparent, foster parent or a relative.

MAINTENANCE   **18–04**

Under section 6 of the F.L.R.A. 1969, the court has power to order either parent to make periodical payments to the person having care and control of the ward or to the ward himself.

CARE AND SUPERVISION ORDERS   **18–05**

The F.L.R.A. 1969, s.7, also gives the court power to make care and supervision orders in respect of wards. These orders can be made only in the same "exceptional circumstances" as apply in the custody jurisdictions considered in Chapter 16.[3]

PRINCIPLES ON WHICH WARDSHIP ORDERS ARE MADE   **18–06**

In *J. v. C.*[4] the House of Lords emphasised that what is now section 1 of the G.M.A. 1971 applies just as much to wardship cases as to other cases involving the custody or upbringing of a minor. In other words, the minor's welfare is the first and paramount consideration. In *J. v. C.* itself the House of Lords decided that the welfare of a boy of 10 required that he be allowed to remain living in England with foster parents who had cared for him for seven years, rather than that he should

---

[3] Where it is impracticable or undesirable for him to be in the care of either parent, or of any other individual. See *Re Y. (A Minor) (Child in Care: Access)* [1976] Fam. 125.
[4] [1970] A.C. 668.

be returned to his natural parents who were Spanish and wanted their son to return to Spain.

Of course, in deciding what is best for the child, the court may have to take into account a number of factors, similar to those considered in all cases involving disputed custody.[5]

The uses to which the wardship jurisdiction can be put are so wide, however, that they may go beyond questions of custody and upbringing, in which case other factors may prevail over the child's welfare.

For example, in *Re X*,[6] wardship proceedings were used in an attempt to prevent publication of a book which contained details of the "revolting" sexual behaviour of the ward's deceased father, which might have caused her psychological damage if she were to have seen it. The Court of Appeal discharged an injunction restraining publication of the book on the ground that the ward's interests could not be allowed to prevail over the public interest in freedom of speech.[7]

18–07 USES OF WARDSHIP

Re X was clearly an exceptional case. But the fact that the general object of the wardship jurisdiction is the protection of the ward means that there can never be an exhaustive list of the circumstances in which a wardship order might be sought. All that can be done here is to give some examples of cases where wardship proceedings will be appropriate.

18–08 **(i) Custody disputes**
Parents and parties to a marriage generally have no need to invoke the wardship jurisdiction to resolve custody disputes, because of the range of alternative and more specific remedies available elsewhere. These were discussed in Chapter 16. However, people with no *locus standi* to apply for those remedies may use the wardship jurisdiction as a means of obtaining care and control of a child. In the past, foster parents and potential adoptive parents have used wardship to retain the care of a child against the wishes of natural parents. The introduction of custodianship[8] and the procedure for

[5] See 16–12 to 16–17, above.
[6] [1975] Fam. 47.
[7] Note *Re C. (No. 2)* [1989] 2 All E.R. 791, where the court did restrain publication of information relating to the identity of health care staff responsible for care of the ward.
[8] See 16–08.

freeing a child for adoption[9] will make such applications less common in future.

Local authorities too may use the wardship jurisdiction as a means of obtaining a care order in their favour, without having to satisfy the technicalities of the child care legislation (see 18–29 to 18–41, below).

(ii) Kidnapping   18–09

Once a minor is made a ward of court, anyone who takes the minor out of England or Wales without the leave of the court commits a contempt.[10] Therefore if, for example, a custodial parent suspects that the other parent is about to take the child abroad, it may well be wise to make the child a ward as a means of preventing the child's removal. This is no longer essential owing to the "port alert" procedure considered below, although warding a child may still be advisable, to encourage the police to instigate that procedure (see 18–23).

(iii) Undesirable associations   18–10

Parents of teenage daughters have sometimes sought to have them made wards of court, in order to prevent them marrying men whom the parents regarded as unsuitable. It is a contempt of court to marry a ward without the court's consent, so that, even if the wardship proceedings do not prevent the marriage, the girl's parents will have the satisfaction of knowing that their new son-in-law may be sent to prison.

Similarly, the wardship jurisdiction can be used to prevent a minor associating with people of whom his or her parents disapprove. Having made their child a ward of court, the parents can seek an injunction forbidding a person considered undesirable from having any contact with the ward.

Although applications of this kind were once quite common, they are rare nowadays.

(iv) Permitting and preventing medical treatment   18–11

Wardship proceedings can be used as a means of obtaining consent to an operation on a minor whose parents are opposed to it. In *Re B*.[11] a baby suffering from Down's Syndrome was made a ward by a local authority, in order to

---

[9] A procedure whereby a child may be declared "free for adoption," after which the child may be made the subject of an adoption order without further parental consent. See the C.A. 1975, s.14.

[10] This is subject to the provisions of the Family Law Act 1986, s.38, which allow, in very limited circumstances, the removal of a ward to another part of the U.K.

[11] [1981] 1 W.L.R. 1421.

get the court's consent to a life-saving operation. The parents of the baby thought it would be kinder to allow her to die.

Conversely, a child may be warded in order to prevent an operation. In *Re D.*[12] an 11-year old mentally retarded girl was made a ward in order to prevent a sterilisation operation being performed on her, even though her mother wanted the operation to take place.[13]

Once a child is a ward, the court's consent is not always necessary before any medical treatment is performed. Such a rule would be, at best, irksome in routine matters and, at worst, fatal in emergencies. In general, the consent of the person having care and control of the ward should suffice. However, *Re D.*, in particular, suggests that it would be wise to obtain the court's consent before any important non-therapeutic treatment is performed on a ward of court.

18–12 **(v) Children born to surrogate mothers**
In *Re A Baby*[14] a child had been born to a surrogate mother. The natural father applied in wardship proceedings for care and control which was granted by the court. The local authority had previously obtained a place of safety order. As will be seen (at 18–44, below), in such circumstances a wardship order is rarely made, the courts preferring to leave the matter to the juvenile court. Nonetheless, the judge pointed out that in urgent cases of this type the matter should be dealt with by the High Court in wardship proceedings.

18–13 PROCEDURE

It is not within the scope of this book to cover in detail the procedure in wardship cases, and therefore this will be dealt with in outline only.

18–14 **(i) Jurisdiction**[15]
The court may ward any minor who is a British subject, whether or not the minor is physically within the jurisdiction. Any minor ordinarily resident in England and Wales may also be made a ward, and it has been held that even a minor temporarily present here can be warded. The court does not,

---

[12] [1976] Fam. 185.
[13] Where an operation to sterilise a minor is contemplated, the High Court should almost always be consulted in wardship proceedings. Practice Note [1989] 2 F.L.R. 447.
[14] *The Times,* January 15, 1985.
[15] If an order for care and control is sought in wardship proceedings certain statutory restrictions on jurisdiction apply. See Family Law Act 1986, ss.2 and 3.

however, have jurisdiction over a minor with diplomatic immunity.[16]

(ii) The application[17]   18–15

The application is made in the Family Division of the High Court, by originating summons issued out of the Principal or a District Registry. The urgent nature of the procedure can be seen from the fact that, as soon as the *application* is made, the minor becomes a ward of court, although, if the wardship is to continue, it is essential that an application for a hearing date should be made within 21 days after the issue of the summons.[18]

The summons should contain:

   (i)   the name of the minor;

  (ii)   a statement of the orders the plaintiff claims. (*e.g.* that the minor be made a ward and costs);

 (iii)   the relationship of each party to the minor or his interest in the minor[19];

 (iv)   the date of birth of the minor;

  (v)   the minor's present whereabouts (or a statement that the plaintiff is unaware of his whereabouts);

 (vi)   a notice to the defendant informing him of his obligations to acknowledge service and inform the court and the plaintiff of his own and the minor's address.

The summons will also contain a warning that it is a contempt of court to take the minor out of the jurisdiction.

Supporting documentation   18–16

Any relevant legal aid documentation should be filed in the usual way, together with a certificate as to the existence of other court proceedings pending in relation to the child (*e.g.*

---

[16] As the jurisdiction is dependent on allegiance to the Crown. See *Re D. (an infant)* [1943] 2 Ch. 305.

[17] See R.S.C., Ord. 90.

[18] Supreme Court Act 1981, s.41 and R.S.C., Ord. 90, r. 4.

[19] Although anyone can apply to have a minor made a ward of court, the court has power to dismiss the application as an abuse of the process of the court if there is no good reason for it. Practice Direction [1967] 1 All E.R. 828.

matrimonial proceedings). It will also be necessary to file the child's birth certificate, or a certified copy of it.

18–17 Subsequent procedure
The summons should be served on the defendant and an application for a hearing date should be made within 21 days. At the hearing, wardship may either be confirmed or revoked and any other orders made.

18–18 TRACING A MISSING WARD

Although the defendant is required by the summons to reveal the whereabouts of the ward where this is unknown to the plaintiff, there are obviously some cases, such as kidnappings, where the defendant is unlikely to comply. Indeed the whereabouts of the defendant may not be known, so that service of the proceedings cannot be effected.

In such cases there are various ways in which the whereabouts of the ward, or the person believed to have possession of the ward, may be discovered.

18–19 (i) Publicity
The court has power to permit publication of information relating to a ward. The applicant's solicitor should seek permission to publish as much information as is necessary to attract publicity, or the judge may adjourn a hearing briefly to enable the press to attend.[20]

18–20 (ii) Police
The police will assist by making inquiries in the area in which the child is thought to be, and brief details of the ward will be circulated in the Police Gazette.

18–21 (iii) Government departments[21]
Various government departments may be able to provide the current address of a missing ward, or the person with whom the ward is said to be. The department most likely to be able to help is the D.S.S., which may be able to provide an address from national insurance, health service or welfare benefit records. Alternatively the Passport Office may have the current address, especially if the person sought has recently applied for a passport. In the case of these, and other departments, the applicant's solicitor should ask the court to make the request for information through the registrar.

---

[20] Practice Note [1980] 2 All E.R. 806.
[21] See Practice Direction [1989] 1 All E.R. 765.

Where the person sought is serving, or has recently served, in the armed forces, the applicant's solicitor may obtain the address for service of wardship proceedings direct from the appropriate service department.

PASSPORTS   **18–22**

Where it seems likely that a ward will be taken out of the country, it may be wise to give notice to the Passport Department at the Home Office that the ward should not be issued with a passport without leave of the court.[22] It may well be, however, that the ward already has a passport, or is on the passport of the person suspected of the kidnapping. In such cases the court can order the surrender of the passport and will notify the Passport Office of this to prevent a replacement being issued.[23] It would seem, however, that this cannot stop a British visitor's passport being issued by a post office.

2. The Removal of a Child from the Jurisdiction

PREVENTION; THE "PORT-ALERT" PROCEDURE[24]   **18–23**

If it is thought that a child is about to be removed from the country, the "port-alert" system should be used. It is a criminal offence under the Child Abduction Act 1984[25] to remove a child under 16 from the United Kingdom where removal occurs without the consent of, *inter alia*, both parents *or* of any person who has been awarded custody *or* of the court. As a result, the police will inform the sea- and airports whenever there is a threat that a child is about to be removed unlawfully from the country. The police will, however, need to be satisfied that the threat is "real" and "imminent," which means that the "port-alert" is not being sought merely by way of insurance, and that removal is likely within 24 to 48 hours.

This procedure is available to attempt to stop the removal of any child under 16 from the United Kingdom. It is not necessary to obtain a court order in respect of such a child before police assistance is sought. However, in many cases where no custody order has been made, it might be advantageous to ward the child, as inevitably care and control

---

[22] See Practice Direction [1986] 1 W.L.R. 475.
[23] Practice Direction [1983] 1 W.L.R. 558.
[24] See Practice Direction [1986] 1 W.L.R. 475.
[25] ss.1 and 2.

would be in dispute. The wardship summons or order may well prove invaluable in persuading the police of the serious nature of the matter.

Application is made to a police station (preferably the applicant's local station) and, in the case of a ward, should be accompanied by a wardship order or an injunction or, in urgent cases, a copy of the originating summons bearing the seal of the court. The applicant should also provide all relevant information concerning the child, and the person accompanying the child, as well as (*inter alia*) information about the likely port of embarkation and the likely destination.

If the police decide the "port-alert" system should be used, the child's name will be put on a "stop list" which is circulated to the ports. The child's name will be removed after four weeks unless a further application for inclusion is made.

18–24 PASSPORTS

It is also worth noting that the Family Law Act 1986 gives a court which has made an order prohibiting the removal of a child from the United Kingdom[26], power to order the surrender of any United Kingdom passport relating to the child. This extends the power, which is also available in the High Court in wardship proceedings (see 18–22, above), to all courts with jurisdiction to forbid the removal of a child.

18–25 RECOVERING A CHILD FROM OUTSIDE THE JURISDICTION

Even though an attempt to prevent the unauthorised removal of a child from the jurisdiction may fail, the person who effects such a removal may be guilty of an offence under the Child Abduction Act 1984 of kidnapping at common law,[27] and of a civil contempt of court. But this in itself may be of little comfort to the parent or party from whom the child has been taken. What concerns them is whether the child can be recovered, or whether any domestic custody order that may have been made can be enforced in the jurisdiction to which the child has been taken.

18–26 If a child under 16 has been wrongfully removed to any state which is party to the Hague Convention on Interational Child

---

[26] Also see 16–41 and 16–42.
[27] See *R.* v. *D.* [1984] A.C. 778.

Abduction, then, under Part I of the Child Abduction and Custody Act 1985 (C.A.C.A. 1985), it is possible to request the return of the child. This will normally be ordered if less than a year has elapsed since the removal. Even if more than a year has elapsed, the child should still normally be returned, unless he has become settled in his new environment.[28] The main aim of this procedure is to secure the speedy return of the child. No attempt is made to determine the merits of any custody issue.

If a child under 16, in respect of whom a custody order has **18–27** been made, has been improperly removed to a state which is a party to the European Convention on Recognition and Enforcement of Custody Decisions, then, under Part II of the C.A.C.A. 1985, an application may be made for enforcement of the domestic order, and the Convention, as incorporated by the C.A.C.A. 1985, requires such orders to be recognised and enforced in every contracting state. In general, this should lead to the return of the child, although there are various grounds (such as the fact that the original decision is manifestly no longer in accordance with the child's welfare) which could justify a refusal to enforce the order.

Under the Family Law Act 1986, custody orders made in **18–28** respect of children under 16 are recognised in all parts of the United Kingdom. Custody orders made in one part of the United Kingdom may be registered in another part and the order may then be enforced there.[29]

3. Local Authorities' Powers over Children **18–29**

It is beyond the scope of this book to deal with this topic in detail. This area of practice is now usually dealt with by specialist lawyers who are on the child care panel administered by the Law Society.

Although local authorities' powers over children are not confined to receiving and removing them into care, these are the most important of the powers they exercise, and they affect large numbers of children. At any one time there may be between 70,000 and 80,000 children in the care of local authorities in England and Wales. These children come into care under a wide range of statutory provisions, but the great majority are in care under either the C.C.A. 1980 or the C.Y.P.A. 1969.

[28] See *Re G.* [1989] 2 F.L.R. 475.
[29] Family Law Act 1986, ss.25–32.

CHILD CARE ACT 1980

18-30   **(i) Reception into care**
A local authority has a duty under section 2 of the C.C.A.
1980 to receive into care any child within its area who is
believed to be under 17, where it appears that:

> (i)   the child has neither parent nor guardian, is lost or
> abandoned;

or

> (ii)   the child's parents or guardian are incapable of
> looking after him;

and

> (iii)   in either case, the intervention of the local authority is
> necessary in the interests of the child's welfare.

This latter condition is designed to encourage the local
authority to place the child with a friend or relation where
possible, rather than regard reception into care as a first
resort.

The main purpose of the section is to provide for short-term
care and it would seem that over half of all children received
into care under section 2 leave care within six months.[30]

18-31   **(ii) Parental rights**
The voluntary nature of this process, whereby the child is
received into care, is reflected in the limited powers of the
local authority. Section 2(3) of the C.C.A. 1980 provides that
the local authority does not acquire any right to keep the child
in care against the wishes of its parents. The local authority
cares for the child, decides where he should live and where
he should go to school, but these decisions are subject to the
parents' wishes.

18-32   **(iii) Duration**
The local authority's duty ends when the child attains the age
of 18. Meanwhile the parents can ask for the child to be
returned at any time. However, the local authority may be
able to pass a resolution assuming parental rights, which will
enable them to keep the child. They can only do so if grounds
exist as discussed below.

It is provided that 28 days' notice must be given of the
parents' intention to remove the child, if he has been in care

---

[30] See further Stephen M. Cretney, *Principles of Family Law* (4h ed., 1984),
p. 494.

for six months or more. This also allows the local authority time in which to consider whether or not to assume parental rights, or alternatively, to take wardship proceedings.

(iv) Grounds for assumption of parental rights[31]

18–33

Under section 3 of the C.C.A. 1980, the local authority may resolve to assume parental rights and duties over a child against his parents' will, if the child is in care under section 2,[32] provided that certain grounds exist. For example, that the child's parents are dead, or that a parent is, for various specified reasons, unfit to care for the child, or the child has been in care for three years.[33]

(v) Effect of assuming parental rights

18–34

The section 3 resolution vests in the local authority most of the parental rights and duties of the parent or parents named in the resolution. It does not, however, affect the parents' rights to withhold consent to the child's adoption[34] nor their right to choose the religion in which the child should be brought up[35]; neither does it affect their duty to maintain the child.[36]

In any case, the resolution may name only one of the child's parents, in which case the unnamed parent's rights and duties are unaffected. The local authority will, however, remain free to exercise its powers under the C.C.A. 1980 unless that parent signifies disapproval.[37] If this happens, the authority may consider whether it has grounds for passing a resolution in respect of that parent too, or, alternatively, it may take wardship proceedings.

(vi) Procedure for assuming parental rights

18–35

Once a resolution has been passed assuming parental rights, the local authority must immediately give notice to the parents named in the resolution. The parents then have one month to object by serving a counter notice on the local authority. If a parent does object, the local authority must make a complaint to the juvenile court within 14 days, otherwise the resolution will lapse.

---

[31] C.C.A. 1980, s.3.
[32] It is uncertain whether the child continues to be in care, despite his parents' request for his return, when he has been in care for less than six months. See *Lewisham London Borough Council* v. *Lewisham Juvenile Court JJ.* [1980] A.C. 273.
[33] C.C.A. 1980, s.3.
[34] C.C.A. 1980, s.3(10).
[35] C.C.A. 1980, s.4(3).
[36] C.C.A. 1980, s.4(2).
[37] C.A. 1975, s.85(3).

The court will confirm the resolution if it is satisfied:

(i) that the grounds on which the local authority passed the resolution existed when the resolution was passed; and

(ii) that a ground (not necessarily the one relied on in the resolution) exists at the time of the hearing; and

(iii) that it is in the interests of the child that the resolution should remain in force.[38]

Subject to a right of appeal to the High Court, the resolution then continues in force until the child attains the age of 18 or until it is rescinded by the juvenile court[39] or by the local authority.[40]

18–36 CHILDREN AND YOUNG PERSONS ACT 1969

A local authority may take care proceedings in the juvenile court in respect of a child under 17, on various grounds set out in section 1 of the C.Y.P.A. 1969. One possible outcome of such proceedings is that the court will make a care order vesting most parental rights and duties over the child in the local authority, subject only to restrictions similar to those outlined at 18–35, above. The local authority might choose this course of action if the parents were unco-operative from the outset, so that the child could not be received into voluntary care under section 2 of the C.C.A. 1980; or if the grounds provided by section 1 of the C.Y.P.A. 1969 were more appropriate than those provided by the C.C.A. 1980.

18–37 (i) Grounds
Before making an order the juvenile court must be satisfied that one of the conditions specified in section 1(2) of the C.Y.P.A. 1969 exists. The court must also be satisfied that the child is in need of care or control which he is unlikely to receive unless an order is made under the Act. The section 1 conditions may be summarised as follows:

(i) The child's proper development is being avoidably prevented or neglected or his health is being avoidably impaired or neglected, or he is being ill-treated. (This condition is the one most frequently

[38] C.C.A. 1980, s.3(6).
[39] C.C.A. 1980, s.5(4).
[40] C.C.A. 1980, s.5(3).

relied on in care proceedings. It may be proved by inference, either from the fact that the condition has been established in respect of another child in the same household, or that a person already convicted of an offence against a child is, or is about to become, a member of the household).

(ii) The child is exposed to moral danger;

(iii) The child is beyond the control of his parent or guardian;

(iv) The child is of compulsory school age and is not receiving efficient full-time education suitable to his age, ability and aptitude;

(v) The child is guilty of an offence, excluding homicide. (This condition is little used. The child is usually prosecuted for offences instead.)

(ii) Who may apply
18–38

Most care proceedings are brought by a local authority, but police constables may apply too.[41] Officers of the National Society for the Prevention of Cruelty to Children are authorised[42] to bring proceedings under the first three conditions summarised above. Proceedings based on lack of full-time education can be brought only by a local education authority.[43] If the local authority is not the applicant, it must be notified of the application.[44]

(iii) Orders
18–39

Section 1(3) of the C.Y.P.A. 1969 sets out the orders which can be made as a result of care proceedings.

Care order

This vests most of the parental rights and duties in the local authority. The child may then be removed from home and be placed in a local authority home or boarded with foster parents. The local authority has power to regulate or even terminate access to the child, although, if access is terminated, the authority is bound to give the person concerned notice of the decision and that person can then seek an access order from the juvenile court.[45] Children made the subject of a care

---

[41] C.Y.P.A. 1969, s.1(1).
[42] Under the C.Y.P.A. 1969, s.1(6).
[43] C.Y.P.A. 1969, s.2(8).
[44] C.Y.P.A. 1969, s.2(3).
[45] C.C.A. 1980, s.12C.

order are not necessarily removed from their home, however, although the local authority could remove them at any time if it thought it right to do so.

Once made, a care order can normally last until the child is 18,[46] but the juvenile court may discharge it earlier on the application of the local authority, the child or his parent or guardian.[47] The order also ceases if the child is adopted or freed for adoption.[48]

18–40 *Supervision order*

The child may be placed under the supervision of the local authority or, in certain circumstances, a probation officer. The supervisor is under a duty to "advise, assist and befriend"[49] the child, and, to this end, the order will normally require the child to maintain contact with the supervisor, giving him notice of any change of address or job, and to receive home visits from him.

A supervision order lasts only for a maximum of three years, and, if made in care proceedings, must in any case cease when the child reaches 18.[50] Besides this, either the child or the supervisor can apply for the earlier discharge of the order.[51]

18–41 *Other orders*

The juvenile court has power to make a number of other orders under the C.Y.P.A. 1969. Mentally disordered children may be made the subject of hospital or guardianship orders; parents can be bound over to exercise proper care and control, and, where the offence condition is proved, a child over 14 can be bound over to keep the peace and be of good behaviour.[52]

18–42 PLACE OF SAFETY ORDERS

In an emergency it may be necessary to remove the child from his parents as quickly as possible for his own protection, and take him to a place of safety. "Place of safety" usually means a local authority community home or foster home, but it

---

[46] C.Y.P.A. 1969, s.20(3).
[47] C.Y.P.A. 1969, s.21(2).
[48] C.Y.P.A. 1969, s.21A.
[49] C.Y.P.A. 1969, s.14.
[50] C.Y.P.A. 1969, s.17.
[51] C.Y.P.A. 1969, s.15(1).
[52] C.Y.P.A. 1969, s.3(7).

includes police stations, hospitals and surgeries as well.[53] There are several statutory provisions which allow this to be done, but the one most often used is section 28 of the C.Y.P.A. 1969.

Under section 28(1) anyone can apply to a single justice for authority to detain a child under 17 and take him to a place of safety, if there is reasonable cause to believe (*inter alia*) that any of the grounds on which care proceedings can be brought are satisfied in respect of the child.

A place of safety order lasts for a maximum of 28 days. Such orders are, however, often followed by applications for an interim care order (which can itself last for up to 28 days) and by full care proceedings under section 1 of the C.Y.P.A. 1969.

SEEKING A CARE ORDER BY WARDSHIP PROCEEDINGS 18–43

The High Court has power, under section 7 of the F.L.R.A. 1969, to make an order that a ward be placed in the care of the local authority. In making such an order the court is guided simply by the requirement in section 1 of the G.M.A. 1971 that the welfare of the child must be regarded as the first and paramount consideration. So, for example, where the local authority doubts whether it could establish one of the grounds contained in section 1 of the C.Y.P.A. 1969 on which a care order might be made, it might apply instead for the child to be warded, to enable the High Court to decide the matter simply by reference to what is best for the child.

CHALLENGING A LOCAL AUTHORITY BY WARDSHIP 18–44 PROCEEDINGS

When a child is in the care of a local authority, the authority has wide powers to control his upbringing. If the child is in care as a result of a parental rights resolution under section 3 of the C.C.A. 1980, or under a care order, then most of the parental rights and duties are vested in the authority.

However, cases are bound to arise in which the child's parents, or some third party, wish to challenge the local authority's exercise of its statutory powers and duties. For example, parents may want to object to the place where the child is living, or they may wish to apply for the return of the child. The prospects of a successful challenge being made are, however, very limited. Apart from applying to the juvenile

---

[53] C.Y.P.A. 1933, s.107.

court for the discharge of the resolution or the order, the only alternative is to take wardship proceedings. These are unlikely to succeed. In *A.* v. *Liverpool City Council*[54] the House of Lords held that the wardship jurisdiction should not be used as a means of reviewing a local authority's exercise of its powers over children in care, unless it can be shown that the authority has acted improperly or in breach of disregard of its statutory duty. Although there are cases in which this has been done,[55] such cases are unusual.

---

[54] [1982] A.C. 363.
[55] *e.g. Re L.* (A.C.) [1971] 3 All E.R. 743 in which an authority misled the mother's solicitor about the need to object in time to the passing of a parental rights resolution.

19. Protection of Children after the Children Act 1989

1. Introduction

The radical effect of the Children Act on the whole area of the law relating to children was explained at 17–02 above. The Act has a similar impact on the powers of the court to make public law orders, for example, care orders.

Although the Act is not in force at the time of writing, this chapter has been written as if it were. Most of the Act is not expected to come into force until, at the earliest, October 1991. Before the Act is in force this chapter will only be of academic interest, and the reader is referred to Chapter 18 for the existing law.

2. Wardship

19-02

The Act has not affected the general wardship jurisdiction of the High Court (except as regards its use by local authorities in general matters and its power to make care or supervision orders). Therefore, for a coverage of these powers see 18–02 to 18–22, above. However, the need to resort to the use of wardship will be reduced because of the availability of the "prohibited steps order," (see 17–22, above).

REPEAL OF POWER TO MAKE CARE OR SUPERVISION   19-03
ORDERS

The Act repeals the power of the High Court to make care or supervision orders in wardship proceedings.[1] This should substantially reduce the work currently undertaken by the High Court in exercising its wardship jurisdiction. Up until now local authorities have tended to use the wardship jurisdiction where they found difficulty in proving the necessary grounds to obtain an order in the magistrates'

[1] C.A. 1989, s.100(1).

court.[2] As will be shown below, this problem should not longer exist. It therefore follows that the so-called "wardship challenge" of local authorities[3] by parents is also no longer possible.

Should the High Court feel, when exercising its wardship function, that a care or supervision order might be more appropriate, it can direct the local authority to investigate the child's circumstances and, if the statutory conditions are satisfied, make an interim care or supervision order. (See below 19–12).

19–04   LOCAL AUTHORITIES AS APPLICANTS FOR WARDSHIP

A local authority has, effectively, no *right* to apply for a child to be made a ward of court.[4] The sort of situations which might have required the local authority to apply for wardship, as opposed to a care order, for example, to enable life saving operations to take place, or to prevent sterilisation, would be covered by the power of the local authority to apply for a specific issue order.[5]

19–05   **3. The Removal of a Child from the Jurisdiction**

The Act has not affected the law relating to the prevention of children being removed from the jurisdiction. In the same way the law relating to the recovery of a child from outside the jurisdiction remains unchanged. This area has been dealt with at 18–23 to 18–28 above. However, one consequential change that has taken place is that a person who has a residence order in their favour is permitted to remove a child from the U.K. for less than one month (see 17–25). This is to facilitate foreign holidays.

19–06   **4. Local Authorities' Powers Over Children**

It is beyond the scope of this book to deal with this area in any detail. Some guidance is given to the new powers of local authorities under the Act, but for a full understanding the reader is recommended to one of the standard works on this

---

[2] See 18–43.
[3] See 18–44.
[4] However, leave may be given. See footnote 7.
[5] See 17–20. There is a residuary power for a local authority to apply to invoke the inherent jurisdiction of the High Court. It is very difficult to conceive of circumstances which might justify such an application and in any event leave will be required. C.A. 1989, s.100(2).

subject. This area of law is now, for practical purposes, beyond the competence of the general practitioner and is usually dealt with by lawyers who are on the child care panel administered by the Law Society.

INTRODUCTION

19–07

The previous law had come in for a great deal of criticism, principally because there was a variety of statutory provisions which enabled courts to make care and supervision orders. These orders were made on proof of different grounds and with different effects.

There is now only one set of grounds which must be established before a child can be taken into care, although proceedings can be taken in a number of different courts. Under the previous law it was possible for a child to be taken into care by the local authority resolving to assume parental rights after the child had been voluntarily placed in care.[6] This has been abolished by the Act. There is, however, instead, a requirement that a child must be provided with accommodation in certain circumstances. This terminology is obviously less threatening and less suggestive of parental failure than the former terminology of "voluntary reception into care."

ACCOMMODATION FOR CHILDREN IN NEED

19–08

The Act provides[7] that local authorities shall provide accommodation for any child in need[8] who appears to require it as a result of:

(a) there being no person who has parental responsibility[9] for him; or

(b) his being lost or abandoned; or

(c) the person who has been caring for him being prevented (whether or not permanently, and for whatever reason) from providing him with suitable accommodation or care.

However, the essence of this provision is that it is voluntary and if a person with parental responsibility objects this cannot

[6] See 18–29 to 18–34.
[7] C.A. 1989, s.20.
[8] See C.A. 1989, s.17(10).
[9] See 17–11.

be done.[10] Such a person can remove the child from the local authority accommodation at any time without notice.

19–09 CARE AND SUPERVISION ORDERS

(i) Grounds

The court may make a care or supervision order if it is satisfied[11]:

    (a)   that the child concerned is suffering, or likely to suffer, significant harm; and

    (b)   that the harm, or likelihood of harm is attributable to:

        (i)   the care given to the child, or likely to be given to him if the order were not made, not being what it would be reasonable to expect a parent to give him; or

        (ii)   the child's being beyond reasonable control.

19–10 The court must also be satisfied that it would be better for the child to make an order than to make no order.[12] Further, the welfare principle and the checklist of factors as set out at 17–09 applies to care and supervision as much as to section 8 orders.

The grounds set out above deal with one of the fundamental defects of the old law. It now enables the court to make care orders on the basis of anticipated risk. The previous absence of this was a prime factor in the extensive use of wardship by local authorities.

19–11 **(ii) Jurisdiction**

A care or supervision order cannot be made in respect of a child who is over 17, or 16 if married.[13]

It can only be applied for by a local authority or an authorised person. The N.S.P.C.C. are authorised for these purposes.[14]

The application can be made on its own or in other family proceedings.[15] The High Court, county court or magistrates'

---

[10] Subject to certain conditions, see C.A. 1989, s.20(7) (8) and (9).
[11] C.A. 1989, s.33(3).
[12] C.A. 1989, s.34.
[13] C.A. 1989, s.31(2).
[14] See C.A. 1989, s.11(5).
[15] C.A. 1989, s.31(3).

court (the domestic section of which is renamed "the family proceedings court") are given concurrent jurisdiction. Rules of court are to be made to deal with such matters as where such proceedings are to be initiated, transfer of cases between courts, and procedure. It is expected that most of the applications will start in the family proceedings court. As yet no rules have been made.

A court hearing an application for some other order in family **19–12** proceedings, for example, a residence order, can, if it thinks it appropriate, direct the local authority to investigate a child's circumstances with a view to applying for a care or supervision order.[16]

The local authority must then consider whether to:

(a) apply for a care or supervision order; or

(b) provide services or assistance for the child or his family; or

(c) take any other action in respect of the child.

If the local authority decides not to apply for a care or supervision order they must notify the court within eight weeks (or such other period as the court may direct) of the reasons for their decision and of any action they propose to take with respect to the child.

At the same time as directing the investigation by the local authority the court could make an interim care or supervision order but it cannot make a full order unless an application is made for one which satisfies the grounds.

(iii) Care orders: **19–13**

(a) *Effect*

A care order places the child in the care of the local authority. It gives the local authority parental responsibility for the child and the power to determine the extent to which a parent or guardian may meet his parental responsibility.[17] A parent will not lose his parental responsibility on the making of a care order but his rights will be effectively curtailed. A parent is entitled to reasonable contact with his child, subject to the right of the local authority to apply to the court for authority to refuse contact.[18]

---

[16] C.A. 1989, s.31(9).
[17] See 17–11.
[18] C.A. 1989, s.37.

(b) *Duration*

A care order will continue in force until the child is 18 unless it is brought to an end earlier.[19] It can also be brought to an end if a residence order is made.[20]

19–14 **(iv) Supervision orders**

(a) *Effect*

This is an order which places the child under the supervision of a local authority or, in certain circumstances, a probation officer. The duties of a supervisor are:

(a) to advise, assist and befriend the supervised child;

(b) to take such steps as are reasonably necessary to give effect to the order;

(c) to consider whether or not to apply for a discharge or a variation where the order is not wholly complied with or may no longer be necessary.[21]

(b) *Duration*

The order will last for one year unless it is extended. It may not last more than three years in all and will cease in any event when the child is 18.[22]

19–15 OTHER RELATED ORDERS

The Act contains other supplementary powers including the power to appoint a guardian *ad litem* to represent the child and to make an education supervision order to deal with non-school attendance. It is worth noting that the court has power on an application for a care or supervision order to make a section 8 order instead.[23]

19–16 EMERGENCY POWERS

Again the Act seeks to redress some of the problems associated with the old law. There were various overlapping jurisdictions but the most commonly used one was the application for a place of safety order.[24] The Act replaces them

[19] C.A. 1989, s.91(11).
[20] See 17–16.
[21] C.A. 1989, s.35(1).
[22] C.A. 1989, Sched. 3, para. 6, and s.91(13).
[23] See 17–36.
[24] See 17–42.

all with two provisions: the child assessment order and the emergency protection order.

(i) Child assessment order[25]

19–17

This can be applied for by the local authority or an authorised person. It is to be used where there is reason to suspect that a child is being abused or neglected but, because of an inability to be able to examine the child, evidence cannot be obtained.

(ii) Emergency protection order[26]

19–18

If there is an immediate need to take the child away, an emergency protection order may be obtained. It may be obtained by anyone, including a local authority, if the court is satisfied, broadly, that the child is likely to suffer significant harm. Further, in circumstances where the local authority is unable to gain access to a child at risk then it alone may apply for an order. The order authorises the child's removal to accommodation provided by or on behalf of the applicant. The order lasts for eight days with a possible maximum extension of seven days.[27] This should enable the local authority to apply for a care order or obtain an interim care order which can last for, initially, eight weeks.[28]

(iii) Jurisdiction

19–19

In theory these orders may be made by the High Court, the county court, or the family proceedings court, although it is anticipated that the regulations will specify that the family proceedings court is to deal with the majority of these applications.

---

[25] C.A. 1989, s.43.
[26] C.A. 1989, s.44.
[27] C.A. 1989, s.45.
[28] C.A. 1989, s.38.

PART IV

FAMILY VIOLENCE

20. Injunctions and Family Protection Orders

1. Introduction

20–01

This chapter is primarily concerned with the private law remedies available to adults seeking protection against domestic violence; protection for their children is considered as an incidental matter. Whilst it is, of course, possible for children to be assaulted in the context of marriage break-down, the wife is far more likely to be the victim of such violence. The problem of providing protection specifically for children, as victims of domestic violence in the broader context, is essentially a matter of public law and is dealt with in Chapters 18 and 19 above.

Throughout this chapter, for ease of reference, it will be assumed that the wife is the applicant seeking an order against her husband, although orders can be made against a wife.

20–02

The police might seem the obvious agency to turn to for protection from violence. Unfortunately they are often reluctant to bring prosecutions unless serious physical injuries have been inflicted. This may be because in such "domestic" matters, they find that the wife often changes her mind, and fails to provide the evidence to secure a conviction. Therefore, it is often necessary for the victim of violence to look to the civil courts for a remedy.

20–03

The wife may need to be protected in various ways. She may, for example, want an order restraining her husband from molesting her, or an order excluding him from the home. It is not uncommon, however, for a wife to be forced to leave the matrimonial home herself to escape her husband, sometimes with her children, and seek temporary accommodation with relatives or friends, or in a women's refuge. In these circumstances she will normally require an order removing her husband from the matrimonial home and reinstating her in the property.

However, it is also important to appreciate that, despite the fact that she may have suffered serious cruelty, the wife may not wish to end the marriage. It would be wrong to assume that a wife in such a position must want a divorce and to force her along that road. There are, as will be seen, jurisdictions available under which orders preventing violence and regulating occupation of the property can be made without the need for a decree.

2. The Types of Orders

20–04 ORDERS FOR THE PROTECTION OF A PARTY AND CHILDREN

Orders which restrain one party from assaulting, or interfering with, the applicant or a child are called "non-molestation" orders in the county court and High Court, and "personal protection orders" in the magistrates' court. The details are dealt with below.

20–05 ORDERS TO EXCLUDE ONE PARTY FROM OCCUPATION OF THE MATRIMONIAL HOME

These orders exclude one party from the matrimonial home and may order him to allow the other to enter the property. They are commonly called "ouster injunctions" in the county court and High Court, and "exclusion orders" in the magistrates' court. Both such orders may exclude, either by "putting" a party out of occupation, if he refuses to go, or by "keeping" him out, if he has already left. Again, the details are examined below.

20–06 EMERGENCY ORDERS

The court is often asked to make an immediate order where there is a serious risk to the applicant or the children. These orders may be made at first instance in the absence of the respondent. In this case they will only last for a few days. They are called *"ex parte orders"* in the county court and High Court, and "expedited orders" in the magistrates' court.

20–07 UNDERTAKINGS

The parties are sometimes prepared to compromise an application. For example, the husband may deny the specific allegations made by his wife, but will be prepared to agree not to molest her. She may be prepared to accept this in lieu of an injunction. Indeed in some cases an undertaking may be preferred to an injunction in that, as it is given voluntarily, it is more likely to be complied with. If it is not complied with, an undertaking may be enforced by proceedings for contempt of court, and is therefore, in theory, as good as an injunction, although, unlike an injunction, no power of arrest can be attached to it.[1] In practice, if an undertaking is broken, the court, on being asked to enforce it, is likely to grant an injunction.

3. The Jurisdictions   20–08

The law relating to injunctions is in an unsatisfactory state. Development over the last few years has been piecemeal and hurried, with various Acts passed to deal with "specific situations or to strengthen the powers of specific courts."[2] The law can, therefore, be somewhat confusing, as the jurisdictions overlap in some areas and provide exclusive relief in others. The jurisdictions are dealt with in detail below.

The main jurisdictions are:

(i) Domestic Violence and Matrimonial Proceedings Act 1976.

(ii) Matrimonial Homes Act 1983.

(iii) Jurisdiction ancillary to a petition.

(iv) Domestic Proceedings and Magistrates' Courts Act 1978.

Applications under the D.V.M.P.A. 1976 will usually be made in the county court, although such applications may also be made in the High Court. Both High Court and county courts have the power to make orders under the M.H.A. 1983, but, as will be seen, this jurisdiction is rarely used on its own. If proceedings are taken for an injunction ancillary to a petition, then the court in which the petition is proceeding has power to make the appropriate injunction. This will usually be the divorce court. The D.P.M.C.A. 1978 confers

---

[1] See below, 18–69.
[2] *Per* Lord Scarman in *Richards* v. *Richards* [1984] A.C. 174.

jurisdiction solely on the magistrates' court to make family protection orders. This will be dealt with separately later in the chapter.

20–09 DOMESTIC VIOLENCE AND MATRIMONIAL PROCEEDINGS ACT 1976

The D.V.M.P.A. 1976 was passed to provide a specific remedy to protect spouses, children and cohabitants from domestic violence. It did away with the rule which prevented the court from granting injunctions unless these could be shown to be needed as an incidental to other proceedings. Although the Act only empowers the court to make orders for protection, it is open to the applicant to seek other forms of relief (*e.g.* maintenance) if she is eligible to do so, in other proceedings.

Section 1(1) of the D.V.M.P.A. 1976 provides that the court shall have power to grant an injunction containing one or more of the following provisions:

20–10 (i) A provision restraining the other party to the marriage from molesting the applicant
The word "molestation" is not statutorily defined, but certainly extends beyond violence, and has been construed to mean the same as "pester."[3] It will cover, for example, the husband who persistently telephones his wife, calling at her place of work, calling at her house early in the morning and late at night.[4] The court usually expands on the word "molestation" in the terms of the order, to make its meaning clear to the husband. The order may thus require him, "Not to molest, assault, annoy or otherwise interfere with the applicant, nor to communicate with the applicant save through her solicitors."[5]

20–11 (ii) A provision restraining the other party from molesting a child living with the applicant
A non-molestation injunction under the D.V.M.P.A. 1976 can extend to protect a child other than the applicant's, as well as a child who is not a child of the family. It would cover, for example, foster children living with the applicant. However,

---

[3] *Vaughan* v. *Vaughan* [1973] 1 W.L.R. 1159, 1165, *per* Stephenson L.J. See also *Horner* v. *Horner* [1982] Fam. 90.

[4] See *Vaughan* v. *Vaughan* (above).

[5] Stephenson L.J. stated in *Vaughan* v. *Vaughan* (above) that whether communication amounts to a molestation is a question of fact and degree. It might be argued, therefore, that this form of wording is outside the courts' powers, going beyond "molestation." Nonetheless, this is a common form of wording found in many injunctions.

children of the family who were living with other people (*e.g.* grandparents) would not be within the protection of this Act.

(iii) A provision excluding the other party from the matrimonial home or from a specified area in which the matrimonial home is situated   20–12
This is a very wide power, but it has certain limitations. In particular there is no power to exclude a third party (*e.g.* the husband's mistress) from the home. Also it would not be possible to exclude the other party from some other place (*e.g.* the wife's place of work), unless this happened to be in the same area as the matrimonial home. Nevertheless, the power to exclude from an area in which the home is situated is particularly useful, as it may be used to exclude a husband from, for example, the housing estate on which the home is situated, or an area which includes local shops and schools. There is no defined limit beyond which the husband cannot be excluded, although, of course, an unreasonably wide exclusion zone would be liable to reduction on appeal.

(iv) A provision requiring the other party to permit the applicant to enter and remain in the matrimonial home or a part of the matrimonial home   20–13
This would normally only be ordered in conjunction with an order requiring the occupying spouse to leave.

THE POSITION OF COHABITANTS UNDER THE D.V.M.P.A. 1976   20–14

As mentioned above, the powers of the court under the Act can be invoked by cohabitants. Section 1(2) of the D.V.M.P.A. 1976 provides that section 1(1) shall apply to a man and woman who are living with each other in the same household as husband and wife as it applies to the parties to a marriage, and any reference to the "matrimonial home" shall be construed accordingly.

The courts have given this provision quite a wide interpretation. First, they have been prepared to allow a party to invoke the court's jurisdiction under the Act provided that the parties could be said to have been cohabiting, rather than living together as husband and wife in the strict sense. Thus, the woman might not have taken the man's name, and might indeed have made it quite clear that she did not regard herself as his wife and did not see their relationship as a stable or permanent one. For example, in *McLean* v. *Nugent*[6] the

6 (1980) 1 F.L.R. 26.

applicant alleged that the respondent had forced her to share her flat with him for several months. She later returned to live with her parents to avoid his violence, but when he continued to pester her at her parents' house she applied for a non-molestation injunction against him. The Court of Appeal accepted that, on these facts, the parties should be regarded as having lived together as husband and wife for the purposes of the D.V.M.P.A. 1976, and upheld the woman's application for the injunction. Similarly, in *Adeoso* v. *Adeoso*,[7] the Court of Appeal accepted that the parties (who were not married to each other) were living together as husband and wife in the same household, even though they lived their lives as separately as possible in a very small flat. They occupied separate rooms, which were kept locked, and there was no sharing of cooking or laundry facilities. Certainly under the divorce jurisdiction they would have been regarded as living apart (see 3–41 above).

It is, of course, clear that, however wide an interpretation is given to section 1(2) of the Act, the parties must at some time have actually lived together. Thus, in *Tuck* v. *Nicholls*,[8] one of the issues in dispute was whether or not the parties were living with each other in the same household as husband and wife. The parties had obtained a joint tenancy of a council house, but at the time of the woman's application for a non-molestation and ouster injunction, they were still only in the process of moving into this accommodation. Some furniture had been moved into the property, but the woman had spent at most only two nights in the new house, and remained living most of the time in her parents' home. The Court of Appeal took the view that, if this was the full extent of the parties' cohabitation, they could not be said to be living together as husband and wife in the same houshold within section 1(2) of the 1976 Act.

A second respect in which the courts have taken a broad view of section 1(2), is in their acceptance that, as long as the parties were living together as husband and wife at the time of the incidents relied on, the fact that they are not living together at the time of the application should not be a bar to that application succeeding. This point was established by the House of Lords decision in *Davis* v. *Johnson*[9] and, indeed, the application of the principle can be illustrated by reference to the facts of *McLean* v. *Nugent* discussed above. This broader

[7] [1980] 1 W.L.R. 1535.
[8] [1989] 1 F.L.R. 283.
[9] [1979] A.C. 264.

interpretation of the wording of section 1(2) was, of course, essential if one of the main aims of the provision was not to be frustrated. In many cases couples separate as a result of domestic violence and Parliament cannot have intended that an unmarried partner should have to go on cohabiting in the face of such violence before an application for an injunction to restrain it could succeed. It must be added, however, that the Act does not provide protection for a partner who suffers molestation of some kind only after the parties have separated. Nor, of course, does it provide a remedy at all for a partner in a homosexual relationship.

In cases where the D.V.M.P.A. 1976 does not apply, it should, nevertheless, be remembered that the necessary injunctions may be obtained in an ordinary action in tort. It may, for example, be possible to obtain an injunction in an action for assault and battery, or in trespass. It should be noted, however, that the law does not recognise separate torts of molestation or harassment, and that therefore no separate action will lie for appropriate injunctions on these grounds alone. It should also be borne in mind that, where one party either uses or threatens violence against another, he may well have committed a number of criminal offences. It is therefore possible, at least in theory, to invoke the aid of the police in such cases, with a view to criminal proceedings being instituted against the offender.

MATRIMONIAL HOMES ACT 1983   20–15

The purpose of this Act was not to provide injunctive relief, although it does enable the court to regulate the occupation of the matrimonial home. Broadly, it gives a spouse[10] a statutory right of occupation so that, even though that spouse may have no legal or equitable interest in the property, nor any rights as a tenant, she cannot be evicted by the other spouse without a court order.[11] Applications for orders regulating the occupation of the matrimonial home may also be made under this Act by spouses who are joint owners or joint tenants of the home. If the home is held in the joint names of the husband and wife, the application is made under section 9 of the M.H.A. 1983; if one spouse is the sole owner or tenant the application is made under section 1(2).

---

[10] It does not apply to parties unless they are married.
[11] See Chapter 9 for further details of the statutory rights of occupation, and the possibility of registering them as protection against a purchaser or mortgagee of the property.

20–16 **The powers of the court**
The court can make one or more of the following orders:

(i) an order declaring, enforcing, restricting or terminating the statutory rights of occupation of a non-owner or non-tenant spouse;

(ii) an order prohibiting, suspending or restricting the exercise by either spouse of the right to occupy the dwelling-house;

(iii) an order requiring either spouse to permit the exercise by the other of that right.

20–17 It will be seen from this that the Act contains no provision allowing the court to restrain one spouse from molesting the other. The M.H.A. 1983 powers can be compared with the powers of the court under the D.V.M.P.A. 1976, discussed at 20–10 to 20–13, above. As can be seen, there is very little distinction between the two in so far as they regulate the occupation of the matrimonial home. However, *on its own* the M.H.A. 1983 is inadequate as it does not allow for the control of molestation, nor can it be used to exclude a spouse from an area in which the home is situated.

In practice the main use of the M.H.A. 1983, in this field, i to provide the statutory authority under which the divorce court makes ouster injunctions during matrimonial proceedings. This is in addition to the divorce court's powers to make other injunctions discussed below.

20–18 ANCILLARY TO A PETITION FOR A DECREE

The necessity for injunctive relief arises most commonly during the turbulent process of marriage breakdown. Although all the following powers may be used by the court ancillary to a claim for a decree of judicial separation or nullity, it is assumed, for the sake of brevity, that the powers are being exercised ancillary to a petition for a divorce.

20–19 **(i) Non-molestation injunctions**
It is now settled[12] that the court has the power to grant injunctions ancillary to divorce by virtue of section 37 of the Supreme Court Act 1981 and section 38 of the County Courts Act 1984.

---

[12] *Richards* v. *Richards* [1984] A.C. 174.

Section 37 of the Supreme Court Act 1981 provides that the High Court may by order grant an injunction "in all cases in which it appears to the court to be just and convenient to do so." Section 38 of the County Courts Act 1984 confers the same powers on the county court.

These are often termed the "inherent" powers of the court, although, strictly speaking, they are now subsumed under these statutory provisions. Under these provisions the court may grant injunctions against molestation (this term has been explained at 20–10, above). However, the power to make injunctions excluding a spouse from the matrimonial home no longer derives from these provisions.

(ii) Exclusion from the matrimonial home   20–20
In *Richards* v. *Richards*,[13] the House of Lords established that the jurisdiction of the divorce court to make orders regulating the occupation of the matrimonial home derives, not from any "inherent" jurisdiction, but from the provisions of the M.H.A. 1983, set out at 20–16, above. Hence an application made in divorce proceedings by, for example, a wife wanting to exclude her husband from the home, is in fact made under either section 1 or section 9 of the M.H.A. 1983 (see 20–15). The procedural aspects of this are considered at 20–33 to 20–52 below.

(iii) Exclusion from places other than the matrimonial home   20–21
Where one party to divorce proceedings is seeking to exclude the other from some other place, for example, a place where they work, or an area around the matrimonial home, resort must still be had to the "inherent" powers, which are now covered by the Supreme Court Act 1981 and the County Courts Act 1984.

(iv) Ouster injunctions against third parties   20–22
Again, under the Supreme Court Act 1981, it is possible for the court to exclude someone other than a party from the matrimonial home. In *Jones* v. *Jones*,[14] for example, the Court of Appeal granted an ouster injunction against the husband's mistress, whom he had installed in the matrimonial home. Of course, following *Richards* v. *Richards* it would seem to be necessary for the party seeking such an injunction to be able to establish some legal or equitable right on which to base the application. This could, at least in some cases, be founded on the wife's right as an occupier to exclude a trespasser.

[13] [1984] A.C. 174.
[14] [1971] 2 All E.R. 737.

20–23 **(v) Injunctions after decree absolute**
As the decree absolute terminates the marriage, the M.H.A. 1983 can no longer apply, unless, before the decree, the court made an order extending the statutory rights of occupation beyond divorce. The D.V.M.P.A. 1976 also would not apply, unless the parties are living in the same household as man and wife, which is most unlikely, even if they are still living in the same house after the divorce.[15] In any case, the Act could not assist where one party wants to exclude the other by keeping him away from a home which he has already left.

20–24 *Non-molestation injunctions*

If it is necessary to protect the children of the family, then the court does have power to make such an order under its "inherent" jurisdiction referred to above.[16] Furthermore, in *Webb* v. *Webb*[17] the Court of Appeal held that this jurisdiction, when read together with the Rules of the Supreme Court Order 29, r. 1(1), could be used to grant a wife a non-molestation injunction (and an injunction keeping her ex-husband away from the home) even though the decree absolute had been granted some 18 months previously. Order 29, r. 1(1) provides that: *"An application for the grant of an injunction may be made by any party to a cause or matter before or after the trial of that cause or matter. . . . "* The Court of Appeal held that a matrimonial cause was a cause within the meaning of Order 29, and, therefore, an injunction could be granted even though the case has ended.

It must be emphasised, however, that Order 29 is a procedural provision and cannot confer on the court a jurisdiction which it would otherwise lack. It is not clear from *Webb* v. *Webb* on what jurisdiction the injunction was based. In *Richards* v. *Richards* the House of Lords held, that, where the M.H.A. 1983 and the D.V.M.P.A. 1976 do not apply, and an injunction is sought under the Supreme Court Act 1981, the application must be based on some legal or equitable right. Presumably in the case of an application for a non-molestation injunction after the divorce, the application is based on a general right not to be molested, which everyone enjoys, whether they are married or not.

---

[15] See 3–41 above, where the meaning of this term is considered in relation to divorce. Though compare also *Adeoso* v. *Adeoso* [1980] 1 W.L.R. 1535 considered at 20–14 above.

[16] *Beasley* v. *Beasley* [1969] 1 W.L.R. 226.

[17] [1986] 1 F.L.R. 541. See also *Ruddell* v. *Ruddell* (1967) 111 S.J. 497; also *J. (H.D.)* v. *J. (A.M.) (Financial Provision Variation)* [1980] 1 W.L.R. 124 and *Bardsell* v. *Bardsell* [1982] 3 F.L.R. 375.

Ouster injunctions   **20–25**

In *Webb* v. *Webb* (above), the Court of Appeal also held that
there is "inherent" power to grant an ouster injunction after
decree absolute. The court did not consider on what legal or
equitable right the application was based. It may be that Mrs.
Webb had a proprietary interest in the house, and certainly,
in the past, exclusion injunctions have been granted on this
basis. The position may, however, be more complicated
where the parties have a joint interest in the property. In
Waugh v. *Waugh*[18] the court held that it had no power to grant
an ouster order to one joint tenant, because a joint tenant has
no legal or equitable right to exclude the other.

Another situation which has, in the past, been held to
justify the granting of an ouster order after the divorce, has
been where it was needed for the protection of children.[19] It is
not clear whether this possibility has survived the decision in
Richards v. *Richards*. Certainly in that case the House of Lords
emphasised that the interests of the children are not a
paramount consideration in deciding an application for an
ouster order.

Subsequently in *M.* v. *M. (Custody Application)*,[20] the Court
of Appeal held that there is no inherent jurisdiction to make
an exclusion order in custody proceedings against a divorced
spouse unless the applicant has a sufficient proprietary
interest in the property in question. In this case the former
husband was the sole tenant of the property, and so could
not be excluded. In contrast to this, however, in *Wilde* v.
Wilde,[21] a differently constituted Court of Appeal held that,
despite *Richards* v. *Richards*, the court retained an inherent
jurisdiction to exclude where this was necessary for the
protection of children. It is clearly desirable that the court
should have such a jurisdiction, but it is one which now
needs to be properly established either by a further appeal to
the House of Lords, or better still, by amending legislation.

ANCILLARY TO OTHER PROCEEDINGS   **20–26**

There are still a number of situations where parties (such as
partners to a homosexual relationship) may have to seek the
protection of an injunction ancillary to some other claim (*e.g.*

---

[18] (1982) 3 F.L.R. 375.
[19] See, *e.g. Quinn* v. *Quinn* (1983) 4 F.L.R. 394.
[20] [1988] 1 F.L.R. 225.
[21] [1988] 2 F.L.R. 83.

an action for assault, trespass or nuisance). In the case of children, a claim for a non-molestation injunction might be made ancillary to a claim for custody under the G.M.A. 1971.[22] It is important, however, that there should be some link between the substantive claim and the injunctive relief required. For example, it would not be possible to seek a non-molestation injunction ancillary to a claim for a declaration of property rights under section 17 of the M.W.P.A. 1882.

20–27 ## 4. Principles Applied to the Granting of Injunctions

In this section the principles governing the orders made by the county court under the D.V.M.P.A. 1976, the M.C.A. 1973 and the M.H.A. 1983 are considered. The approach of the courts to making such orders is the same whichever jurisdiction is used.

20–28 ## NON-MOLESTATION INJUNCTIONS

No real objection can be made to an application for an order not to molest anyone, although the courts have stressed that injunctions are not to be granted lightly, and the overriding principle is that the order must be necessary for the protection of the person on whose behalf it is sought. Nonetheless, providing there is evidence of actual or threatened molestation, the court will readily grant an injunction. In serious cases, the court can grant such an injunction without the need for the attendance of the respondent.[23]

20–29 ## OUSTER INJUNCTIONS

The House of Lords decision in *Richards* v. *Richards*[24] has settled the principles which govern ouster injunctions. The M.H.A. 1983, s.1(3) lays down the only criteria which will apply to applications for these orders, whether sought under the M.H.A. 1983, the D.V.M.P.A. 1976 or the Supreme Court

---

[22] Although not for an ouster injunction, see *Ainsbury* v. *Millington* [1986] 1 F.L.R. 331.
[23] See 20–46, below for further details.
[24] [1984] A.C. 174.

Act 1981. These criteria will also apply in cases involving cohabiting couples.[25]

The criteria are:

(i) the conduct of the spouses in relation to each other and otherwise;

(ii) the spouses' respective needs and financial resources;

(iii) the needs of any children; and

(iv) all the circumstances of the case.

It is now clear that none of these criteria is to be treated as paramount, so that, for example, the needs of the children will not always predominate. Having weighed all the factors, the court may then make such order as it thinks just and reasonable.

The relevance of these statutory criteria must now be considered in more detail.

THE SPOUSE'S CONDUCT   **20-30**

In many cases the most relevant conduct will be the respondent's violent behaviour. Violent conduct of any significance will often be the decisive factor in any particular case, and will often result in the exclusion of the party who has been violent. It is, however, well established that it is not essential to be able to adduce evidence of violence in order to succeed in an application for exclusion. Another important factor is whether the applicant may be said to have acted reasonably in bringing the application for the injunction. This aspect is well illustrated by reference to the facts of *Richards* v. *Richards* itself. In this case the wife had filed a divorce petition relying on the husband's unreasonable behaviour, which consisted largely of showing a lack of affection and concern for the wife's well-being. Mrs. Richards's own counsel had admitted at one stage of the proceedings that these allegations were "flimsy in the extreme," the trial judge had described them as "rubbishy" and the husband was defending the petition. Some time after filing the petition the wife left the matrimonial home, and, taking the two children of the family with her, went to stay in accommodation which was overcrowded and clearly unsatisfactory for both her and the children. She now sought an ouster injunction to exclude the

---

[25] *Lee* v. *Lee* [1984] F.L.R. 243.

husband from the matrmonial home, saying that she would not return to the property until the husband had left. The House of Lords held that the injunction should not be granted, finding that Mrs. Richards's refusal to live in the matrimonial home was unreasonable.

THE PARTIES' NEEDS AND RESOURCES

In most applications the main consideration under this heading will be the need of the parties for a home. Where the court is considering granting an exclusion injunction it will always have to consider the availability of alternative accommodation for the party to be excluded. This means that, for example, the court will always inquire where the husband is going to live if he is to be excluded. The lack of alternative accommodation, which many husbands may plead in these circumstances, is not likely to prevent an injunction being granted altogether. It will, however, often have a bearing on the length of time which the husband will be allowed before being required to vacate the property. A court has a complete discretion as to this matter, as the legislation makes no reference to it. Consequently the time allowed for compliance with the order may vary between, for example, 24 hours and four weeks.

THE NEEDS OF ANY CHILDREN

As mentioned above, in *Richards* v. *Richards* the House of Lords emphasised that, unlike disputes as to custody, injunction proceedings do not require the welfare of the children to be treated as the first and paramount consideration. This means that if, for example, the wife is being unreasonable in refusing to return to the matrimonial home until the husband is excluded, an injunction may well be refused even if the children are clearly living in unsuitable accommodation. The facts of *Richards* v. *Richards*, set out above, are a clear illustration of this point. Nevertheless, the children's need for a secure home is obviously a very important factor in these cases and, in general, it may be said that the custodial parent will usually be allowed to remain in or return to occupation of the home, even if this means excluding the other party. The point may be illustrated by reference to the facts of *Lee* v. *Lee*.[26]

---

[26] [1984] 1 F.L.R. 243.

418

Mr. and Mrs. Lee were unmarried. Mrs. Lee had two **20–31** children, a boy and a girl. Whilst Mrs. Lee was in hospital the daughter had been placed in local authority care, because of the alleged indecent behaviour of Mr. Lee towards his daughter. When she left hospital, Mrs. Lee discovered the allegations against Mr. Lee and refused to return to him. She went to live in cramped accommodation. The juvenile court then discontinued the care order, but made a supervision order, under which the child was not to be brought into contact with Mr. Lee, nor return to her mother until her mother had suitable accommodation. The child went to live with her grandmother.

On Mrs. Lee's application for an ouster injunction, the Court of Appeal held, granting the ouster injunction:

(i) The principles of the M.H.A. 1983 should apply even though the application was made under the D.V.M.P.A. 1976.

(ii) In considering those factors, no weight could be attached to the conduct of either party, both being of stormy temperament. The applicant needed a home for herself and the children, whereas the respondent only had to provide for himself. So far as resources were concerned, both parties were dependent on state benefit. However, the needs of the children to be re-established in the family home carried the greatest weight.

ALL THE CIRCUMSTANCES OF THE CASE

This wide "catch-all" phrase allows the courts to consider any other matter that may be relevant to the particular application. This is not to say, however, that a judge is entitled to take into account any matter that strikes him as relevant. The Court of Appeal will be prepared to interfere with the discretion of the judge at first instance if it considers that he has taken into account factors which really are irrelevant. This point can be illustrated by reference to *Summers* v. *Summers*.[27]

Mr. Summers was aged 20 and his wife 23. There were three **20–32** children of the family. Mrs. Summers petitioned for divorce and left the matrimonial home with her children. She applied for a non-molestation order and an ouster injunction. The

[27] [1986] 1 F.L.R. 343.

court found that there had been no acts of violence by Mr. Summers against his wife and refused to grant the non-molestation injunction. The judge did, however, grant an ouster injunction because he felt that it was not right for the children to be living in a small flat with their mother and their grandparents; he also said that it might "ease a reconciliation."

Mr. Summers appealed and the Court of Appeal held:

(a) There might be some cases where the interests of the children are paramount.

(b) The statute did not require the court to consider making an order as a means of promoting a reconciliation.

(c) The judge should have borne in mind the draconian nature of an ouster injunction.

(d) As the judge took into account matters which he ought not to have taken into account, and probably did not consider matters which he should have considered, the appeal would be allowed.

It will be apparent from what has been said above that it is not possible to extract any simple rule from the case law to indicate when an ouster injunction will be granted. However, in cases where there is a serious risk to the applicant's or a child's physical or mental health, and the only effective means of prevention is an ouster injunction, it is likely that the court will make such an order.

20–33 5. Procedure

This section deals with the procedure for obtaining injunctions under the D.V.M.P.A. 1976 and ancillary to divorce.

20–34 LEGAL AID AND LEGAL ADVICE AND ASSISTANCE

As this topic has been dealt with in general in Chapter 2, only those additional matters which relate to injunctive relief will be dealt with here.

The initial advice will, subject to the usual limits, be covered by the Green Form in the normal way. As it is necessary to apply for an injunction as a matter of urgency, there is an emergency procedure available to obtain legal aid.

When the application form for legal aid is submitted, a second application form for emergency legal aid is also completed and forwarded. This enables the Area Director to grant an emergency certificate on the assumption that the financial and other matters referred to in the application forms are correct. Should it later transpire that this is not so, the certificate may be revoked and the applicant will be personally liable for the solicitor's costs.

Where the matter is one of extreme urgency and the applicant **20–35** wishes to apply for an *ex parte* injunction (as to which see 20–46, below) the Area Director can be telephoned to inform him that an application for an emergency certificate is being made. In these circumstances the Area Director may sanction the grant of an emergency certificate from that moment. An undertaking to forward the application forms must be given by the solicitor, if these have not already been submitted.

Alternatively, where emergency work has to be done outside office hours, it is now possible to do the necessary work without having made a prior application for emergency legal aid, provided an application for an emergency certificate is made at the first available opportunity afterwards.[28] In these circumstances, the certificate can be backdated to cover work already done. If for some reason this is not feasible, a last resort might be to seek the approval of the court itself to be allowed to represent the client under the Green Form. The court has power to grant such representation for a person "who is not receiving and has not been refused" a legal aid certificate for the proceedings concerned.[29] The court must be satisfied that the hearing should proceed on the same day, and that that party would not otherwise be represented. If these conditions are satisfied, the court can approve a proposal from a solicitor within the precincts of the court that he represent the unassisted party under the Green Form.

THE APPLICATION **20–36**

The procedures for applying for injunctions under the D.V.M.P.A. 1976 and ancillary to divorce, whether for a non-molestation injunction, or under the M.H.A. 1983, are very similar. They are summarised together below, and the minor divergences between them are indicated.

If the application is made ancillary to divorce for a non-molestation injunction, the same procedure will be followed

---

[28] See Civil Legal Aid (General) Regs. 1989, reg. 103(6).
[29] See Legal Advice and Assistance (Scope) Regulations 1989, reg. 8; see also 2–36, above.

as for an ouster injunction under the M.H.A. 1983 ancillary to a divorce. For the sake of brevity this jurisdiction is referred to below as "ancillary to divorce." It should be noted that the procedure summarised is that ancillary to divorce, although the procedure ancillary to one of the other decrees (*i.e.* judicial separation or nullity) will be similar.

(i) "On notice" injunctions

20–37 *File documents*

The applicant's solicitor will commence proceedings by filing:

(i) An *originating application* containing the terms of the injunction sought (D.V.M.P.A. 1976); *or*

a petition and supporting documents (unless, of course, these have already been filed) and a *notice of application* for a hearing date, containing the terms of the injunction sought (ancillary to divorce).

(ii) A copy of the application for sealing by the court and return to the applicant.

(iii) An affidavit in support.

(iv) The legal aid certificate (if relevant). At this stage the certificate will probably be the emergency certificate. When it arrives, the full certificate will also have to be filed.

(v) A draft of the order sought is also required by the rules[30] except where the case is one of urgency; in many courts it will be sufficient if the draft order is submitted to the judge at the hearing.

(vi) The court fee.

20–38 The application should be made in the appropriate county court, *viz.*:

D.V.M.P.A. 1976—in the county court for the district in which the applicant or respondent resides, or where the matrimonial home is situated.

Ancillary to divorce—any divorce county court. If the petition has already been filed, then the application for the injunction must, of course, be made in the same county court.

---

[30] C.C.R. Ord. 13, r. 6.

In the majority of cases the distinction is academic, as the application will simply be made to the local county court.

Court returns a copy of the application for service—If the application is made under the D.V.M.P.A. 1976, the court will also send a separate notice of the hearing date to the applicant's solicitor, for service on the respondent. Where the application is made ancillary to divorce, the hearing date will be entered on the notice of application itself. **20–39**

Service—The applicant's solicitor will then effect personal service[31] of the copy of the application on the respondent, together with a notice of issue of legal aid and a copy of the applicant's affidavit. Under the D.V.M.P.A. 1976 the minimum period of notice of the hearing is four days; under the procedure ancillary to divorce, it is two days. Again the distinction is likely to be academic, owing to the congested nature of the court lists. **20–40**

File notice of issue—The applicant's solicitor should then file a copy of the notice of issue of the legal aid certificate served on the respondent. **20–41**

Proof of service—An affidavit of service should be obtained from the process server to prove that service has been effected. **20–42**

Affidavit in reply?—It may be that the respondent will file an affidavit in reply and send a copy to the applicant, but this is rare. **20–43**

Hearing—The hearing will take place before a judge in chambers, when evidence on oath will be taken from the applicant and any witnesses she may have. The respondent will also give oral evidence if he is present, and any witnesses he may have will be heard. The judge will then make an order. **20–44**

Service of order—Assuming the judge has granted the injunction, a copy of the order will be prepared by the court and served by the applicant's solicitor on the respondent personally. Even if the respondent was present in court when the order was made, this should be done, as it is required by the rules. For further details about this see 20–55 below. **20–45**

(ii) *Ex parte* injunctions **20–46**
There are occasions where the risk of immediate assault on the applicant is so great that she wishes to seek the protection

---

[31] See 20–55.

of the court as soon as possible. In cases of emergency, an application for an injunction may be made without the respondent attending. Should such an order be made it must be followed within a matter of days by a full hearing on notice, to avoid any miscarriage of justice. Where an *ex parte* injunction is sought, the procedure outlined above is subject to the following modifications:

20–47   —It will be necessary to telephone the county court to arrange a hearing time.

20–48   —If the application is being made ancillary to divorce the petition and accompanying documents may be omitted at this stage if there is insufficient time to prepare them. However, an undertaking will be required from the solicitor to file these within a short period of time (*e.g.* seven days). The same point applies in the case of injunctions under the D.V.M.P.A. 1976, where an undertaking can be given to file the originating application.

20–49   —The draft order may be omitted.

20–50   —The applicant should attend at court to give oral evidence in support of her application. If time permits, it will be helpful for the applicant, the judge and the applicant's solicitor, if the application and affidavit in support can be available at the hearing. In some circumstances a draft of the order applied for can also be extremely helpful in expediting the preparation of the court's order.

20–51   —Assuming the order is made, it will be necessary for this to be served personally on the respondent as before. Afterwards the procedure for obtaining an injunction on notice, set out above, must be followed.

20–52   A Practice Note[32] emphasises that an application for an *ex parte* order should only be made if there is a "real immediate danger of serious injury or irreparable damage." Further in *Masich* v. *Masich*[33] the court stated that ouster injunctions would only be made at a hearing on notice, and not *ex parte*. The court went on to warn solicitors against making such applications *ex parte* otherwise they might be made personally

---

[32] [1978] 2 All E.R. 919.
[33] (1977) 7 Fam. Law 245.

liable for the costs. Nevertheless there are some judges who are prepared to grant ouster injunctions *ex parte* where they feel the circumstances warrant it.[34] In general, there should be less difficulty obtaining an *ex parte* order *keeping* a party out of the house than one which *puts* him out.

Draft order

To a large extent, orders made ancillary to divorce and the D.V.M.P.A. 1976 are very similar. The main difference is the headings appropriate to each jurisdiction. The heading for orders under the M.H.A. 1983 (ancillary to divorce) is the same as the heading used on the other divorce papers.

Illustrated below is a draft of a final order made under the D.V.M.P.A. 1976.

20–53

IN THE CHRISFORD COUNTY COURT

No. of Application..........

IN THE MATTER OF the Domestic Violence and Matrimonial Proceedings Act 1976

AND IN THE MATTER OF Dunromin, Acacia Avenue, Chrisford, Bogshire.

BETWEEN

JANE SMITH   Applicant

and

PETER SMITH   Respondent.

Before His Honour Judge .... sitting at Court Square, High Street, Chrisford, on the ...... day of ...... 199 .

Upon hearing the solicitor for the applicant and upon reading her affidavit sworn the ...... day of ...... 199 and upon hearing her oral evidence and upon hearing the solicitor for the respondent and upon his oral evidence.

NOW IT IS HEREBY ORDERED[35] THAT:

---

[34] See *G. v. G.* (1989) *The Times*, November 23.

[35] Note that C.C.R., Ord. 47 r. 8(5) (as amended) requires that those provisions of the injunction to which a power of arrest is attached are to be set out in separate clauses of the injunction without including references to any forms of molestation to which a power of arrest cannot attach.

1. The respondent shall be excluded from the matrimonial home known as Dunromin, Acacia Avenue, Chrisford, from a time twenty-four hours after the service on him of this order.[36]

2. Having vacated the said premises, the respondent shall not return to them, nor to the road known as Acacia Avenue, Chrisford, for three months, or until further order.[37]

3. The respondent shall not use violence against the applicant.

4. On or before the expiry of twenty-four hours after service on him of this order, the respondent shall deposit all the keys to those premises in his possession with the applicant's solicitors, Snoggle and Co., of High Street, Chrisford.

5. The respondent shall further not threaten violence against the applicant, or otherwise molest, interfere with or (save through a solicitor) communicate with her until further order.

6. Either party may seek to have these orders reviewed rescinded or revoked upon giving not less than 7 days notice to the other party and the court.

7. The respondent shall pay the costs of the applicant. Order for legal aid taxation of the applicant's costs.

Dated this .... day of 199   .

....
Judge

PENAL NOTICE

To: Peter Smith of Dunromin, Acacia Avenue, Chrisford

---

[36] A judge has a discretion as to how long to allow a party to vacate the home. Even where a period of four weeks was allowed, the Court of Appeal refused to interfere with this. See *Hopper* v. *Hopper* [1979] 1 All E.R. 181. However, one or two weeks would be the normal maximum; see *Burke* v. *Burke* [1987] 2 F.L.R. 71.

[37] The court has a discretion to decide for how long an injunction should operate. In practice some non-molestation injunctions may be granted without such a time limit, when, in theory, they would remain in force indefinitely. In the case of ouster injunctions a period of three months is usual or, in the case of injunctions ancillary to divorce, until decree absolute. See Practice Note [1978] 2 All E.R. 1056; *Davis* v. *Johnson* [1979] A.C. 264; *Hopper* v. *Hopper* [1979] 1 All E.R. 181.

YOU MUST OBEY THE DIRECTIONS CONTAINED IN THIS ORDER. IF YOU DO NOT YOU WILL BE GUILTY OF CONTEMPT OF COURT AND YOU MAY BE SENT TO PRISON.

....
Registrar

Dated this .... day of .... 199 .

POWER OF ARREST ATTACHED

POWER OF ARREST   20–54

It is unlikely that a solicitor drafting an injunction order for consideration by the judge would go so far as to draft out the full form of the power of arrest. This would depend on local practice, but it would probably be sufficient to indicate on the draft order that a power of arrest was being sought (as shown above). This is because the power of arrest is now prepared, by the court office, on a separate form, which is additional to the order, a copy of which can be given to the police. Clearly both orders would be served on the respondent.

The power of arrest is thus a complete document containing all the information which the police would need to know in order to arrest the respondent. The power of arrest is explained at 20–58 to 20–59 below. For completeness, an example of the final power of arrest form is set out below.

Domestic Violence Injunction

Power of Arrest

In the Chrisford County Court

Case No.

Applicant's Ref:

SEAL

Applicant

Respondent

(Here set out the provisions of the injunction to which the power of arrest relates)

1. The respondent shall be excluded from the matrimonial home known as Dunromin, Acacia Avenue, Chrisford, from a time twenty-four hours after the service on him of this order.

2. Having vacated the said premises, the respondent shall not return to them, nor to the road known as Acacia Avenue, Chrisford, for three months, or until further order.

3. The respondent shall not use violence against the applicant.

POWER OF ARREST

And the judge being satisfied that the respondent has caused actual bodily harm to the applicant and being of the opinion that he is likely to do so again, a power of arrest is attached to this injunction, whereby any constable may arrest without warrant the respondent if he has reasonable cause for suspecting the respondent of using violence, or entering any premises or area in breach of clauses 1, 2 and 3 of this injunction, as mentioned in section 2(3) of the Domestic Violence and Matrimonial Proceedings Act 1976.

This power of arrest shall expire on the ...... of 199   .

[*There then follows a note to the arresting officer explaining his duties with regard to the arrested respondent. This is explained further in 20–59.*]

6. Enforcement

20–55 COMMITTAL

The primary method of enforcement of an injunction is by committal to prison for contempt of court. For this to be possible a penal notice, warning the respondent of the consequences of breaking the injunction, must be indorsed on the order. An example of this can be seen in the draft order above. It is also necessary to be able to prove to the court that the respondent was aware of the terms of the order. The order should be served personally on the respondent and this is normally proved by means of an affidavit of service. This should be done even though the respondent was in court when the injunction was made, although enforcement may be possible if service was not effected.[38] Where the respondent gave an undertaking rather than submit to an injunction, the undertaking may also be enforced by committal.[39] A form of undertaking is prescribed for this purpose, and this, like an order, sets out the terms of the penal notice. The form also allows the judge to direct that the party giving the undertaking shall sign in court an acknowledgment of his undertaking. This ensures that the consequences of a breach are brought directly to the respondent's attention.

The procedure for applying for an order for committal is as follows[40]:

20–56

File:

(i) notice of application for the respondent to show cause why he should not be committed and a copy;

(ii) affidavit in support containing details of breaches.

Serve:

The stamped copy of (i) above when this is returned by the court plus a copy of (ii).

It is possible that at this stage the respondent may file an affidavit in reply.

At the hearing, which will normally be in open court, the judge may make an order that the respondent be committed to prison for a period of time not exceeding two years.[41]

20–57

---

[38] An order requiring a person to abstain from doing something may be enforced even if service has not been personally effected, provided he has had notice of it. See C.C.R., Ord. 29, r. 6. Furthermore r. 7 gives a general discretion to the court to enforce without service even in the case of mandatory injunctions. See *Husson* v. *Husson* [1962] 3 All E.R. 1056 and *Turner* v. *Turner* (1978) 122 S.J. 696.

[39] County Court (Amendment) Rules 1988 (S.I. 1988/278).

[40] C.C.R., Ord. 29.

[41] Contempt of Court Act 1981, s.14; County Court (Penalties for Contempt) Act 1983.

Alternatively, a suspended committal order might be made, or, of course, there may be no order. In *Goff* v. *Goff*[42] the Court of Appeal reviewed some of the relevant factors that the court should take into account in deciding whether an immediate committal order is justified. The factors mentioned by the court include such matters as the previous character of the party in contempt, the effects a committal order might have on the children of the marriage, and the effect on the financial position of the party in contempt. In general, an immediate committal order will be reserved for serious breaches of the injunction or undertaking. For example, in *Brewer* v. *Brewer*[43] the Court of Appeal upheld an immediate committal for two months after the husband had entered the home, damaged property, and made threats, including threats to kill the wife, in public. At the far end of the spectrum comes *Mesham* v. *Clarke*[44] where the Court of Appeal upheld a maximum two-year sentence. In this case there had been repeated breaches of a non-molestation and exclusion injunction, culminating in an express warning from the judge of the consequences of another breach.

20–58 POWER OF ARREST

The procedure for seeking committal might prove too cumbersome to deal with a violent respondent whose first reaction on being served with a copy of the injunction might be to assault the applicant. In certain circumstances, therefore, the court may empower the police to arrest a respondent without warrant if they have a reasonable suspicion that he is in breach of the injunction.

20–59 The court may attach a "power of arrest" to the injunction if the judge is satisfied, "that the other party has caused actual bodily harm to the applicant or ... to the child concerned and considers that he is likely to do so again."[45] Actual bodily harm has been defined as including any hurt or injury calculated to interfere with the health or comfort of (the applicant).[46]

It must not be assumed, however, that the judge will attach a power of arrest if these statutory criteria are met. In *Lewis* v.

---

[42] [1989] 1 F.L.R. 436.
[43] [1989] 2 F.L.R. 251.
[44] [1989] 1 F.L.R. 370.
[45] D.V.M.P.A. 1976, s.2.
[46] *R.* v. *Miller* [1954] 2 Q.B. 282 at p. 292.

Lewis[47] the Court of Appeal emphasised that the power of arrest should not be regarded as a routine remedy, and suggested that it should be reserved for cases of persistent disobedience. Although the discretion to attach a power of arrest derives from section 2 of the D.V.M.P.A. 1976, the discretion can be exercised in relation to injunctions granted under other jurisdictions, for example, ancillary to divorce. It must be remembered, however, that a power of arrest can never be attached to an undertaking. It should also be noted that orders made under the M.H.A. 1983 are not, strictly speaking, "injunctions," so that section 2 does not apply to them. In most cases, however, a non-molestation injunction would be sought as well, and a power of arrest could be attached to this. Even when this is not done the court may be persuaded to overlook the technicality.

The Act is silent as to the length of time for which the power of arrest should last. However, a Practice Note[48] suggests that the power should normally be limited to a period of three months, in line with the normal duration of an injunction granted under the D.V.M.P.A. 1976.

Once the power of arrest has been attached to the injunction, a copy of it should be delivered by the court to the police station nearest to the applicant's address. It is good practice for the applicant's solicitor to deliver a copy to the police as well, on the day of the injunction, as the court may well effect delivery by post.

An injunction with a power of arrest attached may be enforced by detention of the respondent by the police. The power may be exercised wherever a constable has reasonable cause to suspect the respondent of being in breach of any term of the injunction which restrains him from using violence *or* from entering the premises or an area in which the premises are situated. Assuming the power of arrest is exercised (and this, of course, is a matter of discretion for the police), the respondent must not be released for a period of 24 hours without the authorisation of a judge, and must, within that time, be brought before a judge. The judge can either order his release or order his committal for a period of time, in the same way as if the respondent had been brought before him on an application for committal. There is, however, no need for the injunction, nor any notice to show cause, to have been served on the respondent first.[49]

---

[47] [1978] Fam. 60.
[48] [1981] 1 W.L.R. 27.
[49] C.C.R., Ord. 47, r. 8.

20–60 7. Proceedings in the Magistrates' Court

The D.P.M.C.A. 1978 confers powers on magistrates to make orders for protection against family violence, similar in scope to those available in the county court. Section 16 of the D.P.M.C.A. 1978 gives the court power to make two types of order, generally known as personal protection orders and exclusion orders.

20–61 PERSONAL PROTECTION ORDERS[50]

These order the respondent not to use or threaten violence against the person of the applicant and/or a child of the family. They may also include a provision that the respondent shall not incite or assist any other person to use such violence. It will be noted that in two respects this order is narrower than the county court order which prohibits molestation generally. First, it restrains the respondent only from using or threatening violence. Magistrates have no power to prohibit a respondent from pestering or communicating with the applicant or children in a general way. Secondly, any child referred to in the order must be a child of the family and not simply a child living with the applicant.

20–62 EXCLUSION ORDERS[51]

The court can order the respondent to leave the matrimonial home, or prohibit the respondent from entering the matrimonial home. The court can also, where it makes an exclusion order, order the respondent to permit the applicant to enter and remain in the matrimonial home.

It is worth noting that (unlike the county court) the magistrates have no power to exclude the respondent from an area in which the home is situated.

20–63 GROUNDS FOR MAKING THE ORDER

The D.P.M.C.A. 1978 sets out the grounds which must be established before an order can be made.

(i) Personal protection orders
The court must be satisfied that the respondent has used, or threatened to use, violence against the applicant or a child of

---

[50] D.P.M.C.A. 1978, s.16(2).
[51] *Ibid.* s.16(3).

the family, and that the order is necessary for the protection of the applicant or a child.[52]

(ii) Exclusion orders   20–64
The court must be satisfied:

(i)   that the respondent has used violence against the applicant or a child of the family; *or*

(ii) that the respondent has *threatened* to use violence against the applicant or a child of the family, and has *used* violence against some other person; *or*

(iii) that the respondent has, in contravention of a personal protection order, threatened violence against the applicant or a child of the family.

In addition to any of the above conditions, the court must be satisfied that the applicant or a child of the family is in danger of being physically injured by the respondent.[53]

It will be noted that the above criteria require more than just the threat of violence coupled with a risk of physical injury. In this respect they are not only more stringent than the criteria according to which personal protection orders are made; they are also much more specific than the criteria employed by county court judges in deciding whether to grant ouster injunctions. As seen, at 20–29, above, the criteria laid down in section 1(3) of the M.H.A. 1983 give county court judges a much wider discretion in exercising their powers.

As in the county court, the magistrates' court is required to enter a date for the expiry of an exclusion order.[54] It is likely that the magistrates' will follow the practice of the county court and select, in most cases, the period of three months.

PROCEDURE

(i) Legal advice and assistance and legal aid   20–65
The initial advice and assistance will be covered by the Green Form in the usual way.[55] Once it has been established that the client wishes to apply to the magistrates' court for relief, it is

---

[52] *Ibid.* s.16(2).
[53] This does not have to be an immediate danger; see *McCartney* v. *McCartney* [1981] Fam. 59.
[54] D.P.M.C.A. 1978, s.16(9) and Magistrates' Courts (Matrimonial Proceedings) Rules 1980, Schedule, Form 14.
[55] See Chap. 2.

necessary to apply to the Area Director for A.B.W.O.R. This procedure has been covered in detail at 2–35, above.

As in the county court, it is possible in urgent cases to make an application for approval over the telephone. Of course, this should only be done in cases of genuine emergency, and an undertaking must be given to submit the completed forms forthwith.

Once A.B.W.O.R. has been granted, the solicitor must notify the other party and the court as soon as practicable.[56] There is no prescribed form for this.

20–66   It is possible for a client to have too much capital to be eligible for Green Form advice, but still be elgible for A.B.W.O.R., because of the higher capital limit prescribed for this form of assistance. Furthermore, a client may very occasionally be ineligible for A.B.W.O.R., but still be eligible for ordinary legal aid. In these circumtances a client may apply for legal aid for the magistrates' court proceedings using application form SJ1, and, if appropriate, an emergency certificate, as discussed at 20–34, above.

20–67   **(ii) Non-expedited procedure**
Essentially the procedure is the same as that followed for all other domestic proceedings in the magistrates' court.[57] This has been dealt with at 14–47 to 14–50, above.

In outline, the steps are as follows:

(a) File complaint at court. Printed forms are available from magistrates' courts for this purpose.

(b) Summons prepared by court. Again a printed form is used containing a notice of the court's powers to make orders under section 16 of the D.P.M.C.A. 1978. The summons will normally contain the date when the application will be heard, which, in the case of an application for an exclusion order, must be within 14 days.[58]

(c) Service of summons. This may be effected by a court officer, or, in some cases, the applicant's solicitor will arrange for it to be served. Whenever possible personal service should be effected in order to be able to establish that the respondent has received the summons, if he fails to appear at the hearing. However, it is also possible to effect service by post,

---

[56] Legal Advice and Assistance Regs. 1989, reg. 24.
[57] Note that when s.92 Children Act 1989 comes into force domestic proceedings in the magistrates' court will be known as "family proceedings."
[58] Magistrates' Courts (Matrimonial Proceedings) Rules 1980, r. 13(2).

or the summons may be left with a person at the respondent's last known or usual place of abode.[59]

Proof of service is normally effected by the process server sending to the court a copy of the summons with a certificate of service indorsed. Service should be effected a "reasonable time" before the hearing,[60] but this is not further defined.

(d) *The hearing*. At the hearing evidence is given orally by the applicant and the respondent in the usual way. The only difference is that it is not necessary for a "domestic panel"[61] of magistrates to hear the case.

(e) *The order*. Assuming the order is made, it will contain a statement explaining to the respondent the penalties for disobeying the order in much the same way as the "penal notice" which is endorsed on county court orders. It may also contain a power of arrest (see 20–69, below).

(f) *Service of order*. This should be effected in the same way as the summons. Again, personal service should normally be used.

(iii) Expedited procedure   20–68

It is possible to obtain an emergency personal protection order from the magistrates' court. It should be noted that it is not possible to obtain any form of exclusion order by this process.

Having obtained A.B.W.O.R. or legal aid, probably as an emergency, the steps are as follows:

(a) *Statement of imminent danger*. A statement that there is imminent danger of physical injury to the applicant or a child of the family must be made to the court. This can be made orally, but some courts require it in writing. No form is prescribed for this statement.

(b) *Service of summons not required*. There is no need for *service* of the summons. However, many courts would seem to require a written complaint to be filed (or "laid"—as it is often called) and a summons to be issued.

(c) *The order*. This may be made by a single justice, who will grant a personal protection order if he is satisfied that there is imminent danger of physical injury to the applicant or a child

[59] *Ibid*. r. 20.
[60] Magistrates' Courts Act 1980, s.55(3).
[61] See 14–50, above. Under s.92 of the Children Act 1989 the domestic panel will become known as the "family panel."

of the family. Although a power of arrest could be attached if the conditions are satisfied (see 20–69 below) it is unlikely to be attached until both parties have been heard.

(d) Service of order. Unlike a non-expedited order, an expedited order *must* be served personally on the respondent[62] and the order is ineffective until served.

The expedited order can only last for 28 days from when it was made (or until the making of a full order, if earlier). The expedited order must therefore be followed quickly by a full hearing of the application. Normally, at the same time as the expedited order is served, the summons will be served as well, containing the hearing date of the application. The subsequent procedure is then as set out at 20–67, above.

ENFORCEMENT

20–69 **(i) Power of arrest**
When the magistrates have made either a personal protection order, or an exclusion order, they may add a power of arrest to the order if they are satisfied:

  (i) that the respondent has actually caused physical injury to the respondent or to a child of the family; and

  (ii) that he is likely to do so again.

This should only be attached when necessary and not as a routine measure.[63] Where a power of arrest is attached, a constable may arrest the respondent if he has reasonable grounds for suspecting that he is in breach of the order. The respondent must be brought, within 24 hours, before a justice of the peace, who may remand him in custody or on bail pending a hearing.

20–70 **(ii) Committal after the issue of an arrest warrant**
Where the order has been broken and the respondent has not been arrested under the terms of any power of arrest, then the applicant can apply to a justice of the peace for the issue of a warrant of arrest. Evidence must be given on oath, and the J.P. must be satisfied that there are reasonable grounds for believing the respondent has disobeyed the order. Once brought before the court, whether under a power of arrest, or

---

[62] Magistrates' Courts (Matrimonial Proceedings) Rules 1980, r. 19(1).
[63] *McCartney* v. *McCartney* [1981] Fam. 59. *Widdowson* v. *Widdowson* [1983] F.L.R. 121.

under a warrant, the respondent is liable to maximum penalties of two months' imprisonment or a fine of £2,000.[64]

CHOICE OF JURISDICTION 20–71

As will have been seen throughout this chapter, some jurisdictions provide only limited relief. For example, if a couple are unmarried, they cannot use the D.P.M.C.A. 1978 or go ancillary to divorce, or use the M.H.A. 1983, and therefore the D.V.M.P.A. 1976 may provide the only practical remedy. However, all the jurisdictions provide an adequate remedy in most cases. It will therefore often be necessary to consider certain extrinsic factors in deciding which jurisdiction to choose.

(i) Availability of courts 20–72
There are parts of the country where access to a magistrates' court is much easier than to a county court, which may be many miles away. Also, some county courts do not have divorce jurisdiction. In these courts only the D.V.M.P.A. 1976 may be used.

(ii) Legal aid principles 20–73
Two principles of legal aid administration have a bearing on the choice of jurisdiction.

The Legal Aid Board in its *Legal Aid Handbook*, emphasises the need to avoid a multiplicity of actions.[65] If, therefore, the client wishes to obtain a divorce then, unless there is some special reason for preferring another jurisdiction (*e.g.* the need to protect a child who is not a child of the family) the application should be made ancillary to divorce proceedings.

The Legal Aid Board encourages the use of the magistrates' court where possible because it is the least expensive forum.[65] Again, however, there may be pressing reasons for not applying to the magistrates' court (*e.g.* the need for protection from "molestation" as opposed to "violence").

(iii) Checklist 20–74
Most of the factors that will influence a choice between jurisdictions have already been referred to in this chapter. For the purposes of clarification these are summarised below, in a chart which shows how a particular factor may dictate the choice of jurisdiction.

---

[64] Magistrates' Courts Act 1980, s.63(3) and Criminal Penalties, etc. (Increase) Order 1984 (S.I. 1984 No. 447).
[65] *Legal Aid Handbook* (1990), Note for Guidance 11.

FACTOR	Ancillary to decree	D.V.M.P.A.	D.P.M.C.A.
Applicant is married to respondent	*	*	*
Applicant and respondent are unmarried		*	
Protection wanted for "child of the family"	*		*
Protection wanted for child "living with applicant" who is not a child of the family		*	
Protection from violence wanted	*	*	*
Protection from molestation wanted	*	*	
Exclusion of respondent wanted from area in which home situated	*	*	
Further orders for financial provision wanted	*		*
Further orders for property adjustment and a decree wanted	*		

FUTURE REFORM

20–75 It will be apparent from the above checklist that there are at present many inconsistencies and deficiencies in the range of protection offered to victims of domestic violence. The law is clearly in need of reform, and in a working paper published in 1989 the Law Commission put forward proposals for change.[66] The Law Commission identifies two possible approaches to reform. The first would be to retain the basic structure of the present law, but to seek to remove as many inconsistencies, gaps and deficiencies as possible. The alternative would be to restructure the law in a more radical way, so as to provide a single consistent set of remedies

[66] Working Paper No. 113.

beween different courts. The Commission will in due course publish a report taking account of the response it receives to this working paper. It may then become apparent which, if either, of the two options is to be adopted.

21. The Local Authority and Housing

21–01 This chapter briefly considers the ways in which the client who has to contend with domestic violence may be able to invoke the help of her local housing authority in resolving her problems. This mainly entails a consideration of the duties of local authorities to rehouse the homeless, although the chapter concludes with a look at the position of the client who is already living in council housing. As in the previous chapter, it is generally assumed that it is the woman who is seeking assistance.

21–02 ## 1. Housing the Homeless

Local housing authorities are under certain duties to provide help for people in their area who are rendered homeless, or who are threatened with homelessness. These duties arise under Part III of the Housing Act 1985. The precise extent of a local authority's duties towards homeless people varies according to which of three categories they fall into, and these are considered below. Many matrimonial clients, however, will not be concerned to obtain long-term housing under the Act. It will often simply provide a short-term remedy for a woman who has been compelled to leave her own home as a result of domestic violence, and cannot find temporary accommodation with friends or relations, or in a local women's refuge. Although she can obtain an order to exclude a violent man from the home, and an order allowing her to reoccupy the home, she cannot generally obtain an exclusion order *ex parte*. This means that she may need immediate short-term accommodation before her application can be heard. There are also some clients, however, who have such bitter memories of the ill-treatment they have suffered in the former home, that they cannot contemplate the prospect of ever returning, and they may require long-term rehousing.

21–03 THE MEANING OF "HOMELESSNESS"

A person is homeless within the meaning of the H.A. 1985[1] if there is no reasonable accommodation which he and his

---

[1] H.A. 1985, s.58, as amended by the Housing and Planning Act 1986, s.14.

family are entitled to occupy in England, Wales and Scotland. However, a person may have reasonable accommodation and still be homeless if:

(i) he cannot secure entry to it,

or

(ii) it is probable that occupation of it will lead to violence or threats of violence, which are likely to be carried out by someone else living in the accommodation.[2]

It has been held in *R.* v. *Ealing London Borough, ex p. Sidhu*[3] **21–04** that the fact that a woman is being accommodated in a refuge for battered wives does not mean that she is not homeless for the purposes of the Act. Refuges of this kind are temporary crisis accommodation, and to treat them as accommodation within the meaning of the Act would deprive many victims of domestic violence of its protection.

Nevertheless, the House of Lords has held, in *R.* v. *Hillingdon London Borough Council, ex p. Puhlhofer*,[4] that the question of whether accommodation is to be regarded as "accommodation" for the purposes of the Act is a question of fact for the housing authority. The effect of this decision may be to make it very difficult for applicants to challenge successfully an authority's decision that they are not homeless.

A person may also be entitled to help from the local housing **21–05** authority under the Act if he is "threatened with homelessness," which means that he is likely to become homeless within the next 28 days.[5]

THE DUTIES OF HOUSING AUTHORITIES **21–06**

As mentioned above, the duties of local housing authorities vary according to the category into which an applicant falls. The three categories will be considered in turn.

(i) The homeless person with a priority need who did not **21–07** **become homeless intentionally**
Housing authorities' obligations are greatest towards applicants in this category. Under section 65(2) of the H.A. 1985, they are under a duty to "secure that accommodation

---

[2] *Ibid.* s.58(3).
[3] (1982) 80 L.G.R. 534.
[4] [1986] A.C. 484.
[5] H.A. 1985, s.58(4).

becomes available" for such applicant's occupation. This may well take the form of an offer of council accommodation, although it can be seen from the wording of the section that this is not essential. An authority could, for example, satisfy its statutory duty by giving the applicant financial assistance with the cost of privately rented accommodation. In all cases, however, the authority must ensure that the accommodation provided is "suitable," and, in deciding whether this description is satisfied, must have regard to their other statutory duties of promoting slum clearance and avoiding overcrowding.[6]

In deciding whether the applicant qualifies for this assistance, the housing authority will obviously have to consider whether she has a "priority need" and whether she became homeless "intentionally." These terms are defined in the Act.

21–08 *Priority need*

Section 59(1) of the H.A. 1985 defines this term to include:

    (i) a pregnant woman

   and

    (ii) a person with whom dependent children reside or might reasonably be expected to reside.

It can be seen from this that many victims of domestic violence should be able to establish a priority need. However, a difficulty which some applicants face is that some housing authorities may refuse to treat a battered woman as having a priority need until she has obtained a custody order. This puts the woman in a dilemma; she may not be rehoused until she gets a custody order, and a court may refuse her a custody order until she is rehoused. In fact, in *R. v. Ealing London Borough, ex p. Sidhu,*[7] Hodgson J. held that the authority had been wrong to insist on a final custody order as evidence of priority need, but this does not seem to have stopped authorities from taking a similar approach in other cases.

21–09 *Intentionally homeless*

Section 60(1) of the H.A. 1985 provides that a person is intentionally homeless if she deliberately does or fails to do

---

[6] H.A. 1985, s.69(1), as substituted by the Housing and Planning Act 1986, s.14.
[7] See note 3, above.

anything in consequence of which she ceases to occupy accommodation which is available for her occupation, and which it would have been reasonable for her to continue to occupy.

This final qualification is obviously important in the case of a victim of domestic violence. A woman may, for example, have deliberately left the matrimonial home as a result of her husband's violence, but should not be regarded as intentionally homeless if it would be unreasonable to expect her to return while her husband was still there. This point is reinforced by the Code of Guidance, to which local housing authorities must have regard in exercising their powers under the Act. Paragraph 2–16 of the Code expressly states: "A battered woman who has fled the marital home should never be regarded as having become homeless intentionally."

The position has, however, been complicated by dicta of Woolf J. in *R. v. Wandsworth London Borough, ex p. Nimako-Boateng*,[8] in which he suggested that in some cases it would be reasonable for the woman to remain in the home, and to seek non-molestation and exclusion injunctions against the man. This has encouraged some authorities to take the view that a woman who leaves without first seeking an injunction has acted unreasonably, and is, therefore, intentionally homeless.

Interim duty   **21–10**

Where a housing authority thinks that an applicant may be homeless and have a priority need, it is under a duty, imposed by section 63 of the H.A. 1985, to ensure that accommodation is made available for the applicant pending a final decision.

(ii) The homeless person with a priority need who did **21–11**
become homeless intentionally
The duty of housing authorities to applicants in this category is a duty:

   (a) to secure that accommodation is made available to them for such period as they consider will give them a reasonable opportunity of finding their own accommodation, and;

---

[8] [1984] 1 F.L.R. 192.

(b) to give them advice and assistance towards finding their own accommodation.[9]

This in effect means that the housing authority will find temporary accommodation for the applicant. The authority clearly has a discretion that must be properly exercised in each case. It has been held unlawful for an authority to impose a fixed period of two weeks as the maximum period allowed in temporary accommodation.[10] Again, the accommodation need not be in council property. It could, for example, be in a hostel or in bed and breakfast accommodation.

21–12 **(iii) The homeless person with no priority need who did become homeless intentionally**
The duty of housing authorities to applicants in this third category is restricted to giving advice and assistance to help the applicant find accommodation.[11] In practice this may not be of much value to the applicant.

21–13 THE LOCAL CONNECTION PROVISIONS

Section 67 of the H.A. 1985 contains provisions which are primarily designed to prevent local authorities having to assume responsibility for homeless applicants who have no local connection with the area. For example, authorities in seaside resorts, or with large prisons in their area, might find themselves shouldering a disproportionately large burden if they could not refer applicants back to the area with which they have a local connection.

Accordingly, under section 67, where an applicant has a priority need and did not become homeless intentionally, the authority need not rehouse her if certain conditions are met, but may instead refer her to the local housing authority with which she has a local connection. The term "local connection" is defined, by section 61, to include connections through normal residence, employment or family associations.

The conditions that must be satisfied to justify the referral to another authority are, essentially, that the applicant has no local connection with the authority to whom she has applied, and does have such connection with the authority to whom she is referred. However, section 67 also provides that the applicant is not to be referred to a district in which she will

---

[9] H.A. 1985, s.65(3).
[10] *Lally* v. *Kensington and Chelsea Royal Borough, The Times*, March 27, 1980.
[11] H.A. 1985, s.65(4).

run the risk of domestic violence. It should, therefore, be possible for a woman to seek refuge from violence in an area in which she has no local connection, if the only connections she does have are in an area where she is at risk. However, the question of whether the woman will run the risk of domestic violence in that area is ultimately one for the local authority itself. As long as the authority has properly considered the matter, it will be very difficult to mount a successful challenge to the authority's decision to refuse the woman accommodation in their area.[12]

2. Local Authority Tenancies   21–14

A council tenancy is a secure tenancy under the H.A. 1985. This means that a council tenant enjoys substantial security of tenure. In particular, the tenant cannot be evicted by the landlord without a court possession order, and such orders can be obtained only on specified grounds, such as non-payment of rent.[13] This security depends, in part, on the tenant remaining in occupation of the home, or, where there is a joint tenancy, on one of the tenants remaining in occupation.[14]

Where a divorcing couple occupy a council house, the divorce **21–15**
court has power to order the tenant spouse to transfer the tenancy to the other, and when this is done the security of the tenancy is not lost. (This is considered in more detail at 6–123, above).

However, a spouse subjected to domestic violence will not **21–16**
always wish to take immediate divorce proceedings. Furthermore, the parties occupying the property may not be married, and so the powers of the divorce court to transfer the tenancy cannot be invoked. The question, therefore, sometimes arises as to whether there are alternative means whereby a secure tenant may be deprived of his tenancy.

Where the property is in the name of a sole secure tenant, it **21–17**
may be that the security will be lost if the other party obtains an exclusion injunction against him. As security depends on the tenant's continued occupation, his exclusion under the injunction may cause this to lapse, leaving the local authority free to serve a notice to quit on him without a court order, and, if it wishes, to grant a new secure tenancy to the other

---

[12] See R. v. *Bristol City Council ex p. Browne* [1979] 1 W.L.R. 1437.
[13] *Ibid.* s.84 and Sched. 2.
[14] *Ibid.* s.81.

party. It is arguable, however, that exclusion under an injunction should not have this effect. Certainly it has been held that exclusion injunctions are not capable of interfering with property rights.[15] However, in *Warwick* v. *Warwick*[16] the Court of Appeal assumed that an exclusion injunction would have this effect.

21–18 Where the property is in the names of both parties under a joint tenancy, the position is clearer. In *Greenwich London Borough Council* v. *McGrady*[17] the Court of Appeal held that one joint tenant of a secure tenancy can serve a notice to quit on the council without the agreement of the other, and that this will bring the tenancy to an end. When the notice to quit expires, the local authority will be free to grant a new secure tenancy to the party who gave notice to quit.

In conclusion, however, it should be added that some commentators have questioned whether the adoption of this device might not leave the woman open to an action for damages for breach of trust by the man. Furthermore, if she remains in occupation of the property as a sole tenant, it might still be argued that she is a trustee attempting to benefit from her breach of trust. In this case, she would hold the equitable estate on trust for herself and the man.

---

[15] In *Davis* v. *Johnson* [1979] A.C. 264.
[16] (1982) 12 Fam.Law 60.
[17] (1982) 81 L.G.R. 288.

Index

(All references are to paragraph numbers.)

447

ANCILLARY RELIEF—*cont.*
hearing, 10–26
inheritance, relevance of, 6–49
lump sums, 6–10, 6–11, 6–12
maintenance pending suit, 6–04,
  6–05, 6–06
needs, relevance of, 6–51
net-effect approach, 6–86 *et seq.*
obligations, relevance of, 6–52, 6–53
one-third approach, 6–81, 6–82
"package deal," 6–80
pensions, 6–66
periodical payments, 6–08 *et seq.*
procedure, 10–01 *et seq.*
property adjustment, 6–13 *et seq.*
remarriage,
  prospects of, 6–50
  trap, 6–22, 10–09
rule 77 letter, 10–21
subsistence level, 6–47
third parties,
  beneficial owners, 6–116
  creditors, 6–117, 6–118, 6–119
  evidence from, 10–24, 10–25,
    10–26
  income of, 6–45
  landlords, 6–121, 6–122, 6–123,
    6–124, 6–125
  mortgagees, 6–114, 6–115
variation, 12–13 *et seq. See also*
  VARIATION.
welfare benefits, relevance of, 6–46
welfare of children, 6–35, 6–36
welfare of family, contributions to,
  6–59
ANSWER, 4–88, 4–89, 4–90
APPEALS,
ancillary relief, 12–02
ARREST, POWER OF, 20–54, 20–58,
  20–59, 20–69
ASSISTANCE BY WAY OF
  REPRESENTATION. *See* A.B.W.O.R.
ATTACHMENT OF EARNINGS, 13–09,
  14–60
AUTOMATIC DIRECTIONS, 10–02, 10–15

BACKDATING PERIODICAL PAYMENTS,
  6–17, 6–23, 10–10
BAILIFF SERVICE, 4–41, 4–43
BANKRUPTCY,
matrimonial home, sale of, 6–117,
  6–118, 6–119
Married Women's Property Act
  1882, application under, 6–129
rights of occupation, effect on, 9–13
BAR TO DIVORCE, 3–05, 3–06, 3–07

BARS TO NULLITY, 5–16, 5–17, 5–18
BEHAVIOUR,
affidavit in support of petition, 4–60
cohabitation after final incident,
  3–29, 3–30
examples of, 3–27
magistrates' court, complaint in,
  14–07
mental illness, caused by, 3–28
particulars in petition, 4–20
test of, 3–24, 3–25, 3–26
BENEFITS IN KIND,
ancillary relief, assessment of, 6–44
BREACH OF ORDERS. *See* ENFORCEMENT.
BREAKDOWN, IRRETRIEVABLE, 3–08,
  3–09

CALDERBANK LETTERS, 10–27
CAPITAL GAINS TAX,
annual exemption, 7–29
cars, 7–37
chattels, 7–37
elements of, 7–27 *et seq.*
indexation, 7–30, 7–31
main residence exemption, 7–34,
  7–35, 7–36
Married Women's Property Act
  1882, application under, 6–130,
  7–46
matrimonial home, disposal, 7–38 *et
  seq.*
Mesher orders, 7–43 *et seq.*
rebasing, 7–28
spouses, disposals between, 7–33
sterling, 7–37
CARE AND CONTROL,
definition, 16–01
wardship cases, in, 18–03
CARE ORDERS,
care proceedings, in, 18–39
Children Act 1989, under, 19–09 *et
  seq.*
divorce, on, 16–23
D.P.M.C.A. 1978, under, 16–30
G.M.A. 1971, under, 16–33
wardship cases, in, 18–05,
  18–43
CHARGING ORDER,
matrimonial home, over, 6–117,
  6–118
lump sum, to enforce, 13–06
CHILD BENEFIT,
amount, 8–06
child, definition of, 8–05
claims, 8–04, 8–07
eligibility, 8–04

WARDSHIP—*cont.*
uses of, 18–07 *et seq.*
WARRANT OF DISTRESS, 14–64
WARRANT OF EXECUTION, 13–04
WELFARE BENEFITS. *See also* individual
benefit headings.
ancillary relief, relevance to, 6–46,
6–47
Green Form advice, 8–02, 8–61
marriage breakdown, on, 8–100 *et
seq.*
WELFARE OF CHILDREN,
ancillary relief, relevance to, 6–35,
6–36

WELFARE OF CHILDREN—*cont.*
custody, relevance to, 16–12
family proceedings, relevance in,
17–07, 17–09
WELFARE OF FAMILY,
ancillary relief, relevance of
contributions, 6–59
WELFARE REPORTS, 16–16, 16–24,
16–36, 16–37, 16–38, 17–24
WILLS,
divorce, effect of, 3–79, 3–82
judicial separation effect of, 5–29
nullity, effect of, 5–20
WITNESS SUMMONS, 10–24, 10–25